THE EVER-CHANGING SEA

THE EVER-

Illustrations by INGRID NICCOLL

CHANGING SEA

David B. Ericson and

Goesta Wollin

ALFRED · A · KNOPF / *New York*

1 9 6 7

THIS BOOK IS FOR

Janet & Karen

ACKNOWLEDGMENTS

No AUTHORS OF A BOOK WHICH RANGES ACROSS A FIELD AS BROAD as oceanography can rightly claim that the product is a result of their efforts only. We have drawn on the work of many scientists and only a relatively few are referred to with specific credit in the text or listed in the bibliography. To these scientists, too numerous to mention, we are extremely grateful.

We feel deep gratitude to Maurice Ewing, director of the Lamont Geological Observatory, Columbia University, for his generous support of our research work and his active participation in it.

This book would not have been written without wise guidance and important suggestions from Angus Cameron, editor at Alfred A. Knopf. We are extremely grateful to him.

We express our sincere appreciation to Janet Wollin and Matilda Flannery for able assistance in the laboratory investigations and in the preparation of the manuscript.

Special acknowledgment with gratitude is due to Ingrid Niccoll for drawing the illustrations. Her work is an important part of this book.

The readers of this book will understand our considerable debt to many of the members of the staff of the Lamont Geological Observatory. While the total list of those who helped directly or indirectly in this book or in the studies that led up to it is too long to print here, the volume would be quite incomplete if we failed to record our gratitude to Allan W. H. Be, Wallace S. Broecker, Paul R. Burkholder, Patrick J. Coyle, Charles L. Drake, John I. Ewing, W. Arnold Finck, James D. Hays, Bruce C. Heezen, Richard Kollin, Teh-Lung Ku, Angelo Ludas, Andrew McIntyre,

John E. Nafe, Jack Oliver, J. Lamar Worzel, and Roger Zaunere.

For valuable advice and stimulating discussion of the problems of deep-sea research we are thankful to scientists from all over the world, particularly to Gustaf Arrhenius, M. N. Bramlette, Cesare Emiliani, Fritz Koczy, Ph. H. Kuenen, Börje Kullenberg, Fred B Phleger, William Riedel, Francis P. Shepard, Ivan Tolstoy and John D. H. Wiseman.

The data and material for many of the studies carried out by us and by other scientists of Lamont Geological Observatory reported in portions of this book were obtained during deep-sea expeditions sponsored by the Office of Naval Research. Our studies of cores of deep-sea sediment were supported by the National Science Foundation and has already appeared elsewhere, primarily in *Science*. But the writing of this book has been a private undertaking, carried out entirely at our own expense.

D.B.E. and G.W.

Palisades, New York/February 1967

CONTENTS

1 THE IMMENSE SEA   3

2 THE CIRCULATION OF THE OCEAN   41

3 THE WAVES OF THE OCEAN   91

4 EVER-CHANGING SEA LEVEL   119

5 THE FACE OF THE EARTH BENEATH THE SEA   145

6 THE SEDIMENT CARPET   173

7 THE DEEP SEA AND THE ICE AGES   205

8 THE CRUST BENEATH THE OCEAN BOTTOM   235

9 THE MOHOLE   257

10 LIFE IN GREAT DEPTHS   287

11 THE OCEAN AND THE FUTURE   319

   Bibliography / 351

   Index / follows page 354

LIST OF FIGURES

1 Diagram illustrating the relative proportions of oceanic depth and the emergent land of the earth. [*After Gene Johnson*]   7

2 Comparison of bottom topography based on 13 wire soundings with the same bottom based on over 1,300 sonic soundings. [*After Sverdrup* et al., The Oceans]   10

3 Chart of geologic time, beginning with the first appearance of easily recognizable fossils in the Cambrian Period.   16

4 Layers of the earth: the core, the mantle, and the crust.   18

5 Illustrations of Wegener's theory of continental drift.   20

6 Map of the world drawn so that the edge of the map nowhere cuts the land. [*After Athelstan Spilhaus*]   27

7 A diagram of a water molecule.   42

8 Schematic representation of a wind-driven current in deep water (the Ekman spiral). [*After Sverdrup* et al., The Oceans]   49

9 Coriolis effect.   50

10 Sun's rays heat the equatorial seas, which expand and flow "downhill" toward the poles.   52

11 Surface currents of the oceans.   59

12 The wandering Gulf Stream. [*Woods Hole Oceanographic Institution*]   61

13 Antarctic Circumpolar Current. [*After* Scientific American]   75

14 The Cromwell Current. [*After Mary S. Cowen*]   78

15 Deep ocean circulation. [*After Henry Stommel*]   86

16 Movement of currents measured by Swallow floats. [*After T. F. Gaskell*]   87

17 Drawings demonstrating that wave forms travel, but that the water itself does not. *92*

18 Diagram illustrating how an ocean wave breaks when it enters shallow water. *96*

19 The tidal force in a section through the line connecting centers of earth and moon. [*After Ph. H. Kuenen,* Marine Geology] *99*

20 Spring and neap tides. *101*

21 Diagram showing cause of daily inequality of tides. [*After Ph. H. Kuenen,* Marine Geology] *102*

22 Cotidal lines of the semi-diurnal tide in the Atlantic Ocean. [*After Sverdrup* et al., The Oceans] *105*

23 Illustrating the stages in the evolution of fringing reefs to atolls according to the Darwin hypothesis. [*After Francis P. Shepard,* Submarine Geology] *124*

24 The mechanism of isostasy. [*After Rhodes W. Fairbridge*] *129*

25 Convection currents within the earth. [*After* Scientific American] *132*

26 Diagram showing the relation of altitude to time for the high sea levels of the Pleistocene. [*After F. E. Zeuner,* Dating the Past] *140*

27 Continental margin provinces: type profile off northeastern United States. [*After Heezen* et al., 1959] *154*

28 The Tonga Trench. [*After* Scientific American] *157*

29 Positions of the main oceanic trenches. [*National Institute of Oceanography*] *158*

30 The Mid-Oceanic Ridge. *161*

31 Submarine Canyon. *165*

32 Continuous profiling for normal incidence reflections. [*After J. B. Hersey*] *180*

33 Mechanism of slumping and generation of a turbidity current. *186*

34 Distribution of various kinds of deep-sea sediments in relation to physiographic provinces. [*Data from Ericson* et al., *based on piston cores taken by Lamont Geological Observatory expeditions.*] *188*

35 The Kullenberg piston corer. [*After Hans Pettersson,* The Ocean Floor] *198*

36 The principle of taking a piston core. *210*

37 Species of common North Atlantic planktonic foramini-
    fera. [*After Fred B Phleger*]   217

38 Correlation of precisely defined levels in cores from dif-
    ferent locations—on the basis of changes in coiling direc-
    tion of *Globorotalia truncatulinoides* with depth in cores. 219

39 Discoasters, guide fossils that helped identify the onset
    of the first ice age.   223

40 The "gap" in the deep-sea record of the Pleistocene.   225

41 Schematic drawings of a series of tree sections, illustrat-
    ing cross dating, and how a chronological sequence is
    built up connecting prehistoric timber with modern trees.
    [*After F. E. Zeuner*, Dating the Past]   227

42 Pleistocene time scale and generalized climate curve.   231

43 Illustrations of the human and prehuman skulls in the
    sequence of glacial and interglacial stages of the Pleisto-
    cene.   232

44 Schematic representation of refraction of waves. [*After
    Ph. H. Kuenen*, Marine Geology]   243

45 Illustration of a seismic refraction method. [*After T. F.
    Gaskell*]   245

46 Cross section of the earth's crust showing typical land
    and sea forms.   267

47 Illustrations of the theory that the earth's magnetic field
    flips over periodically converting the North Pole, mag-
    netically, into a "south" pole. [*After* The New York
    Times]   274

48 Gulper, or pelican eel. [*After* Dana *expeditions*]   305

49 Female angler fish and a parasitic male. [*After* Dana
    expeditions]   307

50 Coelacanth fish *Latimeria chalumnae*.   313

51 Beard worm, member of the Pogonophora. [*After* Traité
    de Zoologie]   316

52 Oceanographic buoy.   321

53 The *Aluminaut;* world's first aluminum submarine.   324

54 New fishing system. [*After T. F. Gaskell*]   328

55 Deep-sea mining machines. [*After* Scientific American]   336

THE EVER-CHANGING SEA

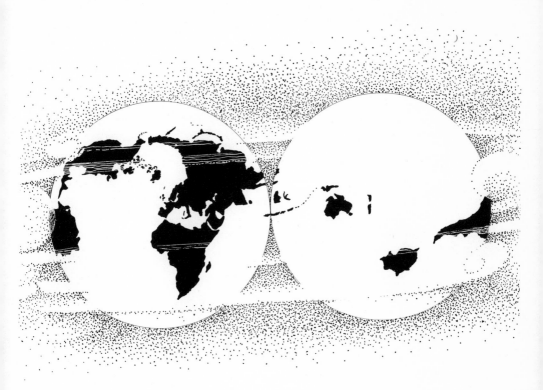

CHAPTER I

THE IMMENSE SEA

Aeons ago, when the universe was young, our planet was a swirling cloud of dust and gas. As time passed mutual attraction gradually brought the particles together, and as this condensation proceeded impact and compression generated enough heat to melt the hardest substances. Eventually, as the youthful planet lost heat by radiation to outer space, its temperature fell low enough to permit its surface to solidify. At the same time various elementary substances entered into combination; from the union of the gases hydrogen and oxygen sprang the water of the primeval ocean. During the following 2,000–3,000 million years conditions here and there on the earth's surface must have varied through an almost infinite series of infinitesimal gradations, until pure chance brought together the exquisitely precise combination of circumstances and substances necessary to set going the self-perpetuating chemical reaction that is the essence of life.

Then as our planet swung through its orbit about the sun many millions of times, competitive selection—by favoring the more effectively coordinated systems of living chemicals that arose by chance variations—has so unified the simple reactions to temperature, light, touch, and time, that at last an organism has emerged that can form mental images and can trace sequences of events. Thus after many aeons the swirling cloud of disorganized matter, transformed by condensation, has brought forth beings capable of forming a mental image of that swirling cloud of disorganized matter.

One senses a vast span of time in this development of awareness. Since the complex substances that are life can exist only at

3

temperatures well below the boiling point of water, we could set a limit to the antiquity of life, if we could measure the age of the ocean.

In 1899 an Irish physicist, John Joly, attempted to calculate the age of the ocean by dividing the total amount of salt in the ocean by the amount of salt brought to the ocean each year by all rivers. By his calculation the ocean was 90 million years old. In 1899 this age was considered astonishingly great.

Since then chemists have discovered various ways of determining the ages of rocks by means of the rates of decay of radioactive substances. For example, they have shown that a certain limestone containing carbon in the form of graphite is 2,700 million years old. But layered limestones such as this can accumulate only under water. Furthermore, this particular limestone contains concretionary structures that are very probably the remains of primitive aquatic plants. If so, the climate of the world at that early time must have been much as it is today.

In 1966 two scientists at Harvard published descriptions of microscopic rod-shaped objects much like bacteria, which occur in water-laid rocks of the eastern Transvaal, South Africa. According to the radioactive clock these vestiges of life are even older than the concretions of southern Rhodesia; they are not less than 3,100 million years old. In the same sedimentary rocks, which by all evidence accumulated in a body of water, occur substances called hydrocarbons which the Harvard scientists believe to be "of definitely biological origin."

Why, one wonders did Joly's calculation fall so far short of the real age of the ocean? Perhaps, in part, because of the very slow release of salt from continental rocks by chemical decay during the thousands of millions of years before there were land plants to supply the organic acids that accelerate the chemical breakdown of rocks.

But probably a much more important reason for the failure of Joly's method is the extraordinary nature of the epoch of earth history in which we live. Ours is a time of high continents studded with lofty mountain ranges. In the record of the rocks geologists read a different account of the past. During by far the major part of the past several thousand million years, low and featureless continents have been flooded by shallow seas. Under such conditions the rate of chemical decay of surface rocks, and therefore the rate of release of salt, must have been only a tiny fraction of the present rate. In this way Joly's calculation helps us to realize that we live during the exciting times of a "geological revolution."

Geologists find unmistakable evidence of earlier revolutions, that is of comparatively short interludes in the drama of the earth when mountain building was rife, when the continents stood high above deep ocean basins, and volcanoes poured forth quantities of molten rock and ash. Then, as the forces within the earth entered a phase of decreasing energy, the wearing-down process of erosion by streams, glaciers, and powerful sand-driving winds took its toll. First to go were the mountains; over their roots crept shallow seas teeming with life; and then the world settled down for another one hundred million years of quiescence.

The source of the colossal amount of energy expended during these spasms of mountain building or geological revolutions is the most critical problem confronting earth scientists.

Impressed by the shortening of the earth's crust that must have accompanied the crumpling together of great thicknesses of sediments (which gave rise to mountain ranges like the Appalachians, the Alps, and the Himalayas), earlier geologists concluded that the earth was shrinking. The resemblance between the wrinkles of the earth's surface and the wrinkled skin of a dry and shrunken apple was too obvious to be disregarded. Furthermore, the shrinkage theory was consistent with the then prevalent view that the earth was slowly cooling.

But geologists now realize that this explanation has fatal flaws. Evidence of tension in the earth's crust, though less conspicuous, is as prevalent as evidence of compression, according to the recent findings of marine geologists. Detailed charting of the ocean basins in the past fifteen years has uncovered a rift, or steep-walled valley, that winds down the middle of the Atlantic, around the southern tip of Africa, and sends a branch northward into the Indian Ocean, while the main part ranges eastward south of Australia and thence across the Pacific. From this and other evidence it now appears that local stretching of the earth's crust has roughly equaled compression elsewhere. The evidence supports neither contraction nor expansion of the earth as a whole; instead

it points to movement of certain parts of the earth's crust in relation to others. We will come back to this problem later.

The earth well deserves to be called the "watery planet";
water covers 71 per cent of its surface. The Pacific, by far the
largest of the oceans, accounts for one half of the area covered by
water; the Atlantic covers one quarter, and the Indian Ocean
about 15 per cent, the remaining 10 per cent being covered by the
Arctic Ocean, Mediterranean, Caribbean, North Sea, and other
minor seas.

The ocean basins are topographical features of the first order.
If the surfaces of the continents were leveled by a cyclopean
bulldozer, they would everywhere stand 875 meters (2,870 feet)
above sea level, but the ocean floors after similar leveling would
lie at a depth of 3,800 meters (11,600 feet) below sea level.

The total area and average depth of the oceans are great in
comparison with the area and height of the land, and the disparity in volume is greater still. If rock were taken from the continents and put into the ocean basins until the surface of the earth
were quite smooth, the earth would be enveloped by a continuous
ocean with a depth of more than 2,430 meters (8,000 feet).

Oddly enough the greatest depths are not found in the central
parts of the oceans; instead they are concentrated within furrows
or trenches that run close to and parallel with some coasts and
island arcs, such as the Aleutians and the Antilles. In these
trenches have been found such record depths as the Cape Johnson Deep in the Mindanao Trench off the east coast of the Phil-
lipines—which is 10,033 meters (32,907 feet) deep—and the still
greater Challenger Deep southwest of Guam, with a maximum
depth of 10,915 meters (36,800 feet). This is a good deal greater
than the height above sea level of the world's highest mountain,
Mount Everest. (The diagram shown in Figure 1 dramatically
illustrates the relative proportions of oceanic depth and the
emergent land of the earth.)

The Indian Ocean has only one deep trench, the great Sunda
Double Trench along the south coast of Java. Its maximum depth
is 7,252 meters (23,787 feet).

The greatest depth in the Atlantic Ocean is in the Puerto Rico
Trench, which goes down to 9,392 meters (30,184 feet). Less
impressive but of more geological interest is the Romanche Deep,

named after the French surveying ship *La Romanche*, which discovered it in 1883. Its depth is 7,635 meters (25,050 feet). What sets it apart from all other deeps is its unique position halfway between continents and along the trend of the Mid-Atlantic Ridge. Because all other great depths occur near continents or on the convex sides of island arcs, the very existence of the Ro-

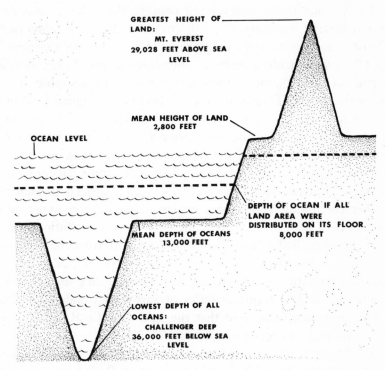

FIGURE 1   *The stretching of the oceans over some 70 per cent of the earth's surface makes our planet an ocean world; the depth of the water emphasizes the fact. This diagram illustrates the relative proportions of oceanic depth and the emergent land of the earth.*

manche Deep was doubted for many years. But in 1901 a sounding by the German research ship *Gauss* proved that it was a reality.

The topography of the earth may be divided into three classes of first-order features. The continents and oceans come readily to mind, but few people are aware of the third. This is a continuous submerged mountain range that winds its way along the ocean floor for 40,000 miles and covers an area equal to that of all the continents. The existence of this vast mountain system is a relatively recent discovery. Thanks to the method of measuring depths by sound waves, which we will explain in Chapter 5, the charting of the Mid-Ocean Ridge has advanced rapidly in recent years; even so, long stretches of it are still known only in bare outline.

The portion of the ridge lying beneath the Atlantic was discovered first; it has received more attention than any other part. Its existence came to light in 1873 when scientists on the British ship *Challenger* made a series of soundings at one hundred mile intervals in the Atlantic in the course of an oceanographic cruise around the world. Their sounding method was primitive and time consuming; they lowered a 200-pound weight on a hemp line. The soundings revealed the unexpected fact that there is a middle zone in the Atlantic where the water depth is less than one half as great as it is in the troughs lying on both sides and adjacent to the continents. But the soundings were too widely spaced to indicate whether the middle zone was a system of jagged mountains or a broad smooth rise. The answer came only after a revolution in the art of sounding had taken place. From 1924 to 1926 the German research ship *Meteor* made a thorough survey of all aspects of the equatorial Atlantic. This included the first extensive use of echo-sounding gear. The resulting series of east-west trending profiles of the ocean bottom showed that the Mid-Atlantic Ridge was an enormous range of rugged mountains.

At the turn of the century soundings made by Alexander Agassiz while on the *Albatross* in the eastern Pacific southeast of Mexico had led to the discovery of a broad rise, which thenceforth was called the Albatross Plateau, although the widely spaced soundings were inadequate to prove that the feature was really a plateau. In 1929 the nonmagnetic brigantine *Carnegie* made a series of echo-sounding profiles in the area, which showed that the Albatross Plateau was in reality a region of serrated mountains. In the meantime, in the late 1920's the Danish oceanographic ship *Dana* had discovered a similar topographical high in the northern Indian Ocean. This was called the Carlsberg Ridge. It was realized that the Mid-Atlantic Ridge, the so-called Albatross Plateau, and the Carlsberg Ridge were similar in their rugged relief and occupied corresponding positions in their respective oceans, but as no connecting links were known it was supposed that they were isolated features.

About 1960 Bruce Heezen and Maurice Ewing of the Lamont Geological Observatory of Columbia University surmised from geophysical evidence and theoretical considerations that the three ridges were probably parts of a continuous world-girdling system. Since then the *Vema*, research vessel of the Lamont Observatory, and other ships too have made a large number of echo-sounding profiles with the express purpose of testing Heezen and Ewing's theory. These have confirmed the continuity of the ridge and have established it as a topographical, and probably structural, feature of importance second only to the continents.

Until recently it was customary to distinguish three major divisions of the ocean floor: that is, the shelf, the continental slope, and the abyss. The shelf is the shallow platform which surrounds the continents. Structurally shelves are really parts of the continents, but since they are covered by water they must be considered in connection with the oceans. The edge of the shelf lies at a depth of about 425 feet or 130 meters, but it also frequently approaches a depth of 650 feet or 200 meters. The average width of the shelf is 30 miles, but it varies greatly from place to place. Off steep coasts such as those of the west coast of South America or Spain the shelf may be only a few miles wide. The widest shelf is that connecting Java, Sumatra, Malacca, and Borneo. Nearer home we have the wide shelf of the Grand Banks of Newfoundland.

An abrupt change in slope occurs at the edge of the shelf, from which the sea floor rapidly descends to abyssal depths, that is to about 12,000 feet (3,600 meters). This steeper part is called the continental slope. Beyond the depth of 12,000 feet the sea floor becomes more nearly level across the abyss, as the deeper parts of the open ocean are called.

Before the extensive use of echo sounding the abyss was thought to be a smooth, mud-covered plain pretty much devoid of well-defined relief. This conception of the abyss was largely based on the theory that a continuous rain of sediment since the very beginning of things must have buried practically all initial relief of the ocean floor. The widely spaced soundings, the only

kind available until about 1925, did nothing to dispel this conception of the abyss. In the early days of oceanography there was
only one way to measure depth; one lowered a weight on the end
of a line. In deep water a single sounding would take hours, and
then the length of line paid out was likely to be a good deal
greater than the real depth because deep currents pulled the
hemp line into large S-shaped curves. Later the substitution of
piano wire for the hemp line improved the accuracy since the fine
wire was less liable to be deflected by currents, but at best the
method was slow and therefore hopelessly inadequate for detailed charting. Today echo-sounding instruments measure the

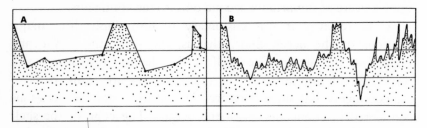

FIGURE 2   *Bottom topography in the South Atlantic Ocean. (A) Profile
of the bottom between the South Shetland Islands and Bouvet Island
based on 13 wire soundings. (B) Profile of the same bottom based on
over 1,300 sonic soundings. Vertical exaggeration about 200:1.*

greatest depths in the few seconds that it takes a sound wave to
travel to the bottom and its reflected echo to return to the ship.
Until World War II the instruments gave depths as numbers,
which could be converted into profiles of bottom topography only
by hand plotting. During the war instruments were developed
that automatically converted the echos into a continuous profile
of the bottom traced on a moving strip of paper (see Figure 2).
To stand before an echo sounder as the ship crosses a previously
unsounded region and watch the revolving stylus slowly trace the
profile of a mountain range of Alpine proportions is an experience
well worth a few days of seasickness.

From the new information obtained in this way marine geologists are learning that the most rugged topography anywhere to
be found on our planet lies at abyssal depths in the ocean basins.
The features include great trenches, vast mountain ranges, can-

yons, and isolated nearly circular mountains, known as sea-mounts, which are probably submarine volcanoes.

Even though only about 3 per cent of the ocean bottom has been thoroughly surveyed, enough has been learned to make oceanographers alter radically their conception of the ocean floor. It is now realized that if the oceans were drained of water, the exposed landscape would include mountains taller than Everest, plains vaster than the Russian steppes, and canyons rivaling the Grand Canyon. In addition to the enormous mountain ranges of the mid-ocean ridges, there are swarms of isolated seamounts.

Apparently, something was wrong with the theory that billions of years of sediment accumulation would smother ocean bottom topography under a universal blanket. The most probable reason for the discrepancy between theory and fact is that the "new look" provided by the echo sounder is indeed just that; the ocean floor is seething with geological activity. Geologists have long known that the last few million years of the earth's history have been a time of mountain building on the continents. Now we are learning that the forces of mountain building must have been no less active on the ocean floor; only thus can we explain the rugged relief so little subdued by sediment cover that we find there.

On the other hand, it is undeniable that sediment accumulation has had an influence upon ocean bottom topography, but the effect has been local. For example, the bottoms of the troughs on both sides of the Mid-Atlantic Ridge are broad and almost perfectly smooth plains. Yet profiles drawn by much more sensitive echo sounders—designed to record not only the echo from the top of the sediment but also that from the interface at the base of the sediment where it rests on hard rock—show that the surface of the basement has a degree of relief comparable with that of the Mid-Atlantic Ridge, but at a generally lower level. Evidently concentration of sediment accumulation in these troughs has masked the original rugged topography as completely as a mud-pack hides a woman's face.

Thus recent exploration with improved equipment is making it necessary to unlearn a good deal of what was once accepted without question. Although new discoveries answer some old questions about the oceans, plenty of enigmas remain. One of these concerns the origin and age of that enormous depression in the earth's crust, the basin of the Pacific Ocean. In 1881 Sir George Darwin, son of the author of *On The Origin of Species*, proposed the hypothesis that the moon was composed of continental rock torn from that part of the earth now occupied by the Pacific Basin. Astronomers know that the density of the moon is comparable to that of continental rocks. Furthermore, its volume is about right to fill the Pacific and Atlantic basins. If used to fill in the ocean basins, it would provide the earth with an almost continuous continental crust. However, astronomers have also concluded from mathematical studies that the separation of the moon from the earth would be an astronomical impossibility. More probably the Pacific Basin, as well as the other ocean basins, is a creation of the earth's own internal workings.

To sweep together the less dense mineral fraction of the primeval earth in such a way as to form the continental masses as we know them today would require a vast amount of energy. If the earth's supply of energy included nothing more than the residual heat left over from the time when the earth condensed from a cloud of dust and gas, sufficient energy to effect the segregation of the continents would be hard to find. But if we can regard the earth as a huge atomic energy plant, and recent advances in geochemistry suggest that we can do so, we need not look to astronomical forces outside the earth to explain the ocean basins.

On the other hand, some earth scientists question whether a scum of light material could ever separate out from the dense ground mass of our planet. To get around this difficulty, W. L. Donn, a geophysicist, B. D. Donn, an astronomer, and W. G. Valentine, a geologist, have recently suggested that the continents may have originated from the impact of one or more bodies of continental size and low density from outer space. Most meteorites consist of iron or dense rock, and therefore do not meet the requirements of the theory, but, as these scientists point out, the moon has just about the right density. If the moon formed separately from the earth, there is no reason why other objects of low density should not have existed in outer space.

However this may be, we still have to explain abundant and world-wide evidence of local stretching and shortening of the crust, and this has happened since the formation of the continents. Not only that, but a significant amount of this differential movement has taken place within the last million years or so. Flow of material at depth brought about by energy released by radioactive decay seems to provide the only satisfactory explanation.

The prevalence of certain fossils, particularly the remains of extinct creeping plants, in ancient sedimentary rocks of South America, Africa, India, and Australia has led to speculation about the origin of the Indian Ocean and the South Atlantic. According to one theory, what is now the basin of the Indian Ocean was occupied until about 100 million years ago by a vast continent known among geologists as Gondwanaland, which linked Australia, India, Arabia, and Africa, extending over to Brazil. Very recently fossils representing several species of creeping plants belonging to the characteristic flora of Gondwanaland have been found in Antarctica. Accordingly that continent as well must have been a part of the Gondwanaland complex.

But did Gondwanaland really exist? One wonders because its disappearance seems to require a rare bit of geophysical thaumaturgy. One principle of geophysics has stood every test. It is that the continents stand above the ocean basins because they are made of lighter or less dense rocks than those underlying the basins. Each continent consists of a "shield" or nucleus of granitic rocks having an average thickness of some twenty-two miles, and surrounded by younger mountains and shelves, all resting on a bed of denser material. The important point is that they do not stand higher because they are supported by a rigid pedestal, but rather because they "float" on denser material, as a cork floats on water. To sink, a continent would have to undergo an increase in the density of its rocks; there is no evident way by which this could come about. Thus the problem of how to get rid of a continent is more difficult than it might seem at a glance. Probably the continents have existed since a very early stage in the development of the earth, but not necessarily in their present positions or in their present shapes. The puzzling distribution of the fossil creeping plants probably indicates that the continents on which they occur were at one time in contact. Since then the continents have moved apart, carried along by convective flow of the denser material upon which they ride, and the Indian Ocean is the depression that was left after the continents had drifted apart. According to the chronology of geological events this happened a little more than 100 million years ago.

Two important kinds of evidence found during recent exploration of the oceans have a bearing on the age and origin of the basins. In the Atlantic, Pacific, and Indian oceans old sediments containing the remains of various extinct forms of life occur. Samples of these sediments have been obtained from the tops and flanks of seamounts and ridges where younger sediments have been removed by slumping[1] or where, because of deep current scour,[2] younger sediments have not accumulated. On the evidence of the fossils in these old sediments, the oldest that we or any other investigators have ever found is no more than about 100 million years old.

The second kind of evidence comes from the application of geophysical methods of measuring the thicknesses of unconsolidated sediment on the ocean floor. In the Atlantic the average thickness is in the order of about 750 meters (2,400 feet); in the Pacific it is as little as 300 meters (1,000 feet). In terms of time these thicknesses are probably about equivalent, because the average rate of sediment accumulation in the Pacific is approximately one half that of the Atlantic. This is due to the much greater size of the Pacific, a good deal of it being far from sources of land-derived sediment, and to the trenches, particularly off the American continents, which trap turbidity currents and prevent the sediment-laden water from reaching far out into the Pacific Basin. From the ages of layers of sediment in sediment cores de-

[1] Masses of water-saturated sediment on slopes are necessarily somewhat unstable. As the rain of fine particles from above slowly adds layer upon layer of sediment, the instability becomes critical. Any disturbance, such as a minor earth tremor, suffices to trigger a debacle. The initial result is what on land we would call a landslide. In the ocean it is called *slumping* (the process is described in more detail and illustrated in Chapter 6).

[2] Almost the only kind of sediment that can reach seamounts far from the continents consists of extremely finely divided mineral particles wafted by oceanic currents from the continents, and of the little shells of planktonic animals and plants that perpetually rain down from the upper layers of water. In recent years, oceanographers have become more and more aware of the importance of deep currents. These are not very swift, but they do possess enough energy to remove almost all of the fine material that reaches the tops of seamounts and ridges. This process is called *scouring* (the process is described in more detail in Chapter 2).

termined by the radiocarbon method of dating, we know that the average rate of sediment accumulation in the Pacific is about 0.014 foot or 4.3 millimeters per 1,000 years; in the Atlantic the rate is about twice as fast. When we divide the thicknesses of sediment on the floors of the two oceans by their respective rates of accumulation, we find that the total time represented is somewhere between 70 and 80 million years. However, as we said earlier, present conditions are exceptional. Probably the rate of accumulation was somewhat slower most of the time, and therefore 100 million years may be a more reasonable estimate of the total time span represented by the sediment in both oceans. Thus two independent methods of investigation, geophysical and paleontological, yield converging evidence suggesting that sediments older than about 100 million years are absent from the floors of the Atlantic and Pacific oceans.

Apparently, some drastic reorganization of the floors of the oceans must have taken place roughly 100 million years ago, that is, during the Mesozoic Era of the geological time scale (see Figure 3), the era when the animal world was dominated by giant reptiles. This is a rather startling conclusion, which flies in the face of the well-entrenched conception of the ocean basins as permanent features. The new evidence drives us to the opposite view, that the ocean basins are probably the most geologically active regions of the surface of the earth. In spite of all the evidence on the continents of folding, fracturing, subsidence, and upheaval of blocks of the crust, together with intrusion and outpourings of molten rock, it seems that the continents have been stable in contrast to the ocean basins.

If there were people on the moon with telescopes, the first thing that would catch their attention would be the contrast between the continents and oceans. To the moonlings this would be particularly surprising because their own sphere lacks corresponding depressions of global proportions. But as we have already mentioned, the moon is homogeneous in make up; apparently it has about the same density throughout. In view of this, uniformity of its surface features would be expected. The moonlings would be quite right; our earth really is a rather peculiar sphere.

For as long as some men have had the leisure to think, instead of hunting and fighting, they have wondered and thought up theories to explain the nature of our world. Two thousand years ago, the Roman philosopher Seneca concluded that the earth came from the sea. He envisioned the world at its birth as completely covered by water in which all the elements were dissolved. His universal ocean was hot and circulating in violent

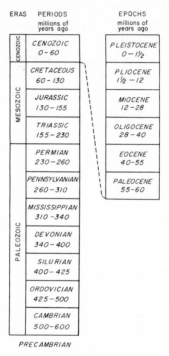

ERAS	PERIODS millions of years ago	EPOCHS millions of years ago
CENOZOIC	CENOZOIC 0 - 60	PLEISTOCENE 0 - 1½
MESOZOIC	CRETACEOUS 60 - 130	PLIOCENE 1½ - 12
	JURASSIC 130 - 155	MIOCENE 12 - 28
	TRIASSIC 155 - 230	OLIGOCENE 28 - 40
PALEOZOIC	PERMIAN 230 - 260	EOCENE 40 - 55
	PENNSYLVANIAN 260 - 310	PALEOCENE 55 - 60
	MISSISSIPPIAN 310 - 340	
	DEVONIAN 340 - 400	
	SILURIAN 400 - 425	
	ORDOVICIAN 425 - 500	
	CAMBRIAN 500 - 600	
	PRECAMBRIAN	

FIGURE 3　*Geologic time chart beginning with the Cambrian Period, in which easily recognizable fossils first made an appearance. (Right) An expanded time scale of the Cenozoic Era.*

confusion. In time the world cooled, the water became quiet, and the dissolved matter precipitated out to become the continents.

Thirteen hundred years later, during the Middle Ages, Dante revised the story of the earth. He agreed with Seneca; the lands came from the sea, but he thought that they were raised from the waters by the attraction of the stars "as a magnet draws iron."

Five hundred years later, in 1749, Georges-Louis Leclerc, Comte de Buffon, theorized that the earth came from the sun. He supposed that a huge comet, hurtling out of space, had crashed into the sun. The force of the collision sent balls of swirling incandescent gas spinning into space. Some of the gas bodies fell back into the sun, and others wandered off into space, but nine of the globes went into orbits around the sun. In time they cooled and condensed into the planets as we know them.

In 1900, Thomas C. Chamberlin, an American geologist, and F. R. Moulton, an American astronomer, suggested that the collision was not necessary. They also replaced the comet with a star, because by that time it was known that comets are mere wisps of dust and gas with negligible mass. The gravitational pull of a star passing close by the sun would raise a tide on the sun hundreds of thousands or even millions of miles high. If the other star was ten times as large as the sun, the two bodies would have had to approach to within 20 million miles of each other to raise a sufficiently high tide on the sun. Chamberlin and Moulton thought of the tide as cresting like a breaking wave, some parts of which the attraction of the intruding star tore off much as a gale whips off the top of a white cap. Some of the drops of the hot spray were pulled into the other star, while the main body of the wave fell back into the sun. But nine drops received enough momentum from the encounter to enter into orbits of their own around the sun.

In 1960, M. Woolfson of Manchester, England, proposed a new modification of this theory. He believes that all the planets were drawn from the sun within twelve hours by the approach of another star which came as close as 4 million miles. Woolfson's intruding star, one hundred times larger than the sun and traveling 60 miles a second, created a succession of tidal waves whose crests were pulled away from the sun and into orbit by the attraction of the giant star. Pluto, Neptune, Uranus, Saturn, and Jupiter were torn away as the star approached, the asteroids when it was nearest the sun, and Mars, Earth, Venus, and Mercury as it passed on its way.

The various modern theories of origin agree that some 5,000 million years ago our planet started as a great cloud of dust and gas. Then as it cooled a central sphere of molten liquid condensed. As the center gradually grew larger, gravitational separation of the components took place. The densest substances, probably mostly iron and nickel, sank to the center and formed the earth's core. According to students of earthquakes, the *core* of the earth has two parts: an inner solid sphere, surrounded by liquid (see Figure 4). The radius of the whole core is about 2,200 miles. Around the core is a wrapping of less dense rock called the *mantle*. This is 1,800 miles thick and forms the main mass of the earth. The third layer is called the *crust;* as its name implies, it is the outermost, surface layer of the earth. It is composed of less dense material than that of the mantle. It is really a very thin skin, averaging no more than 20 miles (or 32 kilometers) in thickness.

Presumably the crust was the first solid layer of the earth to

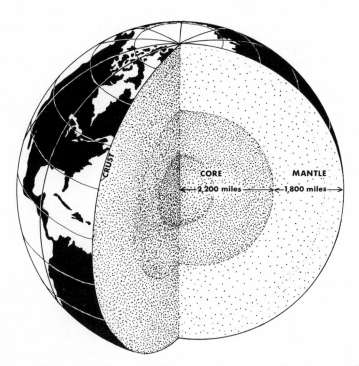

FIGURE 4 *Layers of the earth. The core, about 7,000 km. (4,400 miles) in diameter, consists of exceedingly hot, dense material. It is thought to have two parts: a solid center and a liquid outer layer. Surrounding the core is the mantle, about 2,900 km. (1,800 miles) of dense rock. Next is the crust, or outermost layer of the earth. This is very thin in comparison, its thickness varying from as little as 5 km. (3 miles) to at most 50 km. (30 miles).*

be formed. It must have floated on the molten mantle rock, like the skin on a pan of hot sauce. Then as the underlying mantle cooled, quantities of steam and other gases were expelled from the solidifying crustal rock. Thus the atmosphere came into being. Finally the temperature of the crust fell below the boiling point of water. Now, when rain fell, it was not immediately boiled back into the atmosphere. Whatever initial depressions there may have been at that remote time were flooded by primeval oceans.

Earth scientists disagree as to how the continents came into existence or why they are arranged as they are. One school of thought holds that the present arrangement of the continents dates from an early stage of the earth's development before life had evolved and even before the condensation of the oceans. But on one thing they all agree; that is, that the continents are made up of less dense rocks than those under the ocean basins. One can imagine that this segregation of lighter rock may have come about when the mantle was so hot as to be essentially a liquid. As the mantle material flowed in great eddies, it swept together a viscous scum of lighter material into the masses which we know as the continents. When the mantle "froze," the relative positions of the continents and ocean basins became fixed forever after.

An opposing school has been influenced by an Austrian meteorologist, Alfred Wegener. About half a century ago he observed, as others had before him, that the opposing shores of the North and South Atlantic "fit" when viewed on a globe. Because the fit seemed too good to be due to mere coincidence, he conjectured that the land masses of the old and new worlds had once been locked together like the pieces of a jigsaw puzzle, and that they had later broken apart and drifted away from each other (see Figure 5). Perhaps if Wegener had been more of a geologist, he would have recognized the objections to his theory set forth by most geologists, especially concerning the unknown enormous force required to cause the continents to move apart, and would have promptly forgotten about it. But for better or for worse, he did not. Instead he spent a large part of the remainder of his life looking for evidence to support this fascinating theory.

Wegener started out to tackle his scientific problems with only quite normal gifts in mathematics, physics, and other natural sciences. He had, however, the ability to apply these gifts with

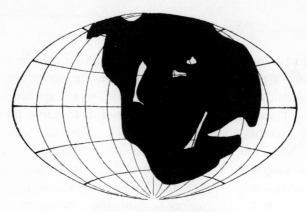

200 MILLION YEARS AGO

50 MILLION YEARS AGO

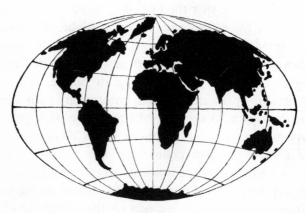

TODAY

FIGURE 5 *Illustrations of the theory advanced by Alfred Wegener that one original land mass had split up and the fragments slowly drifted apart. It was based on the apparent "fit" between opposing shores of the North and South Atlantic and on geological and biological evidence.*

great purpose and conscious aim. He had an extraordinary talent for observation, for knowing what is at the same time simple and important, and what can be expected to give a result. Added to this was a rigorous logic, which enabled him to assemble rightly everything relevant to his ideas.

The "grand old man of meteorology," W. Köppen of Hamburg, with whom Wegener had close contact from 1910 onwards and whose daughter became his wife, advised Wegener to stick to meteorological research and not to waste time with geological problems. Köppen foresaw the drawback from which Wegener was later to suffer:

To work at subjects which fall outside the traditionally defined bounds of a science naturally exposes one to being regarded with mistrust by some, if not all, of those concerned, and being considered an outsider. The question of the displacement of continents involves geodesists, geophysicists, geologists, paleontologists, animal- and plant-geographers, paleoclimatologists and geographers, and only by consideration of all these various branches of science, as far as is humanly possible, can the question be resolved.

Scarcely had Wegener started to devote himself to the theory of continental drift than he was caught up into the maelstrom of World War I and was twice wounded. His friends have often pointed out that Wegener took his military service very hard. Not because of dangers and hardships, since they would probably have appealed to a nature like his, but because of the inevitable conflict between his duty to his fatherland and his inmost conviction of the futility of war. Wegener was one of those rare men who do not willingly stop at duty for the good of self, family, or native land, but who rather see in the promotion of the well-being of mankind as a whole the true purpose of life.

Because of Wegener's interest in many fields of science it was a long time before he achieved a regular professorship at one of the many universities and technical high schools in Germany. It was said time and again that he had been turned down for a certain chair because he was interested also, and perhaps to a greater degree, in matters that lay outside its term of reference— as if such a man would not have been worthy of any chair in the wide realm of world science. In 1924, however, when Wegener was forty-four, a regular professorship in meterology and geophysics was created especially for him at the University of Graz in Austria.

Searching for evidence to support his theory of continental drift, Wegener found a good deal. For example, there are remarkable similarities between rocks of the same ages on opposite sides of the South Atlantic. Then he found suggestive correspondence between the Appalachians and their Canadian extension and the geological structure of the highlands of Scotland and Scandinavia. Furthermore, the remains of many fossil plants and animals in ancient sediments on the opposite shores of the Atlantic are strikingly similar; one can hardly doubt that they lived under similar conditions.

Some meteorologists and zoologists were impressed by the evidence, but most geologists were critical of the idea of drifting continents. They pointed out that no internal force was known that could cause the continents to move apart for large distances —let alone split them into fragments. Any force from outside the earth sufficient to move North America westward by fifty degrees of longitude in about 60 million years, would, they calculated, have halted the earth's rotation. They were inclined to be skeptical of the "jigsaw" argument, if only because the pieces were really not so close-fitting anyway. Further more, they held that the material underneath the earth's crust was solid and that there was no more chance of continents "drifting" about in it than there would be of a cement block drifting about in a concrete floor. Then it was argued that if the continents had drifted in the past, they ought to be drifting still, and yet the best measurements failed to reveal any change in the distance between the continents.

Now, after half a century, the theory of continental drift has received powerful support from what is called *paleomagnetism*. Working from the knowledge that some kinds of rocks become magnetized when they are formed, and the polarity of the magnetism conforms to the direction of the earth's magnetic field at that time, geophysicists have been able to get "fixes" on the position of the North and South Poles relative to the continents during earlier geological periods.

They have found that the magnetic polarities of rocks formed in earlier geological times are different from what they would be if formed today. Thus, whereas rocks laid down during the last 50 to 100 million years have magnetizations that point on the average north, rocks older than this do not. The older the rocks, the further their mean magnetization departs from the present north. What is especially interesting for the theory of continental drift is that in rocks believed to be more than 100 million years old, the track of the North Pole based on American rocks is some thirty degrees west of the track based on British rocks. The only way, seemingly, in which these two tracks can be reconciled is to suppose that 100 million years ago the Atlantic Ocean was one half its present width.

In 1963, to cite another example, Australian scientists E. Irving, W. A. Robertson, and P. M. Scoll announced that their measurements of magnetization of rocks indicated that Australia has been moving at the rate of 5 centimeters (2 inches) a year. They conclude that this wandering of their continent began about 100 million years ago. At its beginning Australia was somewhere near the South Magnetic Pole. Now it lies about 3,400 miles away.

In the meantime what has become of some of the serious objections to continental drift? One was the supposed rigidity of the dense rocks beneath the ocean basins. The reality of the matter is that their behavior when subjected to stresses lasting no more than a fraction of a second, as in transmitting earthquake waves, has no bearing on their behavior when subjected to long period stresses. One can cite many substances that behave in a dual way; for example, strike a piece of ice with a hammer and it shatters like a brittle, rigid solid, and yet glaciers flow like rivers, though of course, much more slowly. Pitch behaves in the same way, and so does ordinary glass, for that matter, but in the latter the deformation is extremely slow under normal conditions.

In fact, proof that material beneath the continents flows when subjected to long continuous stress has been known for some time, but oddly enough the importance of the evidence to the theory of continental drift has been largely overlooked. During the last ice age the Scandinavian Peninsula and a large part of Canada and some of the northeastern states were deeply buried under ice; the enormous weight pressed down these continental masses. Now that the great burden has melted these same regions are slowly rising, as is shown by raised beaches along the coasts. In some places the rise is fast enough to be measurable. Vertical movement of such large parts of the earth's crust cannot possibly take place unless there is flow of material beneath. When they were depressed, material must have flowed away from beneath them; now that the weight of the ice is gone, the dense material below is flowing back and in so doing is pushing up the land surface. The Scandinavian Peninsula is rising just as a ship rises when unloaded; the "rock" beneath the peninsula is behaving like a very viscous fluid.

In this example there is no mystery about the motive force. The sun was the source of the energy; its heat evaporated water in low latitudes, and then the water fell as snow in high latitudes and thereby built up the continental glaciers. Eventually the heat of the sun melted the continental glaciers. But the apparent lack of an adequate source of energy to move the continents was a serious embarrassment to the early advocates of continental drift. Among brave attempts to find one was the tidal theory, which appealed to the drag of the gravitational pull of the moon and sun. Others saw the continents as sliding down into the Pacific Basin after it had been created by the birth of the moon, but the theory that the moon was torn out of the Pacific has never attained really good standing. Appeal has also been made to the centrifugal effect of the earth's rotation, but it seems that the effect is not nearly large enough.

The relatively recent discovery of the prevalence of radioactive isotopes of various common elements has come to the rescue of the theory of continental drift. It is most probable that the internal heat of the earth is due to release of atomic energy. In the long run this continuously generated heat must be drawn off; otherwise in time the earth's temperature would rise to incandescence. There are several ways by which heat can move. One is by conduction; we all know how hot the handle of a spoon becomes even though only the bowl of the spoon is in the hot coffee. Another is by convection; in this case heat is conveyed by movement of the hot substance itself, which implies that the hot substance must be fluid. Convection is the principle by which a hot-water heating system works. As water is heated by a furnace, it expands and therefore becomes less dense. In consequence the hot, less dense water rises from the furnace to displace water that has become less warm and therefore denser by loss of heat while passing through the radiator. Thus heating by the furnace and cooling by radiation result in a continuous circulation of water through the system, at least as long as the furnace is fed fuel.

Within the mantle, flow induced by change in density due to heating and cooling is very probably intermittent, or episodic, because of the great viscosity of the mantle material.

Let us start with the mantle material at rest. Accumulation of heat in the basal layer of the mantle is particularly probable because of the proximity of the earth's core, which must be intensely hot to remain liquid in spite of being under enormous pressure. Furthermore, dissipation of heat from the basal layer by conduction is not likely to be very effective because of the great distance to the earth's surface where loss of heat by radiation occurs. As heat accumulates, temperature rises; as temperature rises, the material of the lower part of the mantle inevitably expands, or, which amounts to the same thing, becomes less dense, or lighter. Eventually gravitational instability within the mantle results; the upper part is actually heavier than the lower part. At sometime in the heating cycle, stress due to this unstable distribution of weight becomes great enough to overcome the viscosity of the mantle material. Just where flow first occurs must depend upon local differences in temperature, and therefore in density, within the upper level of the mantle. Wherever the densest mantle material is concentrated, there sinking should begin. Regional differences in temperature and density in the upper mantle are quite expectable; the rate of loss of heat by radiation from the earth's surface varies considerably from continents to ocean basins.

As some particularly dense part of the upper mantle sinks, nearby material moves in horizontally to take its place, and the laterally moving material in turn is replaced by hot, less dense material rising from the lower mantle; as it reaches the level of the upper mantle, it pushes aside still more of the denser upper mantle material. Soon, that is within some tens of millions of years, the vast heat engine is running at full speed. Volcanoes burst forth, mountains rise by compression, rift valleys open by tension, shallow seas drain from the continents which now stand exceptionally high in relation to the ocean floors; in short, one more geological revolution renovates the face of our ever youthful earth. But half-turns of the flywheels of convection cells should be enough to re-establish gravitational equilibrium, for by that time all the densest material should have sunk and been replaced in the upper part of the mantle by less dense material. Now flow within the mantle ceases; the tensions and compressions within the crust relax, and shallow seas again spread widely on the continents as the contrast between the average elevations of the continents and the floors of the oceans becomes less extreme. According to the geological record on the continents, the intervals of rest within the mantle last some 200 to 300 million years.

As yet, convection flow of the mantle is still hypothetical; we have no direct proof that this kind of flow occurs. However, the great Netherlands geophysicist F. A. Vening Meinesz, in his book *The Earth's Crust and Mantle*, published in 1964, says after summing up the evidence that he thinks the existence of mantle currents may be considered practically certain.

There are at least two ways of looking at the over-all distribution of oceans and continental areas. If you partially close your eyes to avoid seeing detail, and look at a globe, you see the land mostly in the northern hemisphere as an almost continuous ring around the Arctic Ocean, which connects three petal-shaped lobes that reach down into the southern oceans. It is as though four major continental land masses, the three great continents and Antarctica, occupy positions opposite to four oceanic areas. This symmetrical distribution has led to the conjecture that the basins and the continents were formed by four great convection cells in the mantle.

Another way of seeing global patterns is to look at a map of the world drawn in such a way that the edge of the map nowhere cuts the land, as illustrated in Figure 6. On this kind of map you will find that, except between Antarctica and Cape Horn, separated by 700 miles of sea, you could go overland from one continent to all the others without having to cross more than 60 miles of shallow sea. This map shows the land areas as a single island in the world ocean. It suggests that perhaps the continents once formed a single land mass that broke apart, and the fragments, having drifted various distances, are the continents as we know them today.

Of the many theories that attempt to explain the origin of continents and ocean basins, the convection theory seems to us to be the most satisfactory because it can explain in a consistent way not only the major but also many minor features of the earth's

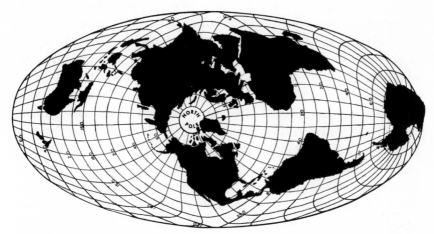

FIGURE 6 *Looking at the world in a slightly untraditional way, one can see on this map that the continents form a ragged island in the middle of the world ocean. How closely the world's entire land mass is tied together is illustrated by the fact that one could travel to all the continents (with the one exception of Antarctica) without at any time having to cross more than 60 miles of shallow sea.*

surface. But still it remains an unproved hypothesis. Perhaps, if the present rapid accumulation of information about the earth continues, we will one day be able to single out the correct hypothesis.

Since prehistoric times men have looked to the sea for food, as the great mounds of sea shells near their camping sites prove. Later, men learned to use the sea as a highway for their ships, but the immensity of the ocean inspired fear, which long delayed exploration and discovery. As late as the 1800's many intelligent people believed that the ocean was bottomless except for the shallow waters off coasts. According to another superstition foundered ships stopped sinking a mile or so down, and hung there forever. It was thought that deep water was very dense because of great pressure at depth. In reality, the increase in density of water under pressure is very slight; a ship heavy enough to sink below the surface would certainly go on down to the bottom. Buoys designed for certain kinds of oceanographic work can be made to sink to, and remain at, predetermined levels, and submarines can hover, but this takes very nice adjustment of ballasting. You may be quite sure that if you throw anything heavier than water overboard, it will sink to the bottom, just as do the skeletons and shells of organisms that drift about in the upper layers of water during their lifetimes, and as do the tiny particles of dust from outer space which rain down on the oceans.

The pioneer who first turned men's rambling questions about the sea into exact science was Matthew Fontaine Maury (1806–73), an American naval officer, who saw far ahead of his contemporaries. Although he had the mind of a scientist, he was keenly aware of the practical value of knowledge about the sea. Before Maury, mariners paid little or no attention to ocean currents or to consistent patterns of wind directions and storms. Maury, by his study of currents, and above all by his organization of a system of world-wide observation of currents, founded the modern science of physical oceanography.

To Maury the sea was a dynamic whole, with "a system of oceanic circulation as complete, as perfect and as harmonious as that of the atmosphere or the blood." Maury fairly earned the right to the titles "father of American oceanography" and "the pathfinder of the sea," as he is sometimes called, by writing the first English-language textbook on oceanography, *The Physical Geography of the Sea*, in 1855. When he began his work, any knowledge of currents, prevailing winds, and storm tracks, was part of the trade secrets of a handful of the most experienced and shrewdest mariners; when he had finished, his charts of ocean currents and prevailing winds had just about revolutionized traffic on the high seas. As the officer-in-charge of the Depot of Charts and Instruments, the precursor of the U.S. Navy Hydrographic Office, he made the first chart of the floor of the North Atlantic based on all soundings then available. By his almost unaided effort he put the United States to the forefront in marine science. His accomplishments were fully appreciated by the governments and navies of Europe, from whom he received the highest honors. In his own country he was inadequately rewarded; innovations, regardless of how useful, were frowned upon.

Maury was born in 1806 in the country near Fredericks, Virginia, where his father was an unsuccessful farmer. Hoping for greener pastures, the family moved to a new farm near West Harpeth River, Tennessee, in 1811. Conditions in the pioneer school that Maury attended were almost unbelievably primitive; there were no textbooks and no blackboards.

When twelve years old, he was sent to Harpeth Academy where he learned some Latin, but what pleased him most was mathematics. Soon he had outgrown Harpeth, but to go to an expensive school in the East was out of the question; his father's farming was as unsuccessful as ever. To gain the education that he wanted, he made up his mind to join the Navy. Without much trouble he secured a midshipman's warrant, went to sea, and learned as much about navigation as was possible on board a man-of-war in those days before the existence of the Naval Academy. Had he done no more than that, he would probably have become a very efficient naval officer, but he did more because he had an innate curiosity about the world around him. Furthermore, he had the ability to observe for himself without need of textbooks or instructors. The sea was his field of observation. Not an impractical dreamer, he set himself a very practical goal, which, always articulate, he described as "nothing less than to blaze a way through the winds of the sea by which the navigator may find the best paths at all seasons." He was awake to the potential value of charts that would show the average directions and strengths of winds at various seasons, as well as currents, and such charts he intended to make.

His first book, *New Theoretical and Practical Treatise on Navigation,* came out in 1836. It was a success; he was already making a name for himself. In 1839 he began abstracting data on winds, currents, and temperatures from ships' logs. Realizing the value of such data, he also knew how useless they were unless coordinated. In 1842 he was appointed superintendent of the Navy's Depot of Charts and Instruments, and the Naval Observatory. He now had at his disposal a wealth of raw material in the form of the files of old logbooks.

But he was not satisfied; he needed more data based on better observations made with up-to-date instruments. His next step was to enlist the help of navigators all over the world. Maury felt sure the routes then in use were merely traditional, handed down from one generation of seamen to another and followed just because these were the ways that ships always went. Most of the routes were crooked and wasteful. For example when a vessel sailed from the United States to the Cape of Good Hope, it crossed the Atlantic three times. He was convinced that by setting down on a chart the records of many ships, much safer, shorter, more economical paths across the oceans could be followed. He explained that "by putting down on a chart the tracks of many vessels on the same voyage, during all seasons, and by projecting along each track the winds and currents daily encountered, together with the latitude and longitude, it was plain that navigators hereafter, by consulting the charts, would have for their guide the results of the combined experience of all ships whose tracks were recorded." On the charts (twenty-four records were to be taken each day, some of them every two hours) he asked that certain conditions be noted by using colors and symbols—a comet tail for wind, an arrow for currents, Arabic numerals for temperature, Roman numerals for barometer readings, broken and dotted lines for months, and colors for the four seasons.

For the most part Maury received enthusiastic cooperation. Mariners are practical people; they have to be to survive, and the same can be said of shipowners. The U.S. Navy was so impressed by the possibilities of the charts that all public carriers were authorized to gather daily information on latitude and longitude; hourly rate of the currents; speed and direction of the winds; temperatures; barometric pressure before, during, and after a storm; and other phenomena such as fogs, whales, birds, islands, and shoals sighted, and errors in earlier charts.

Maury started to publish his famous *Wind and Currents Charts* in 1847. By following the charts the mariners found that the far corners of the world were brought closer together by many days. Everywhere routes were shortened. For example, the average sailing time between Rio and New York was cut from 55 to 35 days by using the newly available knowledge of currents and prevailing winds. Between New York and San Francisco around Cape Horn, a distance of 14,000 miles, the time was cut from 183 days to 135 days. These and other developments were not overlooked by the governments of the maritime nations of the world. They began to appreciate the importance of coordinated knowledge of sea conditions. Only nine years after the publication of Maury's first chart, one thousand navigators were at work collecting weather and current data according to a uniform plan. When new charts were published they represented more than a quarter of a million days of observations.

But there was still more to do. Maury now wrote letters to scientists all over the world urging them to support a universal system of meteorological observations on land and sea. The response was gratifying. In August 1853, representatives of all the maritime nations of the world met in conference in Brussels. At the opening session Maury was asked to state the purpose of the meeting. When he had finished, the members of the conference stood up to applaud "the representative of the youngest nation among them." In a letter to his wife he said: "Rarely has there been such a sublime spectacle presented to the scientific world; all the nations agreeing to unite and cooperate in carrying out one system of philosophical research with regard to the sea. They may be enemies in all else, but here they are to be friends."

As was proper, Maury played the leading role at the conference. He would have liked to have considered cooperation in making weather observations on land. But there was not quite enough international friendship for that; the majority decided to limit cooperation to observations at sea. Nevertheless, his inspiration led to the establishment of official meteorological offices in Great Britain and Germany. As a further outcome of the conference and Maury's influence, other maritime nations established hydrological services, which to a considerable extent cooperated with one another and with Maury in charting the seas. Thus international cooperation in the study of the seas had an early start, thanks to Maury's inspiration.

Although Maury was interested in the nature of the bottom of the sea, his observations of the bottom were almost entirely limited to soundings. Perhaps it is not surprising that when a rather startling discovery was made, it came by accident. The transatlantic cable, laid in 1858, broke two years later at a depth of

6,000 feet. When it was brought to the surface for repairs, many strange things were found clinging to it. That these things could be animals was scarcely credible because theory forbad the existence of life below 1,800 feet. But animals they were, though unlike any that marine biologists had ever seen before. Evidently at great depths in the oceans there was a world of life that scientists had never dreamt of.

So much interest was aroused among scientists and laymen by this find that the British Navy and the Royal Society decided to send a ship on a cruise around the world to study the oceans and what was in them. The emphasis was to be on biological problems, particularly to look for new species and to chart their distribution. To gain a better understanding of the geographical ranges of populations in the seas, it would be necessary to study the chemical properties of sea water, to learn to what depth light penetrated and to record temperatures at various depths. Also needed was more information about ocean currents and the topography of the floor of the ocean.

On December 21, 1872, less than two months before Maury died, the *Challenger*—a full-rigged corvette of 2,306 tons with auxiliary steam power—set out on the first world-encircling oceanographic expedition ever undertaken. During the summer of 1872 she had been remodeled for scientific research. Her guns had been sent ashore and the main deck partitioned off into laboratories and workrooms.

Wyville Thomson, a Scottish naturalist, headed the scientific staff. His job was to find out "everything about the sea." To this end he planned to go back and forth across the Atlantic, Pacific, Indian, and Antarctic oceans. The investigations were to include everything that had a bearing on the biological and physical conditions of the oceans. The scientists were to record temperatures both at the surface and at depth, study movements of tides and currents, chart the relation of barometric pressure to latitude, keep records of the chemistry of the water, make soundings and take samples of bottom sediments, and collect and classify animals and plants.

Were they permitted to relax on those few occasions when the *Challenger* touched at some exotic shore? No! England expected every man to do his duty; when ashore they were to study the geology, investigate plants and animals, observe types of government and the habits and customs of the people.

When one considers the vastness of the problems they attempted to solve, and the inadequacy of the equipment, some of which had never been tried out before, one can scarcely blame them for failing to achieve fully their goals. Even today, after more than ninety years, oceanographers with all kinds of modern instruments and equipment at their disposal are still wrestling with some of the problems that Wyville Thomson tried to solve in three and a half years. Even though the expedition fell short of its goal, it brought back an enormous amount of new information and invaluable collections; it set the pattern for oceanographic investigations from that day to this.

The equipment was the best that nineteenth-century technology could provide. In addition to the finest navigational instruments there was an assortment of equipment for hydrographic, magnetic, and meteorological observations. There were water-sampling bottles, dredges and trawls for catching animals on the bottom and at intermediate depths, and, of course, miles of sounding line and heavier rope for lowering the dredges.

To make a sounding a 200-pound weight was lowered on a hemp line spooled on a 10-foot-diameter drum. By the time the weight reached bottom in deep water, the line would continue to pay out under its own weight. Consequently, the only way of telling when the weight had reached bottom was to time the rate at which the line payed out. When the speed of the running line decreased, the scientists assumed that the weight was on the bottom. The whole operation of lowering and heaving in took several hours in deep water. And then there was no assurance that the recorded depth was at all accurate. Errors were particularly difficult to avoid in regions of strong currents, as along the track of the Gulf Stream, where the sounding line took on great S-shaped curves.

Technically the *Challenger* was the first steamer to cross the Antarctic Circle. Actually, however, she generally traveled under sail and reserved her 1,234 horsepower steam engine for holding position on station and for running the winches that hauled in the various lines. Without steam power the expedition would not have been feasible. Much of the sampling gear was too heavy to be handled by hand. Moreover, making a "station" meant staying as nearly as possible in one place whose latitude and longitude had been accurately determined. Sometimes a station dragged on for two days while the scientists made the necessary measurements and took samples. Except in unusually favorable weather, making such long stations under sail would have been out of the question.

The *Challenger* made 362 stations. At each the sounding line was lowered, a bottom sample was taken, water samples were collected near the bottom, and the temperature of the water near the bottom was recorded. Direction and speed of currents were measured. Whenever possible the dredge was lowered to collect animals from the bottom, and water samples and temperatures at intermediate depths were taken. Sometimes nets were towed at intermediate depths to catch whatever life might be there. As the many new plants and animals came on board, the scientists were crowded out of their laboratories. To make life at all possible on board, quantities of specimens had to be sent home from the ports at which the ship touched. These were stored at the University of Edinburgh until the expedition should return.

The *Challenger* reached England on May 24, 1876; the expedition had been a great success. Before the *Challenger* cruise, knowledge of the deep sea had been almost nonexistent. At the end of the cruise and after publication of the many reports on the collections, the ocean was still largely unknown, but at least much basic knowledge had been gained. Every ocean except the Arctic had been sounded, and 140 million square miles of the ocean bottom had been charted. Among the strange animals collected, 4,717 new species and 715 new genera were eventually identified by specialists.

The homecoming of the *Challenger* was an occasion for rejoicing; but for the scientists there was no rest. Wyville Thomson plunged into a round of conferences, lectures, and social engagements. The Royal Society awarded him a gold medal, and he was knighted. Above all there was the long task of organizing the vast accumulation of information and material. A government department was set up in Edinburgh to examine the biological collections, coordinate the oceanographic data, and publish the results. Sir Wyville was placed in charge of the department, and he continued at its head until he died in 1882 at the age of fifty-two. Very probably his life had been shortened by the fatigue and strain of the expedition. The direction of the work passed to his first assistant, John Murray, one of the naturalists on the expedition.

The fame of the expedition and the unique collection of biological material attracted specialists to Edinburgh from all parts of the world. Sir Wyville realized that only through international cooperation could the tens of thousands of plants and animals be adequately described. Never before had so great a pooling of scientific knowledge on a common project been undertaken.

Twenty-three years passed before the last of the fifty large volumes setting forth the results of the expedition was published in 1895. The volumes included 29,500 pages written by seventy-six authors from all countries engaged in the study of the oceans.

If the scientists on the *Challenger* did not learn "everything about the sea," they had clearly shown the way and set the pace for all future investigations of the waters that dominate our planet.

With the *Challenger* expedition a whole series of investigations and surveys began. While the *Challenger* was bound around the world a German ship—the *Gazelle*—began a similar cruise through the South Atlantic, the Indian Ocean, and the Pacific. A little later the U.S.S. *Tuscarora* began a cruise across the North Pacific, interested primarily in surveying for a Pacific cable, but concerned also with oceanographic problems of every other kind. Two French ships—the *Travailleur* and the *Talisman*—engaged in important biological surveys in the Atlantic, and other ships were soon to be at work all about the world.

Working separately, the various national fishery organizations in Europe proved unable to cope with problems in the North Sea and other European waters. Largely at the instigation of Otto Pettersson of Stockholm's Tekniska Högskola, King Oscar IV of Sweden convened an international conference in 1899 on the application of oceanographic studies to fisheries. The conference prepared a joint plan of investigation, which included provision for the establishment of the International Council for the Exploration of Sea at Copenhagen in 1902. The conference is one of the milestones in the history of oceanography.

In the United States the Coast Survey, which was redesignated the Coast and Geodetic Survey in 1878 and transferred to the Department of Commerce in 1903, conducted a series of studies of the Gulf Stream between 1870 and 1890, including some remarkable current observations, from the steamer *Blake*. This work had to be abandoned in favor of coastal surveys until the 1930's, when the development of the echo sounder led to the necessity of knowing the speed of sound in sea water, which in turn required sampling for salinity and water temperature.

The *Challenger* expedition is one of the great achievements in the history of scientific exploration. A quarter of a century later, oceanographers had gained a general picture of the earth's oceans; and another quarter of a century after that, oceanography entered upon a new era with the *Meteor* expedition of 1925–7.

During the half century from the *Challenger* to the *Meteor*, oceanographic research had consisted mostly of isolated and widely scattered observations. The emphasis was on the amount of territory covered rather than on systematic research. The most notable exceptions to this rule were the Norwegian studies of the North Atlantic and the Norwegian Sea, begun shortly after the turn of the century. When the German South Atlantic Expedition embarked on the *Meteor* in 1925, it undertook what had never before been attempted—the systematic study of a single ocean. In a period of twenty-five months, the *Meteor* crossed the South Atlantic more than a dozen times. The data obtained included some 70,000 soundings of the ocean depths. It was the *Meteor* expedition that first revealed the ruggedness of the ocean floor.

While these and other important oceanographic explorations were under way, many institutions ashore were taking up the study of the sea. The Zoological Station of Naples, founded in 1872, and the Marine Laboratory of the Marine Biological Association of the United Kingdom at Plymouth, founded in 1888, are outstanding among those started early. Prince Albert of Monaco, after operating a series of research vessels, in 1906 endowed an oceanographic museum at Monaco and an oceanographic institute at Paris.

The first oceanographic laboratory in America was the Hopkins Marine Station of Stanford University, established at Pacific Grove, California, in 1892. In 1905 the Marine Biological Association of San Diego was founded at La Jolla, California, with an endowment from members of the Scripps family; it became part of the University of California, as the Scripps Institution for Biological Research, in 1912, and was redesignated the Scripps Institution of Oceanography in 1925. Three of the staff members of the Scripps Institution, H. U. Sverdrup, M. W. Johnson, and R. H. Fleming, wrote the first modern reference work on all phases of oceanography, *The Oceans*. Published in 1942, it is still the most comprehensive textbook on oceanography available.

Today there are more than five hundred marine research stations scattered around the world. Many have their own ships, which remain at sea for months at a time while studying one, or more often, many aspects of the sea.

The oceanographic institutions vary in size, equipment, and staff. There are large, diversified institutions, usually attached to a major university, either as departments of oceanography or as semi-autonomous marine research institutions. These institutions customarily carry out research projects in all fields of oceanography and the atmospheric sciences. There are smaller facilities, offering work in many phases of marine science, but specializing in marine biology. Then there are laboratories subordinate to federal agencies. These are the laboratories that perform research of extremely broad scope in direct application to mission-oriented problems facing the parent agencies. In addition, especially in this country, a certain amount of important oceanographic research is conducted in industrial laboratories.

The first really large-scale exploration in oceanography got its start from World War II. National defense could command financial support and general interest on a scale that pure science could not. By World War II the seas were no longer the sure protection that they had been, largely because of the success of modern submarines. With a shock it was realized that greater knowledge of the oceanic environment was needed urgently. Larger and better equipped ships were built for the specific purpose of studying the sea. And, incidentally, pure science prospered. Instrumentation improved by leaps and bounds. Echo-sounding gear was perfected, electronically controlled nets for biological sampling were devised, and piston core bottom samplers came into general use.

The conclusions of scientists on the ship or in the laboratory on land depend almost exclusively upon the records. In oceanography direct observations are rarely possible. The important advances in oceanography that have come since World War II are in large measure attributable to a revolution in instrumentation and to the application of new materials.

Investigation and exploitation of the world's oceans has been stimulated by naval and maritime requirements. But in recent years scientific and development programs have been paralleled by a new or enlarged commercial interest. A vast global enterprise is now charting the mysteries of the deep and exploiting the oceans' resources.

From the beginning, men have recognized the sea as a supreme wonder and paradox of the natural world—at once a thing of beauty and terror, a barrier and a highroad dividing and uniting mankind, a source of life and a fearful and capricious destroyer. The sea poets of every land have sung in exaltation of its sunlit moods and in awe of its fury and fathomless deeps.

Today in the wider perspectives of man's awareness of the universe it has become clear that the sea is in many ways a miracle. We know now that we are dependent on the sea not only for certain accessories of existence but for the very character of existence itself. The entity called life emerged from the sea; the basic fabric of all living things was initially determined by it; the entire system of nature composing man's environment is governed by it. More than any other physical feature of the planet it is the sea that makes the earth unique.

THE CIRCULATION

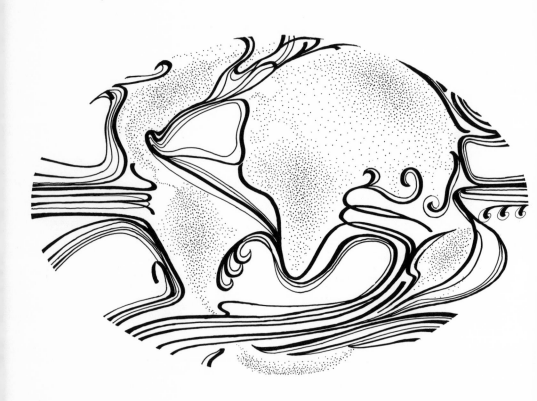

)F THE OCEAN

THE OUTER ENVELOPES OF THE EARTH, THE ATMOSPHERE AND the world ocean, determine the destiny of life. The vast diversity of living things and their distribution on our planet are largely a consequence of the interactions of the perpetual streaming motions of the atmosphere and the discontinuous envelope of water, the hydrosphere.

Because we live at the bottom of the atmosphere and can look up through it, and because its constant changes take place before our eyes, we feel that we know the atmosphere. But this familiarity does not include real comprehension of the complex interactions of the various processes that bring about ceaseless change within the atmosphere, or what we call the changing weather. The inadequacy of our understanding is evident in the well-known difficulty of correctly forecasting the weather for only two or three days in advance. However, the subtle sequence of cause and effect is becoming clearer, particularly through fuller knowledge of that patchy envelope, the hydrosphere. Its influence on weather is important, and in determining long-period variations of climate its effect is critical. Because of the extraordinary capacity of water to store and transport heat, oceanic circulation is a powerful stabilizer of climate. It has been called, with reason, "the flywheel of climate."

Water is such a common substance that we, who are three quarters water ourselves, tend to lose sight of its almost unique properties. These are due to its peculiar molecular structure. The two hydrogen atoms are not directly opposite each other with the oxygen atom halfway between; instead the three atoms form a triangle with the angle at the oxygen atom equal to $105°$, as shown in Figure 7. With this arrangement the negative charge of the oxygen atom is not quite cancelled by the positive charges of the hydrogen atoms. Consequently, the water molecule has polarity; its "ends" are differently charged. Because of polarity the molecules cluster together as loosely joined supermolecules consisting of from two to eight unit molecules. At the boiling point 80 per cent of the molecules are combined in clusters; before the change of state from liquid to vapor can occur, most of

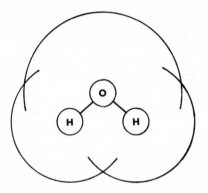

FIGURE 7   *Water molecule. The angle of about 105° between the hydrogen atoms accounts for the polarity of the molecule. If the angle were 180°, the molecule would be nonpolar.*

the clusters must break up. This is why water, a combination of two gases, boils at so high a temperature. If water consisted entirely of unclustered molecules, it would boil at 80° below zero Celsius. Since, in that case, all water on earth would be constantly in the form of vapor, life as we know it could not exist.

As water cools it behaves like most other substances; its volume decreases, but only down to 4° C. Below that point an increase in the proportion of supermolecules to uncombined molecules occurs; since the supermolecules take up more space than the unit molecules, water expands as it cools below 4° C. At the freezing temperature, 0° C., water expands considerably so that the volume of ice is 10 per cent greater than that of the same weight of water at 4° C. Water shares this property of expanding when it freezes with only very few other substances, such as silver and bismuth. And this property in water is crucial to the existence of life. When the temperature of the surface waters of lakes and rivers falls to 4° C., the temperature of greatest density, the heavy cold water sinks to be replaced at the surface by warmer water from below. Such overturn continues until the temperature of the whole water mass has reached 4° C. Further cooling now brings about a decrease of density; overturn ceases, and soon the surface water freezes.

If water became denser as it froze, like most other substances, ice forming on the surfaces of ponds and lakes would sink. With surface water constantly freezing and sinking, ice would soon fill ponds and lakes solidly from top to bottom. At the same time water vapor from equatorial regions would collect as frost or fall as snow on such solidly frozen bodies of water until much, if not all, water had become locked up in masses of ice at the poles. A world in which almost all water were solid would be as little favorable for life as we know it as one in which it were all in the form of vapor.

Ice at the surface of a body of water acts as a barrier to the flow of heat. Once a layer of ice has formed, the rate of cooling or loss of heat of the water beneath becomes much slower, with the result that only very shallow ponds ever freeze solidly from top to bottom. A layer of sea ice not thicker than about 10 feet (or 3 meters) prevents almost all further loss of heat from the water below. This is the reason why the surface of the sea rarely freezes to a greater depth than about 3 meters. As we all know, enormous masses of ice much thicker than 3 meters occur in polar waters and may drift into lower latitudes where they become a hazard to shipping, but these floating mountains of ice are not composed of frozen salt water. They are instead detached fragments of glaciers that flow into the sea or tabular masses of ice that have broken away from a continental ice sheet as it spreads out over the sea. Enormous masses of this kind are common in the Antarctic Ocean. They are composed of ice formed from snow that fell thousands of years ago in the interior of the Antarctic continent, which, having become part of the continental ice sheet, has crept under the pull of gravity toward the sea.

The salt in sea water has an important influence on its reaction to temperature. The freezing point of sea water is two degrees lower than that of fresh water, and unlike fresh water its density increases as it cools below 4° C., almost, but not quite, down to the temperature −2° C. at which it begins to freeze. Therefore, the heaviest sea water is that which is almost cold enough to freeze. This means that sea water at the surface in high latitudes keeps on sinking until its temperature is almost six degrees below the temperature at which fresh water begins to become less dense. It is this extremely cold water from the surface that sinks and fills the deep parts of the ocean basins. Thus, because of saltiness, the deepest layers of the oceans are much colder than they would otherwise be. This intensification of the temperature effect promotes oceanic circulation, tends to equalize climates at all latitudes, and provides a supply of oxygen to the deepest parts of the ocean basins. If sea water reacted to cooling in the same way as fresh, it is probable that the climates of the continents would be distinctly different.

Water is extraordinary in another property; its capacity to store heat is surpassed by that of only one other substance, liquid ammonia. To raise the temperature of a given volume of water by one degree requires 2.2 times as much heat as is needed to raise the temperature of an equal volume of mercury one degree. Similarly, in cooling it gives up 2.2 times as much heat as mercury. Furthermore, when water changes from solid to liquid it absorbs a certain amount of heat without rise of temperature; this is what is known as its heat of fusion. Only ammonia has a greater heat of fusion than water.

In another thermal property water is truly unique; no other substance has so great a heat of vaporization—the number of units of heat absorbed or given out without change of temperature in changing from liquid to vapor or vice versa. Although the heats of fusion and vaporization of water have a less important influence on climate than its heat capacity, they are far from negligible in the heat economy of our planet.

Temperature variation from surface to bottom in the ocean is due to the combined effects of input of heat from the sun, transport of heat by currents, and stirring by winds and tides. The stirring is most vigorous near the surface, and, consequently, we find an uppermost layer of water having the same temperature from top to bottom. The lower boundary of this homogeneous layer, which lies at depths between 250 and 500 meters, is marked by a thin zone in which a rapid drop in temperature with depth occurs. This relatively thin zone is called the *thermocline*. Below the thermocline, temperature falls and density increases slowly with depth. The temperature of the bottom water, where it is deep enough, is always close to freezing; it is the densest water in the ocean.

From temperature measurements in the world ocean, ocean-ographers estimate that 93 per cent of all ocean water is colder than 10° C., and 76.5 per cent than 4° C. The temperature of deep water varies within rather narrow limits, from about 0.4° C. below zero to nearly 4° C. above. The stabilizing effect of this great flood of cold water is intensified by the extraordi-narily great heat capacity of water. If, because of some change in the energy output of the sun, the earth received 1 per cent more heat in the course of a year, and if that much heat went into the atmosphere alone, it would raise its temperature by 15° C. (27° F.), enough to make large parts of the earth intolerably hot; but the same amount of heat would raise the temperature of the deep water of the oceans by only 0.01° C.

Without the stabilizing effect of the oceans, conditions on earth would be more nearly as they are on the moon, where the lighted side is burning hot and the dark side some 100° C. below freezing. For this reason parts of the continents farthest from the ocean have more nearly moonlike climates, with extreme differ-ences from summer heat to intense winter cold. Another effect is to make the climates of the west coasts of the continents more uniform; the prevailing winds of middle latitudes blow from east to west, and thus cause upwelling of deep, cold water along west-ern coasts.

The ocean is in constant streaming motion, but friction would bring its motion to a halt without some continuous input of en-ergy. The source of the energy is the same as that which supplies the energy to keep our own blood circulating, that is radiant energy from the sun. Although we cannot convert radiant energy directly into muscular energy, we make use of it indirectly by eating plants (or animals that have eaten plants), which have utilized sunlight to transform water and carbon dioxide into com-plex organic substances. The ocean is almost as incapable of the direct conversion of radiant energy into motion as we are.

Unlike air, water is relatively opaque to radiant energy. The sun's energy, which can pass with little loss through the entire thickness of the atmosphere, is trapped within the uppermost layer of water. Whereas the sun's energy heats the basal part of the air column indirectly by heating the earth's surface, the same energy expends its full force within the uppermost layer of water. Thus the heating effect of the sun's rays increases the stability of the water column by heating, and making lighter, the uppermost layer. Because the earth is round, the slanting sun's rays that fall on the waters of high latitudes are less effective in heating than the vertical rays of low latitudes; the result of this unequal heating together with the pull of gravity should, at least in theory, maintain a sluggish poleward flow of warm surface water to replace cold water flowing toward the equator at depth. But the circulation induced in this way would be weak; if no other process for distributing heat over the earth were at work, we would have to contend with very different climates.

Fortunately for us, the atmosphere reacts to solar energy in a different way. Unlike water, air is largely transparent to the sun's rays, particularly to the longer wave lengths, which are most effective in heating solid objects on which they fall. Unobstructed by the atmosphere, these rays reach and heat the earth's surface. Only by coming in contact with the warm surfaces of land and ocean does the basal layer of the atmosphere become heated. Then as its temperature rises, it expands; when it has become lighter than the overlying air the stability of the air column is upset. Turnover follows, either in the form of the sudden fury of a summer thunderstorm or as the nearly continuous motion of the trade winds. This atmospheric circulation on a planetary scale is the intermediate process that converts solar energy into the constant motion of our oceans. It is the planetary winds that whip the surface waters of the world ocean into motion; in turn, surface currents largely determine the pattern of flow at depths far below the direct influence of the atmosphere.

Matthew Maury more than a hundred years ago first grasped the importance of the streaming motion of ocean waters, which he compared to the circulation of the blood. Ocean currents, he wrote, are the arteries of the earth; they carry warm and cold water around the earth; their influence reaches to the greatest

depths, thereby bringing cold water from the bottom to the surface. Maury's observations led him to the discovery that the
average ocean currents are related to the average winds and can
be characterized as great eddylike motions that change somewhat
with the seasons. This discovery revolutionized the handling of
sailing ships; by taking advantage of prevailing winds and currents, travel at sea ceased to be the hit or miss affair that it had
been for thousands of years. It also marked the birth of physical
oceanography as a science. Maury's findings, followed up by
those of the *Challenger* expedition, as we have seen, provided the
nucleus from which our present understanding of the dynamic
processes of the oceans has grown. Study of the physical interrelationships governing the great machine of oceanic circulation
has been the primary concern of physical oceanography ever
since.

In 1898 Vilhelm Bjerknes, a Norwegian theoretical physicist,
published a paper which provided a basis for predicting the motions of water masses in the sea from measurements of vertical
and horizontal variations in pressure. This paper stimulated a
new school of thought that led to some major contributions in
physical oceanography. To follow the motions of water masses in
the sea by direct observations was, until fairly recently, difficult
because of the absence of convenient and really stationary reference points at sea. To anchor a ship in very deep water is a feat of
seamanship rarely attempted. Handling the weight of cable paid
out is a problem in itself, and heaving it in consumes much time.
Furthermore, except under particularly favorable conditions,
though the anchor is stationary, the ship is free to swing through
an arc usually large enough to introduce serious errors into the
measurements of slowly moving currents. On the other hand, a
drifting ship can lower and retrieve a series of Nansen bottles in
relatively short time. These bottles, named after Fridtjof Nansen,
are provided with thermometers from which temperatures at various levels reached by the bottles are read; at the same time they
provide samples of water from the same levels that can be
analyzed for salinity. From these properties of the samples oceanographers can calculate the densities of the water masses at the
different levels and from the densities in turn they can deduce
their relative motions. The practical application of this method of

solving problems of oceanic circulation was developed early in this century by Björn Helland-Hansen, Johan Sandström, and several other Norwegian and German oceanographers.

The beginning of the century also brought two other advances toward the modern conception of circulation. Maury's observations on the relationship between winds and surface currents received physical clarification from the Swedish oceanographer, Vagn Walfrid Ekman. In 1905 he showed mathematically that the effect of a wind blowing steadily over the ocean is to drive the surface layer at an angle of 45° to the right of the wind direction in the northern hemisphere and to the left in the southern hemisphere. A further effect is to move successively deeper layers of water at increasingly greater angles to the wind direction, until at a depth of 60 to 100 meters (200 to 330 feet) the direction of motion is opposite to that at the surface. In addition to the shift in direction of flow at each lower level, there is a gradual decrease in velocity. To visualize what happens it is helpful to think of a spiral staircase that becomes narrower downward. The radial arrangement of the steps then represents the gradual shift in current direction and the decrease in width of each lower step represents the decrease in velocity. This "stairway" is known as the *Ekman spiral* (see Figure 8). At first sight the angle between wind direction and the resulting direction of the motion of the water appears paradoxical, until one realizes that wind and water are moving on the surface of a rotating sphere. The resultant motion of each little unit of water is influenced both by the motion of the air above and by the rotation of the earth. The effect of the rotation of the earth is known by the name of its discoverer; it is the *Coriolis force*, or better, *Coriolis effect*, since it is not really a force (see Figure 9).

The effect stems from Newton's law that a moving object left completely to itself moves in a straight line. During the time that a bullet flies in a straight line from a rifle to a target, the rotation of the earth causes the target to shift position a little. Because of the convention of relating motion to the earth's surface, it is customary to say that the path of the bullet has been "deflected by a force," but it seems to us a pity to hide the simplicity of what really happens with the useless fiction of a "deflecting force."

A simple way of simulating the Coriolis effect is to draw a

pencil in a straight line across a pad of paper while at the same time rotating the pad. Of course, the line traced on the paper will turn to the right or left depending upon the direction of rotation of the paper. If the paper is rotated counterclockwise, the pencil line will curve to the right, as the paths of moving objects do in the northern hemisphere. To simulate the Coriolis effect in the southern hemisphere, rotate the paper clockwise.

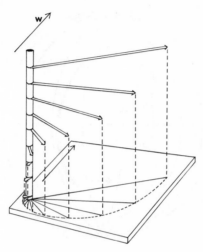

FIGURE 8 *Schematic representation of a wind-driven current in deep water, showing the decrease in velocity and change of direction at regular intervals of depth (the Ekman spiral). W indicates direction of wind.*

The Coriolis effect is greatest at the poles, and diminishes as one approaches the equator. This is because the angle between the horizontal plane and the earth's axis of rotation decreases as one approaches the equator until at the equator, the horizontal plane being parallel to the axis of rotation, the plane does not rotate at all and consequently the Coriolis effect is zero. The decrease in the Coriolis effect from poles to equator is expressed mathematically by saying that the effect is proportional to the sine of the latitude.

Attempts to prove the reality of the Ekman spiral in the open ocean have not been entirely successful, although examples of water transport according to the Ekman theory are well known.

On the Lofoten fishing grounds off the coast of Norway, for example, the prevailing southwest winds have the effect of driving
the water toward the coast instead of to the northeast. This is of
practical importance because it leads to sinking of water near the
coast, so that the layers of the coastal waters as determined by
differences in temperature and salinity are bent downward
enough to intersect the continental shelf. The result is a spotty

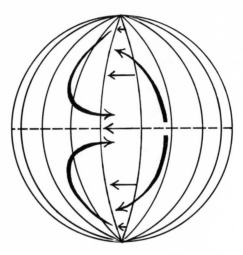

FIGURE 9   *Coriolis effect, caused by the earth's rotation, deflects winds
and currents—to the right in the northern hemisphere, to the left in the
southern hemisphere.*

distribution of the cod hovering near the bottom, because of their
narrow preference for water of a certain temperature and salinity.
To determine the most profitable deployment of the fishing fleet,
surveys of the water structure are made at regular intervals.

Conditions along the coasts of California and Peru are also influenced by wind-driven upwelling which occurs when the prevailing
winds blow toward the equator, thus causing surface water to move
away from the shore; deep water then rises to take its place. As
the rising water, bringing chemicals essential to life, comes within
reach of sunlight, photosynthesis by microscopic drifting plants,
the tiny first links in the nutritional chain, occurs on a massive
scale. Exceptional poleward winds reverse conditions with consequences that may be catastrophic. The coast of Peru provides a

famous example of how a change in atmospheric circulation may alter living conditions drastically. During exceptional years a current of warm, less saline water creeps southward along the coast of Peru, and may even pass Callao. This current is called *El Niño*, the Christ Child, because it arrives near Christmas; but it brings no blessings. On the contrary, disaster follows in its wake. As the warm water mixes with the normal, cold coastal waters, marine life from the lowest forms of plankton to fish suffer mass mortality. Dead fish, littering the beaches, decompose and befoul both the air and the coastal waters. Hydrogen sulfide is released in such quantities that it blackens the white lead paint of ships, a phenomenon known as the "Callao painter." The guano birds, because of the dearth of fish, die or leave their nests, so that the young perish, bringing enormous loss to the guano industry.

By means of Ekman's theoretical model and the accumulation of reliable observations of conditions in the oceans at all depths, the German oceanographer Otto Krümmel was able to develop in 1907 physical justification for many of his views on ocean structure and circulation. Krümmel and later Georg Wüst, another German oceanographer, have shown that the salt concentration in the surface layer of the open ocean is in general related to the local balance of evaporation and precipitation, and is to be regarded largely as dependent upon latitude. Similarly, the temperature of the ocean surface is directly influenced by the amount of sunshine reaching it (see Figure 10), but, in this case, the simple relationship to latitude is complicated by currents carrying warmth to higher latitudes and others returning colder water.

Knowledge of the patterns of circulation in the deep oceans has come largely through tracing the distributions of certain properties of water masses such as temperature, salinity, and oxygen content as they are modified with increasing distance from their sources. The scientists who have contributed most to the development of this approach are probably Krümmel and Wüst.

But the study of the oceans is expensive; to find money to support what appeared to most people to be little better than an interesting hobby was difficult until a sea disaster underscored the practical need of more knowledge of those seven tenths of the earth's surface, the oceans.

On April 14, 1912, the largest ship of her day, the *Titanic*, was steaming west on her maiden voyage at 22 nautical miles an hour in the North Atlantic some 500 miles ESE of Cape Race, Newfoundland. At 11:40 at night in calm and clear weather, one of the lookouts notified the bridge that an iceberg lay right ahead. The first officer Murdock leapt to the engine room telegraph, rang

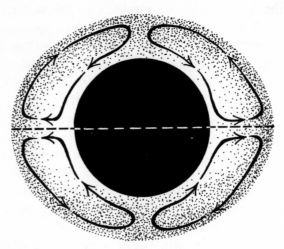

FIGURE 10 *Sun's rays heat the equatorial seas, which expand and flow "downhill" toward the poles. The polar waters sink, flowing toward the equator on the sea floor.*

it over to Stop, and shouted "Hard a-starboard"[1] to the quartermaster at the wheel. Probably Murdoch's order was a mistake, one for which he paid with his life, but to have grasped the full consequence of his order at that moment would have required almost superhuman foresight.

Had the *Titanic* struck the berg head on, it is likely that her watertight compartments could have kept her afloat at least until the arrival of the *Carpathia* on the following morning. Because the bow swung to the left in answer to the rudder, the ship struck a glancing blow. As she slowly ground past the berg, a deep projection of ice tore a gash 300 feet long in her right side below

[1] At sea "starboard" means right. Given the order, "hard a-starboard," the quartermaster in accordance with custom among English-speaking seamen before 1931 was to push a no-longer existing tiller all the way to the right, thus causing the bow to swing to the left.

the water line. The wound opened six of the sixteen watertight compartments that were intended to make her "unsinkable." When the sun rose the *Titanic* was on the bottom; of her 2,224 people, 1,513 were lost.

In January 1914, the representatives of nineteen world powers met in order to plan ways of preventing future calamities. The outcome was the establishment of an International Ice Patrol. It was decided that the task of tracking bergs and predicting their drift in the northern sea lanes should be carried out by the United States Coast Guard. In the establishment of the Ice Patrol the practical importance of oceanography gained new recognition.

On board one of the Coast Guard cutters assigned to the Ice Patrol was a young ensign named Edward Hanson Smith, whose keen interest in ice conditions attracted the attention of his superiors. After serving overseas during World War I, Smith studied at Harvard, and then at the division of oceanography of the Geophysical Institute of Bergen, Norway. He returned to the Patrol as Chief Observer, but to do a good job merely observing was not enough for Smith; he was determined to gain an insight into the processes at work in distributing the bergs. In 1926 he showed how the mathematical principles of Bjerknes could be used to explain the circulation of the Labrador Sea and Baffin Bay, waters into which many bergs are calved. In 1928 Smith, now lieutenant commander, led an expedition along the west coast of Greenland to Melville Bay to explore the principle source of icebergs. The information he gathered there became the subject of a thesis that earned him a doctor's degree from Harvard. The studies of high latitude circulation carried out by the group of scientists under Smith's, and later F. M. Soule's, direction have provided convincing evidence that the indirect methods of describing ocean currents developed by the Norwegian oceanographers are useful for practical purposes.

In 1931 a marine biologist at Harvard, Henry B. Bigelow, realizing that better understanding of life in the sea demanded fuller knowledge of the environment, summed up the problems in his book, *Oceanography: Its Scope, Problems, and Economic Importance*, and thereby helped to bring in a new era of oceanographic research in the United States. Because many of the puzzles to which he called attention remain unsolved, the goading effect of his problem-posing approach is still felt. With Bigelow's guidance the Woods Hole Oceanographic Institution was founded in 1930. It is now one of the five or six most important oceanographic institutions in the world.

In the development of the Woods Hole Oceanographic Institution Columbus Iselin has played the leading role. Iselin was born in New York in 1904. It is a little surprising that the socially prominent Iselin family—originating from landlocked Switzerland and with a tradition in banking—should have produced a hard-working and dedicated oceanographer; or, at least it is until one learns of the devotion to sailing of his near relatives; his great-uncle, C. Oliver Iselin, was a defender of the cup won by the *America* four times, and his father, Lewis Iselin, had a fondness for small-boat racing on Long Island Sound.

At the age of eleven his own feeling for the sea inspired Columbus to learn the use of tools from the carpenter employed at the family's summer house at New Rochelle in order to build a boat. It was called the *Sponge* and it leaked! While in preparatory school he showed his mettle as a sailor by devoting his vacations to cruising along the coast of Maine and into the treacherous waters of the Bay of Fundy.

When Columbus Iselin entered Harvard in 1922 he specialized in mathematics. Was this because he looked forward to a career in banking? Or was it a lurking thought that he would need mathematics to find his way about the sea? However that may be, banking lost out when he met Professor Bigelow during his third year at Harvard. From that time on he knew what he wanted to do. Realizing that he would need a boat when he graduated, he ordered a 72-foot schooner to be built in Nova Scotia. He named her *Chance*. As soon as he had his degree, he and a crew of fellow students set sail for the coast of Labrador.

From our own experience on the coast of Labrador we know that the weather "down there" can be rugged to really dangerous. To find shelter from a gale one must enter poorly charted, reef-strewn waters. When not stormy, the weather is often miserably cold and wet. Well, that was part of the adventure. To make up for it there was some skylarking now and then, or a trip ashore to make the acquaintance of the Eskimos. But through it all Iselin's leadership was firm; the scientific observations went on. For him they were probably the best part of the adventure. When the *Chance* came home she brought significant new information on the Labrador Current—the current which has so important an influence on the climate of New England, and often makes the water of the north shore of Cape Cod numbing cold.

At about this time Bigelow was writing a report on oceanography for the National Academy of Science. Iselin's success with the little *Chance* was opportune. It proved a point which Bigelow stressed in his report; that small vessels could gather valuable scientific information. With the reassurance that the heavy and continuing expense of keeping large research vessels in commission would not be necessary, the Rockefeller Foundation provided Bigelow with $3 million to outfit and endow an oceanographic institution. He chose Woods Hole on Cape Cod as the site. The town already had a world-famous scientific organization, the Woods Hole Marine Biological Laboratory.

Together Bigelow and Iselin planned the new institution's ship. She would be the first vessel designed from keel to truck specifically for oceanographic work, and such she remained until the 1960's. Her building was entrusted to Burmeister & Wain of Copenhagen. When she was ready and had received her name, *Atlantis*, Iselin took command and sailed her to Woods Hole.

The *Atlantis* is (for she is still in existence) a steel-hulled, 142-foot, double-ended ketch, which means that she has two masts of which the tallest is stepped forward. She has a diesel engine capable of pushing her along at 8 knots or about 9 miles an hour. Her ketch rig was an excellent choice; in a gale the big mainsail could be furled, leaving in perfect balance the relatively small mizzen near the stern and one or two staysails forward. When making frequent stops for hydrographic stations, the sails were a good deal of a nuisance and were usually furled, but on long runs they helped save fuel, and in an emergency, as when she lost her propeller in the middle of the equatorial Atlantic, they made the difference between utter helplessness and a glorious westward sail in the trade winds. What she lacked in size, she made up for by her fine design; no weather was too rugged for her.

During the following ten years Iselin spent much of his time

with the *Atlantis*. As she crossed and recrossed critical parts of
the North Atlantic, he and other scientists studied the ocean's
structure by lowering strings of Nansen bottles to bring up samples of water. In addition each bottle carries two thermometers;
from the temperatures and salinities at the various depths the
densities of the layers of water may be calculated. Through observations of this kind carried out largely by workers of the
Woods Hole Oceanographic Institution today we have an excellent understanding of the circulation of the North Atlantic.

Shortly before the beginning of World War II, the experimental use of sound navigation ranging or *sonar*, for short, ran
into trouble. Sonar is a method of detecting objects under water
by sending out sound waves or "pings," and recording the echoes
that rebound from an object back to the searching ship. From the
known speed of sound in water and the time interval between the
instant of sending a ping and the arrival of its echo, one can
locate a motionless submarine. But in the warm waters off Guantánamo, Cuba, gear that had worked well elsewhere saw "ghosts";
at the same time it missed targets that really were there. Baffled
by this strange behavior of the sonar, the Navy sought the aid of
the Oceanographic Institution. In response, Woods Hole sent the
Atlantis to Guantánamo with a group of oceanographers on
board. Led by Iselin, the scientists lowered reversing thermometers to various depths and soon found the explanation for the
erratic behavior of the sonar. Because of the intense heating by
the tropical sun, a sharply defined change in temperature occurred at a depth of 50 feet (15 meters). At that level the velocity
of sound in the water changed abruptly enough to render the
lower layer of water essentially opaque to sound, thereby hiding
objects, for example a submarine, as effectively as if behind a hill.
Submarine men were quick to see the usefulness of this phenomenon; during the war many United States submarines escaped detection by hiding beneath levels of abrupt change in
temperature. Of the greatest help in the game of hide and seek
was a device developed at Woods Hole called the *bathythermograph*, BT for short. In only a few minutes a BT traces a continuous curve of temperature change from the surface to a depth as
great as 900 feet or 275 meters and it can do this, if necessary,
from a ship traveling at 18 knots.

Full and cordial cooperation between Navy men and oceanographers followed the incident off Guantánamo Bay; it dispelled
once and for all the Naval conception of the oceanographer as a
mere trifler at play with silly contraptions. How Maury would
have welcomed the change!

During the next few years hundreds of naval officers came to
Woods Hole and its sister institution at La Jolla on the Pacific,
the Scripps Institution of Oceanography, for training. Submarine
men learned how to elude the hunter by taking advantage of the
complexities of oceanic structure, while destroyer men learned to
spot their prey in spite of the same complexities.

The war years were a busy time for oceanographers. By charting currents they helped air rescue ships to find airmen downed
at sea. Understanding of the behavior of waves on various kinds
of beaches gained from studies of the thundering surf along the
coast of southern California near La Jolla, and along the south
beach of Martha's Vineyard enabled them to predict surf conditions for the landings on Sicily, Normandy, and the islands of the
Pacific. Their studies of the effects of current and wave scour on
various kinds of bottom sediments led to improvements in the
design and laying of mines. By prying into the habits of barnacles
and other organisms that attach themselves to the hulls of ships
they found out how to formulate a paint that kept off the un-
wanted passengers; this cut the Navy's fuel bill by 10 per cent,
and increased the time that ships could stay at sea without over-
hauling.

Then one day the sorry business of war came to an end. With
a general sigh of relief the scientists went back to pure science,
the pursuit of knowledge for its own sake, which had been their
real interest all along.

Woods Hole is a pleasant village with a few fishing boats in a
well-protected harbor. Nearby is the "hole," a narrow passage
connecting Buzzards Bay and Vineyard Sound. During the summer it is fairly lively what with vacationists and people passing
through to take the steamer to Martha's Vineyard and Nantucket.
But in the raw, wet weather of winter the place must seem almost
intolerably bleak to an outsider. When the air is full of the sea as
the fog rolls in, it grows dark early. So, perhaps at four o'clock one
breaks off work to go across the street to the Rendezvous for a hot

buttered rum and a bite to eat before a driftwood fire. Then back to
the lab; at midnight, or it may be later—why bother to look at the
clock?—one feels one's way home along the dark, foggy street
with no other company than the doleful wail of the foghorn at
Nobska Point. Dismal and bleak? Far from it. That last batch of
figures made sense; just possibly they contain a clue to something
really big. In the euphoria granted now and then to artists and
scientists one breathes in the fishy fog with relish and delights in
the melody from Nobska Point.

Despite important progress in recent years, there is still a
great deal left to learn about the circulation of the world ocean,
and the driving forces that control it. Although revised theory
and information obtained with new instruments indicate that
deep circulation may be far more vigorous than was once
thought, it remains true that the really powerful currents are the
wind-driven currents at the surface, shown in Figure 11.

If no continents stood in the way, the trade winds in the
equatorial zone would keep in motion a westward-flowing, world-
encircling current. Because of the obstruction of the continents
and the deflection of the Coriolis effect, the surface circulation
of the world ocean is broken up into five great eddies or gyres. In
the northern hemisphere there are two eddies turning in a clockwise direction: one in the North Atlantic and the other in the
northern Pacific; the three others are in the southern hemisphere
and turn in a counterclockwise direction, one being in the South
Pacific, one in the South Atlantic, and the third in the Indian
Ocean. The directions of rotation of the gyres are determined by
the Coriolis effect (see page 48).

One striking feature of the great eddies of both hemispheres is
their asymmetry; the points about which the eddies turn are not
at the centers of the eddies but considerably to the west. In consequence, the segments of swiftest flow are on the western sides
of the gyres. Here again we see the effect of the earth's rotation or
the Coriolis force.

Most elements of the circulation of the world ocean are remarkably constant from season to season and from year to year.
Storms may stir surface waters temporarily, but the final effect on
a current such as the Gulf Stream is too small to be observed.
However, the circulation of the northern Indian Ocean is an ex-

ception to the rule that seasonal changes do not affect ocean currents. The seasonal winds, arising from the summer heating and winter cooling of the southern part of the Asiatic continent, know as monsoons, have so powerful an effect on the northern Indian Ocean that they actually cause reversals of the currents, with the consequence that from April to October, while the mon-

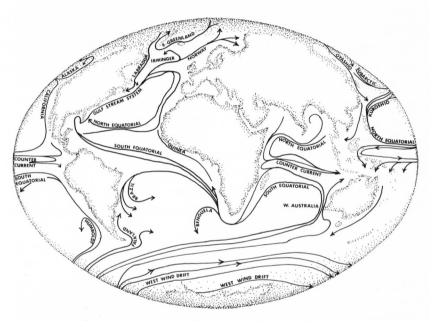

FIGURE 11 *Surface currents of the oceans. A great circular current system exists in each of the North and South Atlantic Oceans, the North and South Pacific, and the Indian Ocean. Coriolis effect, produced by the turning earth, makes the major currents rotate in a clockwise direction in the northern hemisphere, and in a counterclockwise direction in the southern hemisphere.*

soon blows from the ocean over the continent, the North Equatorial Current, normally flowing from east to west, is replaced by the eastward-flowing Monsoon Current. This seasonal change is confined to the northern part of the Indian Ocean; in the southern part the typical counterclockwise motion persists. South of the equator the flow is westward, then south along the coast of Africa as the Agulhas Current, a part of whose water rounds the Cape of Good Hope to join the Benguela Current while the rest turns east toward Australia, then northward to complete the circuit.

In 1959 the International Indian Ocean Expedition was organized with thirteen nations participating. Among these were India, the United States, the Soviet Union, the United Kingdom, Japan, Australia, France, the Federal Republic of Germany, and the Union of South Africa. The formal organization ended in 1965, but it will have a long informal sequel; quantities of data remain to be worked up, and very probably the new information will stimulate future expeditions sent out by national institutions to follow up unsolved problems.

In organizing this adventure in international cooperation many scientists hoped to encourage basic studies of the ocean and atmosphere by countries surrounding the Indian Ocean, in the expectation that new knowledge might help to reduce shortages of food. Consequently, study was particularly focused on the physical conditions that favor abundant marine life. But this practical purpose did not exclude a purely scientific spirit from the organization. Physical oceanographers were interested in the Indian Ocean as a model of the world ocean. It is like other oceans in having eastern and western boundaries and in being under the influence of the earth's rotation. It differs from all others in that the motions of its surface waters are influenced by winds whose directions vary with the seasons. This changing system of winds and circulation of the Indian Ocean strongly attracted oceanographers who wanted to put to the test their theories of coupling between winds and currents.

Among important results of the expedition was the discovery that a strong, though seasonal, western boundary current, the Somali Current, develops along the Somali Coast during the southwest monsoon. The velocity of this current exceeds 6 knots or 310 centimeters per second. During the same season intense upwelling off northern Somalia brings to the surface the coldest water found anywhere in the world so near the equator.

The most famous and best-known of ocean currents is the Gulf Stream, which is really only one segment, though the swiftest, of the North Atlantic gyre. The Gulf Stream proper extends from Cape Hatteras to the region east of the Grand Banks of Newfoundland at longitude 45° west. The eastward extension, called the North Atlantic Drift, is more diffuse and tends to branch. However, there is no well-defined boundary separating one from the other. According to observations by scientists of the Woods Hole Oceanographic Institution, the Gulf Stream develops large eddies or meanders, as illustrated in Figure 12. Sometimes the meanders, like the oxbow lakes of meandering rivers, become separated from the main current and travel along as closed eddies. In

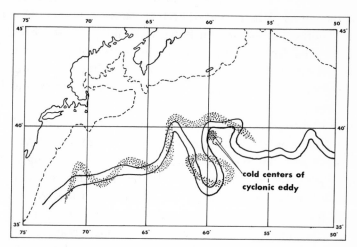

FIGURE 12 *The wandering Gulf Stream. From June 8 to 12, 1950, it followed the path shown by the dark lines. From June 19 to 22 it shifted to the route shown by the cross-hatched lines, and a huge eddy broke off, pushing enormous quantities of subarctic water into the subtropical Atlantic Ocean.*

some measure the diffuseness of the North Atlantic Drift is due to the increasing tendency of the stream to meander.

But even immediately northeast of Hatteras the Gulf Stream is now known to be not so much a broad river in the ocean as a series of narrow, swift bands of flowing water overlapping each other like shingles on a roof.

As the North Atlantic Drift moves east it fans out in two directions: toward Iceland, England, and Norway in the north, and south toward the coasts of Portugal and Spain. The latter branch eventually swings southwest as the sluggish Canaries Current. There are also lesser streams, the smaller vessels and capillaries of the circulation, entering and leaving the main circuit with varying pulse. Part of the northern branch enters the English Channel and the North Sea; another part flows into the Norwegian Sea, then into the Barrents and even far into the Arctic Ocean where Fridtjof Nansen, while drifting on the *Fram,* recognized Atlantic water as a layer of surprisingly warm water between the depths of 800 and 2,200 feet (250 and 670 meters). He sampled this layer and found that it was saltier than the surface water, in fact salty enough to be Atlantic water. Because of its salinity it is denser, and therefore sinks beneath the Arctic water. Another minor branch flows west along the south coast of Iceland as the Irminger Current, then south along the east coast of Greenland, rounds the southern tip of Greenland, and turns north to follow the west coast as the mild West Greenland Current.

As we have said before, the primary transformer of heat energy from the sun into streaming motion of ocean waters is the atmosphere, but the final pattern of motion is strongly influenced by the rotation of the earth. If the earth did not rotate, the warm, and therefore less heavy air of the equatorial zone would rise and flow at a high level toward the poles. There, having lost heat and become heavier, it would sink and stream back again toward the equator to take the place of constantly rising warm air. The directions of flow on a nonrotating earth would be entirely meridional, that is along north-south lines.

Actually, however, because of the deflecting effect of the earth's rotation and because of friction with the earth's surface, what would otherwise be simple meridional circulation breaks up into a system of separate cells and eddies. Air rising near the equator comes down at about 30° north and south of the equator where its descent creates a region of high pressure. At the same time streams of cool air flowing into the equatorial region of low pressure are deflected by the earth's rotation to the southwest in the northern hemisphere and to the northwest in the southern hemisphere, thus creating a zone of powerful winds, known as the *trade winds,* which completely encircles the globe.

As these winds drive forward the waters over which they blow, the deflecting effect of the earth's rotation again comes into play; the wind-generated currents do not flow directly before the wind, but instead swing to the right of the wind's direction in the northern hemisphere and to the left in the southern. In this way two westward flowing streams are kept in motion, the North and South Equatorial Currents.

Between the trade winds in the area just north of the equator is a zone of calms beneath which the water streams to the east. This is the Equatorial Counter Current. It is really a downhill flow of water piled up on the western margins of the ocean basins by the trade winds. Since the atmospheric conditions responsible for these currents are circumglobal within the equatorial zone, North and South Equatorial Currents separated by a countercurrent are common to all oceans.

When the South Equatorial Current of the Atlantic reaches the bulge of South America it separates; the southern branch joins the Brazil Current, southern counterpart of the Gulf Stream; the other branch, deflected northwestward by the coast of South America, flows into the North Equatorial Current. By this inflow from the South Atlantic, the great eddy of the North Atlantic gains water to make up for that lost to the Norwegian Sea and Arctic Ocean. A large part of the combined waters passes through the islands of the lesser Antilles into the Caribbean, and through the Yucatán Channel between Cuba and the Campeche Peninsula into the Gulf of Mexico.

The energy of flow through the Straits of Florida is due, at least in part, to the fact that the water is running downhill. The powerful drive of the east wind crowds so much water into the western end of the Caribbean and Gulf of Mexico that sea level there is higher than it is in the open Atlantic. Off the southeastern tip of Florida the sea's surface stands 19 centimeters higher than at St. Augustine on the east coast of Florida. Furthermore, the surface of the stream slopes from side to side; the earth's rotation deflects the lighter water to the right side of the stream, so that along the coast of Cuba the sea is about 45 centimeters higher than it is along the mainland.

North of the Bahamas the Gulf Stream is joined by a large volume of water that left the main stream just before entering the Caribbean and flowed northward along the outside of the Antilles. This is called the Antilles Current. In fact, there is no direct evidence of the existence of an Antilles current; what is known with certainty is that the volume of the Gulf Stream off Charleston is 1.8 fold greater than it is in the Straits of Florida. A hypothetical Antilles current offers a reasonable explanation for the remarkable increase in volume.

Beyond Cape Hatteras the stream leaves the continental shelf, swings to the northeast, and commences its journey across the deep Atlantic. South of the Grand Banks of Newfoundland the Gulf Stream and the westward-flowing Labrador Current run side by side and so close to each other that the bow of a ship can be in one current when its stern is in the other. As the icy water of the Labrador Current chills air warmed and filled with moisture by the Gulf Stream, dense and almost constant fog settles over the Banks, the fog that used to hamper the New England cod fishermen.

The region within the current gyre of the North Atlantic is called the Sargasso Sea. It takes its name from the sargassum weeds or algae that float about in clumps near and at the surface. The weed itself owes its name to Portuguese sailors who saw a resemblance between its air-bladder floats and a kind of small grapes called sarga in Portuguese. Grisly legends have grown up about the Sargasso Sea and its weeds. Many sailors who had never been there firmly believed that even large sailing vessels could become helplessly entangled among the masses of sargassum weed until their crews went mad or died of thirst and starvation. Well, we have been through the thick of it on board the *Atlantis;* the patches of weeds that we saw could do nothing worse than perhaps retard slightly the progress of a sailing dinghy if sailed deliberately into the patches.

The numerous patches of weeds give the Sargasso Sea a deceptive appearance of fertility. When one dips up some of the weed and throws it on deck, out tumble all sorts of weird little passengers: tiny crabs, snails, a small fish that mimics the weed so faithfully that only its flipping about on deck betrays its fishy nature. By careful search one may find sea slugs also masquerading as sargassum weeds. With a hand lens one can discern the limy, spiral shells (all turning in the same direction) of little worms, attached to the fronds of the weeds; various species of clinging foraminifera, or microscopic, shell-building protozoa, are also there.

But in spite of the abundant weeds and the variety of the odd little creatures living among its fronds, the Sargasso Sea is an oceanic desert. Although its deep-blue water, because of evaporation under an almost perpetually clear sky, is the saltiest of all Atlantic waters, it lacks the particular fertilizing chemicals necessary for large-scale blooms of diatoms—the microscopic, single-celled plants that drift about near the surface and are the real fodder of the sea—the first links in the food chain. The Sargasso Sea as a water mass is too stable; the same water, thoroughly depleted of fertilizing substances, slowly and endlessly revolves without addition of new water by upwelling from below or by incursions of surface water from outside. And yet, with a prevailing clear sky, it receives an enormous amount of radiant energy; with enough of the right kind of chemicals it could swarm with life.

It was once thought that the sargassum weeds originated in shallow water probably somewhere in the West Indies. Having been torn from the bottom by storms, the weeds then drifted into the Sargasso Sea. But it was difficult to understand how so many weeds—the total mass in the Sargasso Sea has been estimated in the order of 10 million tons—could be supplied by such a source. Albert E. Parr, director of the American Museum of Natural History in New York, who studied the life of the Sargasso Sea while cruising on the *Atlantis,* found that most of the drifting algae belong to only two species, *Sargassum natans* and *S. fluitans.* These highly specialized plants, floaters by nature, have never been found attached to rocks. They grow and reproduce by budding as they endlessly circle the Sargasso Sea.

In speculating about the causes of the ice ages of the past one and a half million years, it is tempting in imagination to tamper with the great current gyre of the North Atlantic. What if the Gulf Stream ceased to flow? Might not continental glaciation follow? But the Sargasso Sea is the essence of the Gulf Stream. In fact, Henry Stommel of the Woods Hole Oceanographic Institution, the author of a book about the Gulf Stream, says that the Gulf Stream and the Sargasso Sea are really one and the same thing.

Now, it is utterly beyond credibility that the sargassum weeds and their highly specialized hangers-on could have evolved within the time since the end of the last ice age about 11,000 years ago.

It seems rather unlikely that even the one and a half million years since the beginning of the first ice age would suffice for the development of the adaptations of the inhabitants of the Sargasso Sea through the slow process of natural selection of random mutations.

Very probably at times during the Pleistocene, the epoch of the ice ages, the extent of the Sargasso Sea has varied, and no doubt its position has shifted somewhat as the pattern of prevailing winds has shifted; but the fact that the weeds and the animals survived is a good indication that at no time during the Pleistocene did the Sargasso Sea completely lose its character, which is the same thing as saying that the Gulf Stream must have kept right on rolling along all through the ice ages and interglacials, though from time to time its volume and course may have changed somewhat.

The Gulf Stream system has been likened to a great artery, a salt stream of life within the salt ocean, helping to regulate and sustain the life on land and sea around and in the Atlantic. It has been called the Ocean River, the bringer of warmth and energy to northern Europe, which would otherwise remain a northern wasteland. But new discoveries and more sophisticated theory make it necessary to revise, even to abandon, this old conception of the Gulf Stream.

Recent studies, especially those by Henry Stommel, show that the Gulf Stream is not an ocean river of warm water. The temperature of the water of the stream is not significantly different from that of the mass of water lying to the right of its direction of motion, that is the Sargasso Sea. If the Gulf Stream were a river of warm water flowing through a colder environment, there would be little doubt that it should be considered as a distinct physical phenomenon. Today it seems that there is little justification for treating the Gulf Stream system as a physical system in any sense separable from the general circulation of the North Atlantic Ocean. The most clear-cut feature of the Gulf Stream system is the fact that it is really a flow along the junction of a mass of cold water and a mass of warm water.

There is scarcely any more firmly rooted idea in the mind of the layman than the notion that the Gulf Stream makes the climate of Europe mild. As long as it was thought that the Gulf

Stream was a river of warm water, this idea was reasonable. Now we realize that it is not so much the Stream itself that is important; it is rather the position and temperature of the mass of water on its right flank that influence the European climate. Westerly winds blowing across the vast heat reservoir, the Sargasso Sea, absorb heat and carry it over Europe. Iselin has even suggested that increased transport by the Gulf Stream might be associated with cooler conditions in Europe.

Because of the reversed effect of the rotation of the earth in the southern hemisphere, the gyre of the South Atlantic flows in a counterclockwise direction. The southern current system is not quite a mirror image of that in the North Atlantic; the dominant current flows along the eastern side of the basin instead of the western as in the North Atlantic. This is the Benguela Current, which streams northward along the west coast of Africa. Under the influence of the prevailing southerly and southeasterly winds the surface layers of water are carried away from the coast, so that upwelling of water from moderate depth takes place. This upwelling is of great importance biologically; it brings up to within reach of the sunlight water rich in chemicals needed by diatoms, the grass of the sea. Off Walfisch Bay on the coast of Africa the reaction of radiant energy from the sun with a seeding of diatoms and chemicals in upwelling water is as nearly explosive as a biological reaction can be. Periodic blooms of diatoms and the proliferation of creatures that feed upon them lead to an accumulation of organic matter on the sea floor. Bacteria attack this organic matter and soon all oxygen in the bottom water is used up. At that point another kind of bacteria take over, bacteria capable of living without oxygen. These produce quantities of poisonous hydrogen sulfide, which rises to the surface and causes mass mortality of the fish population. The dead fish sink and add more fuel to the fire, as it were. In the oxygen-depleted bottom waters of the Walfisch Bay region the bottom-dwelling animals, which normally devour organic matter and reduce it to its elements, cannot live. Consequently, the sediment accumulating there is saturated with organic matter that the sulfur bacteria cannot destroy. Not improbably, what is going on now in that region exemplifies the first stage of the development of a petroleum deposit. After the organic sediment has been deeply buried and several million years have passed, during which the organic matter will be subjected to high temperature and perhaps the action of various other kinds of bacteria, it may come to include that complex of organic substances called petroleum. It is significant that sediments made up almost entirely of the siliceous skeletons of diatoms occur in California in association with prolific pools of petroleum.

As the Benguela Current makes its way toward the equator it gradually leaves the coast and blends into the northern part of the South Equatorial Current, which flows west across the Atlantic between the equator and latitude 20° south. As we mentioned earlier, nearly half of the South Equatorial Current crosses the equator to become part of the North Atlantic current system, while the rest flows south as the Brazil Current. The gyre of the South Atlantic is completed by the South Atlantic Current, which flows east from South America toward the southern tip of Africa. In general, the current system of the South Atlantic is weaker and the volumes of water transported are less than in the North Atlantic. It is a system of shallow currents; near the equator the surface flow is probably limited to a depth of less than 200 meters or about 600 feet.

Like the Atlantic, the Pacific has a North Equatorial Current driven by the prevailing northeast winds. This is the longest westerly running current in the world; it flows without interruption from Panama to the Philippines, a distance of 9,000 miles or 14,500 kilometers. Deflected by the barrier of the Philippine Islands, most of its water swings northward (see Figure 11) as the Japan Current or Kuroshio, (the Black Current, so called because of the deep Prussian blue of its water). However, a small part of its water persists in a westward course among the Asiatic islands, while another branch turns back and flows east as the Equatorial Counter Current.

The Kuroshio where it sweeps along the coast of Japan is in some ways similar to the Florida Current, as Wüst has mentioned. It, too, leaves the continental shelf partly under the influence of the eastward guiding Coriolis effect and partly also because of the cold Oyashio which, pouring out of the Sea of Okhotsk and Bering Sea, thrusts itself between the Kuroshio and the Asiatic continent. In this encounter the Oyashio plays a part similar to that of the Labrador Current in the Atlantic, which shoulders aside the Gulf Stream and makes its chilly presence felt as far south as the north shore of Cape Cod.

The meeting of these warm and cold streams here engenders fogs and storms, just as the meeting of the Gulf Stream and Labrador currents does off the Grand Banks.

Along the boundary between the conflicting streams numerous eddies develop, within which complete mixing takes place. From this mixing arises the water that flows toward the east along the Aleutian Islands as the Aleutian Current, a part of whose waters turns north and enters the Bering Sea, where it first flows along the northern side of the islands, then swings counterclockwise finally to emerge at the western outlet of the Bering Sea, its waters now thoroughly chilled, as the cold Oyashio—thus closing the circuit of the Oyashio system.

The major part of the Aleutian Current, however, persists in its eastward course along the southern side of the islands, but before reaching the American coast it separates into two branches. A minor branch flows northward into the Gulf of Alaska and becomes part of a counterclockwise gyre there. Since it comes from the south, its water is relatively warm in spite of some admixture of subarctic water. Its influence on the local climate is, therefore, similar on a small scale to that of the North Atlantic and Norwegian currents on the climate of northwestern Europe. It makes the coastal region of Alaska habitable.

The major branch of the Aleutian Current turns south and follows the west coast of the United States as the California Current. Beginning in March and continuing until July, north and northwest winds prevail off the coast of California. In accordance with the Ekman spiral these winds cause the surface water to flow away from the coast. The result is a coastal region of upwelling. Although the rate of this upwelling is very slow (probably the rise of water from below is no faster than 20 meters a month), it nevertheless suffices to bring waters full of essential chemicals to within reach of the life-giving energy of the sun.

During the entire season of upwelling a subsurface countercurrent containing considerable quantities of equatorial water flows close to the coast at depths below 200 meters. This is the northern equivalent of the subsurface current off the coast of

Peru. During spring and early summer the currents off the coast of California are nearly a mirror image of those off the coast of Peru, but the similarity holds true only seasonally because the prevailing winds off California change in the summer, whereas off Peru they blow from almost the same direction throughout the year.

In the autumn upwelling ceases and a countercurrent, the Davidson Current, develops in the surface waters and runs north along the coast at least as far as 48° North. The Davidson Current is probably a seasonal extension to the surface of the continuously flowing subsurface countercurrent.

The California Current has an important effect on the climate of the west coast of America, acting as a stabilizer to prevent extremes of temperature. Off Lower California it turns west into the North Equatorial Current.

Temperature and salinity measurements show that a distinctly different water mass is present in the region east of the Hawaiian Islands. This leads oceanographers to conclude that a clockwise gyre is present in the eastern North Pacific with its center to the northeast of the Hawaiian Islands.

But now we must return to the Kuroshio. After its encounter with the cold Oyashio it turns eastward and becomes the North Pacific Current. In its *Drang nach Osten* across the north Pacific it suffers desertions of numerous southward-curving branches until only straggling remnants of its original volume survive to flow south between the Hawaiian Islands and the west coast of North America. Eventually its waters close circuit by joining the North Equatorial Current.

Actually the real pattern of circulation east of the Hawaiian Islands is probably a little more complicated. The eddy of the South Pacific is unimpressive in power, in spite of the wide area of its field, the broad South Pacific Ocean. The probable reason is the breaking effect of the South Sea Islands, through which the South Equatorial Current must find its way. In fact, the islands present so baffling an impediment to its progress that among the islands it degenerates into a confusion of minor currents without discernable pattern. However, east of Australia and New Zealand the dominating influences, prevailing winds and the earth's rotation, take over once again; the sweeping curve from southward to westward of the southwestern quarter of the gyre takes shape; its circuit is completed by flow toward South America, deflection to the north and finally northwestward into the South Equatorial Current (see Figure 11).

The waters of the South Pacific gyre do not approach close enough to the coast of South America to influence the climate there. An offshoot of the Antarctic West Wind Drift, the Humboldt Current, flows north between the coast and the waters of the gyre.

It was the Humboldt Current that carried the raft Kon-Tiki from Lima, Peru, northward into the South Equatorial Current, which in turn brought the raft after 101 days at sea to its destination, Tahiti. If Thor Heyerdahl—anthropologist, archeologist, and leader of the Kon-Tiki Expedition—is right, and he has assembled impressive evidence to support his theory, Polynesia was colonized by people from South America who took advantage of the same wind and current system to help them on their way.

Earlier in this chapter we mentioned the vast fertility of the cold upwelling water of the Humboldt Current off the coast of Peru, where great flocks of pelicans, cormorants, and gannets feed on the anchovies and produce the guano of commerce, which contains in concentrated form the fertilizing minerals of the sea.

The sediments beneath the Humboldt Current, like those beneath its counterpart, the Benguela Current off the coast of Africa, are rich in the remains of microscopic organisms that secrete skeletons of opal, or silica combined with some water. Most important among these organisms are the single-celled algae, the *diatoms*. A group of protozoa, the Radiolaria, also makes an important contribution to the silica content of the sediments. In the Humboldt Current the supply of silica and fertilizing chemicals is probably replenished as the current flows along the coast by the quantities of finely divided volcanic glass which have been and still are thrown into the sea by explosive eruptions of the Andean volcanoes. Of course, upwelling is none the less important to biological productivity; were the chemically enriched waters not constantly to come within reach of sunlight, the prodigious blooms of diatoms and other marine plants could not occur.

Paradoxical as it may seem, the same upwelling that gives rise to the teeming marine life makes a desert of the coastal region of Peru. Although the coast is cooled by the upwelling and its sky is overcast during most of the year, it is one of the most arid regions in the world. Air masses coming in from the sea are cooled by the upwelling water; then as they move over the land they are warmed and their capacity to retain water vapor is increased. In consequence, the inhabitants of the coastal region are forced to depend for their water upon some fifty small rivers fed by rainfall in the Andean highlands. Even *El Niño* is not a dependable bringer of rain. Although it has sometimes in the past brought torrential and destructive rain, it has not done so recently. No rain has fallen in the region north of Lima for forty years, in spite of the visitations of *El Niño* in 1932, 1941, and with particular severity in 1953.

The climate of the region has not always been this way. The topography of the country gives evidence of more rain in the past; gullies eroded by running water scar the hills. Furthermore, archeologists find evidence that the so-called *lomas,* or isolated patches of vegetation in the midst of the desert, now kept alive by fog from the ocean, were once more widespread. Their former extent is indicated by the shells of snails, feeders on vegetation, strewn about the country. Bits of wood perfectly preserved by the arid climate have been shown to be 10,500 years old by the radiocarbon method of dating. Evidently, the climate has been about as dry as it is now for almost that long. Very probably the climatic change which put an end to the rainfall that eroded the gullies was connected with the end of the last ice age about 11,000 years ago.

More extensive mountain glaciers in the Andes during the last ice age may have cooled the land, and thereby reduced the difference in temperature between land and sea enough to have promoted greater rainfall. But this explanation avoids the main issue; why were there more extensive glaciers in the Andes to begin with? To put the horse before the cart, probably the more copious precipitation built up the glaciers. Of one thing we can be sure; whatever the basic cause of the climatic change, its effect was not confined to the west coast of South America. If circulation and the heat properties of the ocean off Peru changed at about the end of the last ice age, they must have changed in many other parts of the oceans. Convincing archeological and other evidence shows that deserts all over the world had moister climates some 10,000 or 11,000 years ago.

The reaction between the opposing forces of the Humboldt Current and *El Niño* is tantalizing in its suggestiveness. Why has *El Niño*, former bearer of deluges, brought little or no rain during the past forty years? A climate change, of a kind that could be disastrous in some parts of the world, has occurred as it were before our eyes, and yet we cannot put a finger on the primary cause. We can only guess that this changed behavior of *El Niño* may be related to the world-wide retreat of glaciers during the past half century, and perhaps also to decrease in rainfall, at least locally, in scattered parts of the world. A world-wide effect should have a world-wide cause, and so we look askance at the sun. A change in the amount of radiant energy from the sun would, beyond shadow of a doubt, bring about the kind of variation in volume of ocean currents, evaporation from the oceans, and consequent rainfall on the continents that have been observed.

Yet direct measurements of solar radiation have not been successful because of interference by changing atmospheric conditions. The obvious solution is to take measurements by satellite, but to have meaning the observations will have to extend over at least several years, if not several decades. Such information may very well solve the riddle of the periodic spread of continental ice sheets during the last one and a half million years.

The Antarctic or Southern Ocean is an oceanographic entity rather than a geographical one. The distinctive properties of its waters and their motions set it apart from the adjacent southern regions of the Atlantic, Pacific, and Indian oceans into which it would otherwise dissolve. Its southern boundary is the coast of Antarctica. Its northern boundary may be drawn at the Antarctic convergence between 50° and 60° south latitude, where surface waters flowing north meet waters flowing generally south. At the convergence an abrupt change in temperature and salinity occurs, and an even more striking change in the character of marine life. The waters around Antarctica support few species, but astronomically large numbers of individuals of those few; the region is one of the most productive biological provinces on earth.

In spite of storms and danger from drifting ice, ships of the Lamont Geological Observatory of Columbia University have raised a sufficient number of long sediment cores from the vicinity of the Antarctic convergence to prove that a change in the character of the bottom sediment takes place roughly beneath the convergence. North of it the sediments are calcareous because they contain great numbers of the microscopic shells of foraminifera. South of the convergence these shells are few or quite absent and the sediments therefore contain little lime, but they may be very high in silica contributed by diatoms. Many samples of sediment from points south of the convergence consist entirely of snow-white, fluffy masses of these skeletons.

Some oceanographers prefer to place the northern boundary of the Southern Ocean at about 40° south latitude, that is at approximately the southern coasts of Africa and Australia. Here there is another transition in flow, temperature, and salinity, called the Subtropical convergence. This boundary has the practical advantage that it marks the northern limit of ice drifting from the Antarctic continent. Within this boundary the Southern Ocean covers some 75 million square kilometers, which amounts to 22 per cent of the total area of all the oceans. However, the heat content of the waters of the Southern Ocean, which vary in temperature from −1.8° to 10° Celsius, is only 10 per cent of the oceanic total. Inevitably this vast volume of cold water influences to some extent the climate of the entire earth.

Strong western winds blowing almost constantly in the belt between 40° and 60° south latitude generate the eastward motion of the Antarctic Circumpolar Current, whose maximum flow is in the zone of the Antarctic convergence (see Figure 13). Unlike all other currents, its course is unobstructed by continents. The narrowest constriction it encounters is the Drake Passage between South America and the Antarctic Peninsula. Elsewhere the distance between Antarctica and the nearest continent is more than 2,000 kilometers.

An important part of the program of the International Geophysical Year of 1957–8 was devoted to study of the interactions of the Southern Ocean and the atmosphere over it. Ships from Argentina, Australia, France, Japan, New Zealand, the United

States, and the U.S.S.R. made extensive oceanographic observations in the Southern Ocean.

Before the International Geophysical Year program it had not been clear whether the Circumpolar Current involved the entire water body from the ocean surface to its floor, or whether a deep countercurrent existed below the eastward surface flow. Detailed deep observations of the distribution of temperature, salinity, ox-

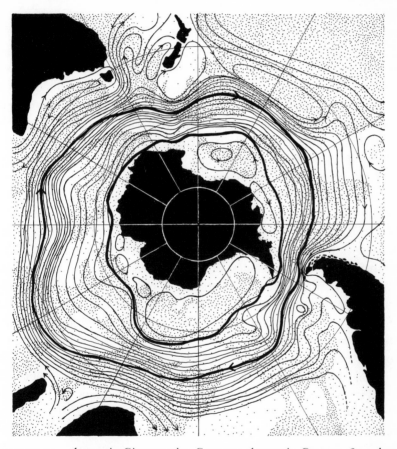

FIGURE 13 *Antarctic Circumpolar Current. Antarctic Current flow has been computed from data collected during the International Geophysical Year by the Soviet Marine Antarctic Expedition. The volume of transport between adjacent flow lines is 10 million cubic meters per second. The Antarctic Convergence (heavy line marked with arrows), where temperature and salinity change abruptly, coincides with the region of heaviest flow.*

ygen, and other substances prove that the eastward motion persists throughout the entire water column. But, as seems to be true of other currents, the total flow consists of a complex of separate streams with fast-moving cores, and even some subordinate countercurrents.

The new evidence that the water motion extends all the way to the bottom explains the influence of bottom topography on the course of the Circumpolar Current. The New Zealand Plateau deflects more than 20 per cent of the water of the Circumpolar Current into the Tasman Sea between Australia and New Zealand. Farther east the Pacific Antarctic Ridge north of the Ross Sea causes the Circumpolar Current to bend sharply northward into the Pacific. These diversions of cold water into the Pacific, shown in Figure 13, make that ocean somewhat colder than the Indian Ocean and considerably colder than the Atlantic.

Another objective of the International Geophysical Year program was to gage the flow of deep water toward and away from the Antarctic continent. More than thirty-five years ago Georg Wüst from analysis of deep observations in the Atlantic concluded that Antarctic waters penetrate to the Arabian Sea and the Bay of Bengal, both north of the equator. Observations by Russians during the International Geophysical Year indicate that the mean northward transport of bottom waters from the whole perimeter of the Antarctic continent is rather more than 800 million cubic meters per second, or more than five times the flow rate of the Antarctic Circumpolar Current itself. To compensate for this enormous outflow a vast layer of deep, warm water of equal volume must enter the Southern Ocean from the north. Thus the thermal influence of the Southern Ocean works in two directions. It takes up from the adjacent oceans a large amount of heat that has a decisive influence on the atmospheric circulation of the southern hemisphere. At the same time, the cold waters of the Southern Ocean creep into the adjacent oceans and cool their deep layers.

In spite of the successes of the International Geophysical Year program and research of recent years, there still remains much to be learned about the current system of the Southern Ocean. The volume of water exchanged between the Southern Ocean and the oceans adjacent to it varies importantly from year to year. This variation must influence its exchangeable heat content and, there-fore, the atmospheric circulation over it. To gain fuller knowl-edge of the quantities involved and the over-all effect on climate, it will be necessary to make systematic observations extending over many years. Such new information will be of the greatest help in compiling long-range forecasts of weather and climate over the entire planet.

Surface currents are vitally important in navigation and in fishing; it is not surprising that they have been intensively studied for more than a hundred years. Furthermore, charts of their gen-eral pattern and useful estimates of their velocities may be made from the observations of ships' captains as set down in logbooks. Only recently with the improvement of methods of measuring currents have oceanographers begun to realize the prevalence and power of currents flowing below the surface, frequently in directions opposite to the surface currents.

In 1951 a ship of the United States Fish and Wildlife Service, while searching for deep tuna in the South Equatorial Current of the Pacific, lowered lines to about 100 meters or 300 feet, but the lines instead of hanging straight down led off to the east at a large angle. One of the scientists on board, Townsend Cromwell, was awake to the possible significance of this. His interest in the prob-lem led to further investigations in 1952 and 1955, which proved that there was a reversal of flow below the west-setting South Equatorial Current at a depth of 45 to 90 meters, or 150 to 300 feet. In 1958 two ships, one from the Scripps Institution of Oceanography and another belonging to the Fish and Wildlife Service, traced the subsurface current from a point at about the same longitude as the Hawaiian Islands to the Galápagos Islands, a distance of about 3,500 miles. In order to have fixed reference points the expedition anchored buoys in 3 miles of water. With current meters they were then able to determine the dimensions of this east-flowing subsurface stream. They found it to be only 200 meters, or about 700 feet from top to bottom and some 250 miles wide. Its upper surface lies at a depth of 20 meters, or 65 feet and its *core*, or level of extreme temperature and salinity, at 100 meters, or 325 feet. The eastward velocity of this thin ribbon of water is between 2.5 and 3 nautical miles an hour, or in the practical units of oceanographers, 130 to 150 centimeters per second, a rate three times as fast as the westward flow of the South Equatorial Current directly above. In fact, it is the fastest current in the equatorial Pacific. In its rate of volume of water transported, 40 million cubic meters per second, it takes second place only to the Kuroshio Current.

Its point of origin in the west has not been determined yet.

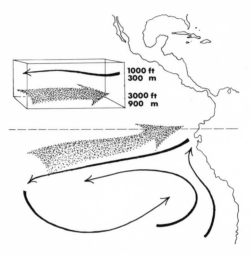

FIGURE 14   *The Cromwell Current: a massive subsurface eastward flow found beneath the westward-flowing South Equatorial Current in the Pacific.*

Probably it flows from somewhere in the vicinity of the Solomon Islands, or it may flow all the way across the Pacific, in which case its length is some 8,000 miles. At the Galápagos Islands it disappears; at least no trace of it can be found on the eastern side of the archipelago. Possibly it loses energy in turbulence among the islands; quantities of water drawn into it by turbulence may dilute its energy quite effectively. Near the end of the survey Townsend Cromwell was killed in a plane crash; the current has been named in his honor. The flow of the Cromwell Current is illustrated in Figure 14.

What of the Atlantic, whose equatorial current system has much in common with that of the Pacific? Should it not also have an equatorial undercurrent? When interest had been aroused by the discovery of the Cromwell Current, oceanographers recollected that J. Y. Buchanan on the *Buccaneer* in 1886 measured an undercurrent in the equatorial Atlantic at a depth of 55 meters. But as sometimes happens in science, this observation was lost sight of. In 1958 W. G. Metcalf of the Woods Hole Oceanographic Institution, while lowering water sample bottles in the equatorial Atlantic, noticed that the wire cable led off at a fairly steep angle and concluded from this that a swift, shallow subsurface current must be running eastward.

Observations made in 1961 during a cruise of the research vessel *Chain* of Woods Hole confirmed the existence of an undercurrent in the equatorial Atlantic similar to the Cromwell Current. Preliminary observations indicate that it is about 300 kilometers broad and more or less symmetrically located about the equator. A velocity of 130 centimeters per second has been measured at a depth of 100 meters. The high salt content of the easterly flowing water suggests that its source is the large reservoir of very salty water lying close to the South American continent south of the equator.

In spite of the aberrations of the Indian Ocean in other respects, it, too, has an equatorial undercurrent, though somewhat weaker than those of the Atlantic and Pacific. This was one of the important discoveries of the International Indian Ocean Expedition.

The fact that these important features of oceanic circulation have been discovered only within the past fifteen years shows how little we really know about the vast realm lying beneath the ocean's surfaces.

Sometimes trivial and seemingly irrelevant observations provide useful clues to what may be going on at depth. Since the *Challenger* expedition of 1872–6 it has been known that individuals of a certain species of foraminifera are abundant in the area south of the Canary Islands but absent north of the islands. This species, *Globorotalia menardii*, is planktonic, which means that it drifts about at the mercy of ocean currents. But the region of the Canary Islands is dominated by the Canaries Current, the eastern segment of the North Atlantic gyre. By all reason this southward-flowing current ought to have swept *Globorotalia menardii* out of the region long ago, and yet sediment samples from the sea floor south and north of the islands show that during the past 11,000 years the geographical range of the species has been limited by a well-defined boundary approximately at the latitude of the islands.

The scientists of the *Challenger* made another, apparently unrelated observation, that the shells of this little creature when found in sediment samples were coated with coarsely crystalline calcium carbonate, whereas the shells of living specimens caught with plankton nets towed near the surface were always smooth and quite without the crystalline layer. A commonly accepted explanation for the difference in the two kinds of shells cited purely chemical precipitation of lime on the empty shells after they had come to rest on the ocean floor. However, this seemed rather improbable, because it is well known that lime tends to dissolve on the deep ocean floor.

Recently the chemical precipitation theory has succumbed to the observation that the glittering layer of calcium carbonate is always thickest on the oldest part of the shells and usually absent from the last-formed part; obviously it is not an inorganic precipitate but must be formed during the life of the animal, but when and where? Evidently not at or near the ocean surface where the living animals were caught. So Lamont Geological Observatory scientists towed nets at greater depths and, as was to be expected, at depths of several hundred meters caught specimens with shells heavily coated with crystalline calcium carbonate. Here was proof that the life cycle of this species includes a vertical migration from the surface down to a depth of several hundred meters, and with it came an answer to the old question: what keeps the population from being swept out of the Canaries region? Apparently what happens is something like this. The immature animals fatten on diatoms in the upper sunlit layer of water, then they start their downward migration and as they sink they add the thick layer of lime to their shells. At some level they reach a countercurrent setting to the northeast, that is in a direction opposite to that of the surface Canaries Current. Finally, they reproduce; the little embryos rise to the surface to enjoy the succulent diatoms of the Canaries Current, but thanks to their ride in the deep countercurrent they will start their feeding just where their parents did, that is in the area south of the Canaries. So far as we know no attempt to detect a countercurrent by direct means has been made, but that it exists we have no doubt. The evidence of the foraminifera is convincing.

What of circulation at much greater depths? As long ago as 1814 Alexander von Humboldt, observing that samples of deep water even in tropical regions were cold, explained the low temperature as being due to the sinking of cold water in polar regions and its flow along the bottom to the equator. If there were no renewal of bottom water by flow from high latitudes, bottom water would become as warm as surface water for the same reason that deep mines are warm, or even very hot—continual generation of heat being caused by radioactive substances in the rocks of the earth's crust. Measurement of the flow of heat upward in the sediments of the deep basins is one of the routine procedures of most oceanographic expeditions nowadays. However, early theory of deep circulation called for nothing more than a very sluggish flow at rates of no more than a few millimeters a day.

Actual measurements of deep flow came as a byproduct from an attempt to wring wealth out of the sea. The Swedish chemist Svante Arrhenius, who won a Nobel Prize for his theory of ionization, found enough gold in some samples of sea water to yield a small profit over the cost of extraction. To Fritz Haber (another chemist, who won a Nobel Prize for the invention of a process of making ammonia out of the nitrogen in the air) the fabulous amount of gold in the oceans seemed to offer a means of paying off Germany's World War I debt. To test the feasibility of winning gold from the sea, Haber organized and partly financed an oceanographic expedition.

In April 1925 the *Meteor,* a converted gunboat, sailed from Kiel to begin the German South Atlantic Expedition. Although the primary objective of the cruise was to assay sea water for gold, the ship was equipped with the best and most up-to-date apparatus for oceanographic work. The chief scientist, Alfred Merz, died soon after the start of the expedition. This left Georg Wüst in charge of the oceanographic investigations. For the next twenty-five months the *Meteor* made a series of fourteen east-west profiles across the South and equatorial Atlantic. In addition to the customary measurements of temperature and sampling of water layers, bottom topography was charted with an early version of the echo sounder, the depth measuring device mentioned in Chapter 1. The time-consuming method of lowering a sounding line had limited the number of soundings made by all expeditions before the *Meteor* to no more than two thousand; in two years the *Meteor* made seventy thousand soundings, and more accurate soundings as well. Another innovation was a bottom sediment sampler that worked a good deal like an apple corer. This had the great advantage that it recovered the layers of sediment just as they had accumulated on the ocean floor. The thicknesses of the sections of sediment brought up were not much more than 1 meter or 3 feet, but even so they represented many tens of thousands of years of sediment accumulation, and the method was a great advance over the earlier scooping up of sediment without regard to its layering. These sediment cores, when studied after the expedition, led to the discovery that the deep-sea sediments of the Atlantic contain a decipherable record of the ice ages and interglacials of the Pleistocene Epoch.

Wüst, whose primary interest was in physical oceanography, was determined to make direct measurements of currents at abyssal depths. To do this it was necessary to hold the ship as nearly stationary as possible, which in turn meant anchoring. This Wüst and Captain Spiess proceeded to do, in spite of the prevalent opinion that anchoring in the middle of the ocean was impossible. Their method was to lower two anchors on tapered steel cables. Lowering the anchors, making the scientific observations, and raising the anchors in 5,700 meters or 3.5 miles of water took as much as four days, but what Wüst learned about deep circulation in this way was worth the trouble.

Wüst's observations led him to conclude that deep water moves south along the continental slope of Brazil in strong, relatively narrow streams. In contrast to the expected sluggish flow, these streams moved faster than the Brazil Current at the surface. Later, in 1938, Wüst anchored the German research ship *Altair* over a seamount in the North Atlantic, where he found evidence of a layer of no flow between 1,500 and 1,800 meters (5,000 and 6,000 feet) beneath the Gulf Stream; below the zone of quiet water, however, he found evidence of a great current moving to the south. In spite of the importance of Wüst's findings and new ideas about deep circulation, his observations were not followed up.

Nevertheless, other kinds of investigations not directly concerned with deep circulation provided scattered evidence of the existence of surprisingly vigorous currents at great depths. Since 1947 Maurice Ewing—director of Lamont Geological Observatory—and his co-workers have been photographing the ocean floor with cameras designed to function at the greatest depths. Some of the earliest pictures showed well-defined ripples on the surface of coarse sediments at depths of about 2 kilometers or 1.5 miles. The form of the ripples was the same as that which one can see on any shallow sandy bottom over which a current has flowed. These pictures were taken on the tops of *seamounts*, ancient volcanoes of mountainous proportions, whose tops stand well above the sea floor. Samples of sediment from such mounts sometimes contain the microscopic calcareous skeletons of planktonic organisms known to have been extinct for many millions of years. Apparently these deposits of ancient sediment have been scoured and partly removed by deep currents, for otherwise they would be deeply buried under layers of younger sediment. In some cases they are covered by a few centimeters of coarse sediment made up of the shells of planktonic snails, fragments of barnacles, and the shells of exceptionally large bottom-dwelling foraminifera. Under present conditions no sediment as fine as the ancient sediments can accumulate on the tops of these seamounts. Does this mean that vigorous deep circulation in the Atlantic is a condition of relatively recent development, that is during the last 2 or 3 million years? Or have the old sediments been pushed up bodily in the process of formation of the seamounts? But magnetic measurements strongly indicate that most seamounts are old volcanoes. Furthermore, samples from their tops sometimes include volcanic detritus. If these submarine volcanoes have grown in anything like the way volcanoes develop on land, it is scarcely conceivable that they could have lifted up masses of soft sediment in such a way as to leave the unaltered sediment capping their summits. It is difficult to avoid the conclusion that these old sediments in their fineness of grain are additional evidence of the exceptional conditions of this remarkable interval of earth history in which man has evolved, that is, the Pleistocene Epoch.

In the past few years more photographic evidence of currents has come from greater depths. Charles Hollister and Bruce C. Heezen, marine geologists at the Lamont Geological Observatory, have found scour marks in photographs from depths exceeding 5,000 meters or 3 miles.

Of course, photographs can yield evidence of only those currents that flow directly over the bottom and are energetic enough to move particles of sediment. To gain a better insight into oceanic circulation we need to know more about currents at intermediate depths, and movements of water masses at velocities too leisurely to leave marks on the ocean floor. Because of the difficulty in the past of making direct measurements with current meters, oceanographers have worked out indirect methods of attacking the problem of deep circulation. For example, it is relatively easy to lower a series of ten or twelve special sampling bottles with thermometers attached. In addition to the temperatures, the water samples make possible determinations of salinity and dissolved oxygen at the various depths.

An example of a water mass traceable by its temperature and salinity is provided by the Mediterranean. Since evaporation at the surface of that almost landlocked sea in summer greatly exceeds gain by rainfall, the surface water becomes increasingly saline and dense. Eventually it sinks as less salty water from the Atlantic replaces it at the surface. This process fills the Mediterranean Basin to overflowing with highly saline and relatively warm water that must escape by way of the Strait of Gibraltar. Because of its density it flows out beneath the eastward inflow from the Atlantic, which replaces it as well as making up the loss from evaporation. At the narrow Strait the incoming and outgoing currents may attain velocites of as much as 4.5 miles an hour or 2 meters a second. During World War II crafty captains of German submarines took advantage of these currents to move in and out of the Mediterranean without use of their engines which would have been heard by the Allied surface patrols. Not until after the war did the Allies navies learn how the German submarines had eluded detection in the Strait.

The salty and heavy water, once having passed through the Strait, pours like a river down the continental slope of the Atlantic until it reaches a level at which the density is equal to its own; there, at a depth of about 1,200 meters, it spreads westward as a layer, which can be detected by its characteristic temperature and salinity over most of the eastern North Atlantic.

The oxygen content of deep water is a particularly good indicator of how long the water has been at depth. Ocean water takes up oxygen only while at or near the surface, that is, by contact with the atmosphere or through the photosynthesis of floating plants, a process that releases oxygen. Once having sunk beneath the level penetrated by light, the supply of oxygen is slowly depleted by planktonic animals and bacteria which float at intermediate and abyssal depths, or below 1,000 meters. Measurements of the oxygen content of many samples of deep water from all parts of the oceans show a systematic variation indicating that there are only two regions where important quantities of water sink from the surface to the abyss. One of these is in the North Atlantic south of the southern tip of Greenland; the other is in the South Atlantic around Antarctica and, particularly, east of the Palmer Peninsula. The oxygen content of deep water in the other oceans gradually diminishes with increasing distance from these sources, until in the bottom of a large basin off Peru it reaches a minimum. From this oceanwide oxygen gradient we can infer that there is a general circulation along the ocean floor from the North Atlantic and the Antarctic Ocean into the other ocean basins.

As already mentioned, additional indirect evidence of at least slow circulation of deep water is provided by its temperature, which is only a few degrees above freezing, even under the equator. The warm water of the tropics is nothing more than a relatively thin surface layer only 450 meters or 1,500 feet deep. Because of the difference in densities of the cold and warm waters they do not mix readily. To maintain this enormous volume of cold water implies a very considerable flow. This has led oceanographers to assume that there is a broad, slowly spreading current flowing down the Atlantic and joining the current from the Antarctic Ocean to form a stream flowing through the Indian Ocean and then up into the Pacific. However, this picture fails to take into account the effect of the earth's rotation and certain considerations of fluid mechanics.

Accordingly, Henry Stommel of the Woods Hole Oceanographic Institution envisions a different pattern of abyssal circulation. A chart of deep circulation according to Stommel is shown
in Figure 15. He reasons that in the open ocean, flow of bottom
water must be different from that of a river—more like the flow of
air in the atmosphere. Air does not move directly from high pres-

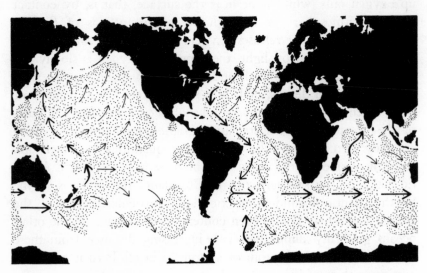

FIGURE 15 *Deep ocean circulation according to Henry Stommel's
theory. The flow away from the sources (arrows with black ovals) is
confined to intense currents on the western edge of the oceans. These in
turn feed a broad flow that carries water toward the poles in each of the
ocean basins.*

sure to low pressure areas; instead it circles around the highs and
lows under the influence of the earth's rotation. In other words,
the air tends to flow along the isobars or lines of equal pressure.
From his own construction of the pattern of isobars in the deep
ocean based on dynamical considerations and on the requirements for the supply of upwelling water, Stommel deduces a flow
from the equator toward the poles. The cold water which sinks in
high latitudes then flows in strong currents along the western
sides of the ocean basins as deep counterparts of the strong currents flowing along the same paths at the surface. In the Atlantic,
Stommel postulates a strong, deep current running down the
western North Atlantic and up the western South Atlantic. When

the currents meet in the South Atlantic they merge and flow east-ward. Stommel supposes that the combined current divides east of the Cape of Good Hope, part flowing north along the east coast of Africa into the Indian Ocean, while the remainder flows south of Australia and northward along the coast of Asia.

Partial confirmation of Stommel's theoretical scheme has

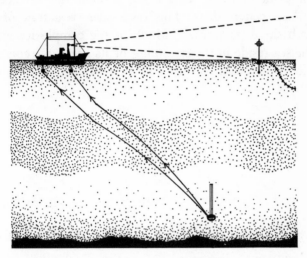

FIGURE 16 *Movement of currents is measured by Swallow floats trans-mitting signals as they drift at various depths. The listening ship's posi-tion is fixed by radar from an anchored buoy.*

come from two independent sources. Wüst, by analysing the pres-sure distribution in the South Atlantic, has shown that the flow of deep water in that ocean is confined to relatively narrow streams along the continental slopes of Brazil and Argentina.

More direct confirmation comes from a relatively new device for measuring deep currents invented by a British oceanographer, John C. Swallow. It is a float which is precisely ballasted so that it will sink to a predetermined depth and remain there. It contains a small ultrasonic pinger that sends out signals at regular intervals. Using the signals, the progress of the float as it is carried along by a deep current can be followed by a surface ship; see Figure 16 for illustration. A Swallow float, at a depth of 2,000 meters or 6,500 feet off Charleston, South Carolina, drifted southward at a

rate of from 2 to 8 miles a day, in good conformity with Stommel's scheme of deep circulation.

As a result of recent explorations, we are having to unlearn a
good deal of what we once believed. Thus, it used to be widely
supposed that the waters above the floor of the ocean were "dead"
—motionless. But the facts, it now seems, are otherwise. All the
waters of the sea even down to the greatest depths are always
going somewhere. In an everlasting motion the surface waters
and the deep waters drift. This restlessness is a trait of the sea
almost as basic as its wetness. Much of the complexity and wonder of the sea reside in the streaming of its great currents, flowing
from pole to pole, east to west and west to east, from sandy shelf
to dark abyss.

CHAPTER 3

WAVES OF THE OCEAN

THE STREAMING MOTION OF OCEAN WATERS HAS POWERFULLY influenced the physical and cultural evolution of mankind by shaping and sometimes changing the pattern of climates on our planet. It has influenced the directions of migrations and trade routes, and thus has led to the fall of empires and the growth of new ones elsewhere. But the effects of oceanic circulation, though powerful, are subtle; only within the past couple of hundred years have men paid much attention to ocean currents.

In contrast, ocean waves must have caught the attention of our earliest ancestors. Wave motion at sea cannot have had much, if any, influence on man's evolution, and not much upon the course of history, with the possible exception of the well-timed storm that broke the power of the Spanish Armada. But storm waves have made a vivid impression on man's imagination, and have shaped his mental image of the sea to such a degree that in some languages the words "sea" and "waves" are interchangeable. Storm waves have provided a theme for folklore as in the old story of Jonah, as well as the inspiration for some of our greatest poetry and prose from Homer to Shakespeare and Conrad.

Waves on and in the sea vary enormously in size, are of many kinds, and due to many causes. But when most people think of waves, they think of wind-driven waves; the kind, for example, that roll constantly onto the outer shore of Cape Cod—their ceaseless attack will eventually destroy the Cape, leaving nothing in its place but a shoal.

Although the cause and effect relationship between wind and waves is obvious, the mechanism by which wind energy is transmuted into wave energy is not clearly understood. It seems to be universally true that the wave form arises, or tends to do so, whenever two surfaces move over each other. Mathematicians can describe these motions by equations in a fairly satisfactory way, but this falls short of real explanation of the effect.

The dimensions of waves are height, length, and period. The height is measured from trough to crest. The amplitude of a wave

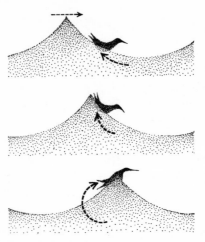

FIGURE 17   *Sea gull demonstrates that wave forms travel, but that the water itself does not. In these drawings, the waves move from left to right as the sea gull (or a water molecule) simply rotates in an imaginary*

is one half of its height. The length is the distance from crest to crest, and the period the time required for two crests to pass the same point. Although waves travel, their motion does not involve net movement of water; it is only the wave form that moves forward. The water particles at the surface and within the wave merely move in more or less circular orbits, which bring them back to their starting points. If you carefully watch a sea gull floating on the sea, you will notice that it moves through a circle in a vertical plane, as illustrated in Figure 17. The crest of the wave carries the gull upward and slightly forward, then the trough takes it down and back to its original position. This rotational motion is greatest in the water near the surface. At a depth of one ninth of the wave length, the movement of the water is halved. Therefore, the depth to which a wave can disturb the sea floor depends more upon its length than height. However, since water motion dies out so rapidly with depth, even the longest wind-generated waves have no effect on the deep ocean floor; it is only when they enter shallow water near coasts that they make themselves felt by stirring up fine sediment on the bottom.

When waves become very long in proportion to their height,

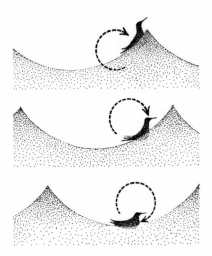

circle, moving slightly to the left up the front slope of an approaching wave, then sliding to the right down the back. When the wave has passed, the gull will not have moved more than an inch or two.

the orbits in which the water particles move become increasingly flattened ovals.

Waves spreading out from some disturbance and no longer under the influence of the wind are approximately sinusoidal in form; that is, the crests are smoothly rounded and are similar in their curvature to the troughs. In contrast, waves making up under the lash of a strong wind approach trochoidal form; the crests rise to sharp ridges while the troughs remain smoothly rounded.

When a strong wind pursues waves over a long enough distance or "fetch" (see page 96), their height increases more rapidly than their length, with the consequence that the crests become steeper and more sharply peaked, until the wind pressure is enough to push the crests forward as tumbling masses of foam, the "white horses" of the sagas. As the wind beheads the most highly crested waves it reduces their height; then as they travel farther their length and velocity increase until at last they travel about as fast as the wind. From then on they are mature; they grow no further.

It is difficult even for those with long sea experience to estimate the heights of waves from a moving ship, because one has no fixed level of reference. Then, too, because of the extreme misery of a rough sea and possible damage and danger from waves, there is an irresistible urge to overestimate their size. When a great liner loses half her lifeboats to a single wave, one supposes that the wave must have been higher than the lifeboats. The more probably explanation is that the liner, because of her own period of rolling and because of a mischance of timing, lurched into the onrushing crest, and the collision of ship and wave imparted kinetic energy to the mass of water which leaped high into the air, lifting lifeboats off their chocks and smashing them.

Newspaper reports of waves 100 feet high are mostly exaggerations. It is easy to overestimate the height of a wave when observing it from a ship whose bow is dipping as the wave approaches. Conrad appreciated this when he wrote that the "size" of waves depends upon whether you look down on them or up at them.

Methodical investigation of waves began relatively recently. During World War II better understanding of waves came through studies inspired by the expectation that waves might afford a way of forecasting conditions at sea and on invasion beaches. To this end continuous wave recorders were developed. In essence, these consist of a device sensitive to changes of pressure, which is placed on the sea bottom and connected to the shore station where the pressure changes are recorded on a revolving drum as waves pass over the pressure gauge. The pressure-sensitive element may be nothing more than an inner tube with enough air to be limply inflated at the depth of water in which it is set. From the inner tube a hose leads ashore to the recording mechanism, which can consist of bellows working against a spring that balances the pressure of the mean head of water. Where the distance between the pressure-sensitive device and the recorder must be greater than 100 meters or about 300 feet the inner tube is not satisfactory, and it is better to convert the pressure changes into electrical pulsations.

This can be done with suitably cut crystals of quartz, that is, silicon oxide, and some other substances. When opposite faces of such a crystal are connected through an electrical conductor and pressure is applied to the faces, a current flows through the conductor. Thus, each wave as it passes over a meter with its sensitive crystal lying on the sea floor generates by its momentary pressure a surge of electricity, an electrical model of itself. Transmitted by cable to the recording apparatus, the electrical surge enters its signature on the continuous record of incoming waves.

The heights of waves as actually recorded are rather unspectacular in comparison with the 100-foot waves of popular fancy. A 60-foot or 18-meter wave is sufficiently exceptional to deserve special mention. 70-foot or 21-meter waves have been recorded in a storm of hurricane force. Fortunately for those who travel on the sea, most waves are much smaller than these examples. Waves higher than 45 feet or about 14 meters are described as "phenomenal" in the sea disturbance scale of the British Admiralty Weather Manual, and are likely to be encountered only in the center of a hurricane. In general, waves in the Atlantic rarely exceed 40 feet or 12 meters in height, whereas in the Pacific 50 feet or 15 meters is about the limit. The largest waves occur in the Antarctic Ocean, where heights up to 60 feet or 18 meters may be reached.

When a storm whips into fury the surface of the ocean over which it drives, the first effect is to raise a confusion of waves of many sizes racing off in various directions and at different speeds, because the velocities of waves in deep water depend upon the wave length or distance from crest to crest. Such a chaotic free-for-all battle of waves where there is no well-defined system of wave fronts traveling in a single direction presents the mariner with a hazard that involves the laws of probability. His ship is constantly menaced by the possible coincidence that several waves of somewhat different wave lengths by overtaking each other at the same time may combine forces momentarily to form a single wave of exceptional height and power. Oceanographers versed in probability theory have calculated, for example, that one wave in 1,175 should rise to three times the height of the average wave.

As waves travel away from a storm region, a sorting process takes effect. The longer waves travel outward faster and leave the shorter ones behind, and long-crested waves take the place of short-crested because the interfering components that give rise to the latter are propagated in different directions.

The *periods*, or times between the passing of two consecutive crests, of the normal run of waves in the Atlantic vary from 6 to 8

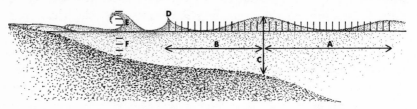

FIGURE 18　*An ocean wave breaks when it enters shallow water. In this diagram, the dotted line indicates the base of the waves. In deep water, the height of ocean swell (small vertical lines) is one twentieth of its length (dimension A).*

In shallow water, the drag of the bottom shortens the wave length (dimension B) to twice the depth of the water (dimension C), and the wave is forced up into a peak (D). The peaking wave breaks when its height (E) is in ratio of 3:4 with the water depth (F).

seconds corresponding to wave lengths of 160 to 320 feet (50 to 110 meters), but occasional wave lengths of 500 or even 600 feet (150 to 180 meters) may occur. Waves of the normal length travel from 20 to 27 miles an hour, while the longest waves do about 35 miles an hour.

In the South Pacific wave lengths of 1,000 feet (300 meters) or even longer are not uncommon. These have a velocity of 50 to 60 miles an hour. Such great wave lengths can arise only where there are long, uninterrupted distances, or *fetches*, over which the generating winds may act; this is why waves of such great velocities are confined to the vast reaches of the South Pacific.

When waves approach a coast the shoaling bottom exerts a breaking effect, as illustrated in Figure 18. The relationship between wave length and velocity no longer holds true; instead, the velocity becomes proportional to the square root of the depth of water. As the water rapidly shoals, the distance between waves shortens, the wave fronts steepen and at last crash forward as breakers. At this point there is a real forward transfer of water, and to this much of the eroding power of waves is due. On long, very gently shelving bottoms, as off Waikiki Beach, the long waves of the Pacific steepen until their forward slopes are deeply concave, and yet because of the nearly horizontal bottom, they rush forward for a quarter of a mile without dissipating their energy by breaking into a smother of foam. Here is the surf-boarder's paradise, well described by Jack London. Let him explain the physics of the sport. "When a wave crests, it gets steeper. Imagine yourself on your board, on the face of that steep slope. If it stood still, you would slide down just as a boy slides down a hill on his coaster." But the moving wave form constantly catches up with you, so that you keep on going without reaching the "bottom of the hill," not, at least, until the wave reaches shallower water and breaks.

But the retarding effect of a shoaling sea floor has more important consequences than the delight of surfboard riders. When a wave enters shallow water obliquely, the retardation sets in first at the end nearest the shore, with the result that the wave front is refracted, or caused to swerve around in such a way as to bring its crest more nearly parallel to the shore line. By the time rollers reach a beach they are often practically parallel to it, regardless of their original direction. This plays an important part in the reshaping of coast lines by wave erosion. In bays, waves fan out thus spreading their energy more thinly there, whereas they converge and concentrate their attacks on the headlands. The ultimate effect is to reduce irregularities of coasts to simple, smooth lines.

To mariners the concentration of wave energy on capes means that they can often find safe anchorage in coves completely open to the sea, provided that the headlands on both sides have gently shoaling floors extending laterally toward the cove.

Records of waves on coasts tell much more than the maximum height of waves that may be expected at a given point. As a rule a wave gage exposed to the open ocean records a mixture of waves of several sizes arriving from different storm centers. The total effect on the record is as confusing as would be several different letters typed one on top of one another on the same sheet of paper. To make sense out of these superimposed messages from distant storms, oceanographers have developed apparatus that can automatically separate out the wave trains of uniform size. Such wave analysis is analogous to the breaking up of white light by a prism into its components of various wave lengths or colors. When wave records made at some point on a coast are analysed, they often show components of long wave length. These long components are called *ground swell*. As we have pointed out, the longest waves travel fastest and, therefore, reach points distant from the storm center ahead of all the others. Under favorable circumstances a ground swell can be watched for several days, during which the wave length becomes shorter as more slowly traveling waves arrive from the disturbance. From the difference in time of arrival of waves of known velocities the distance to the source of the waves can be calculated. In this way, analysis of wave records can be used to trace the paths of storms at great distances. Waves that have traveled enormous distances have been recorded at shore stations. Recording stations on the coast of England have detected waves from the region of the Falkland Islands, 6,000 miles away. The first waves to arrive had a period of 21 seconds corresponding to a wave length of 2,100 feet or 640 meters. Recording stations on the coast of California have picked up waves which had traveled across the Pacific from New Zealand.

Damage and delay to ships because of waves make it desirable to route them in such a way as to avoid areas of severe conditions. By doing so, the United States Military Sea Transport Service found it possible to reduce time of passage by an average of 10 per cent. To plan the best routes they used predictions of conditions in the North Atlantic three or four days in advance, derived from known distributions of storm areas.

In the powerful beat of storm waves one sees a passing phase in the general character of the ocean. The scene is violent and awe inspiring at its height, but it is transient, the product of what might be likened to an emotional outbreak.

In contrast, the pulselike regularity of the rise and fall of the tide brings to mind cosmic causes. In the rhythm of the enormously long waves of the tides, time flows before our eyes. These waves are of global proportions; their wave length is one half the circumference of the earth.

We all realize that the moon is largely responsible for tides; one thinks of its gravitational pull as drawing up the sea surface at high tide. But this simple scheme fails to explain why there are two tides each day. Not only does the ocean surface bulge up directly under the moon, but it also bulges up on the opposite side of the earth. What is the origin of this "force" directed away from the moon?

We are accustomed to think of the moon as circling around the earth; this is a convenient simplification, but in reality both the earth and the moon circle around their common center of

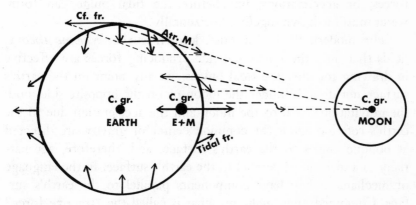

FIGURE 19 *The tidal force in a section through the line connecting centers of the earth and moon. E + M = center of gravity of earth plus moon. Atr. M. = attraction of moon. Cf. fr. = centrifugal force.*

gravity. Because the earth's mass is so much greater than that of the moon, the common center of gravity falls within the radius of the earth, as shown in Figure 19. But although the earth's orbit in the earth-moon system is small, it is none the less important to the stability of the system. Without motion around their common center, and the centrifugal "force" (or better, acceleration) to which the motion gives rise, the two bodies would be drawn to-gether by their mutual gravitational attraction. Since all points on the earth move through the same orbit about the common center, the centrifugal acceleration is the same at all points on the earth, but this is not true of the moon's gravitational pull; it decreases inversely as the square of the distance, and therefore it is greatest directly beneath the moon and least on the farther side of the earth. The consequence is that beneath the moon, its gravitational pull exceeds the oppositely directed centrifugal acceleration, while on the far side the centrifugal acceleration exceeds the gravitational pull. The arrangement works somewhat as if the moon pulled the water away from the earth on the near side and pulled the earth away from the water on the far side. Or on the human scale, it is like pulling a person by one arm. As he moves toward you, his other arm leaves his side because of its inertia. This theory of tides was first developed by Isaac Newton; it is known as the *equilibrium theory*. It appeals only to vertical forces, or accelerations, but before the tidal bulge can form, water must be drawn together horizontally.

The modern theory of tides, known as the *dynamic theory*, holds that only the horizontal tide-producing forces are effective in drawing together the tidal bulges. At any point on the earth's surface not directly under the moon or on the opposite side, both the gravitational pull of the moon and the acceleration due to the earth's rotation about the common center of gravity are directed at oblique angles to the earth's surface, and, therefore, act partially in a directional parallel to the earth's surface. In the language of mechanics, they have components parallel to the earth's surface. Combined, they make up what is called the "tractive force" at any particular point. The amount of the tractive force at any point is given by the following impressive formula:

$\dfrac{3g}{2} \dfrac{M\,e^3}{E\,r^3}$ sin2C, in which g is the acceleration of gravity at the

earth's surface, M is the mass of the moon, E, that of the earth, e the radius of the earth, r the distance between the earth and the moon, and C the angle between the line joining the centers of the moon and earth and a line from the center of the earth to the point of the earth's surface being considered.

The gravitational pull of the sun also has an effect on the tides, and since the sun's mass is 27 million times as great as the moon's mass, one might expect the sun to have a powerful effect. Actually, the sun's effect is rather weak; the little 3 on the shoulder of the r in the formula above is the reason why. The distance between the sun and earth is 389 times as great as the distance between the moon and earth. According to the formula, the sun's tide-raising effect at any point must be $\dfrac{\text{the sun's mass in moon units}}{(389)^3}$ times as great as that of the moon, or $\dfrac{27,000,000,}{58,863,869,}$ which is approximately 0.46. So we see that in spite of the sun's enormous mass, its tide-raising effect is a little less than one half that of the moon. Although the moon's effect is dominant, the sun's is large enough to compli-

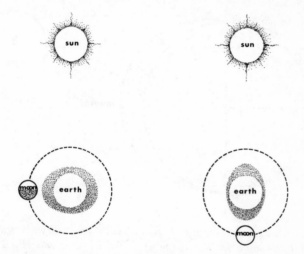

FIGURE 20 *Spring and neap tides: when sun and moon are in line they pull together to produce the highest tides, the spring tides (right). But when they are at right angles to each other their tidal forces are opposed, producing the low neap tides (left).*

cate greatly the procession of the tides. Because of the moon's motion in its orbit, it rises about fifty minutes later each day, and consequently the timing of the moon's effect on the tides falls farther and farther behind that of the sun; twice each month, when the sun, moon, and earth are in line, the effects of the sun and moon reinforce each other and we have particularly high tides called *spring tides;* and twice each month the sun, moon, and earth form a triangle, so that the sun and moon pull at cross purposes, as it were, and we have the smallest tides of the lunar month. These are called the *neap tides*. The making of spring tides and neap tides is illustrated in Figure 20.

To complicate matters even more, the moon swings to 28° north and south of the equator each month. At its extreme positions its tide-raising effect is asymmetrically distributed with respect to the equator. The result is that the two daily tides at any one point differ in height as shown in Figure 21. The sun's varying distance from the equator during the year introduces another

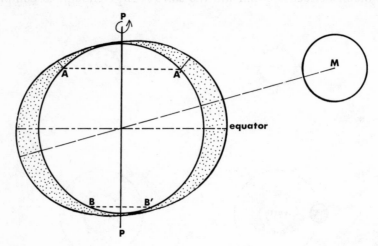

FIGURE 21 *Diagram showing cause of daily inequality of tides. The outer circumference denotes shape of ocean level. A and A¹, B and B¹, successive positions of two points on the earth's surface at half-daily intervals.*

complication. Various other astronomical variables do their bit toward adding complications to the long-run tidal regime. One important variation follows an 1,800-year cycle; because of this the Middle Ages were a time of very high tides. At present, the heights of tides are decreasing and will reach a minimum about the year 2400. We shall come back to this long cycle later.

Action and reaction; the one is inseparable from the other. The tides, which are caused by the relative motions of the earth, moon, and sun, exert a reaction upon these same motions. If the tidal motion of the ocean's waters consisted of nothing more than a rising and falling each day to the extent of a few feet, as is approximately the case with the mid-ocean tide, the tides would represent only a trifling expenditure of energy. But near land this slight oscillatory motion is transformed into the surging back and forth of immense masses of water, which flow into shallow regions like the Sea of Okhotsk, and then out again with much energy lost in fluid friction, and all at the expense of the earth's kinetic energy of rotation. The ultimate effect is that of a break upon the earth's rotation; each year the earth turns a little more slowly and the day becomes a little longer. However, there is nothing here over which to be alarmed; the effect upon the length of our day is really very small, as we shall see.

At first thought, it is difficult to imagine any way of estimating the length of days in the remote geological past. But paleontologists sometimes turn up quite unexpected information.

As corals grow they keep adding lime to their skeletons, or to the conical cups in which some species live. But the rate of adding lime or, in other words, the rate of growth of their living quarters varies with the seasons, probably because of temperature changes, with the result that the cups are marked by encircling corrugations, the distance between which represents one year's growth. Between the corrugations are many fine ridges encircling the cup and parallel to its growing edge.

John Wells, a professor of paleontology at Cornell University who has spent many years studying fossil and living corals, suspected that the fine ridges might represent daily growth increments. This was a reasonable guess because it is known that the uptake of lime in coral tissues falls at night and rises during the day. So he counted the ridges between annual corrugations and found to his gratification that the number of ridges hovered around 360. Then he turned to fossil corals. But the ridges, being very fine, are easily worn away after the death of the animal. After much searching through collections of fossil corals he found well-preserved ridges on some corals that had lived during the Devonian Period, that is about 345 million years ago, and still more on other corals from sediments of Pennsylvanian age, or about 280 million years old. When Wells counted the ridges between the annual corrugations, he found an average of 400 on the Devonian corals and between 385 and 390 on the Pennsylvanian corals.

Wells next turned to the calculations of astronomers. It seems that astronomers agree that the year, or the time it takes the earth to circle around the sun, has remained constant during the past 600 million years, but the best estimates of the effect of tidal friction suggest that each 100,000 years have added two seconds to the length of the day. At that rate, when the first easily recognizable forms of life appeared on earth the day was only twenty-one hours long. It also means that during the Middle Devonian Period the year included about 396 days, while the year of Pennsylvanian time included about 390 days. On the whole the agreement between Wells's counts of ridges and the calculated numbers of days in those early years is extraordinarily good.

Wells, as a paleontologist, views the geochemical methods of dating rocks with a healthy detachment. He points out, quite rightly, that the radioactive decay method of dating stands upon reasonable but unproved assumptions, and therefore acceptance of geochemically determined ages is an act of faith. Confirmation of the ages by some completely independent clock is needed. In Wells's hands, corals in combination with the calculations of astronomers provide just such an independent way of testing the reliability of the geochemical chronology of earth history. It is comforting to find that the corals confirm the generally accepted chronology.

Since astronomers can predict the relative motions of the earth, moon, and sun, they can predict the timing of the tide-producing forces quite accurately. However, the actual reaction of bodies of water to the tidal forces is another matter. Astonishing differences in tidal regime occur within very short distances. The moon and sun set the water in motion, but how far and at what times the local tides will rise depends upon such things as the slope of a sea floor, the dimensions of a gulf, the depth of a strait, or the width of the entrance to a bay. This does not mean that local tides cannot be predicted; it simply means that theory is not of much help. To predict tides at a particular place it is necessary to know what the tides have been doing there in the past and then project that knowledge into the future. In this way, the United States Coast and Geodetic Survey makes up timetables of tides at all points of the American coasts that may be of importance to mariners.

The Atlantic affords an example of the influence of the shape of an ocean basin on the tidal regime. The lines on Figure 22 have been drawn through places where high water occurs at the same time. They are called *cotidal lines*. The broad features of the cotidal system have been constructed from measurements of tides at scattered islands; to observe tides at sea from ships is impracticable. To discover some theoretical basis for the observed pattern we can consider the Atlantic Ocean and its continuation, the

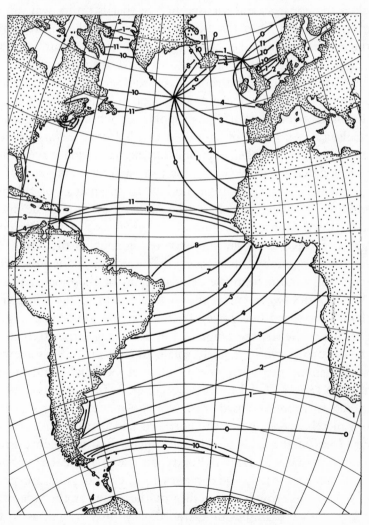

FIGURE 22 *Cotidal lines of the semi-diurnal tide in the Atlantic Ocean.*

Norwegian and Polar Seas, as a long bay closed to the north, but at its southern end in open communication with the Antarctic Ocean. We can now consider the tides of the Atlantic as composed of two parts: a free tide maintained by the direct effect of the tide-generating motions of the earth, moon, and sun, and a co-oscillating tide which is maintained by the tide of the Antarctic Ocean. The northward progress of the tide-wave from the southern ocean is shown by the numbers on the cotidal lines. For example, when it is high tide at Cape Horn, the previous tide has reached the equator, and the one before that is on its way up the English Channel. Thus the tide-wave traverses the entire length of the Atlantic in one day at an average speed of about 350 miles per hour. In the northern half of the chart are three points, one in the Caribbean, one southeast of the southern tip of Greenland, and another between Iceland and Scotland, around which the cotidal lines sweep like irregular spokes of wheels turning counterclockwise. At such points, called *amphidromic points*, there is no tide, but around them continually circles a tide-wave whose motion is determined by the rotation of the earth. As yet, no one has applied the theory of tidal motions to an analysis of the tidal regime of the Pacific, where the difficulties would be much greater. Very probably because of the great size of the Pacific, a progressive wave from the southern ocean such as the South Atlantic is of minor importance, the dominant tide-generating effects arising more from the daily motions of the moon and sun.

When a tide-wave enters the shallow water of the continental shelf, it loses speed because of friction; at the same time it gains height. Nevertheless, the range of the tide along large stretches of the coasts of the world is fairly small, though probably somewhat greater than in the open ocean: tides at oceanic islands rarely have large ranges. Tidal ranges exceeding 20 feet or 6 meters are restricted to more enclosed seas. North American ranges greater than 6 meters are found at the northern end of the Gulf of California, parts of the Gulf of Alaska, Ungava Bay in Quebec Province, and the famous Bay of Fundy on the Atlantic coast. Some cases of unusually large tidal ranges in bays and gulfs are probably due to the crowding together of the water as the tide-wave proceeds. Other examples of extraordinary tidal ranges, as in the Bay of Fundy, must depend upon some more powerful effect. The tidal range of the Bay of Fundy is the greatest in the world. There the critical factor is what is known as resonance. The dimensions of the bay are such that it should have a natural period of oscillation of about 6.29 hours, thus almost exactly fulfilling the conditions necessary for resonance with the tide-raising effect of the moon. The range of the tide increases toward the head of the bay, in accordance with theory although its effect is augmented by shoaling water and by the narrowing and bifurcation of the bay toward its head, where the spring tidal range exceeds 50 feet or 15 meters. In consequence of the rotation of the earth, the range on the southern side of the bay is somewhat greater.

Since any wave involves to-and-fro, as well as up-and-down motion of the water particles, the passage of a tide-wave is accompanied by characteristically reversing tidal currents. In the open ocean these travel only a few miles each way during the tidal cycle, but in shallow water they are much more powerful and may attain speeds of 3.5 miles an hour. In confined passages such as Vineyard Sound south of Cape Cod, they are sometimes alarmingly swift. We remember being at the mercy of a tidal current in a sailboat one calm and dark night off the West Chop, Martha's Vineyard. In the distance we heard a rushing, churning sound, like that of the bow wave of a small steamer, but whatever it was it showed no light; we could see nothing on the dark water. Then as the rushing sound rapidly became louder we realized that we were being hurried by the tidal current directly toward the West Chop buoy; what had sounded like a bow wave was the current churning against the buoy. With no wind we were helpless to avoid a possible collision. As it happened, Neptune was kind; we passed the buoy almost hidden in foam with a few feet to spare.

In the Hole, the narrow passage south of Woods Hole that connects Buzzards Bay with Vineyard Sound, the tidal current at its peak is strong enough to drag the marking buoys completely under, leaving no other sign of their presence than a wake of snarling, violently boiling foam.

When a stiff breeze blows against a tidal current, a steep, choppy, and sometimes dangerous sea results. The names of two points of land in Vineyard Sound, the East and West Chops, attest to the frequency of such sea in their vicinity.

In a few rivers and estuaries about the world the rising tide takes on a spectacular form known as a *bore*. The only bore in the United States occurs in the Cook Inlet of Alaska. At Turnagain Arm the flood tide, if conditions are favorable, advances as a wave from 4 to 6 feet high. The sound of the tumbling water announces its approach half an hour before its arrival at any point, fortunately, because such a wave has no mercy for small boats.

A remarkable bore travels 200 miles up the Amazon and takes so long making the trip that as many as five flood tides may be moving up the river at one time.

A much more famous bore known as the Mascaret occurs in the lower Seine between Rouen and the sea. It has caused a long series of accidents and drownings. In 1843 Victor Hugo wrote a poem to express his grief over the drowning of his eldest daughter and her husband by the Mascaret. The Mascaret attains its greatest height roughly halfway between Le Havre and Rouen, at Caudebec-en-Caux. Its speed is about 15 miles an hour or 24 kilometers an hour. Its height at Caudebec reaches 24 feet or 7.25 meters when the tide is reinforced by a strong westerly wind; it used to be higher before measures were taken to improve the water way, but it still breaks over the quay at Caudebec where it is a spectacle that attracts many visitors.

The most famous bore is on the Chien Tang River in China. Usborne Moore, who studied this bore in 1892, tells how Chinese junks took shelter in specially constructed bays until it had passed, after which they came out to take advantage of the current. He reports that on one occasion: "no less than thirty junks swept up in the after rush and passed Haining with all sails set but with their bows pointing in every direction, several proceeding stern first at a rate of ten knots toward the city of Hang Chau." Of the bore itself he says: "the regularity of its appearance and shape, the distance at which it is heard at night and seen by day; its charge against the sea wall; its speed, height, and gleaming front and thundering roar as it tears past the observer, render it a most impressive phenomenon."

No simple theory satisfactorily explains how a rising tide entering a river mouth becomes the vertical wall of water of a bore. The restriction of their occurrence to only a very few rivers in the world is also a mystery. Why does the Seine have the largest bore in the world and the Thames none? Why does the rising tide in the Hudson behave so differently from that in the Seine? A theory devised by R. A. R. Tricker appears to have much plausibility but it is far from simple and we will not go into it here.[1]

It seems a pity that all this tidal turmoil cannot be put to more useful work than lengthening the day and silting up harbors. To harness the tides is an old dream, one that became a political nightmare at Passamaquody in Maine where the federal government spent millions during the depression years on a scheme to generate electricity by the rise and fall of the tide. In the end the project was abandoned for the ostensible reason that the value of the power eventually developed would be too small to repay the investment of capital. But one wonders if that was the real reason, since elsewhere in the world tidal power has been used profitably on a small scale and will soon be put to work on a vast scale.

Along the Brittany coast of France the tides have turned village mills for hundreds of years. At high tide the millers close the inlet gates of barrages across the mouths of estuaries; then as the tide falls outside, the trapped water inside earns its freedom by turning water wheels as it runs out.

And now a scheme to exploit tidal energy is being planned for installation in the Gulf of St. Malo off the coast of Brittany. To study the feasibility of the project, engineers have mounted a model of the English Channel on a turntable 14 meters in diameter. Rotation of the turntable simulates the effect of the rotation of the earth, a significant factor in the tidal regime of the Channel, which is responsible for much higher tides on the French side. If successful, it is estimated that the yearly output of energy would equal France's total development of hydroelectric energy.

The enormously long waves raised by the moon and sun have every right to be called "tidal waves," but unfortunately because of misuse of the term, tidal wave to most people implies a catastrophic wave generated by an earthquake or volcanic explosion. To avoid this misuse of the term "tidal wave," scientists have been accustomed to use the Japanese word "*tsunami*" to designate dis-

[1] See his *Bores, Breakers, Waves and Wakes* (New York: American Elsevier Publishing Company; 1965).

turbances of the ocean surface generated by earthquakes and volcanic explosions. If lazy, one pronounces the word as *sunami*, but the Japanese manage to put a *t* sound directly before the *s*. The meaning of the word, "large wave in a harbor," is not especially apt; a better term and one now often used is *seismic sea wave*.

A subsea earthquake or sudden displacement of some part of the ocean floor along a fracture in the earth's crust sets in motion two kinds of waves; one is a compression wave or sound wave with a velocity of about 1.5 kilometers per second. Such a wave is not audible, but on a ship it may be felt as a severe shock. Encounters of this kind probably explain reports of mysterious rocks that cannot be found by subsequent soundings. The other kind of motion is a series of surface waves mechanically similar to storm waves but of much greater length and traveling at correspondingly greater velocities. It is this kind of wave that causes much damage and inflicts great loss of life. Quite unlike storm waves, seismic sea waves are harmless at sea; normally they pass under ships without being noticed. Except near the point of origin, their heights are small. The waves of the Hawaiian tsunami of 1946 had a height of only about 1 foot or 30 centimeters in the open ocean. When one considers that the distance between the crests of such waves is about 90 miles, it is easy to understand how they may be overlooked at sea. Why then do they cause so much damage to coastal regions? The answer is that their great wave lengths and velocities more than make up for what they lack in height. Their total energy is enormous.

The Hawaiian tsunami began with a seismic disturbance in the deep trench off the Aleutian island of Unimak. Because the Aleutian Trench runs approximately east and west, the surface waves generated by the sudden release of energy along the trench moved with greatest effect in a north-south direction. The quake occurred at two o'clock in the morning; it reached the Hawaiian Islands less than five hours later. Since the distance traversed was 2,300 miles or 3,700 kilometers, the waves must have traveled at a rate of no less than 460 miles or 740 kilometers an hour. The time interval between arrival of each wave was 12 minutes. Since wave length equals wave velocity divided by period, the distance between crests must have been no less than 92 miles. Thus the energy represented by these fast, long waves was very great even though their height in the open ocean was much less than that of storm waves. Like all waves, tsunamis are sensitive to changes of depth; as they approach a continental shelf they lose velocity and gain height so that their energy becomes more concentrated. This is why a tsunami that passes unnoticed at sea may become ferociously destructive upon reaching a coast. At Hilo on the island of Hawaii the breaking waves rose 30 feet or about 9 meters above still-water level, and in the valley of Pololu the wave left debris at an elevation of 55 feet or about 17 meters. Water from other tsunamis has been driven as much as 2 miles across coastal plains and the uprush of the waves has been reported to rise as high as 135 feet or 41 meters, with rises of 50 feet or 15 meters fairly common.

As expected, the seismic sea waves of 1946 rose to their greatest heights near the source of their energy, that is in the Aleutian Islands. Until the end of March 1946, a two-story reinforced-concrete lighthouse stood on a promontory 32 feet (9.6 meters) above sea level at Scotch Cap on the southwest end of Unimak Island of the Aleutians. Nearby was a coastal lookout station with a complement of twenty men. Behind the lighthouse on a plateau 103 feet (31 meters) above sea level stood a radio mast. On April 1, early in the morning, the seismic sea wave struck. When it receded, the lighthouse, barracks, men, and radio mast were gone.

Following the devastating seismic sea wave of 1946 a warning system was organized by the United States Coast and Geodetic Survey. As a rule the first sign of the approach of a seismic sea wave is the arrival of a rather strong swell-like wave, not different enough from an ordinary wave to alarm a casual observer. Then the first great trough arrives with a vast sucking of water away from the shore. At Hawaii in 1946 the reefs and shallow coastal platforms were uncovered, leaving quantities of stranded fish. During this interval in the drama, the normally continuous sound of the breakers ceased. The sinister hush alarmed many natives, who would not otherwise have known that anything unusual was happening, and large numbers of people ran down to the shore. This seemingly incredible folly is less surprising when we realize that no large seismic sea wave had hit Hawaii since 1877; further-more the tempo of events left little time for reasoning. Many paid for their curiosity with their lives when only minutes later the first colossal wave thundered over the shore.

If lives were to be saved in the future, earlier warning than that provided by withdrawal of the sea would be needed. The present warning system has a center at Honolulu and another in Japan; these receive two kinds of information. Various earth-quake stations in and about the Pacific make preliminary deter-minations of the points at which quakes occur and alert seismic sea wave detector stations at Dutch Harbor and Attu in the Aleu-tians, and at Hilo, Hawaii, where ingenious devices designed by C. K. Green of the Coast and Geodetic Survey Staff measure the rise and fall of the ocean surface. These instruments are so adjusted that they do not react to ordinary wind waves or tides; however, when waves with a period of between 10 and 40 minutes come in, they cause an oscillation of a column of mercury which closes an electric circuit and sets off an alarm. A warning is then sent to the center at Honolulu.

Since 1946 three seismic sea waves have visited the Hawaiian Islands. At five o'clock in the afternoon of November 4, 1952, the seismograph at Honolulu recorded a severe earthquake. Within an hour, with the help of reports from seismic stations in Alaska, Arizona, and California, it was possible to determine the place at which the quake had occurred; it was in the ocean floor off the Kamchatka Peninsula. As reports of the progress of the resulting seismic sea wave came in from various parts of the Pacific, the people at the center in Honolulu calculated that the first wave would reach Honolulu at 23:30 Greenwich time. This seismic sea wave, though somewhat smaller than that of 1946, caused much damage, but thanks to the early warning the only casualties were six cows.

In 1960 a series of cyclopean earth movements along the coast of Chile sent destructive waves all the way across the Pacific to do great damage along the coast of Japan. At Hilo the sea rose to a height of 37 feet or more than 11 meters. The warning system worked very well; the police were notified of a possible disaster hours in advance. But many people, like lemmings, went down to the shore to see the waves! Others simply disregarded the warning to leave their houses. The result was a death toll of sixty-one people.

In Chile at the center of the quake there was no time for warning. Although some deaths were caused by the quake itself, and by a volcanic eruption with avalanches, most of some four thousand deaths were due to a series of waves 30 feet or 9 meters high.

Although the Chilean seismic sea wave of 1960 did moderate damage to yachts and harbor installations at San Diego and San Pedro near Los Angeles, the west coast of the United States has so far escaped serious damage. This is at least partly because of the inclination of the coast line to the sources of so many seismic sea waves, that is, the Aleutians and the deep trenches off the coast of South America. The long diagonal approach of waves from these sources causes the waves to lose energy as they cross a long stretch of shallow water before reaching the shore.

Some catastrophic waves are caused only indirectly if at all by earthquakes. When a child slides down the inclined end of a bathtub, the water swashes up at the other end and overflows on the floor. Such swashes can occur in nature, when a mass of rock or part of a glacier falls from a cliff in a bay or lake. Tremendous waves may result, but their destructiveness is confined to local waters. On July 9, 1958, a few minutes after an earthquake had shaken the coast of Alaska, a volume of rock estimated at 40 million cubic meters fell from an altitude of up to 3,000 feet or 900 meters in the upper Lituya Bay, and generated a surge that rose to 1,700 feet or more than 500 meters up the mountain side across the bay, where it made an almost clean sweep of the forest; only one tree was left standing amidst the ruin. At the same time, a wave moved out of the bay at an estimated speed of 100 miles per hour. This crossed the spit at the bay's entrance with a height of about 50 feet (15 meters). As it did so, it carried a small fishing boat over the tops of the trees on the spit and dropped it outside. It is scarcely surprising that the boat promptly sank; that the owner and his wife were able to escape in their skiff before the sinking is one of those preposterously improbable happenings which only nature dares to write into the story of this world.

The most destructive surge in history was that of May 21, 1792, in Shimbara Bay of Kyushu Island in Japan. An enormous rockfall came down into the bay during a series of earthquakes and raised three waves which drowned fifteen thousand people living on the surrounding shores.

In addition to the sudden local dislocations of the earth's crust that are the cause of earthquakes, release of the earth's energy sometimes takes place through the upwelling of molten rock and the escape of steam and other vapors under high pressure. The eruptions of most volcanoes, particularly those that erupt at frequent intervals, are relatively mild. Their destructiveness, if any, is directly due to the outpouring of red-hot lava.

The really vicious volcanoes are most likely to be those that have been dormant for hundreds or thousands of years, during which time energy has been accumulating beneath them. Such a one was Krakatoa, an ancient volcano rising from the bottom of the Sunda Strait between Java and Sumatra. Except for one small eruption in 1680 it had not erupted in historical time. In 1883 it came to life with a vengeance. First came a series of earthquakes, steam and smoke issued from fissures, the ground became warm, and the natives heard strange rumblings and hissings. Then on August 27 began a salvo of explosive eruptions that would put a whole series of hydrogen bombs to shame. Several cubic miles of rock were hurled 20,000 feet into the air. Two thousand miles away at Manila people wondered at the distant reports, thinking that perhaps some ship in distress was signaling with cannon fire.

When the blasting ceased after two days the northern half of the volcano had disappeared; where the 1,400-foot (420-meter) volcano had stood, there was now a depression 300 meters deep; the only remnant of the island was the southern edge of the crater. The appalling release of energy set in motion waves 100 feet (30 meters) high, which wiped out villages along the Strait and killed some thirty-six thousand people.

Violent storms and hurricanes may lead to catastrophic rises of sea level, which are often called "tidal waves." *Storm surges* is a better name; having no rhythmic motion they are not waves. Instead they take the form of a slow local rise of the sea superposed upon an already high tide. They have a most devastating effect upon low-lying coasts such as surround the Gulf of Mexico. A surge of this kind was responsible for the Galveston flood in 1900 when six thousand people were drowned after the sea had overflowed the sea wall and swept into the town. On August 10, 1856, a storm surge overwhelmed an island on the Gulf Coast south of New Orleans. It had been a fashionable seaside resort of the aristocratic South; at the time the season was in full swing. In *Chita* Lafcadio Hern sketches in imagination the fatal sequence of events; the slow rise of the sea, panic among people at a ball, and the final annihilation of every living thing.

The most massive of all waves are unseen and remained unknown until relatively recently. These are *internal waves,* sometimes called *boundary waves* because they occur at the boundary surface between layers of water of different densities rather than at the interface between air and water. The theory of internal waves had been discussed by Stokes in 1847, but their possible influence on conditions in the oceans was neglected for more than fifty years. In 1904 Ekman appealed to the theory of internal waves to explain what mariners call "dead water," a phenomenon often encountered in the Arctic; sailing ships in light breezes and steamers of low power were sometimes held back by a mysterious drag. Ekman surmised that when a ship moved through a layer of melt water of low salinity resting on denser saline water, its motion would set up waves at the boundary between the two kinds of water. The generation of these internal waves, like the bow wave at the surface, would be at the expense of the ship's motive power, and would, therefore, reduce its speed.

A few years later, the famous Swedish oceanographer Otto Pettersson, who devoted the greater part of his long life's work to study of the sea around Scandinavia and northwestern Europe and who brought into being the International Council for the Investigation of the Sea, discovered curious submarine waves in the Gullmar Fjord on the southwest coast of Sweden. At his research station on Born Island in the fjord was an instrument which drew a continuous record of the depth to the discontinuity between the relatively fresh water of the fjord and the more saline and denser water which flowed in along the bottom of the fjord from the ocean. The pen of this instrument as it moved up and down wrote an exciting account of a powerful rhythmic movement of the deep layer of dense water. As the records unfolded over months and years, the interval of about twelve hours between crests and troughs clearly indicated to Pettersson that these inward surges of deep water were related to the tide-producing forces of the moon and sun, but in their height of nearly 100 feet (30 meters) they were vastly greater than the rise and fall of the tide along the coast of Sweden. Pettersson, who had been born on a small island within sight of the Pater Noster Lighthouse in the Skagerak, was steeped in the history of the Baltic; in the pulsating movement of mountains of water he thought he saw an explanation for the disastrous disappearance of herring from the Baltic and its approaches. During the thirteenth, fourteenth, and fifteenth centuries herring abounded in the Baltic and in the Sund and Belts that connect it with the North Sea. The herring fisheries of the Middle Ages in those waters were the source of the great prosperity of some of the towns of southern Sweden, and the silvery hordes helped to fill with gold the coffers of the merchants of Gotland in the Baltic. Then mysteriously the herring ceased to pass through the Sund and Belts into the Baltic.

By tracing the complex motions of the moon back in time Pettersson calculated that the combined tide-producing power of the moon and sun reached greatest strength during the last centuries of the Middle Ages, the time when the herring were most plentiful in the Baltic. During that period the great submarine waves must have been surging into the Baltic with maximum force, and with them went the herring. Then after the fifteenth century, when the tide-generating power of the moon and sun grew less, the weaker deep surges failed to bring the herring; they remained in the North Sea, to the advantage of Holland.

In 1912 Pettersson published a paper, "Climatic Variations in Historic and Prehistoric Time," in which he presented the hypothesis that climatic cycles may be due to cyclical variations in the heights of tides. Astronomical calculations show that periods of maximum tides recur at intervals of 1,800 years. From the historical record and from hints that he found in myths and folklore he thought he could see an 1,800-year rhythm in climate. But the record is short; it is impossible to rule out coincidence. Perhaps a final answer will come when we know more about tides and the great submarine surges that accompany them.

Not all internal waves are related to the tides; many in the open ocean probably arise when a layer of less dense water flows over a denser layer, the motion at the boundary having an effect similar to that of the wind on the ocean's surface. The wide application of new instruments to the study of the oceans shows that internal waves occur in all oceans and at all depths. Heights as great as 260 feet or about 80 meters have been observed, but the velocities are much less than those of surface waves being generally less than 2 miles or about 3 kilometers an hour.

Very probably the deepest internal waves leave their mark here and there on ocean sediments, particularly sediments on the tops of seamounts. As a rule sediments on the tops of seamounts are remarkably coarse because of absence of the fine clay fraction abundantly present in normal oceanic sediments. Probably the deep currents that sweep across these elevated features prevent the accumulation of fine particles, but it may very well be that the carrying power of such deep currents is greatly increased by internal waves which stir up the fine sediment into suspension where it could not otherwise be lifted by a slowly moving current.

A better understanding of internal waves is of importance to the Navy; at times they may present serious hazards to submarines. This is particularly the case when, perhaps to escape detection, a submarine has descended to a depth close to the limit for which it was designed. If at such a time a submarine encounters large internal waves, the up-and-down motion may cause an unexpected and sudden increase in pressure with disastrous results.

The study of internal waves has made good progress in recent years, but there is still much more that we would like to know about them. For example, are they capable of eroding seamounts in the same way that surface waves by relentless gnawing reduce islands to shoals? Is there such a thing as "internal surf" where internal waves encounter shoals? With the rapid advances in oceanography now we may expect to have answers to these questions before long.

EVER-CHANGING

CHAPTER 4

SEA LEVEL

THE STORY OF A FEARFUL DELUGE APPEARS IN THE LEGENDARY history and folklore of many ancient peoples. A Chaldean legend recorded on tablets found in the ruins of Nineveh is so similar in detail to the biblical story as surely to have had a common origin. In turn the biblical account echoes the Greek myth of Deucalion, who, forewarned by his father Prometheus, survived the futile attempt by Zeus to destroy mankind by drowning. In the *Zend-Avesta*, the sacred book of the old Persian religion, the story of a similar punishment by a deluge occurs. Almost lost in the jungle of Cambodia, the sculpture and bas-reliefs of the ancient temple of Ankor Vat vividly bring to life the Hindu legend that tells how Manu, one of the fourteen progenitors of mankind, saved the life of a fish—for which kind deed the creature rescued him when rising waters overwhelmed the world. Among the far off South Sea Islands they tell of the fisherman who caught his hooks in the water god's hair, which so angered the god that he drowned mankind, but strange to say spared the fisherman. Among northern people the Sagas tell of the Cimbrian flood.

The almost world-wide persistence of a deluge myth suggests some common origin. More than ninety years ago Edward Clodd, in his scholarly book *The Childhood of Religions*, conjectured that fossil sea shells imbedded in rocks now many hundreds of feet above the level of the sea stimulated the imaginations of primitive men to invent stories of a universal flood. Thus, at least some flood stories may have had their origin in what was the first geological hypothesis, and except for the supposed timing of the event and the embellishment of angry gods, one not far from the truth. Geologists believe that there is not a sizable area of any continent that has not at some time been beneath the sea. The sediments laid down during these floodings of large parts of the continents are the pages of the book in which paleontologists read the history of the development of life on our planet.

In the immensely long perspective of geological time it would seem from the sequence of sedimentary rocks on the continents that sea level has never stood still. It is only because our recorded history is an infinitesimal fraction of geological time that sea level can be used as an universal reference level.

The slow but seemingly endless pulsations of relative sea level recorded by ancient sediments are bound up with basic problems of the earth sciences. They are a manifestation of the global forces that have shaped the continents and ocean basins, forces that have raised mountain chains on the continents and still vaster chains of mountains on the ocean floor, and have pushed up islands arcs like the Antilles, Aleutians, and the South Sandwich Islands. Those most spectacular of geological phenomena, volcanic eruptions and explosions, stem from the same causes that have brought about repeated floodings of vast regions of the continents.

As we stated in Chapter 1, geophysicists have inferred from the study of earthquake waves that the earth's interior consists of three zones: a crust varying in thickness from 5 to 50 kilometers; a mantle about 2,900 kilometers thick; and a core of iron and nickel which accounts for about one half of the earth's diameter and nearly a third of its mass.

Speculation about the origin of the earth and its features has led to many hypotheses (some of them discussed in Chapter 1). As scientists learn more about the inner space of our planet and about the behavior of matter, on the gross as well as on the subatomic scale, some hypotheses fall while the plausibility of others grows. In this way the field of reasonably probable theories has become a good deal narrower in the last few years. We may never know how it all started, but at least we can become increasingly sure that certain things did not happen. This process of the survival of the fittest among theories has led to the modern view that the earth began as a rotating cloud of cold cosmic dust, perhaps much the same kind of material that is continually raining in from outer space even now, and minute quantities of which occur in deep-sea sediments. Certainly the cloud included all the sub-stances that occur on earth today, that is the water of the oceans, the gases of the atmosphere, the carbon that makes life possible, as well as the iron and nickel of the earth's core.

Gradually the cloud condensed; a solid nucleus took form; as it grew, compaction, chemical reactions, and radioactivity re-leased enough heat to melt the entire mass. This molten stage seems necessary to account for the concentration of metallic iron and nickel at the earth's center; while fluid, the densest materials could gravitate to the center. After some billions of years of radi-ating heat the temperature of the mass fell sufficiently to permit a crust to freeze. After more cooling, torrential rains set in as the immense volume of water vapor surrounding the young earth condensed. Thus were born the primeval seas. According to meas-urements of radioactive substances and their decay products in the most ancient rocks, the earth reached this stage of develop-ment not less than four and a half billion years ago. By that time rain was falling probably much as now, and rivers were flowing; we know this because some of the most ancient rocks were once gravels, now cemented and altered to hard rock, the pebbles of which must have been transported from uplands and worn to their rounded shape by running water. By that time the tempera-ture of the earth's surface had probably fallen to very nearly its present level and most if not all of its original heat had already been lost by radiation into outer space. Today geologists and geophysicists agree that heat left over from the earth's molten state has not been responsible for the great pulsations of the earth's surface which are so clearly recorded in the book of sedi-ments.

Apparently, much water was entrained with the mantle mate-rial as it condensed. A large part of the "smoke" that adds to the impressiveness of volcanic eruptions is steam, that is, water newly come to the earth's surface from the upper mantle. It is called juvenile water. The prevalence of volcanic rocks scattered through the entire sequence of sediments implies a nearly contin-uous addition of juvenile water to the oceans throughout geologi-cal time. However, for a very long time the net addition of water has probably not been large. Layers of ancient sediments spread widely on the continents show that since the appearance of abundant life about 600 million years ago, marine waters have repeatedly flooded broad areas of the continents and then withdrawn only to return again elsewhere. Many geologists, like detectives at the scene of a crime, have reconstructed conditions in these former seas by comparing the sediments and the traces of once living things that they left, with the kinds of sediments and organisms that are characteristic of various marine environments in the seas and oceans of the present day. From what they have found during many years of search they conclude that, with a very few doubtful exceptions, these seas were always shallow. On the whole, the much older sedimentary rocks laid down thousands of millions of years ago tell the same story of shallow seas, but they speak less clearly because of the alteration that many of them have suffered and the absence in them of the remains of complex forms of life. Apparently, during the last 600 million years, and probably much longer, the earth's supply of water has been just large enough to overflow parts of the continents from time to time but never so abundant as to flood them really deeply. This absence of any discernable trend toward more, or for that matter, less water in the ocean basins is remarkable. Perhaps a gradual increase in the capacity of the ocean basins has occurred, but more probably some process, not now clearly understood, removes water from the oceans at about the same rate as it is added from below by volcanic activity.

The perpetual removal of material from the surfaces of the continents by rain and wind and its final accumulation on the ocean floor should by all reason have a broadly leveling effect. And yet the evidence points the other way; at this moment in geological time the continents stand exceptionally high and some enormous regions of the ocean basins are deeper now than they were some 100 million years ago. As we saw in Chapter 1, intensive studies of the ocean floor by sea-going geophysicists have shown that the layer of soft sediment carpeting the ocean floor is not nearly thick enough to represent accumulation during all of geological time. Instead, the thickness is only about enough to account for accumulation beginning at sometime within the Mesozoic Era when the reptiles still ruled the world about 100 million years ago. This Case of the Missing Sediments is a challenge to detectives among earth scientists. As sometimes happens, the new problem suggests an answer to another; what has become of the water constantly added to the oceans by volcanic eruptions? As each new layer of sediment comes to rest on the ocean floor it traps some water between its particles. Since from one fifth to one third of the volume of the sediments now accumulating in the ocean basins is water, the total volume of water so entrapped is very great. What became of the pre-Mesozoic sediments we do not know, but whatever their fate, it is probable that they took with them a large volume of water, perhaps enough to account for much of the excess water that had been added to the oceans by volcanic eruptions.

In the early days of geology the explanation of mountain building seemed simple. The cooling earth was shrinking like a drying apple; mountains were the wrinkles in the skin of the apple. Then, as geologists came to appreciate the immense age of the earth and found evidence of a succession of episodes of mountain building marching on from the dim beginning of things undiminished into our own time, they recognized the weakness of the shrinking apple theory. At the same time evidence was accumulating and seemingly unrelated observations were turning up. Let us follow some of this evidence to see where it leads.

The theory of organic evolution is so firmly attached to the name of Charles Darwin that most people overlook the impact of his observations and thinking on the development of modern geology. His theory of the formation of coral atolls would have been enough to have made the fame of any ordinary naturalist.

In his autobiography, Darwin tells how his theory took shape:

No other work of mine was begun in so deductive a spirit as this; for the whole theory was thought out on the west coast of South America before I had seen a true coral reef. I had therefore only to verify and extend my views by a careful examination of living reefs. But it should be observed that I had during the two previous years been incessantly attending to the effects on the shores of South America of the intermittent elevation of the land, together with the denudation and the deposition of sediment. This necessarily led me to reflect much on the effects of subsidence, and it was easy to replace in imagination the continued deposition of sediment by the upward growth of coral. To do this was to form my theory of the formation of barrier-reefs and atolls.

He reasoned that if an island with a fringing reef sank slowly, the "various minute and tender animals" responsible for secreting lime would build the surface of the reef upward in pace with subsidence. Since corals build most actively at the outer edge of a reef where they find abundant oxygen and plentiful food, a lagoon would develop between the rising reef and the sinking island. Eventually the central tip of the volcanic cone would disappear, leaving nothing but a coral reef surrounding a lagoon, that is, an *atoll*. The formation of an atoll according to Darwin's theory is illustrated in Figure 23. Darwin realized that his theory

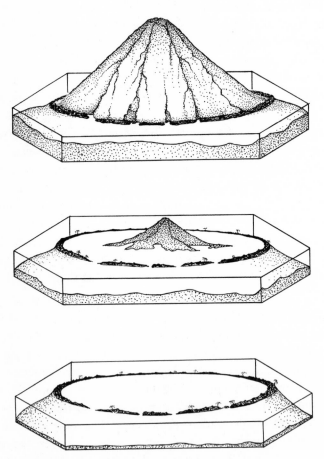

FIGURE 23 *Block diagrams to indicate Charles Darwin's hypothesis of the development of an atoll by the submergence of a volcanic island and the upgrowth of a reef.*

had implications that went far beyond the origin of a kind of islands favored by writers as romantic settings for short stories. From the distribution of atolls and islands surrounded by barrier reefs he outlined regions of subsidence of the floors of the Pacific and Indian oceans. "We are led to conclude," he wrote in *The Voyage of the Beagle* in 1845, "that the great continents are for the most part rising areas; and from the nature of coral reefs, that the central parts of the great oceans are sinking areas."

In 1881, the year before Darwin's death, tantalized by the absence of final evidence by which to test the correctness of his hypothesis, he wrote to the American oceanographer Alexander Agassiz: "I wish that some doubly rich millionaire would take it into his head to have borings made in some of the Pacific and Indian atolls, and bring back cores for slicing from a depth of 500 or 600 feet." Seventy years after Darwin's death his wish was fulfilled, and with the borings came the proof that he had reasoned correctly; his only error had been in underrating the amount of subsidence.

In 1952 two holes were drilled into opposite sides of Eniwetok Atoll by the Atomic Energy Commission and the Los Alamos Scientific Laboratory in cooperation with the United States Geological Survey. Both reached the volcanic basement rock at respectively 4,158 and 4,610 feet or 1,267 and 1,405 meters. The entire thickness of limestone in both holes contained the remains of organisms able to live only in shallow water. However, certain samples of rock from the holes showed that at times the reef had been exposed to weathering and partial solution. These weathered zones contained pollen and shells of land snails typical of islands hundreds of feet high. Evidently sinking of the ocean floor around Eniwetok had been interrupted from time to time by intervals of uplift. The deepest limestone reached was about 60 million years old on the evidence of the fossils it contained.

Fortunately for science, a United States naval vessel cruising in the Pacific during the war was commanded for two years by a geologist, Harry H. Hess, from Princeton University. While looking over the echo-sounder traces he discovered a group of twenty undersea mountains that were peculiar in having broad flat tops. Later by studying charts of the Pacific he inferred the existence of 140 others. Their abrupt rise from the sea floor indicated that they had originated as undersea volcanoes, but at some time in their history the typical conical form had been modified to produce the flat tops. Hess explained the flat tops as due to wave erosion, but since the tops now lie at depths between 940 and 1,730 meters either sea level must have risen since the time of erosion or the volcanoes must have subsided. In 1946 Hess published a paper on these mountains (he called them *guyots* in honor of a nineteenth-century geologist, Arnold Guyot, who was a professor at Princeton for thirty years). In it, he conjectured that guyots were once islands in a primeval sea long before the appearance of lime-secreting organisms. After pounding waves had reduced the islands to shoals, sea level slowly rose. The drowning of the guyots, as Hess saw it, was primarily the result of a world-wide rise of sea level due to the gradual addition of juvenile water to the oceans, though he admitted that some subsidence of the ocean floor might have occurred in response to the accumulating weight of sediment there. By the time lime-secreting organisms evolved about 600 million years ago, the tops of the guyots were too deep for colonization by them. Hess's paper created immediate and widespread interest, and stimulated search for more until now at least two hundred guyots in the northeast Pacific, Gulf of Alaska, southwest Pacific, and northwest Indian Ocean are known.

This hypothetical history of guyots developed by Hess is an interesting example of the revolution in thinking about the deep ocean basins that has taken place within the last twenty years. Formerly, the prevalent view held that the ocean basins had been essentially immutable almost since the beginning of things, in contrast to the continents where ceaseless change has ruled. Now the force of new information gained through intensive exploration of the oceans since World War II has swung the pendulum the other way. Recent thinking with a firmer base of facts tends to see the continents as relatively stable elements of the earth's crust. To a new school of earth scientists the ocean basins are the sites of most active change and renovation not only in topographical detail but probably in gross form as well.

In 1950 an expedition to explore five guyots in the Pacific west of Hawaii was arranged by the Scripps Institution of Oceanography and the United States Navy Electronics Laboratory, led by

Roger Revelle, director of Scripps. During the expedition, dredges dragged over the tops of the guyots brought up surprises in the form of various fossil corals and shells of snails and large clams that lived during the Cretaceous Period, the time of the last great flooding of the continents, more than 100 million years ago. Evidently, the theory of origin of guyots needed revision. Wave erosion of the flat tops had not occurred at a remote time, but at a relatively recent date instead. This meant that the present depths of the tops could not be due to the gradual addition of juvenile water to the oceans; juvenile water would not accumulate nearly fast enough. On the other hand, weight of accumulating sediment as the cause of subsidence was ruled out because the layer of sediment deposited since Cretaceous time would be much too thin to cause the indicated amount of subsidence. In fact, geophysicists now believe that no matter what its age, the entire thickness of soft sediment, on the floor of the Pacific is too thin to cause a significant amount of subsidence.

The failure of guyots to become coral atolls can be explained by a fairly sudden but not necessarily deep subsidence; reef corals and lime-secreting plants cannot grow below the reach of sunlight.

The beauty of this story of the guyots is that it provides further and compelling evidence of the truth of Darwin's early theory that parts of the floor of the Pacific have subsided. Such increase in the capacity of the Pacific Basin by sinking of its floor would lead to what marine geologists call a *eustatic change* of sea level, that is a world-wide rise or fall due either to alteration in the shape of an ocean basin or to the addition or withdrawal of water that occurs when continental ice sheets melt or grow in size. In contrast, are those local and relative changes of sea level due to up or down warping of parts of coasts.

Inevitably, the subsidence recorded by the tops of the guyots must have led to some draining of water from the continents, but the first effect may not have been large; as we have said, the first rapid sinking of the ocean floor need not have been more than just enough to drown the reef-building corals on the guyots. But then as time went on, the sinking floor of the Pacific and probably the floors of other ocean basins so much increased their capacities that a time came when the waters that had flooded the continents during the Cretaceous Period drained entirely back into the ocean basins. This event marked the end of Cretaceous time.

However, according to the record of sediments, several less widespread invasions of the continents by shallow seas have occurred since the great Cretaceous flood. For some reason each of these has been more restricted than the one before, as if the earth were approaching some kind of climax in its life. Evidently, the relation between the average elevations of the continents and the ocean floors has varied now and then since Cretaceous time. We have mentioned how the drill holes on Eniwetok yielded evidence of times of uplift of the floor of the Pacific in the form of shells of land snails, pollen grains, and solution of the coral rock by rainfall.

But in coupling advance and retreat of shallow seas on the continents with rising and sinking ocean floors, have we not explained one mystery by appealing to another? The answer is, No. Bit by bit geochemists, geophysicists, and geologists have assembled facts and observations which converge toward a unifying hypothesis to explain periodic changes in the relative heights of continents and ocean floors, as well as other formerly puzzling features of the face of the earth.

More than a hundred years ago variations in the pull of gravity from place to place led geologists to suspect that the earth's crust floats on a denser plastic material. The continents are rafts of relatively light rock floating high above the floors of the ocean basins, which are composed of dense rock. Large mountain masses are buoyed up by deep, downward extensions of light rock. The awe-inspiring heights of the world's great mountain ranges, like icebergs, are puny in comparison with their downward extensions.

In 1871 Clarence E. Dutton, an American geologist, gave this principle a name, *isostasy*. Since then geologists and geophysicists have collected a wealth of evidence in support of it (the mechanism of isostasy is illustrated in Figure 24). Measurements of gravity not only on continents and islands but also over many parts of the oceans show that all the major features of the earth are in a kind of hydrostatic balance. The last ice age provides a significant example of how isostasy works. Those parts of the continents that were heavily laden by thick ice sheets about 12,000 years ago have been and still are rising, and presumably they will keep on rising until like ships they displace their own weight of the dense mantle material in which they "float." For our purpose the important thing is that such vertical movements of portions of the crust are positive proof that the material of the mantle can flow, at least very slowly. On the other hand, a kind of earthquake wave called *shear wave*—in which the wave motion is across the line of travel of the wave front—passes through the entire thickness of the

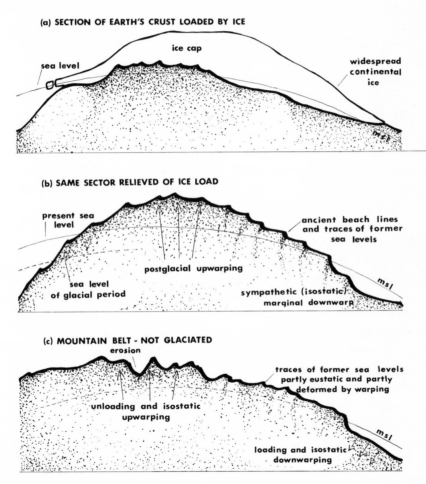

(a) SECTION OF EARTH'S CRUST LOADED BY ICE

ice cap

sea level

widespread continental ice

m s l

(b) SAME SECTOR RELIEVED OF ICE LOAD

present sea level

ancient beach lines and traces of former sea levels

postglacial upwarping

sea level of glacial period

sympathetic (isostatic) marginal downwarp

m s l

(c) MOUNTAIN BELT - NOT GLACIATED

erosion

traces of former sea levels partly eustatic and partly deformed by warping

unloading and isostatic upwarping

loading and isostatic downwarping

m s l

(vertical scale exaggerated)

FIGURE 24 *The mechanism of isostasy in response to: (a) and (b) changes in the ice load, (c) the erosion of mountains.*

mantle. Liquids cannot transmit shear waves; only rigid solids can do so. The resolution of this seeming contradiction lies in the time dimension; the mantle reacts like a rigid solid when subjected to stresses of short duration, and like a very viscous fluid to long-continued stresses. Some familiar substances, like pitch or asphalt, sealing wax, and ice behave in a similar time-dependent way. An iceberg is hard and unyielding when struck by a ship, and yet a valley glacier given enough years will accommodate itself to every turn of the valley down which it flows.

So far the plastic layer of the mantle has appeared only in a passive role. It yields when necessary to maintain isostatic equilibrium as continental ice sheets wax and wane, as erosion reduces mountain ranges to plains, and as rivers build vast deltas, all of which redistributions of mass are brought about by energy from outside the earth, that is from the sun. Can the plastic layer play an active part in changing the expression of the earth's face? Presumably, providing there is a source of energy within it. As we have said, it is unlikely that the interior of the earth retains any heat left from its early molten state. Under any circumstances, such heat would be a dying source of energy, whereas the energy that has raised mountains, fueled volcanoes, and stressed the crust until it has fractured along great rifts, all within the past few million years, is anything but dying.

In the last decades chemists have discovered many different kinds of radioactive substances in rocks. None, fortunately for us, is really abundant, but some are almost universally present. If equally prevalent in the mantle, they should be capable of supplying an almost embarrassingly large amount of heat.

A continuous accumulation of heat within the earth would in time raise its temperature to the melting point. Since such a catastrophe has not occurred within the four and a half billion years recorded by the sedimentary rocks of the continents, the earth's heat budget in the long run must be in balance. Some loss of heat from the earth's interior must take place by conduction, but rocks are not particularly good conductors of heat; that is why deep mines are so hot. Conduction must help a little, but it is unlikely that it can suffice to keep the heat budget balanced, particularly at great depths.

But there is another mode of transfer of heat available; that is, *convection,* or movement of the hot material itself. Convection is constantly at work all around us. We see its effect on a hot summer day when great cumulus clouds rise on the horizon; air heated by contact with the earth's surface and therefore less dense because of expansion rises, and, having pushed its way into the upper atmosphere, loses heat, whereupon its included water vapor condenses into the droplets that form majestic clouds to inspire poets.

The mushroom cloud above an atomic explosion is another example. Intensely heated, and therefore greatly rarified air, rises at hurricane speed to a frigid height where cooling, followed by condensation of water vapor, make the air mass visible.

As millions of years pass heat accumulates in the deeper portion of the mantle, partly because of the generation of heat by nuclear reactions within itself and partly because of contact with the intensely hot fluid core of the earth. As the temperature of the lower mantle rises, it expands and, consequently, becomes less dense; each unit of volume becomes lighter. Like light things generally, this lighter part of the mantle tends to rise. Eventually the tendency becomes strong enough to overcome the viscosity, or resistance to flow of the mantle material. But at the same time parts of the upper mantle through loss of heat by conduction shrink in volume, that is, become denser or heavier, and therefore, like heavy things in general, these localized portions of the upper mantle will tend to sink. Of course, upward and downward flow cannot take place at the same place simultaneously. Instead, hot material, having risen to within a short distance of the earth's surface, spreads laterally and thereby fills the place of less hot material that is sinking in adjacent regions. At the same time the less hot, denser material, having sunk to the lowest level of the mantle region, will spread laterally into neighboring regions where hot material is rising. In this way upward and adjacent downward motions are coupled into systems of continuous motion in closed circuits, as shown in Figure 25. These systems are called *convection cells.* Geophysicists estimate that the rate of flow may be in the order of 2 or 3 centimeters a year. It is unlikely that convection in the mantle is a continuous process; more probably the rate of flow climbs to a climax, then wanes and finally ceases as gravitational stability is restored by half turns of each cell, after which the densest portions will be on the bottom and the lightest at the top. But even the half turn of a large cell should be capable of raising a mountain chain, or an island arc complete with adjacent trench. Each time that overheating at depth again sets the mantle in motion, a new and different pattern of intermeshing cells probably emerges. Forces act at new

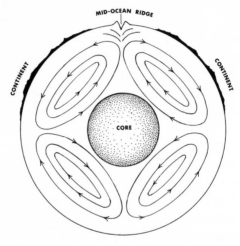

FIGURE 25 *Convection currents within the earth are the basis for a theory of the origin of the Mid-Oceanic Ridge and rift. As seen here, the currents flow up under the rift, push out new material, move laterally under continents and compress them, making mountains rise up.*

angles; tension may take over where compression ruled before. The basic cycle of flooding and withdrawal of waters from the continents repeats itself, but always with differences in detail.

Convective flow in the mantle is still an unproved hypothesis, but the probability that something of the kind really occurs is great. Serious physical or chemical objections do not oppose it. It conforms to the principle of parsimony by its sufficiency to explain and harmonize various scattered phenomena and observations. To the student of ancient sediments it offers a satisfying explanation for the pulsations of sea level that he sees repeated with undiminishing vigor throughout the vast span of the earth's history. At the beginning of the Cretaceous Period about 135 million years ago, before Hess's guyots existed, accumulation of heat deep in the mantle started convection rolling once again. As hot mantle rock rose, it domed upward a broad region of the floor of the Pacific. Under the Indian Ocean another rising flow did the same there. As the intensely hot mantle material came in contact with the thin crust under these oceans, fusion occurred, here and there molten rock broke through the ocean floor to form volcanic islands, the ancestral guyots. In *The Voyage of the Beagle* Darwin wrote: "It would appear that volcanoes burst forth into action and become extinguished in the same spots, accordingly as elevatory or subsiding movements prevail there." The convection hypothesis suggests reasons for the real or apparent absence of a thick layer of unconsolidated sediment on the ocean floors. It may well be that the birth of the ancestral guyots was preceded by a time of drastic reorganization of the ocean floors, when either the physical nature of the older sediments was altered beyond recognition, or, in accordance with a hypothesis advanced by Robert Dietz, a marine geologist at the Scripps Institution of Oceanography, the hot mantle rock as it spread laterally may have swept all older sediment bodily toward and finally under the continents. This theory of Dietz's is a pretty far cry from the generally and firmly held idea of only a few years ago that the crust of the ocean basins had descended unchanged from some four and a half billion years ago when the earth's surface solidified for the first time.

What we know with certainty is that at the time when the tops of the guyots stood near sea level, the continents were inundated on a scale that has not been repeated at any time since. The waters advanced upon North America from the north, south, and east, finally mingling as a warm shallow sea about 1,000 miles wide extending from the Arctic to the Gulf of Mexico and spreading eastward to cover the Atlantic coastal plain from the Gulf to New Jersey. A Cretaceous sea covered most of the British Isles. The famous cliffs of Dover and those on the other side of the Channel, particularly near the mouth of the Seine, and others along the coast of Denmark are masses of lime secreted largely by minute single-celled organisms that swarmed in the warm waters of those days. The name "Cretaceous," from the Latin word *creta* meaning chalk, finds its origin in these characteristic deposits in western Europe. In southern Europe only some ancient highlands stood above the sea, which sent long bays and gulfs far into the interior of the continent. The sea spread into Africa and on its floor sands accumulated; later weathering of the sandstones yielded the desert sands of the Sahara. The waters flowed over Sweden and thence across Russia, covering the site of the Caspian Sea, and reaching as far as the region where the Himalayas were to rise later. Parts of Australia, Japan, and Siberia were flooded. In South America the region of the Andes, then a lowland, was covered by the sea.

The ponderous machine responsible for this almost universal flood moved slowly; so slowly that before it came to rest, the volcanic islands of the Pacific had been worn down by battering waves to mere shoals colonized by various lime-secreting organisms of kinds that lived only during the Cretaceous Period.

Then at last a time came when the excess heat had been dissipated; the floor of the Pacific subsided, carrying down with it the shoals; for their inhabitants this meant death in the lightless depths. With the gradual increase in the capacity of the Pacific Basin, the waters retreated from the continents. When sea level rose again in the Eocene Epoch, the "dawn of the recent," the strange creatures of Cretaceous time had disappeared from the world forever.

The record of the rocks tells that, except for variations of extent and pattern, similar cycles of flooding took place repeatedly before the Cretaceous Period. Since then rises of sea level have occurred, but each succeeding flood has been more restricted. Is it possible that senility is overtaking our earth at last? We doubt it. According to the record, the world has been from time to time for long intervals in the past very much as it is now. The conditions of the present epoch, the Pleistocene, are unusual in the geological record but not unique. Probably things are the way they are because we are living during a time when the system of convection cells inherited from the Cretaceous Period is dying down. In time, we may be sure, a new generation of cells with a different pattern of distribution will take shape. One wonders what kind of beings will be here then to cope with the rising waters.

During rare interludes in the drama of the earth another cause of sea level fluctuations comes into play. Perhaps it is not by mere coincidence that we are living during such a time. The selective effect of the drastic climatic changes of the last one and a half million years has probably hastened the evolution of our species. And the rises and falls of sea level due to the climatic changes have surely had some effect as well, in favoring invasions of new environments at certain times by providing land bridges, and in forcing migrations at others by flooding former hunting grounds.

Heat from the sun is constantly lifting water out of the oceans by evaporation and dropping it on the continents as rain or snow. Normally this water returns to the oceans without much delay, but for some reason as yet unknown, about one and a half million years ago the snow that fell in certain northern regions failed to melt completely during one summer. Whether this was because the winter snowfall had been extraordinarily heavy or because the following summer was unusually cool, we cannot say. All we know is that it was something more than a local, short vagary of weather. From that time on, the winters added more snow to what had become a permanent snowfield. In time the lower part of the mass became solid ice through compaction by the increasing weight of the overlying snow and the freezing of water percolating down from partial melting at the surface. At last the ice became so thick that its rigidity broke down; sluggish flow radially outward from the region of the heaviest snowfall set in; the snow field had become a continental ice sheet. Whatever the prime cause may have been, the effect was widespread; centers of net accumulation of snow appeared at various points in high latitudes both north and south of the equator, and at high altitudes even in equatorial regions. At the same time heavy rainfall in regions now arid created swarms of lakes such as the famous Lake Bonneville, which filled to overflowing the depression on the bottom of which the Great Salt Lake, a mere puddle in comparison, now lies.

At least four times during the Pleistocene, the epoch of man and ice, continental glaciers have spread utter destruction over vast regions of the continents; and each time sea level has fallen as more water was withdrawn from the oceans than was returned. How far sea level fell during the ice ages is still a question; the marks left by former low levels of the sea are under water now and difficult to find. Knowing approximately the land area covered by the continental glaciers, some students of the Pleistocene have attempted to calculate the probable volume of water bound up in ice and from that figure to estimate the lowering of sea level. The estimates vary because one can only guess how thick the ice sheets were, but they provide reasonable limits to the amount of lowering. Probably sea level during the last ice age, the so-called Wisconsin, was at least 100 meters (about 300 feet) below its present position, and probably no more than 200 meters lower.

At some time during the last ice age the floor of the North Sea was dry land. Early men and mammoths roamed the Dogger Bank; North Sea fishermen sometimes find in their trawls the teeth and bones of mammoths and much more rarely flint tools and harpoon points of bone. More often pieces of peat and water-logged stumps of trees come up in the fishing gear. Drowned channels traced by many soundings show that the Elbe and the Weser met and flowed across the formerly exposed sea floor in a single channel. The Rhine and the Thames also became part of a single drainage system.

On the other side of the North American continent, the retreating Bering Sea left open an ample land bridge between Asia and North America. The climate of the Bering Strait region is harsh enough today; one wonders at the hardiness or desperation of the Stone Age men who crossed during an ice age. At least one archeologist, appalled by his own conception of the climate at that time, has suggested that the early immigrants came across the Bering Strait by boat when sea level was higher and the climate was milder. Perhaps, but abundant and unmistakable paleontological evidence tells us that the mammoth, bison, sheep, goat, elk, reindeer, musk ox, black bear, fox, and moose entered North America at about the same time. It is hardly likely that Stone Age men had the fleet of arks needed to transport such a menagerie. If the animals could cross on foot, why not the men?

Possibly the natural assumption that the region of the Bering Strait was encumbered with ice and in a state of desolation during the last ice age is an oversimplification. Abundant bones of large mammals, some even with bits of frozen flesh and hide, found in the frozen gravels of Alaska prove that the general region abounded in big game at a time when the northeastern part of North America was still heavily glaciated. Apparently, the relatively small Atlantic was overwhelmingly dominated by the ice sheets of eastern North America and western Europe; its water, on the evidence of rock fragments transported by drifting ice and now scattered about the floor of the North Atlantic, must have been charged with ice almost as far south as the Azores. It contrast, the temperature of the vast Pacific seems to have remained remarkably uniform during the entire Pleistocene; cores of sediment from the floor of the Pacific even hint that the waters of the Pacific may have been a little warmer during the last ice age than they are now. As Sir George Simpson, a British meteorologist, pointed out nearly thirty years ago, an increase in radiant energy from the sun is a seemingly necessary condition to bring about increased evaporation from the oceans and so supply the copious precipitation that built up the continental ice sheets and filled to overflowing the now empty, or nearly empty, basins of the arid southwestern states. An additional effect of increased radiation would be to heat the earth more at the equator than at the poles, which would accelerate atmospheric circulation. Thus a slightly warmer Pacific may have had a marked influence on the climate of Alaska, the Bering Strait region, and even on that of eastern Siberia. Perhaps an abundance of many kinds of big mammals in Alaska during a time when the northeastern part of the continent was covered with ice is not so paradoxical after all. And perhaps we waste sympathy on the early immigrants into the Americas; the trip over may have been anything but an ordeal.

At the height of the last ice age 27 per cent of the land area of the earth was covered by ice. Then about 12,000 years ago something happened; wasting away of the ice sheets set in. As the ice sheets and glaciers returned their water to the oceans, sea level gradually rose. Certain marine geologists, fascinated by this world-wide upsurge of the oceans, have used the radiocarbon method of dating to measure the rate of rise of the waters. They have searched for submerged deposits of peat, stumps of drowned forests, and shells of clams and snails dredged from the depths exceeding the depth ranges of their now living descendants. At laboratories in Europe and America scientists measure the amount of radiocarbon, the radioactive isotope of carbon, still left in these organic remains and then calculate their ages in years from the known rate of disintegration of radiocarbon. Such dates of former low levels of the sea add up to a remarkably detailed chronology of the step-by-step flooding of ancient coasts. Many tribes of ancient men must have been forced to abandon long-established settlements. Almost certainly such experiences would become part of tribal folklore. Stories improve with telling; possibly what was really nothing worse than a leisurely search for a new cave on higher ground grew after one hundred generations of embellishment into the kind of flood stories that almost every ancient people used to tell.

For some time certain archeologists and geologists have called attention to the archeological riches that must lie at shallow depths along the coasts of Europe and Asia. We have already mentioned the accidental finds on the Dogger Bank. Many tribes of ancient men must have lived close to the sea and near the deltas of rivers and in caves now below sea level. R. A. Daly, professor of geology at Harvard until his death, and author of *The Changing World of the Ice Age* had this to say:

> The last Glacial stage was the Reindeer Age of French history. Men then lived in the famous caves overlooking the channels of the French rivers, and hunted the reindeer which throve on the cool plains of France south of the ice border. The Late-Glacial rise of general sealevel was necessarily accompanied by a rise of the river waters downstream. Hence, the lowest caves are likely to have been partly or wholly drowned. . . . There the search for more relics of Paleolithic man should be pursued.

The shallower parts of the Adriatic should also be rewarding, particularly along the Dalmatian coast where there must be many submerged caves. What would have been difficult and even dangerous exploration when Daly wrote in 1934 would be routine for the scuba divers of today.

According to the radiocarbon timetable the rapid world-wide rise of sea level came to an end about 6,000 years ago. Since then, sea level has fluctuated but always within about 3 meters or 10 feet of its present level. Its failure to rise higher is obviously not due to exhaustion of the ice supply; 10 per cent of the earth's land surface is still covered with ice. If all, or much, of this ice-bound water were returned to the oceans, as it seems to have been during earlier times of warm climate between ice ages, sea level would rise enough to flood almost all the great cities of the world. Until new discoveries solve the basic problem of the cause of climatic changes it is useless to guess about the future course of climate and sea level. Richard F. Flint of Yale, one of the foremost authorities on the Pleistocene Epoch, has pointed out that the present time has more of the characteristics of an ice age than of a fully developed *interglacial*, as the times of mild or warm climate separating the ice ages are called. This suggests that we may be living during a short interval of mild climate, or *interstadial*, within the last ice age. According to the record of climatic changes in the sediments of the deep Atlantic, just such an interstadial did occur between 80,000 and about 60,000 years ago.

Of one thing we may be sure; in the long run climate will fluctuate. If New York is spared a flooding, the alternative will be the advance of a glacier, which creeping forward like an irresistible bulldozer will topple the tall buildings one by one, that is, if there are any buildings left at that time. If the past is a key to the future, our "interstadial" probably has another 10,000 years to run.

Before geologists realized that there had been four ice ages separated by long intervals of mild or even warm climate, they assumed that "the ice age" had come to an end. Accordingly, the majority made a distinction between the "Recent Epoch" and the Pleistocene Epoch, even though Sir Charles Lyell, the founder of modern geology, who introduced the term "Pleistocene" in 1839, had defined it in such a way as to include recent time. Today with clear evidence of not only warmer but also much longer intervals within the earlier Pleistocene, we have no valid reason whatever for setting apart our own little interlude of climate as a distinct epoch. By all evidence and reason we are living in the Pleistocene; we may expect another ice age.

Ancient beaches marking the high sea levels of earlier interglacials have been most carefully studied along the shores of the Mediterranean, but corresponding strand lines are known elsewhere as, for example, along the Atlantic coast of North America. It is a remarkable fact the oldest is the highest, while the younger stand at successively lower levels. This might be construed to mean that the earliest interglacial was warmer than those that came after. It is true, as we have said, that if our climate became warmer, more ice would melt and sea level would rise; but according to the best calculations the rise, if all present-day ice melted, would fall somewhat short of 50 meters or about 150 feet, whereas the highest strand line stands at about 100 meters. An illustration of the relation of altitude to time for the high sea levels of the Pleistocene is shown in Figure 26.

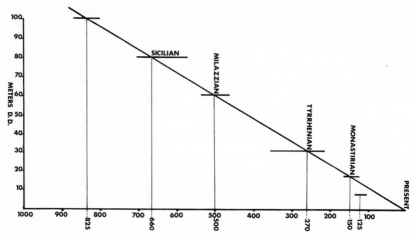

FIGURE 26   *Diagram showing the relation of altitude to time for the high sea levels of the Pleistocene. The horizontal lines represent the Mona-stirian, Tyrrhenian, Milazzian, and Sicilian levels.*

Almost certainly the descending succession of the strand lines is a manifestation of the latest episode of the long-term subsidence of the ocean floors that began with the withdrawal of the wide shallow seas of the Cretaceous Period from the continents.

Although students of the Pleistocene fail to agree on any one primary cause of ice ages, most believe that mountainous continents standing relatively high in relation to the ocean basins are a necessary setting for continental glaciations, the actual timing of which must be determined by some independent cause such as variation in the amount of energy from the sun. If the independent cause asserts itself again, and we have no reason to suppose that it will not, the higher continents and deeper oceans than ever will set the stage for a more severe glaciation than any that our remote ancestors survived.

In the meantime tide gauges all over the world record that sea level is rising, and has been rising for the last fifty years, at an average rate of about 1.2 millimeters a year, or about 4.5 inches per century. The reason is not hard to find; with the possible exception of Antarctica, glaciers all over the world are melting. How long this may keep on and how serious a threat it may be to the great ports and cities of the world are questions for which there are no answers as yet. However, since the record of sea level fluctuations during the last 6,000 years as determined by radiocarbon dating includes a number of ups and downs by as much as several meters, it is most likely that the present rise reflects nothing more than a minor, short-period change in the world's climate.

The invasions and retreats of the sea that we have considered so far in this chapter have been due to world-wide changes in sea level, that is, what are called eustatic changes. Here and there, however, the effect of eustatic oscillations has been complicated by local vertical movements of the land itself. As an example of the gravitational balance among the large features of the earth's surface, we cited earlier in this chapter the recent rise of parts of the continents that were heavily laden with ice during the last ice age. As these lands rose, they raced against the postglacial eustatic rise of sea level. At first, the rising sea pulled ahead, because it responded instantly to the addition of much water from the former ice sheets and glaciers, whereas rise of the land was delayed by the sluggish flow of mantle rock. Then as climate became more nearly stable about 6,000 years ago, the rising shore lines, like the tortoise in the fable, took the lead. Relics of this competition occur in many places along the coast of northeastern North America. For example, in Maine one can find deposits of clay containing abundant shells of marine clams and snails as much as 45 miles or 70 kilometers inland from the coast. These deposits accumulated during the interval after the melting of a large enough part of the ice to cause a considerable rise of sea level and before the land had had time to rise in response to the removal of its load of ice. Since then eustatic sea level has remained fairly still, while the rising land has lifted the ancient clays and shells well above present sea level.

Another, more famous example is the great shell deposit at Uddevalla in Sweden. This is so large that for years the shells were used as a source of lime. Now it is protected as a national monument. It was investigated both by Sir Charles Lyell and by Carl von Linné, the father of modern botany and author of the system of classification used today in both botany and zoology.

Along steep coasts like those of Labrador and parts of Scandinavia, the evidence of the fall of relative sea level as the land has risen is often dramatic. Strand deposits of wave-rounded cobbles mount the slopes of coves between rocky headlands like the steps of giant stairways, sometimes reaching heights of hundreds of feet or even hundreds of meters. Similar uplifted strand lines also occur here and there on the northern coasts of the British Isles.

The uplift recorded by these deposits goes on today. In parts of Scandinavia it is so rapid that harbors are becoming dry and docks are rising out of the water. Evidently, gravitational balance of the formerly glaciated regions has not yet been reached. For this geophysicists have independent supporting evidence; precise measurements of the pull of gravity over these rising lands indicate a consistent deficiency of mass. Until that deficiency is made up by the inflow of more dense mantle rock under these land masses, they will continue to rise.

In contrast to these isostatic readjustments, erratic ups and downs of minor areas, particularly in the vicinity of active volcanoes, sometimes occur. No account of sea level can be complete without mention of that most classic example of submergence and re-emergence of the "temple," really market, of Serapis at Pozzuoli on the Gulf of Naples. The evidence of sea level change here was described by Charles Lyell in 1832. At some time since the Roman period the columns of the market were attacked by a species of clams that bore into rocks in order to make living quarters. The borings in the columns reach to a height above the floor of 16 feet or 4.9 meters and at that level abruptly cease. Since these animals always live between the tides, the market and its general vicinity must have sunk beneath the waters of the Gulf of Naples to a depth of about 4.9 meters, and then after harboring clams for awhile it arose again. Since other classical monuments near shores show no similar evidence of submergence, one can only conclude that the town of Pozzuoli and its immediate surroundings were subject to a local flooding probably in some way connected with the volcanic activity of the nearby Phlegrian Fields and Vesuvius.

Geologists have evidence that the region of the northern Aegean was a land area until late in the Pleistocene. For example, the bones of extinct elephants have been found on Delos and Cerigo. The sinking of this region admitted the waters of the Mediterranean, thereby separating the Cyclades and Euboea. Some scholars have conjectured that this event provided a basis for the classical tales of deluges. This seems reasonable, because the subsidence of this former land may well have been more rapid and impressive as a result of volcanic activity than the very slow rise of sea level caused by the melting ice sheets.

As scientists gradually decipher the history of our planet, never-ceasing change stands out more and more clearly as the central theme, and of all the elements of the earth's surface the most mercurial has been sea level.

But these changes of sea level, which have their origin in variations of climate, the rise of mountain chains, and the depression of ocean basins, seem always to have been cyclical, always returning to the same starting point, and always swinging within rather narrow limits. Against this monotonously repetitious background, the irreversible advance of evolving life stands out in brilliant contrast.

THE FACE OF THE

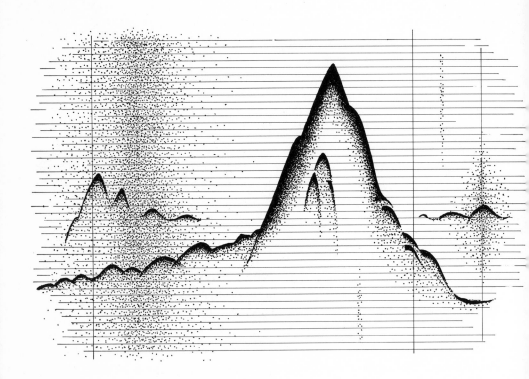

C H A P T E R 5

EARTH BENEATH THE SEA

FRIDTJOF NANSEN, WHO PLANNED AND LED THE NORWEGIAN POLAR Expedition on the *Fram*, once said: "Man wants to know and when he ceases to do so, he is no longer a man."

Probably the first attempt to measure depth by lowering a stone on the end of a line was prompted by that human urge to find out. Later, when larger boats made grounding a hazard, the weight and line method of testing depth proved its usefulness. A wall painting some 3,500 years old shows Egyptian sailors lowering a sounding line over the side of a ship. Was their purpose scientific? Much more probably these ancient mariners were merely using the routine method of finding a safe channel, one still used by some of us who cannot afford the latest electronic gear.

The Apostle Paul gives an early account of the use of the lead line (Acts, XXVII: 27, 28): "But when the fourteenth night was come, as we were driven to and fro in the sea of Adria, about midnight the shipmen deemed that they drew near to some country, and they sounded, and they found it twenty fathoms: and when they had gone a little further, they sounded again, and found it fifteen fathoms." Whereupon they let go four anchors, "and wished for the day." But the day that came was a sad one for the owners; the 276 people reached shore safely, but the ship ended up on the beach, a total loss.

To the crew of the *Santa María* the first encounter with the gulf weed of the Sargasso Sea meant shoal water, but not surprisingly their attempt to reach bottom with a cannon ball and a 200-fathom line failed; many more days of sailing lay ahead of them before reaching the New World.

Until the invention of instruments to measure water depth with sound waves, the lead line was to the mariner in a fog or off an unknown coast what a cane is to a blind man. With a lead line Bering tapped his way through the fog-hidden Aleutian Islands, and Captain Cook used it to find a channel through the intricate maze of the Great Barrier Reef of Australia.

With the age of exploration came deliberate attempts to plumb oceanic depths, but the gear that served the pilot's purpose well enough was not likely to find bottom in the open ocean. In 1521 Magellan while passing the Tuamotu Islands in the the southwest Pacific had his boatswain tie together ten ordinary lead lines to make a total length of 2,300 feet or 700 meters. When even this failed to touch bottom, Magellan concluded that he must be over the deepest part of the ocean.

The importance of soundings in the exploration of the oceans was recognized in 1580 when Captain Arthur Pet sailed from London in the *Barke George* of 40 tons manned by nine men and a boy to explore the Northeast Passage. His instructions read: "At the end of every four glasses . . . sound with your dipsea lead and note diligently what depth you get and also the ground. But if it happens that you cannot get ground, yet note what depths you did prove and could find no ground." According to ancient custom lead plummets for sounding are cast with a depression in the bottom which, when armed with tallow, usually recovers a small sample of sediment; this was the "ground" that Pet was to note. Diligently to note depth and the ground is what all oceanographers and marine geologists strive to do, but Pet's financial backers were probably more interested in the kind of information that would help others to follow his route than they were in pure science.

During the seventeenth and eighteenth centuries other explorers tried to sound the open ocean, but without success; their sounding lines were not nearly long enough. In 1773, however, Captain Constantine Johan Phipps while cruising in northern waters in H.S.M. *Racehorse* succeeded in reaching bottom beyond the continental shelf in a basin between Iceland and Norway. The depth which he found, 683 fathoms, is on Admiralty charts to this day. From then on the problem ceased to be lack of sufficient line. In subsequent attempts, as much as 6,000 fathoms or 11,000 meters of line were paid out before "bottom" was reported. Such spurious "depths" are accounted for by currents and a drifting ship which combined to draw out the sounding line into great S-shaped curves.

Sir James Clark Ross in 1840, while on a voyage to the Antarctic, added an improvement to the technique of sounding by using two of the ship's boats; while the sounding line was lowered from one, the other kept it in position against wind and surface current by rowing. His apparatus consisted of four miles of line wound on a large drum that turned under the pull of the sounding weight. But as the line paid out, its weight alone became enough to keep the drum turning though somewhat less rapidly. In order to tell when the plummet had reached bottom, Ross carefully timed each 100-fathom section of line as it went over the side, and noted the length of line out when an abrupt change in speed occurred. In this way he accurately determined the depth at latitude 27° 26' south and longitude 17° 29' west in the South Atlantic to be 2,425 fathoms or 4,435 meters.

Matthew Fontaine Maury's enthusiasm for innovation led to improvements in the art of plumbing the depths. Instead of the expensive mile-long stout hemp lines used by Ross, Maury introduced a ball of strong twine attached to a cannon shot, which ran it out rapidly; when the bottom was reached, the twine was cut and the depth determined from the length of string left in the ball on board. The time of touching bottom was judged by timing each 100-fathom mark and noting the sudden increase in the time interval when the shot reached the bottom. Maury, however, recognized that in great depth the surest guarantee of bottom having been reached was to bring up a sample of the deposit, but to do so meant hauling up the heavy sounding plummet, and Maury's twine was not equal to the task.

In 1854 J. M. Brooke, a midshipman of the United States Navy, applied a principle already foreshadowed by Nicolaus Cusanus in the fifteenth century and by Robert Hooke in the seventeenth. Brooke's device consisted of nothing more than a cannon ball with a hole through it, and a hollow brass rod about twice as long as the diameter of the cannon ball, which fitted loosely in the hole. On striking the bottom the cannon ball drove the rod into the sediment, but as soon as the line slackened, the cannon ball was released, thus permitting the light brass rod and its contained sample of sediment to be hauled up. This principle was adopted universally for deep soundings. In 1855 Maury published the first chart of the depths of the Atlantic between 52° north and 10° south. At this time a better knowledge of the depths of the ocean took on an unexpected practical importance from the daring project for laying a telegraph cable between Ireland and Newfoundland. Deep soundings were made in the Atlantic for this purpose by vessels both of the British and of the American navies, while in the Mediterranean and the Indian Ocean many soundings were also made in connection with the laying of submarine cables.

Another stimulus came from the biologists, who began to realize the importance of a more detailed investigation of the life conditions of organisms at great depths in the sea. The lead in this direction was taken by British biologists, beginning with Edward Forbes in 1839, and in 1868 a party on board H.M.S. *Lightning* pursued researches in the waters to the north of Scotland. In 1869 and 1870 this work was extended to the Irish Sea and Bay of Biscay in H.M.S. *Porcupine*, and to the Mediterranean in H.M.S. *Shearwater* which secured 157 deep soundings, with samples of the deposits. But these modest expeditions were really only preludes to the great expedition of H.M.S. *Challenger* of 1872–6. Almost simultaneously with the *Challenger*, a German expedition in *Gazelle* conducted observations in the South Atlantic, Indian, and South Pacific oceans; and the American vessel *Tuscarora* made a cruise in the North Pacific, sounding out lines for a projected Pacific cable.

Thanks to these expeditions, the eighth decade of the nineteenth century saw a greater increase in knowledge of the surface of our planet than at any time since the days of Columbus and Magellan. However, the method of sounding was still too time-consuming for detailed charting of the ocean floor. In essence, the method was still that of the Egyptians 3,000 years before. And the Greek philosophers, more interested in logic than in facts gained by experiment, who had argued on purely logical grounds that the depths of the oceans must be about the same as the heights of the mountains on land, had not yet been proved to be just about right.

When the *Challenger* set out on her famous voyage in 1872 she had on board a sounding machine newly designed by the mathematician and physicist, Lord Kelvin. The line, a steel piano wire, had two important advantages over hemp; it needed a much smaller reel for storage and because of its smaller cross section it would have been less seriously deflected by currents. We say "would have been" because the reel collapsed on the first lowering. During the rest of the cruise the *Challenger* sounded with a line of the best Italian hemp. That sounding was still a major operation is clearly shown by the fact that during the three years of the *Challenger*'s cruise she made only 250 deep soundings. Furthermore, we now know that in spite of the care of the scientists, many of the soundings—particularly in regions of strong currents, as in the path of the Gulf Stream—were seriously in error on the deep side; even a 200-pound weight was not enough to draw the line straight down to the bottom. In fairness to Kelvin's invention we must add that it became standard sounding equipment soon after the *Challenger* expedition.

Shortly before the departure of the *Challenger*, a physicist named Alexander Dallas Bache, a great grandson of Benjamin Franklin and for more than twenty years superintendent of the United States Coast and Geodetic Survey, had made some interesting observations and calculations. With an earthquake-recording instrument he determined the time of an earthquake off Japan, and by means of tide gauges he measured how long it took the seismic sea waves generated by the quake to reach the west coast of the United States. Since the velocities of very long waves are directly related to depth of water, he could calculate from these data that the average depth of the Pacific was about 12,000 feet or 3,700 meters. This figure was soon put to the test by the soundings of the *Challenger*, and Bache's estimate proved to a reasonably good average for the abyssal depths of the world ocean. The average depths of the Pacific, Atlantic, and Indian oceans as we know them today are respectively 4,280 meters (14,000 feet), 3935 meters (12,900 feet), and 3990 meters (13,080 feet). Bache's estimated depth was of little value as such, but his method was a new departure; it showed that a form of wave motion might serve to measure oceanic depths in place of the primitive weight and line.

In 1807 François Arago, French scientist and humanitarian who was responsible for the abolition of slavery in the French colonies, had suggested that a sound wave might replace the lead line, if its travel time from a ship to the bottom and back again could be measured accurately. However, more than a hundred years passed before improvement in the technique of measuring short intervals of time made Arago's suggestion practicable.

Between 1900 and 1920 physicists in the United States, Germany, and France were experimenting with the echo method of plumbing ocean depths. In 1922 machines capable of automatically recording depths to 1,000 meters (3,000 feet) became available. Greater depths could be measured by listening for the returning echo with earphones while watching a clock. In the mid-1930's the depth range of automatic recording was extended, but the human ear and eye remained more reliable than the machine for truly oceanic depths. Consequently, all pre-World War II echo soundings exceeding 2,000 meters or 6,000 feet were discrete observations with the human nervous system an essential part of the recording apparatus.

During the war the United States Navy developed the first continuously recording deep-sea echo sounder. This was installed on many United States ships, but even when in good running order its range was less than 3,660 meters or 12,000 feet. Thus, major areas of the ocean floor lay beyond its reach.

In 1945 further improvement of the continuously recording deep-sea echo sounder increased its depth range and an attack upon that vast frontier of exploration, the three quarters of the earth's surface hidden in the darkness of the deep sea, began in earnest.

The modern echo sounder measures the depth under a ship in the few seconds that it takes a sound wave to travel to the sea floor and its echo to return to the ship. Since the velocity of sound in water is about 1 mile or 1,600 meters a second, a depth of 3 miles or 4,800 meters can be measured in 6 seconds. Because it is not necessary to wait for an echo before sending down another sound pulse, it is customary to send them down at regular intervals, such as one every second; consequently, at any one time in deep water several sound waves may be on their way down while others are coming up. As the ship moves forward the closely spaced soundings add up to a practically continuous profile of the steep-sided valleys, monotonous plains, and jagged mountains of the deep-sea floor.

In early models of the echo sounder the sound wave was generated by blows of an automatic hammer on one of the bottom plates of the ship. Today electric oscillators provide ultrasonic pulses; a "pinger" releases sound energy below the water surface. The recording system consists of a stylus on a rotating arm which sweeps across a moving strip of paper. At the instant the sound pulse starts down, the stylus makes a mark near the upper edge of the paper; by the time the echo returns the stylus has moved down from the upper edge of the paper by a distance which is proportional to the time interval; since this is proportional to the depth of water, the distance between the first and second marks made by the stylus is a measure of the water depth. Because of the short time intervals between the returning echoes the marks coalesce into a continuous line on the slowly moving strip of paper. The horizontal scale, of course, depends upon the ship's speed. In order to relate this to the bottom profile the man in charge of the echo sounder at regular intervals notes directly on the paper strip the times of the day and whatever other navigational information may be needed to locate the topographical features geographically.

The principle of echo sounding has various other uses; for example, geologists can map depths of beds of sedimentary rocks on land by exploding small charges of dynamite and timing the return echo from a single layer or the several echoes from a series of layers. Similarly at sea, layers of firmer sediment or hard rock beneath the sea bottom can be detected and their depths estimated by sending down more powerful sound pulses and by listening for the return echoes with more sensitive receiving instruments. Although a large part of the sound energy sent down bounces back from the surface of the sea floor, a part passes through and is reflected upward by deeper layers of denser sediment or hard volcanic rock. Applied in the horizontal dimension sound waves may be used to detect and locate submarines. To oceanographers and geophysicists sound waves are what X rays are to physicians.

As sometimes happens, the powerfully creative process of

natural selection working upon minute variations among the individuals of certain kinds of animals has anticipated man's invention. Experiments with bats show that they can avoid such obstacles as fine wires even in total darkness by means of echoes of the pulsating supersonic note they emit.

Since World War II, use of the continuous recording echo sounder has revolutionized the study of the ocean floor. Except for the excellent profiles of the bottom of equatorial Atlantic laboriously plotted from closely spaced visually timed echo soundings made by the German *Meteor* expedition of 1924 to 1926, and a chart of the ocean floor off the northeastern part of the United States plotted from discrete echo soundings made by the United States Coast and Geodetic Survey, detailed charts of the deep-sea floor did not exist before World War II. What these early surveys revealed was exciting; the deep-sea floor was not the subdued monotonous world that long-held theory had assumed. On the contrary, it was if anything more rugged than the continents. However, these time-consuming, expensive surveys raised questions without being extensive enough to provide answers.

With one of the improved sounders developed during the stress of World War II, H. H. Hess discovered the flat-topped seamounts or guyots of the Pacific described in Chapter 4. Since then the surge of interest in oceans during the last few years has stimulated the development of instruments of extraordinary precision and reliability. While a group of scientists at the Woods Hole Oceanographic Institution were building their Precision Graphic Recorder, another group at the Lamont Geological Observatory of Columbia University developed their Precision Depth Recorder, commonly known as the PDR. Both models record differences of bottom relief with an accuracy of better than 2 meters at a depth of 4,000 meters or 6 feet at a depth of 12,000 feet. The absolute depth cannot be so precisely recorded; this is not because of a shortcoming in the instrument, but because the velocity of sound increases somewhat with depth, depending on the density of sea water, which in turn is influenced by pressure, temperature, and the amount of dissolved salt it contains. Accurate corrections may be made if the vertical variations in the properties of the water column are known, and approximate corrections can be made from tables based on average water properties within the various regions of the oceans. An average correction for a sounding of 5,000 meters is in the order of plus 200 meters.

However, as a rule marine geologists are more interested in differences in depth than in very accurate absolute depths and therefore they commonly use echograms directly without bothering with corrections. This is possible because within any one region the vertical velocity of sound remains fairly constant from place to place.

The marine geologist has other more serious problems to contend with, problems unknown to his counterpart on dry land. He cannot stand on the top of an undersea hill and gain a general picture of the terrain visually. He must do without that powerful tool of the land geologist, aerial photography. He is compelled to hover kilometers above a land which he cannot see and of which he can form an over-all picture only by moving his ship back and forth; as he taps his way along like a blind man, the echo sounder turns out rolls of paper which must be scaled and plotted on a chart before he can trace contour lines, or lines of equal depth, thereby depicting on paper the regional relief. This is a long and tedious task, without the thrill of the original discovery.

Aboard ship the rhythmic sweep of the stylus arm has an almost hypnotic fascination. At each sweep the profile of the bottom advances by a fraction of a millimeter. For miles the bottom had been level and smooth, but now each new mark left by the stylus is higher. As you watch the rising curve you wonder whether the ship is approaching a new seamount. To qualify as a seamount it will have to rise to at least 3,000 feet, (1,000 meters) above the surrounding plain. Now the trace is rising more steeply; perhaps it will be a really big one. But no, before reaching more than about 870 meters, the trace turns down. However, you are not to be misled by that; the trace of echoes is strictly two-dimensional; it tells nothing about what may lie on either side. The trace before you may represent the flank of a much higher mount. So you fetch the officer whose watch it is, and between the two of you, you decide to turn the ship back and recross the region one mile to the east of the first profile. Now the trace of echoes keeps on rising until it has reached a height of 1,400 meters. As a real seamount it deserves more detailed exploration.

By this time it is three o'clock in the morning; although the chief scientist was at work until midnight he must be called. After some plotting of positions and calculations a series of crossings of the region are laid out in such a way as to determine the general form of this newly discovered feature of the earth. By sunrise the survey is done; now a core of sediment from the top of the mount must be taken, and so an early breakfast is eaten to the tune of the deep rumbling of the main winch as it pays out the line with the heavy coring apparatus.

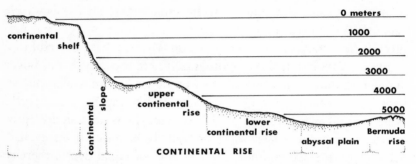

FIGURE 27 *Continental margin provinces: type profile off northeastern United States. This profile is representative of the sector from Georges Banks to Cape Hatteras, eastern United States.*

The hundreds of thousands of miles of echo-sounding tracks now in existence have revolutionized our conception of submarine topography. The new information is bringing within our reach an understanding of the forces and processes that have shaped the world beneath the sea.

In the over-all pattern of this world three broad divisions stand out clearly: the continental margins; the ocean basin floors; and the mid-oceanic ridges.

The continental margins of the Atlantic and Indian oceans include transitional provinces between the continents and ocean floor. These are the continental shelf, the continental slope, and the continental rise (see Figure 27).

The *continental shelf* is really a drowned extension of the adjacent land. In fact, to our ancestors of 18,000 or 20,000 years ago it was part of the land surface, because, as we said in Chapter 4, the continental ice sheets of the last ice age robbed the oceans of so much water that sea level stood somewhere near the outer edges of the continental shelves. The slope of the continental shelf averages 1 in 1,000, but locally it has many irregularities, sometimes even more than the adjoining land. The shelves of the northwest coast of Europe are grooved by valleys in which once flowed rivers of melt water from ice sheets and mountain glaciers. Other irregularities are due to heaps of rubble deposited at the margins of ice sheets that pushed out on the shelves. On the other side of the Atlantic the continental shelf is also traversed by submerged valleys, of which the underwater extension of the Hudson Valley is a well-known example. Long Island, Martha's Vineyard, Nantucket, and Cape Cod are largely masses of rubble that the former North American ice sheet deposited. In the scale of geological time these features are ephemeral; before the ice returns, the pounding waves of the Atlantic will have reduced them to shoals. From the known rate of erosion of Cape Cod by waves William Morris Davis, a famous geographer and student of land forms, predicted that the Cape will disappear in 8,000 or 10,000 years. In his essay on "The Outline of Cape Cod" Davis points to Sable Island, a long sand bar off Nova Scotia, as an example of the vanishing remnant of a mass of glacial detritus.

In low latitudes where the climate is favorable, reef-building corals and lime-secreting sea plants have built deposits of limestone on continental shelves which exceed in massiveness the piles of rubble left by the ice sheets of higher latitudes. The Great Barrier Reef on the continental shelf of eastern Australia, more than 1,000 miles long and several miles wide, is the work of coral polyps and calcareous algae. Beyond the 180-meter (600-foot) depth line the slope of the bottom steepens usually rather abruptly to a gradient varying from 1 in 40 to 1 in 6, the average slope being a little more than 4° down to about 2,000 meters (6,000 feet). Topographically this region beyond the continental shelf, known as the *continental slope*, is the most impressive feature that the surface of the earth has to offer. The continental slopes are the real boundaries of the continents; beyond lie the deep-sea basins. They are the longest and highest escarpments on earth; their average height is 3,700 meters (12,000 feet), but locally they attain the vast height of a little more than 9,000 meters (30,000 feet). Mountain ranges on the continent cannot approach the continental slopes in difference of elevation between foothills and peaks.

In topographical detail models of thoroughly surveyed portions of the continental slope look rather like the slope of a highway embankment, bare of grass, that has been rainwashed. Almost everywhere deep valleys known as *submarine canyons* furrow the continental slopes. Some of these valleys head far back on the continental shelf, in which case they frequently though not always appear to be the seaward extensions of rivers on land. We have already mentioned the Hudson Submarine Valley; another classic example is the submarine valley of the Congo. Their courses are somewhat sinuous, but without the broad meanders of such rivers as the Mississippi. Their gradients are continuous and regular, and in some cases they are joined by one or more other valleys as if by tributaries. At one place the well-surveyed submarine canyon of the Congo is walled in by a cliff more than 600 meters (2,000 feet) high; thus, it lives up to its designation as a canyon.

At the base of the continental slope lies the *continental rise*. It has an average gradient of 1 in 300, but here and there its slope may be as much as 1 in 50 or as gentle as 1 in 700. The larger submarine valleys extend across the continental rise, and more detailed surveys of the future will probably show that many less important valleys do the same.

It is remarkable and significant that the continental rise is almost entirely absent from the margin of the Pacific Ocean Basin. Instead, the boundary between the ocean and continents is defined by an almost continuous line of deep trenches, with the result that the margin of the Pacific consists for the most part of the shelf, the slope, and marginal trench.

One hundred years after the famous mutiny on the *Bounty*, another British ship, H.M.S. *Egeria*, visited the scene of Bligh and Christian's disagreement, that is, the vicinity of the great volcano of Tofua among the Friendly Islands group, better known today as the Tonga Islands. In the course of exploring the ocean floor off the islands, Pelham Aldrich, commander of the *Egeria*, was amazed to have to let 7,315 meters (24,000 feet) of wire run out before the sounding lead reached bottom. When the news of this great depth got about, other nations sent expeditions to explore the region. These traced an enormous trench from the Tonga Islands south to the Kermadec Islands; the deepest sounding here was made in the middle of the 1950's by the research vessel *Horizon* of the Scripps Institution of Oceanography. Her crew found the bottom of the trench to lie at a depth of 10,670 meters or 35,000 feet, that is some 1,800 meters or 6,000 feet farther below sea level than Mount Everest rises above sea level. Yet this profound chasm, as we now know, is only one of the

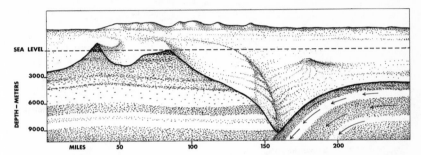

FIGURE 28 *Tonga Trench would appear as in this drawing if viewed northward from a point in the central Tonga Islands, and if vertical distances were exaggerated by a factor of 10 in comparison with horizontal. The exposed land mass in the left foreground is the island of Kao, a dormant volcano. In the distance are the Samoan Islands.*

series of deep and narrow trenches that surround the central basin of the Pacific, running parallel either to strings of islands or coastal mountain ranges on the continents. Along the west coast of South America the vertical distance from the top of the Andes to the bottom of the offshore trench exceeds 12,000 meters or 40,000 feet. The lengths of these trenches are no less extraordinary than their depth; some are 2,000 miles or 3,600 kilometers long. But figures fail to convey their grandeur. The depth of the Grand Canyon of the Colorado is a better unit by which to measure such a colossal furrow in the ocean floor as the Tonga-Kermadec Trench (see Figure 28); seven Grand Canyons would have to be put one on top of the other to equal the depth of the trench. Its length would reach from New York to Kansas City. It follows a nearly straight north-south line east of the Tonga and Kermadec archipelagoes. At its northern end it has a slight hook.

It begins there as a gentle, spoon-shaped depression and runs southeasterly between Tonga and Samoa; then, turning and becoming deeper, it strikes south for 1,300 miles and finally shoals and disappears at a point north of New Zealand. At its deepest central portion its floor is no more than 5 miles wide. Its cross section is an asymmetrical V, with the side toward the islands markedly the steeper; the slope of the steep western side varies from 16 to 30 per cent. For comparison, the average slope of the

FIGURE 29 *Positions of the main oceanic trenches.*

walls of the Grand Canyon at Bright Angel is 24 per cent. In longitudinal section it consists of a series of depressions separated by saddles.

Other great trenches of the Pacific are the Aleutian, Kurile, Japan, Mariana, Philippines, and Java trenches on the northern and western sides and the Acapulco and Peru-Chile trenches on the eastern side of the Pacific (see Figure 29). The Philippines Trench holds the record for depth. In 1962 H.M.S. *Cook* found a depth there of 11,515 meters or 37,782 feet. In general, the deepest trenches all reach approximately the same maximum depth, that is 10,700 meters or 35,000 feet. What significance this common depth may have is not clear at present.

Clearly significant, however, is the fact that the earth's zone of most intense earthquakes coincides with the circum-Pacific trenches. This is particularly true of earthquakes originating at great depths, those of the greatest depths (about 700 kilometers) being associated with the deepest and steepest trenches. This frequency of earthquakes, the almost continuous line of volcanoes parallel to the trenches, and the ranges of high mountains little reduced by erosion along the rim of the Pacific underscore the extraordinary differences between the Atlantic and Pacific basins. The rarity of earthquakes, absence of active volcanoes, and subdued relief of the margins of the Atlantic imply long geological quiescence.

The broad floors of the oceans are the second of the three major divisions of the world beneath the sea. About one third of the area of the Atlantic and Indian oceans and three quarters of that of the Pacific come within this division. Although seamounts occur throughout the oceans, they are most numerous on the ocean floor. From the knowledge of deep-sea physical geography made possible by the echo sounder two subdivisions of the ocean floor stand out: (1) abyssal plains and (2) oceanic rises and lateral or asymmetrical ridges.

Abyssal plains extend over large areas of the floors of the Atlantic and Indian oceans, but their area is very much restricted in the Pacific, where their only important occurrence is off the northwestern part of North America and south of Alaska. They are smooth, almost level regions with gradients not exceeding 1 in 1,000. In the Atlantic abyssal plains vary in width from 100 to 200 miles. At their seaward margins most abyssal plains grade into what is called the *abyssal hills province*. These hills vary in height from about 100 meters (300 feet) to 400 meters (1,200 feet). As a rule, the individual hills vary from 2 to 6 miles across. The abyssal hills provinces of the Atlantic only locally exceed a width of 50 miles, whereas they cover most of the floor of the Pacific.

Oceanic rises are features that stand above the abyssal floor and at the same time are not parts of the continental margin or a mid-oceanic ridge. An example is the enormous mass of volcanic rock in the Atlantic on which perch the islands of Bermuda. The islands themselves are not volcanic; rather they are part of a relatively insignificant cap of limestone built by corals and lime-secreting sea plants that have flourished for scores of millions of years in the shoal water on top of the great pile of cinders of the Bermuda Rise. Although the volcanic rocks are everywhere covered by limestone, their presence directly beneath has been proved by borings. In spite of the ponderous weight of the mass of volcanic rock pressing down on the floor of the Atlantic, subsidence has not occurred since the vast outpourings of lava began in late Cretaceous time, some 100 million years ago. Here again we find a marked contrast between the oceans; the many atolls and guyots of the Pacific, as we said in Chapter 4, have sunk by more than 1,000 meters in some cases.

Oddly enough the Bermuda Islands, those specks of land where the pinnacles of the enormous Bermuda Rise pierce the ocean surface, owe their suitability as sites for hotels to the continental ice sheets of the Pleistocene Epoch. But for the swinging sea levels of the ice ages, it is probable that only coral reefs, awash at low tide, would crown the Bermuda Rise. During each ice age, as the continental ice sheets spread—nourished by snow generated by copious evaporation from the oceans—sea level fell. First the coral reefs were exposed and the animals died; then as sea level receded further a broad zone of the sea floor surrounding the reefs emerged. Here, during the tens of thousands of years of the preceding interglacial age, had accumulated an ample deposit of calcareous sand, the remains of countless lime-secreting marine plants and animals, ground to uniform particle size by the pounding surf. This sand the powerful winds of the ice ages swept up and deposited in the form of dunes on the basement of coral rock. Then as the millennia went by, the loose sands of the dunes were cemented by percolating rain water that dissolved the uppermost layer of the sand and deposited the lime between the particles lower down. Five times during the Pleistocene the sea receded and each time powerful winds added more sand to the dunes until they formed a highland well above the reach of sea level during even the warmest interglacials. Geologists who have studied the limestones of Bermuda believe that they can distinguish the various generations of dunes corresponding to the different ice ages. Today much coral rock also lies above sea level. This is because of the quantity of water still held as ice on Greenland and Antarctica; the present climate, as R. F. Flint has emphasized, is not yet as warm as that of a fully interglacial age.

Another elevated feature of the ocean basins is the asymmetrical ridges that are particularly well developed in the

South Atlantic. The Walvis Ridge discovered by the *Meteor* expedition is one of these. It extends as a continuous ridge from the vicinity of Walvis Bay, southwest Africa, to the Mid-Atlantic Ridge which it joins at the volcanic island of Tristan da Cunha. On the western side of the Mid-Atlantic Ridge its almost mirror-image counterpart, the Rio Grande Ridge, continues to the coast of the province of Rio Grande do Sul in Brazil.

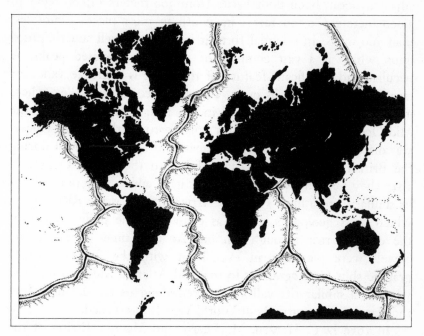

FIGURE 30   *The Mid-Oceanic Ridge runs for 64,000 kilometers (40,000 miles) along the bottom of all the oceans. It is indicated here by the black line and dots. A peculiar feature of the ridge is a riftlike valley or trench running along its crest.*

In addition to the continental margins and the floors of the oceans, there is a third major topographic division of the oceans —the Mid-Oceanic Ridge system. Next to the continents and ocean basins themselves this is the greatest topographical feature of our planet. It is a continuous mountain range extending roughly north to south through the Atlantic into the Antarctic Ocean around the Cape of Good Hope and northeastward into the Indian Ocean where it branches; one branch swings to the northwest and becomes involved with the geological structure of the Red Sea depression and the rift valleys of eastern Africa; the other branch curves to the southeast between Australia and Antarctica, then northward into the Pacific where, following a course roughly parallel to the west coast of South America, it finally enters the Gulf of Lower California (see Figure 30). Its total length is in the order of 40,000 miles. Its elevation above the adjacent ocean basin floor varies from 300 meters (1,000 feet) to 3,000 meters (10,000 feet); its width in most places is not less than 700 miles. In essential form it is a broad swell superimposed upon which is a vast complex of ridges and isolated peaks. A peculiar and significant feature of the ridge is a riftlike valley or trench running along its crest. The existence of this valley where it follows the crest of the Mid-Indian Ridge, or that part of the Mid-Oceanic Ridge which runs northward in the Indian Ocean, was discovered by J. D. H. Wiseman and R. B. S. Sewell during the British "John Murray" Expedition to the Indian Ocean. In 1937 they published a description of it in which they pointed out its similarity to a huge valley in Africa known as the Rift Valley, which most geologists regard as caused by the pulling apart of the earth's crust through tension. At that time Wiseman and Sewell were planning an expedition with the British oceanographic ship *Hydrographer* to the Mid-Atlantic Ridge to find out whether a similar rift valley occurred along its trend, but before the plan could be carried out World War II intervened.

In 1959 B. C. Heezen, M. Tharp, and Maurice Ewing of the Lamont Geological Observatory published a comprehensive account of the topography of the North Atlantic in which they showed that just such a riftlike valley did follow the trend of the Mid-Atlantic Ridge.

The floor of the valley of the Mid-Oceanic Ridge system lies from 2,750 to 4,570 meters (9,000 to 15,000 feet) below sea level, while the crests of the mountains flanking it rise to within 1,100 to 2,200 meters (3,600 to 7,200 feet) of sea level. By way of comparison, the Grand Canyon of the Colorado averages about 1,220 meters (4,000 feet) in depth and from 4 to 18 miles in width, whereas the Mid-Atlantic Rift Valley averages more than 1,800 meters (6,000 feet) in depth and from 8 to 30 miles in width for many hundreds of miles.

Such are the primary lineaments of the topography of the world beneath the sea. They are primary in the sense that they owe their existence to forces working within the earth; forces that, judging from the geological record of the past, are exceptionally active today.

To what extent have the effects of these forces influenced the development of man's culture? Indirectly their effect must have been profound. Students of the ice ages agree that without lofty mountain ranges and emergent continents complemented by deep ocean basins, there would have been no ice ages. Not only must the world-wide climatic changes of the Pleistocene have had an irresistible influence on tribal life, ways of doing things, and even ways of thinking, but the very ice sheets and glaciers themselves, particularly in Europe during the last ice age, must have left some imprint on local cultural development. When one considers that the last ice sheet of Europe began to waste away only about 11,000 years ago, it seems rather extraordinary that among all the legends and myths that older people have been repeating to the young for millennia, there is no mention of anything that can be surely identified as a continental ice sheet. It is really rather disconcerting to have to admit that our European ancestors were so little impressed by anything as awe-inspiring as an ice sheet that they left it out of their folklore.

By a curious perversity a legend dealing with an event that is supposed to go back in time almost as far, that is, 10,000 years, refuses to be downed. This is the legend of the lost Atlantis, the Island Empire that once existed outside the entrance to the Mediterranean, about where the present Mid-Atlantic Ridge rises a mile or more from the ocean floor east of the Sargasso Sea. And yet there is no geological evidence of the former existence of a large island in this part of the Atlantic. In spite of this the literature on Atlantis, which began when Plato first gave an account of the island and its civilization in his Timeas and Critias Dialogues in the third century, has grown to more than a thousand volumes. No doubt much of it is nonsense, but until disproof of the legend has been found, we think it not harmful to consider the essence of the story with an open mind.

Plato's writing on Atlantis is a transcription of what Egyptian priests had told Solon the Athenian lawgiver, when Solon was in the Egyptian city of Sais two hundred years before Plato. The story had been handed down in Solon's family until it came to Plato through Critias. Other ancient writers had written about Atlantis, Homer in the seventh century B.C. for example and Herodotus in the fourth, but Plato's more complete account must be ranked among the most extraordinary records to come down to us from the ancient world. His comparison of the Mediterranean, a harbor with a narrow entrance, to the open Atlantic "which was truly a sea" shows a remarkable understanding of world geography. Most amazing is his reference to another continent, presumably America, on the other side of the Atlantic, and the statement that the Atlantian Empire had colonies there. If there is not convincing geological evidence one way or the other, there are at least some facts of local cultural development that harmonize in a remarkable way with Plato's account. One is the abrupt appearance of the highly evolved culture of Central America at some time before the beginning of our era. Apparently it did not have its origin in America but was introduced full fledged by immigrants or colonists from somewhere else. According to legend among the Mayas, and echoes by the Indians of Mexico and Peru, bearded white men brought their culture from the east. Furthermore a learned protagonist of the Atlantis theory, Lewis Spence, in his book *The History of Atlantis* calls attention to a certain cultural complex distinguished by the practice of mummification, witchcraft, pyramid building, artificial head flattening, the use of three-pointed stones, and some other items, which point to a common origin. These are all collectively to be found within an area stretching from Egypt to the east coast of North America and including the west Atlantic islands and the Antilles. "So far as I am aware," Spence adds, "these elements are not found associated with each other in any other part of the world."

Perhaps future exploration of the ocean bottom will bring up evidence conclusive enough to convince everyone that the legend of Atlantis is only a fascinating myth. Probably we shall not have long to wait; marine archeology is still in its infancy, but with the rapid development of underwater vehicles it should attain maturity soon. Of one thing we may be confident; it has surprises in store for us, just as its elder sister discipline, marine geology, has had.

Of all the unseen scenery of the sea, perhaps none has so evoked the wonder and curiosity of marine geologists as the great mountain ranges whose treeless, snowless, sunless peaks and pinnacles rise out of darkness into darkness, wrapped in eternal night. But of all the enigmas of the sea, none has probably been more spiritedly debated than the mystery of the submarine canyons (see Figure 31).

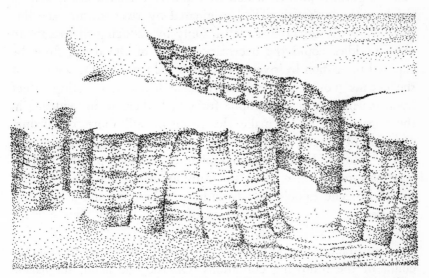

FIGURE 31 *Canyons like this in the continental slope may be cut by turbidity currents carrying river-borne sediments from the continental shelf to the ocean floor.*

The existence of these gashes in the continental slope has been known for more than a century through soundings made by various surveying ships, particularly those of the United States Coast and Geodetic Survey and the British Admiralty, but for a long time they received little attention. Because in form they were strikingly similar to river valleys on land, most geologists who gave them any thought explained them as ancient river valleys that had been submerged by subsidence of the continental margins.

During the last thirty years echo-sounding surveys have shown that submarine canyons are widespread. In fact, they occur off virtually all the coasts of the world, and many have been traced to oceanic depths. The question of their origin has been one of the most tantalizing problems of modern geology. It is not surprising that they have aroused a high degree of interest among many geologists. Probably the greatest authority today on submarine canyons is Francis P. Shepard of the Scripps Institution of Oceanography.

Proof of their apparently universal distribution geographically and the great depths to which they descend dealt a deathblow to the hypothesis that they had originated by river erosion at some time of greatly lowered sea level. Only by reducing the oceans to mere puddles could the necessary depths of the ocean floor be exposed to erosion by rivers. Any such reduction in the volume of the oceans would unquestionably have had a devastating effect upon marine life, a catastrophe for which there is no evidence in the fossil record. To make the problem still more tantalizing, sampling of canyon walls by Henry H. Stetson, a marine geologist at the Woods Hole Oceanographic Institution, proved that at least part of the erosion of the canyons had taken place during the Pleistocene Epoch, that is within the last one and a half million years, a long time in terms of man's history, but a mere moment in geological time.

A satisfactory hypothesis of origin had, therefore, to take account of the following conditions. On the one hand, submarine canyons had almost certainly been eroded by some kind of flow induced by the pull of gravity; their shape and position on the continental slope proved that. On the other hand, the agent of erosion had unquestionably worked beneath the ocean surface, as shown by the great depths to which some descend.

To meet these conditions R. A. Daly, a geologist of great originality at Harvard, proposed in 1936 that the canyons had been eroded by a kind of density current, which he called *turbidity current*, that is, a stream of water containing quantities of fine sediment in suspension. Such turbid water, being denser than clear water, would flow downslope under ordinary ocean water. Daly reasoned that quantities of turbid water must have been generated during the times of lower sea level of the ice ages, when much unconsolidated sediment on the continental shelves was exposed to heavy rains and the attack of storm waves. For some time this hypothesis, without supporting evidence, received little serious attention. Then, shortly after the end of World War II, there began a series of oceanographic expeditions initiated and led by Maurice Ewing, which brought home convincing evidence that Daly's hypothesis correctly explains the origin of submarine canyons and other features of the ocean floor unknown to Daly when he proposed his theory.

An expedition in 1949 led by Ewing followed the canyon of the Hudson almost across the continental rise to a distance of 200 miles from the edge of the continental shelf. Our studies at Lamont Geological Observatory of sediment cores taken along this route proved that the canyon had been eroded in beds of clay many millions of years old. Sediment samples from the floor of the canyon, on the other hand, included sand, gravel, and the shells of various clams and marine snails of species that can live only in shallow water. Horace Richards, an authority on the molluscs of the Pleistocene, examined the shells and reported that all the species are still living but some are now confined to colder waters than those of the shelf off New York and Long Island, thus supporting Daly's conjecture that the last ice age had been a time of particularly frequent and energetic turbidity currents.

In the meantime more cores of sediment had been taken from the continental rise (which lies at the base of the continental slope) of the Hudson Canyon region. Most of these contained an uppermost layer of typical deep-sea sediment from 25 to 30 centimeters thick representing the sediment accumulation of the last 11,000 years, the time since the recession of the last North American ice sheet. Beneath that, however, we found a strikingly different kind of sediment: well-bedded sands, silts, and silty clays containing the shells of foraminifera of species known to live only in shallow water. That these remarkable sediments had somehow traveled down from the continental shelf during the last ice age was a fairly obvious conclusion and one which convincingly reinforced the theory of origin of the continental rise based on its topographical form. Since then similar sediments of shallow water origin have been cored elsewhere on the continental rises of the North Atlantic Basin.

The fact that abyssal plains cover wide areas of the floor of the North Atlantic was an outstanding discovery of the first oceanographic expedition led by Maurice Ewing in 1947. In 1948 the Swedish Deep-Sea Expedition under the leadership of Hans Pettersson discovered a similar plain in the Indian Ocean south of the Bay of Bengal. Since then many others have been found, particularly by Bruce C. Heezen of the Lamont Geological Observatory. However, to verify the apparent smoothness of these plains, a more accurate and dependable echo sounder was needed. Specifically to meet this need Bernard Luskin at Lamont developed the precision depth recorder that we mentioned earlier (see page 152).

An *abyssal plain* has been defined as an area of the ocean floor in which the bottom is flat. But what does flat really mean? Thanks to the PDR we can say that on the relatively well-surveyed abyssal plains of the Atlantic variations in depth do not exceed 2 meters in 2 kilometers (or 6 feet in 1 mile). Such small irregularities as there are always have very gentle slopes. Small, abrupt slopes are never found.

Although some hills and seamounts break the surfaces of abyssal plains, much as islands break the surface of the sea, they do not otherwise disturb the nearly level surfaces of the plains.

For a time the origin of abyssal plains was in question. One formerly popular hypothesis attributed their extraordinary smoothness to enormous outpourings of very fluid lava. However, recent exploration below the surfaces of the plains by means of more energetic sound waves shows that they are underlain by layers of soft sediment resting on hard rock, but the surface of the latter, far from being smooth, is highly irregular in form. The underlying hard rock is probably volcanic; however that may be, it has contributed nothing to the smoothness of the plains. We can only conclude that abyssal plains owe their smoothness to the manner of distribution of the sediment blanket, which has lapped over and finally hidden the original ruggedness of the ocean floor.

At some stage in the evolution of the ocean basins repeated volcanic eruptions probably built swarms of volcanic cones on the ocean floor. No doubt fracturing and tilting of lava flows added to the chaotic ruggedness. But in the meantime the relentless agents of erosion, wind, rain, and chemical decay, were gnawing the rocks of the continents. The detrital products, gravel, sand, and clay carried by rivers and streams to the continental margins, there piled up like snow on a mountainside. From time to time masses of the water-saturated sediment became so unstable that the slightest earth tremor was enough to trigger them into motion and start an avalanche of sediment down the slope. Soon the tumbling, rushing mass of sediment would become completely fluid as it incorporated more and more water through its churning motion. With clear insight Daly saw these torrents eroding deep valleys on the continental slopes; that job done, he lost interest in his turbidity torrents. If he had followed them in his imagination to their final resting place, he would probably have surmised that after leaving the foot of the continental slope the masses of turbid water would flood and come to rest in the deepest nearby depression. In such depressions all sediment in suspension would eventually settle. But concentration of sediment accumulation in the deepest depressions would soon fill them, with the consequence that later floods of turbid water would overflow into slightly less deep depressions, and so on until only a seamount here and there remained above the rising level of sediment.

In the Pacific, however, we do not find the same evidence of the leveling effect of sediment deposited by turbidity currents. This is not surprising; deep trenches lie between the margins of the continents and the broad floor of the Pacific. Turbidity currents that have their origin on the continental slope of the Pacific are trapped upon reaching the bottoms of the trenches and cannot flow out over the floor of the Pacific. But if turbidity currents bring quantities of sediment to the bottoms of the trenches, why have the trenches not been filled to overflowing just as depressions in the floor of the Atlantic have been filled? There seems to be only one answer; the trenches must be of relatively recent origin. Very probably the forces responsible for them are still at work. Frequent, powerful earthquakes and a prevalence of volcanoes attest to release of energy on a global scale throughout the circumference of the Pacific.

To gain insight into what may be contributing to this geological turmoil let us return to the Atlantic. We think it probable—as some earth scientists such F. A. Vening-Meinesz, J. T. Wilson, and Robert Dietz have conjectured—that hot, and therefore less dense, mantle material is upwelling beneath the Mid-Atlantic Ridge. From beneath the ridge the mantel material flows horizontally away both to the east and west. As it does so it carries along on its surface, like a conveyor belt, not only the floor of the Atlantic but also the continents on both sides of the basin of the Atlantic. The absence of trenches off the eastern coast of North America is in harmony with this theory that the North American continent is riding passively on the surface of the westward-moving mantle, and so also is the rarity of severe earthquakes along our eastern seaboard. It is instead along our west coast that collision occurs. There the continental mass runs head on against the either stationary, or more probably eastward-moving floor of the eastern Pacific. As one might expect, the higher continent built of lighter rocks overrides the oceanic crust. Probably it is this still very active overriding of the ocean floor by the North American continent, as well as the other continental masses bordering the Pacific, that maintains the youthful character of the trenches surrounding the Pacific.

Someday fairly soon it will be possible to test the hypothesis of drifting continents by precise measurements across the Atlantic. Geophysicists, reasoning from the probable properties of rocks under the conditions obtaining in the mantle, estimate that the rate of flow of mantle material is somewhere between 2 or 3 centimeters a year. As yet, precision of measurement across the Atlantic is not good enough to detect changes in distance of the estimated amount. But techniques are improving rapidly.

In the meantime there are other ways of approaching the problem. According to Bruce C. Heezen, who has spent years charting the topography of the ocean basins, the Mid-Atlantic Ridge extends through Iceland where a part of the median rift valley may be seen. In fact, all the recent volcanic activity of Iceland has occurred in the rift valley, the floor of which is cut by many active fissures paralleling the larger fractures forming its walls. Measurements by Icelandic geologists show that the width of this valley is increasing at the rate of 3.5 meters per kilometer of width in 1,000 years. While this observation does not prove that the continents are moving apart, it does prove that at least this part of the median valley is truly a rift resulting from tension. The Azores islands, some of which are perched on opposite sides of the rift valley, are also possible sites of future measurements.

Does this evidence of energy very much alive beneath the

floor of the Atlantic lend plausibility to the legend of Atlantis? Alas for romance! Archeology yields no trace of evidence of a highly developed civilization either outside or within the "Pillars of Hercules" so long ago as the hundred centuries of Plato's story. Probably there is no more substance to the Atlantis myth than there is to the other one which tells how Hercules set up his "pillars," the two high points of rock projecting into the sea at the eastern end of the Strait of Gibraltar.

And then one thinks of Homer's Troy and how certainly it seemed nothing but a myth until Heinrich Schliemann proved the contrary. Who knows? As a wise man has said: "One should be skeptical even of one's own skepticism."

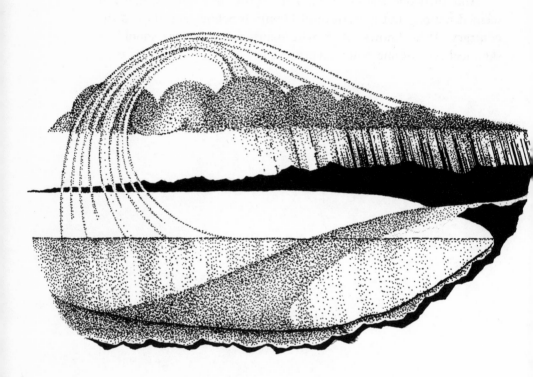

CHAPTER 6

SEDIMENT CARPET

F OR AS LONG AS SHIPS HAVE PLIED THE SEAS, MARINERS HAVE MADE use of local peculiarities of the sediment carpet to help them feel their way at night and in fog. The ancient art of casting the lead or "making the blue pigeon fly" had two purposes; to learn the depth of water and to bring up a sample of sediment beneath the ship. To the latter end the cuplike depression in the bottom of the sounding plummet was "armed" with tallow or some other soft, sticky substance before the casting. Thirty or forty years ago certain skippers of New England coastal schooners had an almost uncanny ability to ascertain their position in thick weather from the kind of sediment brought up by the armed lead; not only did they distinguish different kinds of sands, gravels, and shell deposits, but they could recognize local muds by their smell or grittiness when ground between the teeth.

With the growth of scientific curiosity about the oceans came a need for more effective tools for sampling sediments at great depths. Fine-grained sediments, such as commonly occur below 100 fathoms (180 meters), are poorly retained by the tallow of the mariner's deep-sea lead. Furthermore, when little scraps of sediment are recovered, they are too small for chemical, mineralogical, or biological analysis.

Early in the 1800's Sir John Ross invented the snapper, or "deep-sea clam." It consisted of two brass jaws shaped much like rather deep clam shells and a powerful spring to close them. When lowered the jaws were held open by a trigger mechanism which released the spring when the sampler touched bottom, and permitted it to force the jaws together.

In order to obtain a sample of sediment, whenever they

sounded the scientists of the *Challenger* expedition of 1872–6 added an iron cylinder to the sounding plummet. The cylinder projected fully 18 inches (45 centimeters) below the bottom of the plummet. This worked very well with tenacious clays; with granular deposits it was less successful in spite of an automatic valve that they later fitted to the bottom of the cylinder. Sand quite free of clay has a way of escaping through surprisingly small openings.

By means of this apparatus the *Challenger* collected the first really comprehensive series of samples of deep-sea deposits, which served as the basis for classification and conclusions regarding the geographical distribution of various kinds of sediments. Sir John Murray and A. Renard published a detailed description of this collection, supplemented by samples taken by other expedtions, in one of the volumes of the "Challenger Reports" in 1891. Their work has been the foundation on which all subsequent investigators have built; their classification of deep-sea sediments is still in wide use.

For millions of years sediment particles have been slowly settling one by one to the floor of the ocean, and during hundreds of millions of years sediments have accumulated in essentially the same way in the shallow seas that at one time or another have covered almost all parts of the continents. The leavings of these ancient seas as layers of marine sediment thousands of feet thick on the continents are the source of vast wealth in the form of petroleum, coal, iron ore and other useful minerals, without which we could not maintain our present level of industrialization. To discover more deposits of this kind and so fill the needs of expanding industry and population, an understanding of the processes of marine sedimentation is necessary. To gain this understanding earth scientists turn to the present seas and oceans where they can watch sedimentary processes at work.

But purely material wealth is not the only treasure to be won from these old sediments. The layers of sediment are like the pages of a book and to read what is written there requires patience, but the marvelous story that unfolds is worth the trouble.

All that we know about the development of marine life extending over hundreds of millions of years, we have learned from the study of the remains of creatures left in the layers of sediment spread by the seas that have endlessly overspread the continents and then retreated. From these ancestral traces students of ancient life have pieced together a history of life which establishes beyond suspicion of doubt the validity and reality of the theory of organic evolution, a theory which in its far-reaching implications is the most liberating and enlightening idea ever grasped by men searching for truth.

We concede, a little reluctantly, that raw materials are necessary for the attainment of a high level of culture. And yet some of the most soaring thoughts have been set down by the light of a tallow candle. We hold with Ruskin that "geology does better in reclothing dry bones and revealing lost creations than in tracing veins of lead or beds of iron."

As living things evolve and old forms become extinct, to be replaced by newly evolved forms; as rain, wind, ice, and chemical decay wear down mountain ranges to plains, to be replaced by new ranges elsewhere, the sands of Neptune's hourglass ceaselessly settle to the ocean floor. The settling particles are of many kinds; mere motes of mineral matter wafted from the continents by ocean currents or by high winds, flakes of ash blasted into the atmosphere by explosive volcanoes, shells and skeletons of myriads of minute sea creatures, and the ash of burnt-out meteorites and dust from outer space.

Chemical disorder reigns in sea water; it contains in solution every chemical element and its isotopes. From this broth of all earthly substances, various drifting plants and animals single out certain chemicals with which to construct supporting frames or protecting cases, many of marvelous symmetry and beauty. After death or reproduction of the organisms, the hard parts settle to the sea floor. In this way the unique capacity of living things to bring order out of chaos, either directly or indirectly by means of energy from the sun, generates an important part of the sediment covering vast regions of the ocean basins.

The materials most favored by these organisms are silica, or silicon dioxide, combined with more or less water in the form of opal, and calcium carbonate or lime. When these drifting particles of life die or reproduce by breaking up into many embryonic offspring, the abandoned hard parts, cleansed of organic matter by bacteria, sink to the ocean floor and become a part of the sediment carpet.

These organisms are known collectively as *plankton;* unable to swim, they drift about at various depths wherever ocean currents may carry them. The planktonic population is densest within the upper layer of water penetrated by sunlight; however many, by changing their buoyancy like miniature bathyscaphs, move up and down each day, while some spend each stage of their life cycle at a different depth. Others seem to pass their entire lives at depths of thousands of meters; such deep drifters feed on organic matter that settles from the light-saturated layer of water above.

The contribution of these bits of life to the sediment varies from hardly a trace to by far the largest part, depending upon local conditions influencing their productivity and the extent to which their hard parts are dissolved as they settle through thousands of meters of water. As a rule the calcareous or lime component dominates beneath the warm waters of low latitudes, whereas below the cold waters of high latitudes silica, secreted by diatoms dominates sometimes to the total exclusion of lime. Layers of snow-white *diatom ooze*, almost pure opaline silica, are especially characteristic of the sea floor around the Antarctic continent. Calcareous sediments, of which the shells of foraminifera make up the major part, carpet enormous areas of the world ocean. According to estimates they cover 50 million square miles of the floor of the deep sea, whereas sediment rich in diatoms lags far behind with only 12 million square miles.

However, beginning at a depth of about 4,500 meters (15,000 feet) the fraction of lime in deep-sea sediments rapidly decreases to almost nothing below 5,500 meters (18,000 feet). This is due to solution of the calcium carbonate in the cold, deeper layers of water full of carbon dioxide which combines with the lime to form soluble calcium bicarbonate. At such great depths the so-called "red clay," which is really brown, replaces the light tan to nearly white calcareous sediments of lesser depths. These café-au-lait to deep chocolate brown sediments of the deepest basins owe their color to abundant iron hydroxide and manganese peroxide. Brown clays cover a little less than 40 million square miles of the deepest regions of the ocean floor.

Only in the last two decades have measurements of the thicknesses of the sediment carpet at great depths become possible. This is done by the seismic method—from the Greek word *"seismos"* meaning earthquake, because it uses the same kind of elastic waves as those generated at the sites of earthquakes, the records of which, seismograms, reveal the internal structure of the earth to seismologists well versed in their language. Needless to say, marine geologists cannot wait for earthquakes. They must make their own as needed.

Waloddi Weibull, a Swedish scientist who was with the Bofors Armament Works, developed the method. After experimenting for several years in Swedish coastal waters, he put his equipment on the *Skagerak*, research ship of the Swedish government, and tried it out during a cruise to the western Mediterranean in 1946. Later Weibull employed the same method on the *Albatross* during the epoch-making Swedish Oceanographic Expedition around the world in 1947 and 1948.

Geophysicists of the Lamont Geological Observatory, the Woods Hole Oceanographic Institution, and the Scripps Institution of Oceanography use similar methods in their surveys of the ocean floor.

A few years ago when a ship set out to study the ocean floor it carried thousands of brightly colored toy balloons; those plus several tons of TNT in chests on deck ready to go overboard in case of fire were the main quake-making equipment. Once every hour, and sometimes at shorter intervals, the quake maker on duty fired a "reflection shot" consisting of a length of twine with a block of TNT tied to one end and a balloon at the other, the twine being long enough to let the explosive sink to a depth known by experience to give best results. Just before shot-time he put a blasting cap and fuse into the TNT, lit the fuse, and threw the infernal machine overboard. As the fuse burnt, the ship moved to a safe distance. The explosion sent a handsome geyser into the air and a sound wave down to the bottom, where, as happens at a boundary between two media of different densities and elastic properties, a part of the energy was reflected back to the ship; the rest, however, passed through the boundary surface and continued down through the sediment until it reached another surface of discontinuity, that is hard rock beneath the sediment, where a second partial reflection of the sound energy took place.

Hydrophones, the seismologists' "ears," supported by floats trailing behind the ship and connected to it be conducting cables, picked up the separate reflections, the arrival times of which were recorded on a strip of paper by the recording apparatus on the ship. From the time interval between the arrivals of the two echoes and the known velocity of sound in sediment, the geophysicists could calculate the thickness of the sediment layer.

But this method of exploration was handicapped by the inconveniences and hazards always associated with the handling of large quantities of explosives. Furthermore, even when the shots were fired every quarter of an hour, the distances between the points were too great to show the same degree of detail of the basement surface that the echo sounder could provide for the surface of the sediment. In spite of these shortcomings a quantity of most valuable information about the structure of the ocean floor has been collected by the expenditure of many tons of explosives, particularly during cruises of the *Vema* of the Lamont Geological Observatory under the leadership of Maurice Ewing.

For a better understanding of the structure of the ocean floor some method that could draw a continuous profile of the base of the sediment carpet, a profile as detailed as the echo sounder drew of its surface, was needed. This was very important when surveying an area in which there were several reflecting surfaces beneath the sea floor, in which case correlation between discrete measurements several miles apart was often uncertain. But to make possible continuous profiling of sub-bottom structure it was going to be necessary to develop a way of generating sound waves at short, regular intervals. By the early 1950's the need for such a method of echo exploration was so urgent that several groups of researchers, some commercial, others purely scientific, took up the problem. The Magnolia Petroleum Company made a beginning by developing the *sonoprobe*, which uses a low-frequency sound pulse, that is, relatively long sound waves, generated by a "pinger" that releases sound energy below the water surface. It records the echoes as a continuous profile on a strip of paper. Magnolia developed it for the very practical purpose of exploring possible sites for the large platforms needed for drilling oil wells on the continental shelf. For the oceanographer the sonoprobe, however, was not the answer; it could penetrate unconsolidated sediment to a depth of no more than about 100 meters or 300 feet. Furthermore, to obtain meaningful records of sub-bottom structure as the boat moves along requires the continual supervision of an experienced hand, who knows how to regulate the output of sound in such a way as to compensate for minor changes in the consistency of the sediment along the profile. In addition to Magnolia, various manufacturers of echo-sounding apparatus have been modifying their instruments in order to use lower frequency sound pulses so as to pick up sub-bottom echos as well as that from the sediment surface. Understandably, engineering firms find many uses for these tools in surveying harbors and bridge sites. Perhaps their most brilliant future will be in prospecting for alluvial deposits at shallow depths of such minerals as gold, diamond, tin, and tungsten, to cite a few. In the realm of pure science the method has made possible interesting surveys of shelf areas, in particular that on both sides of the submerged valley of the Hudson eroded during the ice ages. But the geology of the shelf is really only a seaward extension of the geology of the adjacent continent; surveys on the shelf are not likely to yield the kind of information for which marine geologists search.

Once the method had proven itself in relatively shallow water, the instruments evolved, as mechanical things do, by the accretion of small improvements, and each improvement increased the depth range until it is now possible to trace continuously one or more layers of sediment at the greatest depths by means of instruments and methods developed by ingenious men at both the Lamont Geological Observatory and the Woods Hole Oceanographic Institution. (The basic operation of continuous profiling is illustrated in Figure 32.)

In 1961 John Ewing and G. B. Tirey of Lamont Geological Observatory described a method that produced continuous seismic profiles in the greatest depths of water. The records were similar in appearance to standard echo-sounding profiles, except that they showed sediment and rock layers lying as much as 4.6 kilometers (15,000 feet) below the ocean floor. At that time the method consisted of firing 0.5-pound charges of TNT every 2 minutes. The reflections were received by a highly sensitive hydrophone, or underwater "ear," towed by a cable to which several floats were attached. In order to have the hydrophone at rest at the time of each firing of TNT while the ship went on its way at 6 to 8 nautical miles an hour, the cable to the hydrophone was automatically drawn in and then slackened just before each shot. More recently John Ewing and co-workers have substituted a pneumatic sound source for the hazardous shots of TNT. This is essentially a large and powerful air gun, towed behind the ship

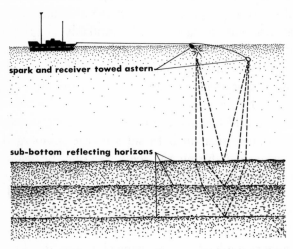

spark and receiver towed astern

sub-bottom reflecting horizons

FIGURE 32 *Continuous profiling for normal incidence reflections.*

and fed air at constant pressure through a hose. In practice it "fires" at intervals of 10 seconds and produces enough energy to penetrate several thousand feet of sediments while the ship proceeds at a speed of about 10 nautical miles an hour. This innovation, which contributes to the peace of mind of seagoing geologists, also very greatly increases the detailed information on the records.

In 1961 the *Vema* using this method charted sub-bottom profiles in the Atlantic as far south as Antarctica and then northward in the eastern Pacific. Since then the method has been used in surveys of all the oceans. One of the first results of these explorations has been the discovery that the "second layer," that is the layer of rock just below the unconsolidated sediment, which was not always detectable by older methods, is universally present.

The most significant outcome of seismic reflection measurements is the evidence that the thickness of unconsolidated sediment in the Atlantic Basin is not more than from 450 to 1,200 meters (1,500 to 4,000 feet) and from 200 to 600 meters (750 to 2,000 feet) in the Pacific.

In 1950 Ph. H. Kuenen, a Netherlands marine geologist and one of the foremost authorities on ocean sediments, published in his book *Marine Geology* estimates of the thicknesses of unconsolidated sediment to be expected in the Atlantic and Pacific. He based these estimates on the thickness of the uppermost layer of sediment in sediment cores from the Atlantic, which had accumulated since the end of the last ice age. Realizing that this rate was not necessarily representative of former times when the continents were less exposed to erosion, and also in order to take into account the effect of compaction of the deeper layers, he adopted one sixth of a centimeter in 1,000 years as a conservative average rate. Then assuming that the age of the ocean was 2 billion years—a conservative assumption because the oldest-known sediments on the continents are more than twice as old—he calculated that the average thickness of sediment should be in the order of 3,000 meters. To check this figure he multiplied the amount of sediment brought to the oceans by rivers each year by 2 billion, and after making allowance for the slower rate of erosion in the geological past, again found that the thickness of sediment ought to be about 3,000 meters.

The serious discrepancy between Kuenen's estimate and the thicknesses actually measured supports our surmise that a drastic geological reorganization of those parts of the earth's surface now covered by the great oceans took place about 100 million years ago, a conjecture diametrically opposed to the older, more generally accepted assumption that the ocean basins as well as the continents have been permanent features which originated, much as they are now, some 4 or 5 billion years ago. As we have pointed out before, one reason for our thinking that reorganization occurred, in round figures, 100 million years ago, is that neither we nor anyone else has yet found fossils older than the Cretaceous Period within the ocean basins, in spite of the fact that in recent years an impressive array of sediments laid down before the Pleistocene has been found by coring and dredging. A second reason is that conversion of the average thickness of sediment into years by assuming a reasonable rate of accumulation gives us in round figures the 100 million years.

Scientists of some of the earlier oceanographic expeditions when taking samples of sediment in deep water far from land were, on rare occasions, astonished to find what looked remarkably like beach sand. We know now that sands, silts, and calcareous gray clays of shallow-water origin occur widely in the ocean basins and are the dominant types of sediment of the abyssal plains of the Atlantic. How did it happen that such widely distributed and strikingly distinct sediments were so rarely found by earlier explorers? Probably because most of these sediments do not lie directly at the surface of the sea floor. For the most part, they were deposited during the last ice age, and since then have been covered by 20 to 30 centimeters (8 to 12 inches) of typical deep-sea sediment. Most early types of samplers only skimmed the surface, and therefore failed to reach the sands. The *Challenger* sampled with a coring tube 60 centimeters (2 feet) long, which must have reached sand fairly often, but clean sand runs out of a coring tube like water unless held in by a valve which the tube used by the *Challenger* did not have. The discovery of the wide distribution of these sands depended upon the invention of a coring tube capable of sampling several meters of sediment.

To the layman, who associates sandy beaches with the sea, it may not seem particularly strange that sand should be found on the floor of the deep ocean, but this is because he has probably not thought much about the origin of quartz sands. The particles of silicon dioxide, the substance of most famous beaches, began in molten rocks within the earth's crust. After tens or hundreds of thousands of years of cooling, the silica and other chemicals crystallized. Then through uplift and removal of covering rocks by erosion, the solidified mass (as granite) was exposed to the disintegrating effect of atmospheric weathering, which released the chemically stable crystals of silica known to mineralogists as quartz. After many thousands of years of knocking about, driven by running water and strong winds, quantities of these quartz particles may become concentrated along shore lines as beaches and dunes. So far as we know, the deep-sea environment does not and never has provided conditions necessary for the release of quartz particles. Furthermore, oceanic rocks are poor in quartz.

All rocks dredged from submarine volcanoes and all rocks found on truly oceanic islands are rich in iron and magnesium and low in silicon dioxide, and in consequence rarely contain quartz. These iron-magnesium rocks are denser than granites; that such heavy rocks dominate the ocean floor, in contrast to the dominance of relatively light quartz-bearing granites on the continents, has been shown by hundreds of measurements of the gravity field over the ocean basins and continents.

We are left with no choice but to conclude that these sands have been carried to the ocean floor from far off sources, but by what agent of transportation? Even the most energetic elements of continuous oceanic circulation are too weak to carry such coarse material. A few geologists have contended that the sands were deposited by streams or along shore lines at some former time of greatly lower sea level. This harmonized with the view that the submarine canyons of the continental slopes had been carved by rivers when sea level was lower. Otherwise the theory had little in its favor; the sands usually occurred under a very thin cover of recently deposited sediment and often contained the small shells of organisms known to be still living, and a few sands actually occurred at the surface as if laid down within the last few hundred years. Apparently their presence called for a process of transportation capable of working under water. Furthermore, many occurred in the deepest parts of the ocean; to account for them as river or beach sands led one to the preposterous conclusion that only a few thousand or even hundreds of years ago the ocean basins had been very nearly empty of water.

Many years ago, before the exploration of the oceans by modern methods, we heard a lecture by an eminent geologist. He described the awful calm prevailing on the floor of the deep ocean; down there in utter darkness and perpetual silence as the millions of years rolled by nothing happened, except for the slow settling of a dust-size particle now and then. According to this conception of the deep-sea world no serious disturbance of the sediment was possible. It encouraged us to expect to find in the layers of deep-sea sediments a record of the earth's history all in orderly pages and going back without omission to the first "great rain" that filled the depressions of the earth's surface.

The exploration of the last few decades has dispelled this vision of appalling calm; it existed only in the minds of imaginative geologists. We now realize that the calm of the ocean floor is disturbed at times by rushing torrents of mud mixed with water which sweep down the continental slopes, across deep-sea fans, and flood far out over abyssal plains, raising havoc with the sedimentary record as they go. They garble the record not only by destroying some of the pages, but also by interleaving irrelevant layers of coarse sediment of shallow water origin from the continental shelves.

These torrents or turbidity currents (cf. page 166) are "storms" of mud, sand, and sometimes even gravel, thoroughly mixed with water, which tumble down undersea slopes like invisible Niagaras. They may be set in motion when sediments heaped on the edges of the continental shelf or upper part of the continental slope are disturbed by a small earthquake, or by an exceptionally violent storm. When this happens a mass of sediment that has accumulated during many years starts to slide downslope. Once in motion the water-saturated sediment becomes quite fluid, and by commingling with more water soon ceases to be so much a mass of sediment as a mass of water saturated with mineral particles. Moving downslope, because of its greater density in comparison with clear water, it nourishes itself by picking up more sediment from the bottom over which it flows. By this "snowballing" effect what may have started as a rather small affair can become a powerful flood by the time it reaches the foot of the continental shelf. In 1929 an earthquake triggered such a turbidity current in the region south of Newfoundland. Within a few hours it had wreaked havoc with a number of transatlantic telegraph cables that happened to lie in its path. From the timing of the cable breaks, as recorded by the interruptions of service, the speed of the current has been estimated at 50 to 60 miles per hour.

As soon as a turbidity current flows out over a gentler slope it loses velocity, turbulence or mixing decreases, the coarser particles settle out, and the loss of density puts a further brake upon it. A consequence of the rapid settling of relatively coarse sediment at the foot of the continental slope is the building up of deep-sea deltas or *fans* off the mouths of submarine canyons. These have the form of extremely low or flattened cones with apices at the points where canyons reach the foot of the continental slope.

However, the loss of the coarsest mineral particles, that is material of sand size, does not end the career of most turbidity currents; quantities of clay particles remain in suspension. Huge volumes of water with clay in suspension have flooded the deep basins of the Atlantic, Caribbean, and Gulf of Mexico from time to time during the relatively recent past. We know this because long sediment cores from the smooth, almost level bottoms of these basins always contain layers of gray, rather limy clay interbedded with the normal brown lime-free clay characteristic of great depths. Without doubt the spreading out of such floods of turbid water over the floors of basins and the settling of sediment from them accounts for the amazing smoothness of the vast abyssal plains of the Atlantic.

The continental slopes are not the only sources of turbidity currents. As the rain of fine particles from above slowly adds layer upon layer of sediment on the flanks of any rise on the ocean floor, the instability becomes critical and slumping or what we on land would call a landslide may occur. Triggered by any disturbance, such as a minor earth tremor, the sliding mass of sediment gathers speed, assumes the nature of a turbidity current, and moves with the energy of a hurricane (see Figure 33).

If it seems strange that a mere suspension of sediment can move under clear water at such high speeds, consider for a moment what avalanches do on land. When avalanches reach velocities of more than 100 miles per hour, it is because the snow has become completely suspended in air; the whole mass can be thought of as floating down a mountainside in suspension.

Similar, far more destructive but fortunately rare phenomena are the *nuées ardentes* which accompany some volcanic eruptions. In 1902 such a glowing horror of incandescent particles of volcanic ash swept down from Mount Pelé at hurricane speed and destroyed the town of St. Pierre on Martinique in the West Indies.

As a result of our study of about 3,000 cores of sediment from the Atlantic, the Caribbean, the Gulf of Mexico, the Mediterranean, and the subarctic seas, we have come to the firm conviction that deep-sea sands and graded sediments (by grading we mean gradual decrease in the size of particles from the bottom of any one layer to the top) were deposited by turbidity currents.

water surface

BEFORE SLUMPING

indicated as a layer only to show
mechanism of slumping

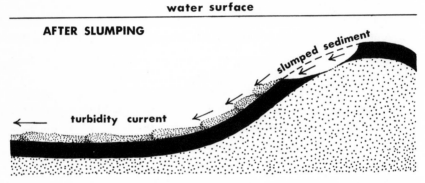

water surface

AFTER SLUMPING

slumped sediment

turbidity current

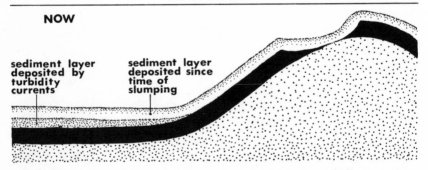

water surface

NOW

sediment layer
deposited by
turbidity
currents

sediment layer
deposited since
time of
slumping

FIGURE 33 *Mechanism of slumping and generation of a turbidity current.
The turbidity current created by slumping erodes sediment as it flows
down the steep part of the slope, thus removing part of the sediment
record. On reaching the nearly level part of the floor of the ocean, however, the mass of turbid water loses velocity and the sediment settles to
the bottom.*

This theory of origin has met every test. Nothing confirms the validity of a theory so well as the verification of predictions based upon it. Here the theory of turbidity currents has come off with flying colors. If turbidity currents owe their velocity to the pull of gravity, their courses along the bottom should be guided by the topography of the bottom over which they flow. With this in mind, one can chart the areas in which deposits by turbidity currents ought to occur, as well as areas where they should not occur. All predictions of this kind when tested have been verified; and many have been tested, as witness the thousands of cores in the collection at Lamont Geological Observatory. We have found sediment layers deposited by turbidity currents in submarine canyons, on plains upon which submarine canyons open, and in deep basins and trenches. But of the many hundreds of cores containing graded layers, not one comes from the top of an isolated rise or from sloping areas with the exception of the gently sloping continental rises. The Puerto Rico Trench afforded a good test of the theory. According to the theory graded layers ought to occur on the floor of the trench, a deep into which turbidity currents must have drained frequently. By splicing together cables from two research vessels, Maurice Ewing, on board the *Atlantis,* succeeded in reaching bottom twice with a coring tube. As predicted, both cores contained ideal examples of graded beds. Like many other similar sediments from great depths, these contained the remains of organisms that live only in shallow water. Among the coarse particles near the sharply defined bases of the graded layers, we found fragments of Halimeda, a bottom-dwelling, lime-secreting plant which cannot grow without sunlight. Many cores have been taken on the sloping sides of the Puerto Rico Trench, but none has contained graded layers.

Turbidites—that is, sediments deposited by turbidity currents —by virtue of their prevalance and bulk, must have a prominent place in the classification of marine sediments. We think that they ought to be recognized as one of two great classes of sediments. The first class should contain the kinds of sediments recognized by the scientists of the *Challenger;* sediments that accumulate through the slow settling of discrete particles. The second group would include graded sand and silt layers, and calcareous gray clays and silts, generally interbedded with sediments of the first

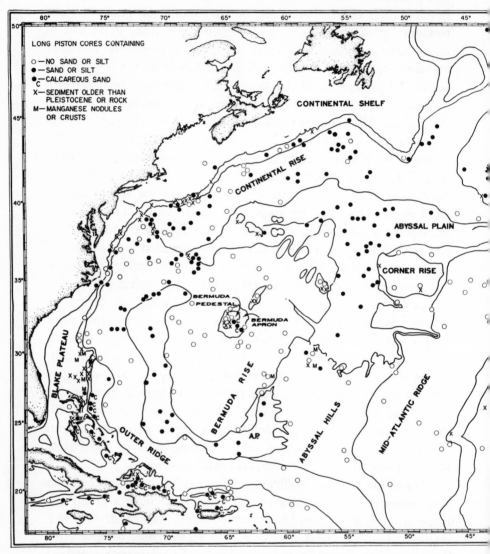

FIGURE 34   *Distribution of various kinds of deep-sea sediments in relation to physiographic provinces.*

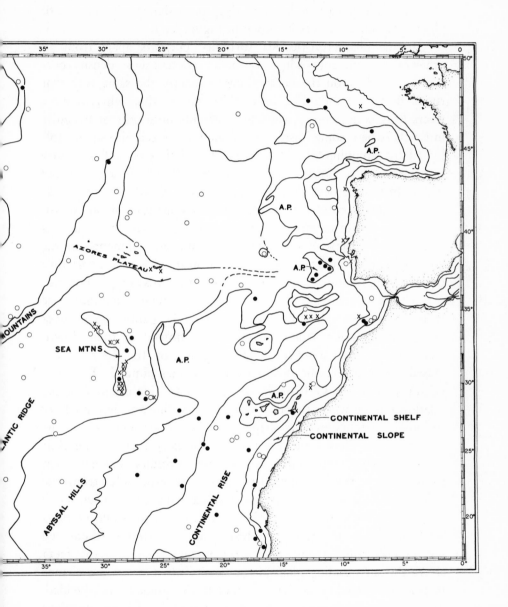

group. Grading, or decrease in particle size from coarse at the bottom to fine at top, particularly well characterizes turbidites. (Distribution of various kinds of deep-sea sediments in relation to physiographic provinces is shown in Figure 34.)

Unique characteristics set turbidity currents apart from all other oceans currents. They are in the strictest sense density currents; they flow on the ocean floor in exactly the same way that rivers flow on land. The only difference is that whereas most rivers flow continuously, turbidity currents flow only at irregular intervals when some disturbance—such as a seismic shock followed by slumping of sediment or the stirring of sediment into suspension by a violent storm—supplies a flood of dense, turbid water. In that respect they are analogous to the destructive walls of water that rage down the otherwise dry arroyos of our southwestern states after heavy rain. To the geologist, whether his interest is in deep-sea sediments or in ancient sediments on the continents, the important point to keep in mind is that a turbidity current can no more flow uphill than the Mississippi. For this reason the rather peculiar kinds of sediments deposited by turbidity currents occur only on relatively gentle slopes over which the sediment-laden currents have flowed in their downward course from a source higher up, and on the floors of enclosed basins where the turbid water becomes ponded. The deep central part of the Gulf of Mexico provides a fine example of the relationship between the distribution of sediments deposited by turbidity currents and the shape of the sea floor. During the last ice age of the Pleistocene, the floor of the deep basin of the Gulf of Mexico was repeatedly flooded by turbidity currents that rushed down the surrounding slopes, and especially from the delta of the Mississippi which in those days must have been much larger than it is now. In 1953 Maurice Ewing and his co-workers while exploring the Gulf of Mexico on the *Atlantis* discovered several hills rising from 180 to 350 meters (600 to 1,200 feet) above the surrounding plain of the deep Gulf. Here was a chance to test the turbidity current theory; if the graded, well-bedded, gray clays and silts of the abyssal plain really had been deposited by dense turbid water from the Mississippi Delta, the upper parts of the hills should be quite free of such sediments. To answer this question several cores were taken on or near the tops of the hills;

as expected they consisted of sediment strikingly different from that of the surrounding plain. It was the classic *globigerina ooze*, a type of sediment that accumulates through the very slow but continuous settling from above of fine mineral particles and hard parts of organisms. As theory had predicted, the floods of turbid water from the Mississippi Delta had flowed completely around the hills without having any effect on their upper parts. Since then the collection of cores at Lamont Geological Observatory has grown greatly; among the several thousand cores from every kind of submarine topographical setting the relationship between kind of sediment and topographical setting has held rigidly true. Without exception the upper parts of isolated features rising above the general level of the ocean floor are quite free of the kind of sediments deposited by turbidity currents.

At what point does a mass of sediment sliding down, let us say, the continental slope become a turbidity current? We have mentioned the characteristic grading of particle sizes in layers of sediment deposited by turbidity currents. That the largest particles should settle out of suspension first and therefore dominate in the basal part of a graded layer is not surprising, but the fact that they can do so is proof that in the suspension of a turbidity current each particle must have been free to move completely independently of those about it. Of course, there is probably some transitional stage between sediment sliding en masse in which the individual particles have no independent freedom of movement and the true suspension of a turbidity current; probably the change-over takes place rather suddenly. At any rate we have not yet found an example of sediment that might have traveled and come to rest in the transitional stage between sediment moving en masse and sediment wholly in suspension. Examples of sediment masses that have come to rest without going into suspension sometimes occur in the cores. Generally, they occur at the bottoms of steep but short slopes as, for example, along the side slopes of the Hudson Submarine Canyon, and at the bottom of the steep slope south of the Gulf of Mexico where it is bounded by the Campeche Peninsula. Characteristically, they show a marbled effect, with two or more kinds of sediments kneaded together in complete confusion.

Sediments from depths not greater than 4,500 meters are

largely made up of the shells or tests of microscopic animals and plants. These parts of once living things tell a fascinating story of changing conditions in the ocean during the one and a half million years of the Pleistocene or Anthropogene Epoch during which man evolved from a subhuman ancestor. Among these little shells, many thousands of which would scarcely fill a thimble, those of the foraminifera are the most abundant and the most useful as indicators of past conditions. From the record of marine sediments on the continents, paleontologists know that foraminifera have been abundant for several hundred million years. More than 25,000 living and fossil species have been identified and more are constantly being added to the list. The majority of species live on the sea floor. While many of these *benthic species*, as they are called, secrete tests of calcium carbonate, some others build houses by cementing together particles of sand, flakes of mica, or even the small discarded shells of other foraminifera. Most species are very small, that is a millimeter or less in diameter, but among the ancient forms there were some giants. The limestone with which the Cheops Pyramid was built is largely composed of the shells of a kind of foraminifera having the size and shape of small coins, for which reason they have been called *nummulites* from the Latin word meaning coin. Cheops, who lived five thousand years ago, is a young upstart in comparison with the foraminifera of his pyramid which lived 60 million years ago. The largest shells of foraminifera that we have ever seen were in a limestone in Syria; much like pancakes in shape, they measure 15 centimeters (6 inches) in diameter.

Of most interest to the oceanographer, however, are those relatively few species which have taken to the planktonic way of life, spending their entire life cycle drifting about in the open ocean. All these species are microscopic, rarely exceeding a millimeter in diameter, and all make their shells out of calcium carbonate precipitated from sea water. At first sight of a quantity of shells seen through a binocular microscope, one gets the impression that most consist of irregular clusters of white bubbles; as a little girl of four said, "They look like popcorn." With more familiarity one sees that there is really a good deal of variation in the form of the bubbles, or chambers, and in the arrangement of the clusters. A spiral arrangement of the chambers is particularly common; this gives the shells of many species a superficial resemblance to tiny snail shells. In addition to a passage from chamber to chamber and an aperture or doorway to the outer world, many fine holes pierce the chamber walls. Through these the animal sends out extensions of itself as pseudopodia or "false feet," by means of which it gathers food. From the many holes in the chamber walls, or *foramina*, the group derives its name, "foraminifera," the hole-bearers.

Calcareous sediments rich in the shells of planktonic foraminifera carpet about 45 per cent of the ocean floor. It would cover a much larger area except for the fact that some of the shells as they sink slowly from near-surface waters dissolve in the frigid water of the deep depressions of the ocean floor.

The planktonic species are young in comparison with the age of the whole group of foraminifera. They first appear in sediments deposited during the Cretaceous Period about 100 million years ago. As an evolutionary experiment they were a great success; the sunlit waters of the open oceans provided them with a favorable and vast new territory in which they proliferated enormously. Ever since then these little creatures have ceaselessly added their limy shells to oceanic sediments.

If one were attempting to invent a class of ideal fossils by which layers of sediment could be marked, one could hardly improve upon the foraminifera. Many of the species have evolved rapidly and have soon become extinct. Such short-lived species are particularly good markers of sediment layers; they permit paleontologists to subdivide the sequence of ancient sediments on the continents in detail, a matter of much importance in the search for deposits of petroleum.

The remarkable evolutionary versatility of the foraminifera has enabled them to colonize virtually every kind of marine environment, with the result that fossil foraminifera are more nearly universally present in the marine sediments of the last 100 million years than any other group of fossils.

In spite of the wide dispersal of the group as a whole, many species are fastidious as to their surroundings; some bottom dwellers will live only within certain depth limits; others must have clear water, while still others get along in relatively muddy water; water temperature influences the distribution of many species. This is especially true of certain planktonic species living in the oceans today, some being confined to equatorial waters, whereas others abound only in high latitudes, and at least one lives among the ice floes of the Arctic Ocean. From past shifts in the geographical ranges of temperature-sensitive species as recorded in the layers of sediment on the ocean floor, we can infer that the earth's climatic zones have moved back and forth in latitude in response to the climatic changes of the last one and a half million years.

Thus, these sediments of slow and orderly accumulation record the climatic and geological conditions under which they were laid down, the deeper layers corresponding to the earlier intervals of time. They provide an ordered record of the ages. But before marine geologists could decipher the record, some way of recovering it intact had to be devised. An instrument capable of sampling a thick sequence of layers without disturbing their order was needed.

Actually, such an instrument was used by the *Challenger*. The "sounding machine" consisted of a tube 60 centimeters (24 inches) long below the sounding lead, the weight of which forced the tube into the sediment. As we have said before, this tube would not be likely to retain sand, but it must frequently have recovered a record of the last climatic changes when the continental ice sheets melted; but as the *Challenger* scientists were not aware of this possibility, they always treated the cores from the tube as bulk samples and destroyed their layering by forcing them into glass jars.

After World War I the German *Meteor* expedition took a large number of cores, some of which were about 1 meter (40 inches) long. Perfectly preserved in glass tubes, they were studied after the return of the expedition by Wolfgang Schott, who made the fascinating discovery that short as the cores were they nevertheless contained evidence of the latest climatic changes of the Pleistocene.

In the 1930's Charles Piggot devised a corer that utilized the energy from a charge of black powder. The coring tube was shot into the sediment by a gun which fired automatically when the lower end of the coring tube touched the sediment surface. Although it never brought up cores longer than about 3 meters (10 feet), it did mark an important advance over all earlier sampling devices. In the meantime, Henry Stetson of the Woods Hole Oceanographic Institution and M. J. Hvorslev of Harvard found that a coring tube with a large lead weight at the top and dropped through the last 25 feet of its descent, penetrated the sediment just as well as the Piggot gun and with much less danger to the lives of oceanographers. However, it did nothing to increase the lengths of cores. More than once we have seen the Hvorslev-Stetson corer come up with mud on the lead weight and even on the tail fins, but our hopeful expectation that it contained a core 5 or 6 meters long was always disappointed; invariably, no matter how deep the tube plunged into the sediment, it yielded a core no longer than about 3 meters. Plainly the problem was not insufficient energy to drive down the corer, but rather the friction within the tube which beyond about 3 meters prevented more sediment from entering.

The next great step, a real revolution in the art of coring, is closely involved with Hans Pettersson and the Swedish expedition of the *Albatross*. It began during Pettersson's student days in London when he met Sir John Murray of *Challenger* fame. This encounter stimulated Pettersson's imagination and he determined someday to explore the mysteries of the ocean floor. His reaction was natural; he had always had salt water in his veins.

His ancestral home had been a rocky island off the windswept shores of the Skagerak, the arm of the North Sea that separated Norway and Denmark. The house was called *Kålhuvudet*, "Head of Cabbage," because the rock it stands on had a fancied resemblance to that vegetable. At night the windows of *Kålhuvudet* were swept by the beam of the Pater Noster Lighthouse, marking a region of strong currents and hidden rocks dangerous enough to have evoked many a *pater noster* from approaching mariners.

Pettersson's father, Otto Pettersson, had devoted a long life to problems of the sea, and died in the midst of his studies at the age of ninety-three. It was he, as we saw in Chapter III, who discovered internal tidal waves at the entrance to the Baltic by means of instruments in his laboratory overlooking the Gullmar Fjord. Although his interest was mostly in the waters around Scandinavia and northwestern Europe, he was also responsible for organizing the International Council for the Investigation of the Sea.

"With such an ancestry and in such an environment the sea is bound to become an obsession," wrote Hans Pettersson in *Westward Ho With the Albatross*, his account of the famous expedition.

He had planned to carry on the work of his father when he went to study in London, but his meeting with John Murray changed all that; thereafter, it was his ambition to attack the problems of the world ocean. After taking a doctor of science degree at the University of Stockholm, and studying at Upsala University, and University College in London, he returned to the Skagerak and carried on his father's investigation of internal waves and currents along the coasts of Sweden while planning for the future. Then from 1923 to 1928 he led a group of workers at the Institute of Radium Investigation in Vienna, but Murray's influence was with him still; he studied the radium content of manganese oxide nodules from the floor of the deep sea.

In the early 1930's Pettersson was appointed professor of oceanography at the University of Göteborg. A step closer to his goal, he now put his prestige to work to interest the people of Sweden in a deep-sea expedition. Cannily, he appealed to national pride and to the Viking heritage.

With imagination, enthusiasm, and native articulateness he told everyone he met about the discoveries to be expected from the application of new methods and newly devised instruments to the study of the ocean floor. It would be a voyage of exploration worthy of a great maritime nation. As the campaign gained momentum, he made broadcasts, lectured, published in newspapers, and even wrote books. But to arouse interest was not enough; money was needed and a great deal of it. To keep a well-equipped ship at sea with a staff of specialists on board long enough to accomplish what he hoped for was going to be costly. So he turned to the wealthy men of Göteborg, appealing to their well-known reputation for generosity to the arts and sciences.

Then as the iron was getting hot, hope-shattering war came. However, as it turned out the war was only a delay, and a delay at that time was an advantage in some ways. It gave the Göteborg scientists a chance to experiment with new instruments and methods and to plan every detail that might promote the ultimate success of the cruise.

One of the important objectives was improvement of sediment-coring techniques so that much longer records of past conditions in the oceans could be obtained. The new Oceanographic Institute in Göteborg, inaugurated in 1939 with Hans Pettersson as director, facilitated the construction of experimental coring apparatus.

The problem was not to find a way of driving the corer into the sediment; a ton of lead and a tripping device to let the apparatus fall freely through the last 10 meters of its descent provided plenty of energy for that. The problem was rather to make the sediment enter the tube. Not only did friction reduce the maximum length of cores to about 3 meters, it also rendered worthless as records of past events the lower halves of the cores because of extreme distortion due to the frictional resistance.

In an early attempt to solve the problem, Pettersson and Börje Kullenberg fastened a high-pressure spherical container to the top of the coring tube. Before lowering, the container was evacuated. On touching bottom, a valve opened to permit water from the tube to flow into the container thereby causing the outside pressure to force sediment into the tube. In 1942 the vacuum corer raised an undisturbed core nearly 15 meters (50 feet) long from the bottom of the Gullmar Fjord, which is not very deep. In really deep water the vacuum corer is not successful because in practice it is impossible to adjust the valve to the vacuum chamber nicely enough to maintain a balance between the rate of penetration of the tube and the completely independent rate of flow of water into the vacuum chamber. When the valve is open too far, sediment rushes into the tube in complete confusion; when too little open, sediment cannot enter. The principle, use of hydrostatic pressure, was sound, but the mechanism by which it was applied was not workable.

Three years later Kullenberg discovered a solution that was as effective as it was simple; he put a freely moving piston into the coring tube and connected it to the main lowering cable with a wire line (see Figure 35). When the tube is 5 meters (17 feet) above the bottom a tripping device, actuated by a weight hanging 5 meters below the lower end of the tube, releases it from the main cable. The apparatus then drops freely until its lower end reaches the sediment surface. At that instant the wire from the piston to the main cable, previously slack, becomes taut, and thereafter it holds the piston stationary, or nearly so, just above the sediment surface, while the tube penetrates the sediment. In

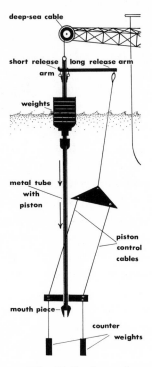

FIGURE 35　*The Kullenberg piston corer.*

this way, friction between the sediment and the inner wall of the tube cannot push the sediment downward without creating a vacuum between the stationary piston and the surface of the sediment which immediately brings into effect the great water pressure outside the tube to push the sediment into the tube. Thus the piston corer uses the same principle as the vacuum corer, but with the critical difference that the rate of penetration of the tube into the sediment and the application of outside pressure to force the sediment into the tube are so interlocked that the two processes necessarily remain in perfect adjustment to each other. The first trial in the Gullmar Fjord yielded a 21-meter (70-foot) core. The sevenfold increase in length over the cores taken by the Hvorslev-Stetson corer opened the way to a new world of discovery for marine geologists.

During this time Pettersson persuaded Waloddi Weibull, the authority on explosives at the Bofors Armament Works, to develop a method of measuring the then unknown thickness of sediment in the ocean basins. Weibull proposed using depth charges that could be detonated at any predetermined depth between 450 meters (1,500 feet) and 6,000 meters (20,000 feet) and recording by means of an oscillograph the echoes thrown back from the sea floor and from the rock surface beneath the sediment, the time interval between the arrivals of the echoes providing a measure of the sediment thickness.

While these important experiments were going on, the indefatigable Pettersson was succeeding in the all-important matter of finding a ship and enough money to run it. No sooner had the war ended in 1945 than the Broström Shipping Company offered him the use of their training ship the *Albatross*, a four-masted auxiliary schooner of 1,540 tons, for a fifteen-month, world-encircling expedition. The Royal Society of Göteborg and various generous citizens offered money for equipment and operation of the ship. The first Swedish deep-sea expedition was to be realized without benefit of governmental financing, a rare phenomenon in this age.

Because of the weight of the new apparatus, particularly the very long and costly piston corer, it seemed best to confine the cruise to the tropics, that is within 30° north and south of the equator, where heavy weather was least likely to make trouble. Futhermore, this zone had not been extensively studied before.

Attention was to be focused on problems of marine geology. This was natural; the long coring tube could not fail to provide new insight into past biological and geological conditions by sampling deep layers of sediment never before accessible to scientists. The echo sounder would outline a continuous profile of the mountains, valleys, and plains of the underwater world, and Weibull's seismic echo method would yield measurements of the thickness of unconsolidated sediment with all that that implied for the age and history of the ocean basins. At the same time, the cruise offered an opportunity to study and chart the layering of ocean waters from surface to bottom, the vertical and horizontal variations in temperature, salinity, and dissolved oxygen, the biologically important nutrient salts, and the distribution of marine organisms; to make the most of this opportunity was a part of the plan.

The Swedish Deep-Sea Expedition of 1947 and 1948 took the *Albatross* across the North Atlantic, the Caribbean, through the Panama Canal into the Pacific, among the South Sea Islands, into the Indian Ocean, the Red Sea, and, finally, through the Mediterranean and home to Göteborg. By the application of powerful new methods and instruments, the *Albatross* brought home outstandingly important new information about the sediments and the geology of the ocean basins.

The long cores of sediment, after years of study by experts, were to lead to a clearer understanding of the changing climates and living conditions of the Pleistocene Epoch during which mankind evolved. The amount of material collected from the depths was so large as to tax the capacities of the scientists and laboratories of any one nation. To expedite the recovery of new knowledge from the wealth of material, international cooperation was needed. Scientists from a dozen institutions in Europe and the United States came to Göteborg to get samples from the cores. Some studied the material in Göteborg; other specialists took the samples back to their own laboratories for analysis. In some cases the investigations still go on, and probably will continue as long as the material lasts. The Oceanographic Institute of Göteborg, which made the expedition possible and assured its success by careful planning and the improvisation of new methods and instruments, still serves as the center of an organization to supply specialists with samples and to coordinate and publish the results of analyses.

Gustaf Arrhenius (now with Scripps Institution of Oceanography), grandson of Svante Arrhenius, the discoverer of ionization and recipient of a Nobel Prize, was the geologist of the expedition. His monumental study of the mineralogical, chemical, and biological composition of cores from the Pacific was a major contribution to our knowledge of deep-sea sediments generally and to our understanding of conditions in the Pacific during the Pleistocene in particular.

Twenty-five years ago R. A. Daly, the Harvard geologist who first appealed to the theory of turbidity currents to explain the erosion of submarine canyons, wrote his book *The Floor of the Ocean* in which he stated that: "The major mysteries of land geology itself are planetary, and to a large extent their secrets lie hidden under the ocean. The learning of those secrets will mean a wide extension of the field of knowledge and therewith a new call on human courage." This was a prophetic statement. Collaboration between geologists and oceanographers, so happily brought about during the Swedish Deep-Sea Expedition, has greatly widened our knowledge of the ocean floor. And by its example it has stimulated subsequent exploration. Already the new knowledge of the geology of the ocean basins is strongly influencing our ideas about the origin and geological history of the continents.

Modern coring techniques have made it possible, with the piston corer, to raise cores about 25 meters (80 feet) long from the sediment carpet in the deep ocean. One of the most important results of this development was the discovery of the complete stratigraphical, chronological, and climatic record of the Pleistocene which will be described in the next chapter.

Improved techniques of drilling through the complete sediment carpet, by which an undisturbed record of the sediment layers may be obtained, are now being developed. Therefore, we should soon be able to solve many problems, such as for instance the fundamental one of the origin or differentiation of continents and ocean basins. This in turn involves the hypothesis of continental drift, the permanence of continents and ocean basins, the possibility of contraction or expansion of the earth, or even of alternating expansion and contraction. The apparent thinness of the layer of unconsolidated sediment under the floors of the oceans is another problem that will be solved by improved drilling techniques. As we have said, according to seismic measurements the thickness of unconsolidated sediment in the Atlantic Basin is not more than from 450 to 1,200 meters (1,500 to 4,000 feet) and from 200 to 600 meters (750 to 2,000 feet) in the Pacific. When calculations are made on the basis of rates of sediment accumulation, we find that the time represented by these layers of sediments is only about enough to go back to the beginning of the Cretaceous Period. Possible explanations come to mind; for example, that the ocean floors may have been flooded by great outpourings of lava. Or that some process of metamorphosis may have altered the physical properties of pre-Cretaceous sediments in such a way as to make them unrecognizable by seismic methods. One way to find out if, as the evidence indicates, an almost catastrophic reorganization of the major part of the surface of the earth took place fairly late in earth history is to drill with improved techniques through the whole thickness of sediment to the hard rock beneath.

Future explorations of the sediment layer will also bring more practical results. Whenever attention is turned to such practical results from deep-sea explorations, mineral resources at once come to mind. The high promise of this aspect of exploration of the sediment carpet has already, of course, been realised in part since important and lucrative oil production is now being found off the coasts of a growing number of countries. Among other minerals, diamonds are recovered along the coast of South Africa, tin is dredged from shallow waters off the Indonesian Archipelago, Japan mines iron from its coastal waters, and sulfur is recovered from beneath the Gulf of Mexico. However, all present exploitation of undersea mineral deposits is in relatively shallow water that is less than 400 feet (120 meters) in depth. There is no true deep-sea mining industry today. Recently researchers have seen indications of very large deposits of several kinds of useful minerals on the deep-sea bottom, some of which seem capable of supporting commercial mining operations. More and more in the future science and technology will turn to the sediments of the deep ocean to solve not only important scientific problems but also many practical problems, including the need for manganese, phosphorus, gold, platinum, tin, and a host of other minerals.

THE DEEP SEA

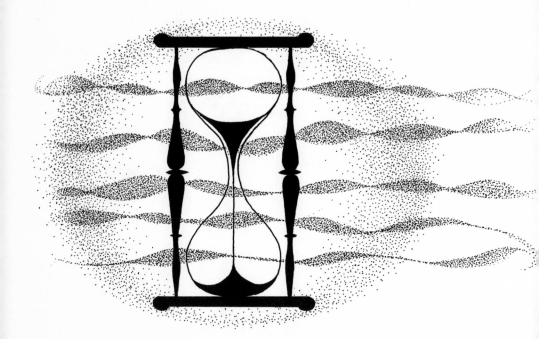

ND THE ICE AGES

THE PLEISTOCENE EPOCH, IN WHICH WE ARE LIVING, IS A CRE-
scendo in the grand opera of the earth. It is a time of emergent
continents, deep ocean basins, active volcanoes, and high mountains; a time of drastic climatic changes marked by repeated
spreading of great ice sheets over wide regions, and a time of
exceptionally rapid evolution of living things.

According to the record of the rocks, short intervals of extreme conditions have occurred before. Geologists call them *revolutions*. Some of the earlier revolutions have also been accompanied by the spread of ice sheets on the continents. This was
certainly true of a revolution in late Pre-Cambrian time before
the appearance of abundant and clear evidence of life 600 million
years ago.

Another time of glaciation occurred during the Permian Period, as a part of the revolution that marked the close of the
Paleozoic Era, the era of "ancient life."

Although fully convincing evidence of glaciation during the
revolution which brought to a close the Mesozoic Era, or era of
"medieval life," has not been uncovered yet, suggestive evidence
of glaciation at this time has led to much debate among geologists.

Perpetual change has ruled the earth's surface even during the
intervals of relative calm between revolutions, but the change
has always been repetitive or cyclical. The world of life has also
varied ceaselessly, but with the all-important difference that its
development has never been repetitive. During interludes between geological revolutions the development of living things
has steadily marched forward; during the brief revolutions it has

leaped ahead. At such moments of geological time major divisions of the animal kingdom have become extinct or have sunk to minor roles forever, their places being taken over for the first time by others better fitted to survive in a fiercely competitive world. For example, the geological processes that gave rise to the Rocky Mountains and thereby brought down the curtain on the Mesozoic Era were no different in kind from those that had raised the Appalachians some 270 million years earlier; but the disappearance of the great reptiles at the close of the Mesozoic and the surge into dominance of the warm-blooded mammals during the Cenozoic, or era of "recent life," were events unique in the history of our planet; survival by virtue of ponderousness gave way to survival through superior nervous coordination.

The Cenozoic Era, now culminating in the Pleistocene Revolution, has not yet brought forth much if anything in the way of mechanical innovations in the organic world; instead, the evolutionary advance has centered in that most extraordinary product of evolution, the brain, and its last moment, the short Pleistocene Epoch, has detonated an explosive development of the human brain in particular.

Has our revolution come to an end already? In the geological literature one often finds references to the "end" of the Pleistocene, supposed to have occurred about 11,000 years ago when the continental ice sheets melted. According to this view we now live in the Holocene, or "wholly recent" epoch, in contrast to the Pleistocene, or "most recent" epoch. At one time it was thought that the Pleistocene included only one long glaciation; had that been true, it would be reasonable to regard the retreat of the continental ice sheets as marking the end of the ice age. But we now know that a series of ice ages occurred during the Pleistocene and that they were separated by interglacials during which the world climate was sometimes even warmer than it is now. Admittedly, it is possible that we are now entering a new era, that there will be no more ice ages for millions of years to come; but the fact remains that there is no valid evidence that this is so. On the contrary, the traces of earlier epochs of refrigeration suggest that they lasted a good deal longer than the one and a half million years of our Pleistocene. We infer from this that we have not yet seen the last ice of our epoch.

The Pleistocene has been a battleground for scientists since it was named more than a hundred years ago. A reason for the great interest in and heated controversy over the Pleistocene is probably its close connection with the evolution of man. If the climatic and topographical changes of the Pleistocene had not occurred, it is doubtful whether *Homo sapiens* could have developed within the short span of one and a half million years. The rapidly changing conditions subjected to drastic selection the primate stock from which man sprang.

The relatively short Pleistocene has already brought greater changes to the face of the earth than has any earlier epoch of the previous 60 million years of the Cenozoic Era, the age of mammals. The continental ice sheets and valley glaciers have been powerful sculptors and modifiers of the land surface. All glaciated regions bear unmistakable signs of their work; over broad areas the old rocks were bared of soil and subsoil and were ground down by the moving ice into rounded, smoothed forms. The soil, the product of millions of years of weathering, or chemical decay, was removed from vast regions and piled up and concentrated in others, thus filling old valleys, diverting rivers from their courses, and creating lakes of great size by damming old outlets. Innumerable lakelets also filled depressions along the margins of the ice sheets and some remained after melting of the ice. At the same time mountain glaciers carved some of the most spectacular features of our present world: the Matterhorn, the Jungfrau, and other famous peaks in the Alps are examples. In our own country the Yosemite Valley and Glacier National Park are the work of Pleistocene glaciers.

Because of the nature of the depositional process, that is, alternating expansion and melting of the ice sheets, the deposits easily accessible to study left on the continents by the ice provide only a discontinuous record at best. Then the difficulty of interpreting the record is compounded by the fact that as each succeeding ice sheet spread over the land it tended to destroy the evidence left by earlier glaciations. Furthermore, the long interglacial ages are often represented by nothing more than a weathered or chemically altered zone, on the surface of glacial detritus left by a preceding ice sheet. As if this were not enough, in many regions the alternative to weathering has been total destruction of the record by erosion, the ceaseless washing away of unconsolidated sediment by rainfall, streams, and high winds which little by little transfer material from the continents to the ocean basins. Under exceptional circumstances where conditions have been favorable Pleistocene events are recorded by deposits of plant detritus, that is peat, or by sediments laid down in closed basins. But because of discontinuity and variability in the rate of accumulation of such deposits, their usefulness to students of Pleistocene chronology is limited to the range of the radiocarbon method of dating, which is not reliable further back in time than about 40,000 years.

Thus the record of the Pleistocene on the continents is like a tattered old book from which many pages or even whole chapters are missing. Because it is so nearly illegible, we turned to the sediments of the deep ocean basins, the universal, ancient archives where we hoped to find a continuous account of our epoch.

Beneath the oceans lie clues to many basic questions regarding the origin of not only the earth's dominant features, the continents and ocean basins, but also the evolution of life, and the climatic history and chronology of the Pleistocene. For millions of years a carpet of sediment has been accumulating on the ocean floor. This unconsolidated sediment covering the bedrock of the basins is much more than mere mud. To the geologist it tells a thrilling story of dramatic events in the history of the earth; the out-pourings of volcanoes, the waxing and waning of the ice sheets and mountain glaciers, the burning dryness of deserts, and the effects of floods and past climatic changes.

In deep water, that is at depths greater than 5,000 meters, the prevailing sediment consists very largely of finely divided clay. This smooth, slippery sediment with a large water content opposes little resistance to the coring tube, so that cores as much as 25 meters (about 80 feet) long can be taken. But such cores are more frustrating than useful; usually they contain few or no shells of foraminifera, or other organic remains. For our purpose they are blank pages. On the other hand, when they do contain enough shells to provide an intelligible record we find that the length of time represented is disappointingly short because of rapid accumulation of the sediment. At lesser depths where there is little clay, much calcium carbonate, and more compaction of the particles because of slow accumulation, sediments offer more resistance to the coring tube. In that kind of sediment we consider ourselves lucky if we recover a core 12 meters (40 feet) long; however, the time span represented by such a core is normally a good deal longer than that recorded by the much longer cores of clay, and with the additional advantage that the record of climatic changes is easily legible.

Maurice Ewing devised a new version of the piston corer which has an important advantage over earlier corers. Whereas the tubes of the Stetson and Kullenberg corers had been especially turned on lathes, like gun barrels, at great expense, the Ewing version uses commercial steel pipe, which is cheap and expendable.

Among the many activities aboard an oceanographic research ship, coring for deep-sea sediments is one of the most strenuous and yet most delicate tasks. The heavy winch amidships is especially designed for this job. The half-inch steel cable stretches from the winch across the deck to the A-frame—the A-shaped steel structure tilted out over the side of the ship from which the corer is lowered into the sea.

The corer is essentially a steel pipe up to 21 meters (70 feet) long, with a cutting edge at its lower end and a 1,500-pound mass of lead at the top. The whole apparatus hangs from a releasing device. The trigger arm off to the side holds the trigger weight on a separate cable. When the coring assembly reaches bottom, the trigger weight hits first and trips the release mechanism so that the corer drops freely. The massive core head plunges the pipe down through the sediments. Inside the pipe a piston held stationary by the taut lowering wire, puts the great water pressure at depth to work to overcome friction as the corer punches out a core. The layers of sediment trapped in the core pipe can now be drawn from the ocean floor to begin the long ascent to the ship far above (see Figure 36).

When the corer breaks the surface it is carefully hoisted to its cradle along the rail. The pipe is brought aboard in sections. A piston on a rod is fitted into the bottom of the pipe. The pipe is pulled over the rod and the piston pushes out the core of sediments. The core is sliced into sections and placed in trays to be carried off to the ship's laboratory where samples are taken for preliminary inspection with a microscope.

After preliminary microscopic examination the core sections are sealed in a protective wrapping. Out on deck they are carefully slipped into metal tubes, sealed again, and stowed in the ship's hold.

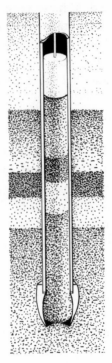

FIGURE 36   *A piston corer consists mainly of a metal tube and an internal piston. When the instrument hits the bottom, the piston stops, but the tube goes on into the sediment, enclosing a sample which is held by clasps at the tip of the tube.*

When cores taken by research vessels of Lamont Geological Observatory arrive back at the Lamont laboratory, we know from preliminary reports via radio and summary reports of shipboard examination which cores are of special interest and to these we give priority.

The core collection at Lamont has grown to over four thousand cores from all parts of the world's oceans. It is the largest collection in the world. These cores have been obtained during more than forty-five expeditions.

Each expedition has its highlights. We remember most vividly the times we went out on expeditions and obtained exceptional cores under difficult circumstances. And particularly the rough and windy days far out at sea in the equatorial Atlantic in 1951.

We had run into a gale that swept over the sea like a broom run wild. The *Atlantis*, the Woods Hole Oceanographic Institution research vessel which we from Lamont Geological Observatory had chartered, was hove to under trysail with the engine at rest. The single sail was too small to drive the *Atlantis* ahead; all it could do was reduce her roll, and it kept her headed more or less in the same direction in relation to the wind. It was useless to think of working on deck. Only the echo sounder kept up its endless routine.

In such weather, sounding by lowering a weight on the end of a hemp line or a piano wire would have been impossible. And yet all through the gale, while the *Atlantis* was rolling her lee rail under, the faithful echo sounder was sending down a "ping" every few seconds.

Off watch, one went below and listened to a monotonous music. There was the sound of the unknown heavy object that constantly rolled a short distance on the steel deck and fetched up with a hollow wooden thud; there was the clinking in unison of dozens of sample bottles, reinforced by a chorus of ticks, chirps, and squawks of mysterious origin, perhaps emanating from the fabric of the straining ship. Through this chaos of sound came a single note of order, the perfectly timed, high-pitched, fluty ping of the echo sounder. Behind a window on the instrument, a stylus on a rotating arm swept across a slowly moving strip of calibrated paper. At each arrival of an echo, a spark passed between the stylus and the specially treated paper, leaving a black mark to indicate the depth. As the closely spaced echoes came in, the black marks coalesced to form a continuous line rising and falling as the *Atlantis* passed over hills and valleys far below the keel. It seemed as if we were flying over an unknown planet hidden from view but outlined on a radar screen.

Up on deck we forgot about unknown planets; monstrous

hissing waves surged up and poured over the deck, adding their voices to that of the wind. When she was on the crest of a wave, the entire ship would vibrate with the force of the gale, and then make a sickening plunge into the trough, only to be wrenched up again like a lift and assaulted by the following mountain of water.

During normal weather, while we were busy testing, measuring, and studying particular aspects of the sea, we tended to lose sight of the whole. But during the gale the sea as an entity forced itself upon us, and the enforced leisure that it brought gave us a chance to see the beauty we normally missed. We could enjoy the dolphins (*Coryphaena hippurus*) sparkling in the waves, their long dorsal fins and backs a brilliant blue shading to silvery white below, with purple and gold reflections. On their heads and backs was a series of bright blue spots; the fins and tails were a dazzling yellow.

Now and then we saw flying fish as they glided alongside the ship. Breaking the surface of the water, they spread their wings, the greatly enlarged pectoral fins, and taxied ahead until they had speed enough for the glide. With their wings motionless while in the air, they looked like small model Spitfires.

Oddly enough, we found the closest intimacy with the life of the sea in our cabin, which was on the lee side and had a single large porthole. At one moment, as the ship rose on a wave, we could look out over the foam-crested waves; at the next, the ship would sink into a trough and roll to leeward. Then as the porthole plunged under, we looked deep into blue-green water. Looking into and not upon the surface of the water gave us a truly fish-eye view of the sea. It was fascinating to watch the bouquets and long garlands of drifting seaweed go by. When the ship surged ahead, these things passed in a blur, but when she was met by a particularly powerful wave, she would come to a standstill, and then we would find ourselves face to face with some big-eyed fish peering out from a bushy frond of weed, or it might be a weird shrimplike creature with eyes on long stalks. Once the many tentacles of a Portuguese man-of-war came into sight. Looking up, we saw the underside of the translucent gas-filled float, glowing pinkish blue in the light from above. We imagined how it would feel to be a little fish caught in the stinging tentacles.

Also across the porthole flowed an endless stream of plankton
—those organisms, mostly small, which cannot swim at all or else
swim so feebly as to be entirely at the mercy of winds and currents. In shape and color these particles of life were infinitely
varied; many were blue, blue-green, or yellowish-green; others
were silvery, deep crimson, or purple. Shapes varied from the
umbrellalike jellyfish to the bizarrely shaped larvae of all sorts of
crustacea.

But it was particularly at night that the plankton appeared in
full glory. What fireworks they displayed then as they glowed,
pulsated, and flashed with yellow, red, blue, and white light. In
some the light was diffused; in others it was emitted by lantern-
like organs with lens and reflector, which threw powerful and
directed beams. A few of the larger forms could eject clouds of
luminous substance to confuse their enemies. Others used their
lights to aid them in catching food; not by lighting it up, but by
setting themselves aglow and acting as a lure. The ability to emit
light, known as bioluminescence, is shared by members of most of
the major animal groups that live in the oceans, from microscopic
single-celled forms to the highly developed vertebrates.

After the storm had calmed down, we ranged over many
square miles of sea and watched the wire meter on the winch tick
off thousands of feet of wire in our attempts to obtain cores.
Sometimes hours of hard work would go for naught when a bent
and twisted coring pipe containing no core was hauled up, or
when we stowed below samples of sediment of no more than
average interest.

Once more we prepared the coring instrument for lowering
and sent it down to the bottom of the sea. When it came back to
the surface we discovered that the pipe was broken off about 10
feet from the top. However, the part that was broken off was not
lost; it was hanging on the wire attached to the piston, which,
fortunately, had caught in the upper part of the broken section
where the wall of the pipe had been squeezed together a little
before breaking. It looked as though the piston would slide
through at any moment. This was alarming; we didn't want to
lose the 30-foot long core the broken section probably contained.

We reached down to haul it up but the coating of mud outside
the pipe made it impossible to lift. Captain Adrian Lane came

over to help, but even the three of us could not lift it near enough to the railing.

"Get us a line," Captain Lane called.

The great weight of the pipe told us that it must be full of sediment. This made us double our effort to hold it. Yet it slid slowly through our hands into the water. One of the seamen came running with a line. The captain reached far over the railing and took a hitch around the coring pipe. We all grabbed the line and heaved away at it, but the line came off the slippery pipe and we all went sprawling on deck.

"We'll have to get a longer line and make it fast below the coupling," said the skipper.

The coupling was about 10 feet below the break. When Captain Lane tried to fasten the line below the coupling, he found that it was beyond his reach. In the meantime, we held onto the end of the coring pipe as best we could.

"Grab my legs and I'll hang over the side. I think I can reach it then," the skipper ordered.

A couple of seamen took hold of his legs while he tried to reach below the coupling. Still it was beyond his grasp.

Again we tried to get it up by brute force, but regardless of how we knotted the line or how tightly we gripped the pipe, it evaded us like an eel.

"Hold my feet," called the captain. So down he went until only his feet were above the gunwale. After several dousings, he succeeded in making the line fast below the coupling.

At last the pipe lay safely on deck and we extruded the core.

A preliminary examination of the core gave us the impression that it was the best we had yet obtained in our efforts to discover the complete climatic history of the Pleistocene. It was just over 32 feet long and consisted throughout of sediment with an abundance of shells of foraminifera. How long a time the sediment in the core represented or how many zones of foraminifera recording climatic changes it included we had no way of knowing until we could give it a thorough investigation in the laboratory.

Examinations of cores on shipboard are never really satisfactory. Cores of ocean sediment are always coated on the outside by smeared sediment, which completely hides the nature of the real core. One can scrape off the smear to some extent, but it is not possible to do so thoroughly enough to reveal all the important details. The only way to do this is to slice the core longitudinally through the center. This is never done on board, because it is impossible to bring the halves back into their original relationship, and to wrap and store the halves separately is to risk serious damage and contamination to the sediment.

At our laboratory at Lamont Geological Observatory the cores are split and carefully measured and marked every 10 centimeters (about 4 inches). This will enable us to know its original dimensions even after it dries and shrinks. Samples are taken at each 10-centimeter interval—so we are not likely to miss an important layer. These samples, carefully labeled, will give us a survey of the entire core. Whatever we find in any one core can be compared with findings in other cores sampled in the same way.

The core samples at this stage consist mostly of a composite of mineral and organic particles of various sizes. To separate the larger particles which we will study, we wash the sample on a .074 millimeter sieve. The residue, called the *coarse fraction*, now consists mostly of the shells of foraminifera which sometimes compose as much as 95 per cent of deep-sea sediments.

After the coarse fractions of the samples have been dried, they are ready for study of the microfossils under a binocular microscope.

At last the day came when with intense interest we studied the microfossils in the core which from shipboard examination had promised to be the best we had yet obtained in our efforts to discover the complete record of the Pleistocene. We found more zones defined by variations in abundance of temperature-sensitive foraminifera than we had ever found before. This was the first core in which we found evidence of more than one ice age. From the chronology of the upper part of the core as determined by radiocarbon dating, we could extrapolate downward and estimate a time scale for an important part of the Pleistocene. This estimate indicated that we had in our hands a record of climatic events spanning the last 450,000 years. Never before in our efforts to decipher the record of Pleistocene climatic changes had we found a core that reached so far back in time.

In order to obtain evidence of past climates and other environmental conditions, the scientist must think of fossils as organisms that were once alive and had specialized adaptations to their particular surroundings. Having learned what kind of environmental conditions are most favorable to still-living near relatives he can attempt to reconstruct the ancient environment. As can be expected, the method becomes less reliable as the evolutionary gap between the fossils and the living organisms increases. A paleontologist must first learn to be a good detective, finding meaning in all sorts of seemingly trivial and irrelevant observations.

To the uninitiated, washed coarse fractions of deep-sea sediments look very much like ordinary beach sand. Except for the fact that the sizes of the particles fall within the size range of sand, the material is very different from the kind of sand that has made some beaches famous. But to appreciate this, one must look at the coarse fractions with a microscope. Then one enters a new world. At a magnification of 30 diameters, the particles of mere "sand" undergo an astonishing change into the chambered shells of foraminifera (see Figure 37).

When one looks at samples of foraminifera with a microscope for the first time, the normal reaction is an exclamation of surprise and pleasure. There is something about the proportions of the chambers, the pattern of their arrangements, and the surface texture of these little shells that appeals to most people.

Studies by W. Schott, J. A. Cushman and L. G. Henbest, F. B. Phleger, C. D. Ovey, F. L. Parker, J. D. H. Wiseman, and others, of the planktonic foraminifera in ocean sediment cores have shown that there is a variation, from level to level, in the relative abundances of the species that are sensitive to temperature. It is agreed by these investigators that the variations record shifts in the geographical ranges of the species and that these shifts were a consequence of climatic changes.

In deciphering the deep-sea record of climatic changes by studying foraminifera in sediment cores, we follow the principle that the present is the key to the past. Our first question, then, concerns the present. How are the common planktonic species distributed in the oceans today? Living foraminifera have been collected in various parts of the oceans, and we have a fairly good general picture of the geographical distribution of most of the species. We know from these data that no species of planktonic foraminifera is completely cosmopolitan and that some species are rather severely limited in distribution. In general, the boundaries of the geographical ranges of the species trend east and west, an indication that temperature is a condition of importance in limiting their ranges.

Since the *Challenger* oceanographic expedition of 1872, many samples of sediment have been raised from the floors of the oceans, particularly from the North Atlantic. For the most part, these samples have been taken close to the surface of the sedi-

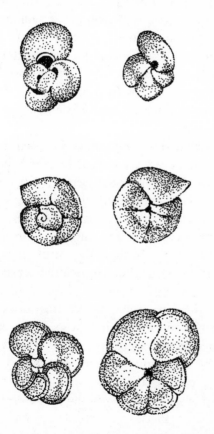

FIGURE 37   *Species of common North Atlantic planktonic foraminifera:* (*upper*) Globigerinoides sacculifera; (*middle*) Globorotalia truncatulinoides; (*lower*) Globorotalia menardii.

ment, or at most only a few inches below the surface. Various investigators have studied the planktonic foraminifera in the samples, and from their data have emerged patterns of the areal distribution of the eighteen most common species now living in the Atlantic. The studies show that water temperature is an important condition controlling the geographical distribution of the species. This is of primary importance in our attempt to decipher the record of past climatic changes. Evidently, some species of planktonic foraminifera are sensitive to temperature and their geographical distributions are limited accordingly.

One soon learns to recognize the various species by the distinctive textures of the shells, the number of chambers, and their shape and arrangement. Then by counting the shells of different temperature-sensitive species in samples of sediment from various depths in a core we can estimate what the climate was like when the layers of sediment accumulated on the sea floor. For example, the relatively large form called *Globorotalia menardii* is abundant today only where the upper layer of water is fairly warm; the population of this species is most abundant by far in tropical waters.

As we go back in time examining the foraminifera in deeper and deeper layers in a core, we come to one in which *Globorotalia menardii* is rare or absent, its place being taken by smaller species which we recognize as living only in northern waters today; we conclude that this layer was deposited at a time of cold climate when ice sheets covered Canada and the northern part of the United States. As we go through the entire core layer by layer noting the abundances of the temperature-sensitive species and plotting the data on a graph, a record of the climatic history of the Pleistocene unfolds before our eyes. We can discern the advances and recessions of the continental ice sheets in the changing populations of these microscopic shells.

Examining the foraminifera more closely we note that, like snail shells, some coil to the right and others to the left. For example, more than 95 per cent of the shells of the species *Globorotalia menardii* in Pleistocene sediments coil to the left. In *Globorotalia truncatulinoides*, in contrast, the ratio of right- to left-coiling shells varies from level to level in the cores (see Figure 38). These ratios plotted on coordinate paper provide us with another indicator of changing conditions as a check on variations in abundance of other species.

As we studied more cores from widely scattered points in the Atlantic, we found that the vertical sequence of changes was repeated from core to core. To us this meant that the changes in living conditions to which the populations of foraminifera reacted must have taken place on an ocean-wide scale. Only such fluctuations of temperature as must have accompanied the growth and shrinkage of the continental ice sheets could account for these

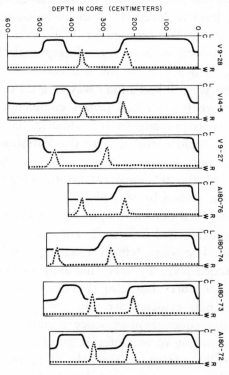

FIGURE 38 *Changes in the coiling direction (dotted lines) of* Globorotalia truncatulinoides *along the length of the cores make it possible to correlate precisely defined levels in cores from different locations. The scale of coiling is 100 per cent left at the left margin of each column to 100 per cent right at the right margin. The solid lines are climate curves based on relative numbers of (C) cold-water and warm-water (W) species of planktonic foraminifera. The distance between core V9-28 and core A180-72 is about 1,300 kilometers, or 700 nautical miles.*

widespread reactions on the part of the foraminifera. Here, then, was a way to trace the sequence of climatic events of the Pleistocene and to estimate their timing.

In our search for the complete record of the Pleistocene we eventually found a core that spanned the last 600,000 years. This core had been raised at a point in the equatorial Atlantic, 3° 13′ South latitude and 32° 12′ West longitude, from a depth of 4120 meters (13,500 feet). It was about 12 meters or 40 feet long and consisted of calcareous clay with an abundance of shells of planktonic foraminifera.

According to our interpretation of the changes in numbers of the shells from level to level, this core included sediment layers deposited during the last ice age or Wisconsin, the preceding time of warm climate or Sangamon Interglacial, the earlier Illinoian Ice Age, and a part of the still earlier Yarmouth Interglacial. However, we still had a long way to go. For one thing, no other core that we had studied passed completely through the sediment layer corresponding to the Illinoian Ice Age and into sediment that we could correlate with the Yarmouth Interglacial. Without another core for comparison, we could not be sure that the lower part of the sequence was really continuous, that is without a gap due to loss by slumping.

We now redoubled our efforts and before long had found six more cores which reached below the zone corresponding to the Illinoian Ice Age. The zones defined by changes in foraminifera in these cores matched layer by layer not only the upper zones of hundreds of other cores but also the newly discovered lower zones. With this new evidence we now felt certain of the continuity of these long sequences of evidence of climatic change.

However, according to our interpretation of the record in the cores we were still far from our goal, the discovery of a complete record of the Pleistocene. We needed to find cores in which the complete Yarmouth Interglacial, the Kansan Glaciation, the Aftonian Interglacial, and the Nebraskan Glaciation were represented, and most important, we needed to find the boundary between the Pleistocene and the Pliocene epochs.

The discovery of a well-defined basal boundary of the Pleistocene was both literally and figuratively basic to the problem of determining the duration of the Pleistocene. At that time, we had no assurance that a clearly defined boundary existed. As we have explained, the record of climatic events on the continents becomes more and more obscure as one tries to trace it farther back in time. This is a natural consequence of the destructive effect of later glaciations. Before finding the boundary in the cores, we had no way of knowing that the change from the nonglacial conditions of the Pliocene to the glacial climates of the Pleistocene had not involved a long series of small, almost imperceptible gradations. In fact, the concept of a thoroughly indefinite transition between the epochs was rather popular among students of the Pleistocene. But as it turned out, the clear definition of the boundary brought the problem of the duration of Pleistocene into clear focus; we now had an excellent level of reference to define the beginning of the new chronology of the Pleistocene.

In 1951 we found the first evidence of the Pliocene-Pleistocene boundary in a single core from the Blake Plateau, a great platform extending from the Bahama Islands to Cape Hatteras. The evidence was in the form of an abrupt and rather drastic change in the foraminifera at a certain level in an otherwise rather uniform core. One particularly striking change was the reversal in the direction of coiling of *Globorotalia menardii*. In all Pleistocene samples that we had ever seen the shells of this species coiled to the left, but here below the faunal change 95 per cent of the shells coiled to the right. But with nothing more to go on than this one core we could not rule out the possibility that the faunal change recorded merely a depositional hiatus, that is, the loss of some unknown thickness of sediment by slumping, in which case it would have little interest for us. On the other hand, if sediment accumulation had been continuous across the faunal change, it represented what must have been an extraordinary change in living conditions, in which case it would be of the greatest interest to us because of its biological and climatological implications.

Admittedly, there was circumstantial evidence for discontinuity because of slumping. The overlying Pleistocene section was far too thin. Some part, probably no less than 18 meters (60 feet) of sediment, must have been removed by slumping; otherwise the coring tube could not have reached the older sediment below the faunal change. But if slumping had taken place during the late Pleistocene, why should it not have occurred earlier as well, in short, at the level of the faunal change? After all, we had seen many cores that contained sharply defined discontinuities with Pleistocene sediment resting directly on Miocene or older sediments.

At the same time, there was something different about this core. In all others there had been a sharply defined change in nature of the sediment at the faunal change, such as a difference in color or in degree of compaction. Furthermore, in the other cores the faunal changes in themselves were enough to prove the presence of a break in the continuity of the sedimentary record; from the microfossils below the changes we could tell with certainty that whole epochs of time were missing. In this core from the Blake Plateau, the microfossils below the change indicated a pre-Pleistocene age, but it was also clear that they were of very late pre-Pleistocene age, and possibly belonged in the latest Pliocene.

At that time, however, we were not in a receptive state of mind. The evidence was suggestive, but we wanted something better than that. For years we had expected a gradual and subtle change in the foraminifera at the boundary between Pliocene and Pleistocene sediments. Not really satisfied one way or the other, we left the core and proceeded with the general study of the sediments.

Years went by. Then one day in 1962 we found more important evidence in a core from the equatorial Atlantic. Here again was the abrupt reversal in the direction of coiling of *Globorotalia menardii*, but more exciting still, we found two additional changes at the same level in the core. One was the absence of *Globortalia truncatulinoides* below the level, although it was abundant above. The other was the presence of abundant *discoasters*, calcareous star-shaped objects much smaller than foraminifera, below the faunal boundary but not above. Discoasters (see Figure 39) are so small that they pass through the sieve which we use to concentrate the shells of the foraminifera; to detect their presence one must smear a little of the fine fraction of the sediment on a glass slide and examine it at a magnification of 1,000 diameters. We had found discoasters frequently in pre-Pleistocene sediments wherever slumping of overlying layers had uncovered them, but we had never found them in sediments of undoubted Pleistocene age except where we had good reason to suppose that the discoasters had been washed out of older sediments and redeposited. For example, layers deposited by turbidity currents sometimes contained them. From our own observations and those of other paleontologists studying ancient marine sediments on the continents, we knew that the discoasters

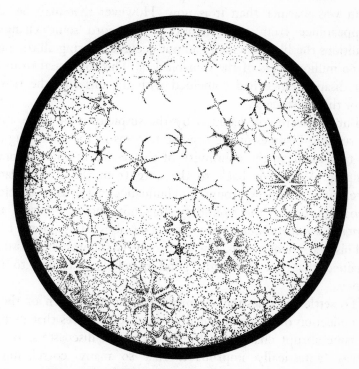

FIGURE 39 *Discoasters. The organisms that secreted these guide fossils became extinct at the onset of the Pleistocene. The discovery of discoaster evolution in the Pliocene was a key in identifying the onset of the first ice age.*

first appeared at about the beginning of the age of mammals, the Cenozoic Era. Then after having swarmed in the Atlantic in astronomical numbers for about 60 million years, the organisms that secreted the tiny stars departed from the waters of the Atlantic, Pacific, and Indian oceans. We thought that they had become entirely extinct, but A. S. Bursa of the Arctic Unit of the Fisheries Board of Canada has found single-celled organism in material from the under surface of the ice in the inshore waters of Devon Island (in the Canadian Arctic Archipelago) which secrete discoasters. Why these organisms should have taken refuge from the conditions of the Pleistocene in the ice-ridden waters of the Arctic Region is a mystery, because if there is anything about their past of which we can be quite sure, it is that they reached their climax of abundance in equatorial waters when the world's ocean was warmer than it is now. However that may be, their disappearance from the Atlantic must record some change in conditions the like of which had not occurred during all the previous 60 million years of the Cenzoic Era. This suggested to us that their disappearance had coincided with the onset of the first ice age of the Pleistocene.

But we were still haunted by the suspicion that these abrupt and striking changes in the organic remains in the cores might be due to a break in the continuity of the record in consequence of slumping. We went back to the core from the Blake Plateau; there, sure enough, we found an abundance of the same species of discoasters below the boundary but not above, whereas *Globorotalia truncatulinoides* was abundant above but absent below it. This was encouraging, but with only two cores the possibility remained that the seemingly good matching was due to mere chance.

To settle the question we made a thorough search of the entire collection of cores and finally found seven cores that included the same abrupt changes in foraminifera and discoasters. Because it was fantastically improbable that so many correlating sequences could be due to chance, we now felt sure that we really had found evidence of the onset of the first ice age, the climatic event which marked the beginning of the Pleistocene Epoch.

An important by-product of the discovery of the lower boundary of the Pleistocene is the evidence it gives us regarding the nature of the climatic change that initiated the Pleistocene. Evidently, there was no transition period of long duration, geologically speaking, between the Pliocene and Pleistocene epochs. From the nature of the sediment at the boundary, we estimate that this thickness represents a time interval of no more than about 5,000 years. As we have pointed out earlier, the Pleistocene is the great backdrop of time for man. When the curtain rose on the drama of man's evolution, it rose with a bang.

Now it was a question of closing the gap (see Figure 40). Our record of the Pleistocene extended from the present through postglacial time back into the latter part of the second inter-glacial age, the Yarmouth. In addition, we had discovered the

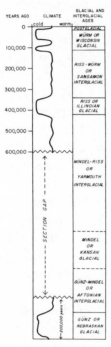

FIGURE 40   *The "gap" in the deep-sea record of the Pleistocene.*

lower boundary of the Pleistocene—the record of the first ice age, the Nebraskan, and the lower part of the first interglacial age, the Aftonian. The combined thickness of sediment in the cores that contained this record added up to about 21 meters (70 feet). On the assumption that this thickness of sediment had accumulated at about the same rate as similar late Pleistocene sediment layers which had been dated by the radiocarbon method, we estimated that the combined thickness represented some 800,000 years. This time interval for only part of the Pleistocene was in itself startling because it was in sharp contrast with the most widely accepted dates for the beginning of the first ice age, which ranged from 300,000 to about 600,000 years ago. The missing section of the record according to our interpretation included a large part of the second interglacial, the Yarmouth, all of the second ice age, the Kansan, and part of the first interglacial age, the Aftonian. How thick the missing section of sediment might be or how long a time interval it would represent, we did not know. Nor had we any idea of how it might look. Furthermore, we could not be sure that we had any cores that contained a record of the gap in time. Since the complete Pleistocene section would be thicker than 21 meters (70 feet) and the longest cores that could be obtained of the type we needed were only about 15 meters (50 feet) long, we knew that we would not discover the complete Pleistocene in any single core. We were also sure that when we found cores containing the missing section, we would be able to fit them into the sequence by correlating the parts of these cores that overlapped with the record we had.

What we planned to do, if we could find suitable cores, was to borrow a trick from the dendrochronologists, who piece together records of past climates based on the studies of tree rings from many trees, each older than the preceding one (see Figure 41). Thus they build up a composite record that goes much farther back in time than the lifetime of any single tree. This is possible because distinctive sequences of thin and thick tree rings can be recognized in trees of about the same age in the same general region. When such a distinctive sequence of several rings near the center of a living tree can be correlated with or matched by the same sequence in the outer part of a tree trunk used to hold up the roof, for example, of an Indian Pueblo, it becomes possible to push the record back beyond that of the oldest living tree. But near the center of the tree trunk from the pueblo is another distinctive group of rings than can be correlated with a corresponding group in a log from a still older pueblo, and so on, as long as the dendrochronologist can find older and older logs. In spite of the fact that this tree-ring method of measuring time of past climatic changes does not reach even the end of the last ice age about 11,000 years ago, it provides important information for the study of past climates. In a way, the layers of sediment on the ocean floor are not unlike the growth rings of a tree. In correlating the layers of sediment from core to core, however, we do not need to rely upon matching thin and thick layers. The method we use depends on correlating zones of distinctive groups of foraminifera from core to core.

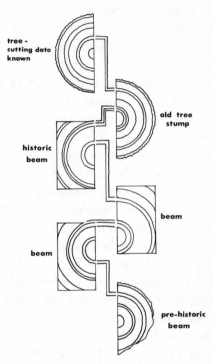

tree-cutting date known

old tree stump

historic beam

beam

beam

pre-historic beam

FIGURE 41 *Schematic drawings of a series of tree sections, illustrating cross dating, and how a chronological sequence is built up connecting prehistoric timber with modern trees.*

Statistically, the probability of finding the complete record of the Pleistocene now seemed quite good. We had at our disposal at the Lamont Geological Observatory by far the largest collection of deep-sea cores in the world. At that time, in 1963, it included more than three thousand and more were constantly being added. We had another great advantage over other scientists who were searching for a complete record of the Pleistocene; we had already studied more deep-sea cores than anyone else. From the start of the investigation in 1947, we had held fast to the principle that every one of the cores should be given some attention. We did not study a few cores in great detail, to the complete neglect of the rest. Rather, we had accumulated a voluminous mass of data from the three thousand cores.

In our search we went through the old data that had built up in more than one hundred notebooks; we re-examined the foraminifera in exceptionally long cores; we studied new cores and eventually, in 1964, we found the missing link. The gap had finally been closed.

Our record of the Pleistocene is the result of piecing together correlating and overlapping sections of twenty-six cores ranging in length from 5.5 meters (18 feet) to 21.9 meters (72 feet). They came from various places in the Atlantic extending from 4° West to 79° West and from 28° South to 28° North latitude. The depths of water from which the cores were taken varied from 970 meters (3,180 feet) to 4,885 meters (16,000 feet).

We had now before us the complete record of the Pleistocene, the epoch of the earth's history in which occurred that momentous step in organic evolution, the emergence of man. We had an absolute time scale from the present back to about 175,000 years ago, established by means of the radiocarbon, protactinium-ionium, and protactinium-231 methods of dating. The ages of various levels in the cores determined show that the sediments of the 26 cores accumulated at the average rate of nearly 2.5 centimeters or 1 inch in 1,000 years. The total thickness of the composite Pleistocene section is about 38 meters or 125 feet. On the basis of the average rate of accumulation and the thickness of the whole section, by extrapolation beyond 175,000 years, we established a new time scale for the climatic events of the Pleistocene Epoch. According to our estimate the Pleistocene began about one and a half million years ago.

Since publication together with Maurice Ewing of the result of our investigations in *Science* in 1964, Teh-Lung Ku and W. S. Broecker of Columbia University and Lamont Geological Observatory have dated by thorium-230 measurements a series of four samples from core V12–122 from the Caribbean, one of the twenty-six cores of our composite section. In addition to checking the reliability of the other methods of dating, they succeeded in pushing back the range of absolute dating to the level corresponding to the end of the Illinoian Ice Age and the beginning of the Sangamon Interglacial, which they determined to be 320,000 ±32,000 years old, in good agreement with our age of 340,000 years estimated from the rate of sediment accumulation as determined by radiocarbon dating of sediment layers near the top of the core. As we had concluded from other evidence, the rate of accumulation indeed remained essentially constant during the last several hundred thousand years.

In the meantime geochemists are trying out methods of dating Pleistocene deposits on the continents. Ratios of thorium-230 to uranium-234 in samples from the Key Largo Limestone and the Miami Oolite of Florida indicate that the ages of these deposits vary from 112,000 ±10,000 to 215,000 ±35,000 years before the present. For many years geologists have assigned these rocks to the Sangamon Interglacial Age when sea level was some 10 meters higher than it is now. A sample of coral collected by Norman D. Newell of Columbia University was dated in 1965 by W. S. Broecker and D. Thurber of Lamont Geological Observatory by measuring uranium, thorium, and radium ratios; the age, 80,000 years, puts it in the warm interstadial of the last ice age, when sea level appears to have been about 3 meters higher than at present.

From Europe we hear some discordant notes. In late Pleistocene time a shallow sea, the Eemian, flooded parts of the Netherlands, Denmark, and the southern Baltic region. By the radiocarbon method a sample of peat from the series of sediments overlying the marine Eemian beds was found to be 64,000 ±1,100 years old. To make any measurement at all on a sample so old, it was necessary to enrich it isotopically. As a *tour de force* in the technique of geochemistry this was admirable. But one wonders; was the minute amount of radiocarbon so detected introduced by percolating ground water long after accumulation of the peat? Furthermore, even if the age of the peat is valid, the marine Eemian itself remains undated. In spite of these uncertainties prevalent opinion holds that the Eemian Interglacial, presumably equivalent to the Sangamon Interglacial of America, ended about 70,000 years ago. We submit that the Eemian deposits may be the time equivalent of a zone (which we have correlated with the last ice age interstadial) of the deep-sea sediment sequence, though there is no proof of this by radiocarbon or any other method of dating.

Then there is the Jüngere Hauptterrasse of the Rhine, considered by most geologists to date from the Mindel Glaciation. Potassium-argon ages of samples of volcanic debris in the terrace fall between 354,000 and 370,000 years.

Another point of interest is the Donau Glaciation or glaciations of Europe, which apparently preceded the so-called "first ice age" or Günz. It is remarkable that no evidence of glaciation antedating the Nebraskan, supposedly equivalent to the Günz, has ever been found in America. The Donau deposits have not been dated by a radiometric method. We mention them here because they, together with the above radiometric ages, suggest that the accepted transatlantic correlation of climatic events may be in error.

A firm intercontinental correlation must await really firm dating of the various deposits. However, the admittedly infirm beginning, taken at face value, suggests that the accepted interpretation of the march of climatic events in Europe maybe out of step with that of America. The supposedly interglacial time of the Eemian Sea may have been really contemporaneous with the warm interstadial of the last ice age represented by the coral collected by Newell, the Mindel Ice Age with the American Illinoian, and so on. Very likely it is wrong; we rather hope it is, but if so, then some of the above-cited radiometric ages must be spurious.

The Pleistocene is familiar to most people as the great ice age, the epoch of cavemen and wooly mammoths and huge continental ice sheets covering much of northern Europe and North America. Actually, as is illustrated in Figure 42, the records show that it was divided into four successive major glaciations separated by long intervals of temperate climate.

During these long periods of oscillating climate it is generally believed that *Homo sapiens*, modern man, evolved from an earlier species and took the first primitive steps toward culture and civilization. The stresses of changing climate and changing environment almost certainly helped shape the course of man's evolution. Survival required intelligence and agility. The environmental vicissitudes of the Pleistocene stacked the cards in favor of the individual best endowed with those qualities.

Previous estimates of the duration of the Pleistocene have ranged from 300,000 to about one million years. From the example of species whose evolution has been traced in detail, these estimates have seemed improbably short to encompass all the sum of small changes that must have gone into the making of *Homo sapiens* from his ancestral species of the earlier period. Our recently discovered new chronology of one and a half million years

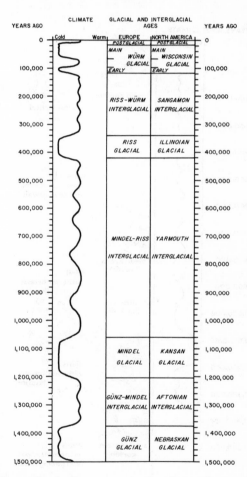

FIGURE 42   *Generalized climate curve based on the study of deep-sea cores, correlated with Pleistocene time scale. In this book, the Pleistocene is considered to begin with the onset of the first glaciation, the Nebraskan, or Günz.*

for the Pleistocene stretches out the span of the evolution of man
and allows time for the slow accumulation of small changes
which Darwin assumed to be the basis of evolution.

Our chronology provides a time scale against which to study
the rate of biological and geological development of the Pleistocene, and it supplies anthropologists with a dated context in
which to place the emerging races and cultures of man and his
primitive predecessors. Figure 43 illustrates the occurrence of the
remains of some early men and their antecedents in the sequence

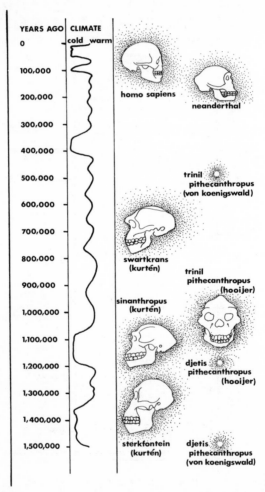

FIGURE 43   *Illustration of the human and prehuman skulls in the sequence
of glacial and interglacial stages of the Pleistocene according to the authors' time scale.*

of glacial and interglacial stages of the Pleistocene according to our time scale.

The study of deep-sea sediments has been fruitful. The first complete record of the Pleistocene is probably the most important outcome of our study of the three thousand cores obtained during forty-four expeditions over the period 1947–64.

In the sedimentary layers that are the product of the slow but constant rain of particles to the floor of the ocean lies a complete history of at least the age of mammals, and perhaps much more than that. More cores, which are being gathered daily, will yield more data, and will take us back in time many millions of years. The development of new coring techniques and methods of drilling at sea will give us sedimentary sections beyond our present reach.

The sampling and interpretation of the complete sedimentary record that will become available on the floor of the ocean is one of the most promising and exciting subjects for scientific study. Here the geologist, biologist, geophysicist, and astronomer will find a record of the evolution of life itself.

THE CRUST BENEATH

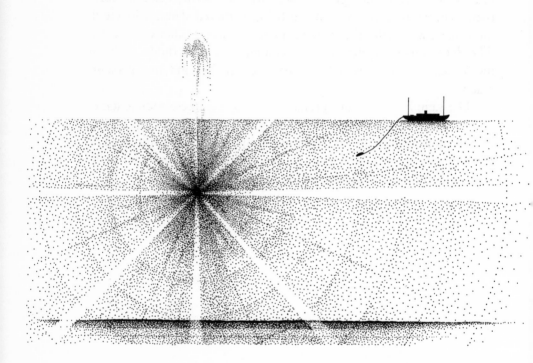

CHAPTER 8

THE OCEAN BOTTOM

ALMOST THE ONLY PART OF THE SEA BOTTOM DIRECTLY ACCESSIBLE
to the sampling devices of the marine geologist is the upper
couple of dozen meters (about 80 feet) of sediment. Somewhere
beneath the sediment we know there must be hard rock, a basement whose time of origin antedates the sediments. The depth at
which the basement lies, its relief, whether smooth or mountainous; its nature, whether composed of frozen lava or thoroughly
altered sediments; its thickness; whether it is at all similar to the
crust beneath the continents—all are questions of profound interest to geologists. The answers can tell us much about the origin of
our planet, its liquid core, mantle of dense rock, the crustal layer,
and its broad features. Within the last few years the intensity of
interest has reached such a pitch that firm plans to drill a series of
holes in the deep ocean basins in an attempt to reach the mantle
rock beneath the oceanic crust have been made. From preliminary tests in the Pacific near Guadalupe Island, a couple of hundred miles southwest of San Diego, California, much was learned
about the great difficulty of drilling in deep water, but little about
the deep structure of oceanic basins. The deepest hole reached
only a few hundred meters. It ended in relatively young volcanic
rock, which was not surprising; the nearby island, Guadalupe, is
volcanic. Before the geologist's questions will be answered in this
way improvements in the technique of drilling at sea will have to
be made; this will take several years at least.

Because scientists are an impatient lot, they have not sat back
to wait for the drillers, but have resorted to various means of
exploring by indirection. During the past twenty years they have
found partial answers, suggesting evidence and hints of what lies

below the sediment carpet by means of sound waves and measurements of gravity and heat flow. An unexpected outcome is the evidence of life in the ocean basins. They are full of geological activity while the continents are, and apparently have been, relatively passive.

The seismic method or use of sound waves to probe the deep rock layers has been by far the most useful tool of geonomists, or geo-scientists. It depends basically upon the measurement of the time of travel of sound waves generated by an explosion, or some mechanical substitute, through the various layers of the earth's crust.

The pioneer in seismic measurements at sea is Maurice Ewing of Lamont Geological Observatory. Under Ewing's leadership, a long series of oceanographic expeditions sent out from Lamont has made more seismic measurements than any other oceanographic institution in the world.

Maurice Ewing established himself as one of the world's outstanding leaders in geophysical and geological research early in life. The big, powerful Texan farm boy worked his way through Rice Institute at Houston, receiving three degrees including a Ph.D. in physics in 1931. He made his first acquaintance with the sea when he took a summer job firing charges of blasting gelatin from a whaleboat off the Gulf Coast for a company that was prospecting for petroleum. From the way the sound waves from the blasts were reflected and refracted by the layers of rock under the sea floor the geophysicists in charge of the work could learn much about the subsurface structure. Ever since then Ewing had been interested in the sediments and the earth's crust beneath the ocean bottom. Ewing had first made his name known by applying sound waves generated by dynamite blasts to the study of sediment layers and hard rock basement. This work was done over the shelf of the east coast of the United States while he was teaching physics at Lehigh University between 1930 and 1943. The completion of his investigation marked an important advance in the earth sciences. But the study had another side which was less well appreciated. The project was carried out at a time when financial support for pure science was difficult to find. Most of the instruments needed to record the sound waves reflected from the deep layers of rock Ewing and a few of his students had to build with whatever odds and ends they could lay their hands on, some of which were literally junk. Then because of Ewing's teaching load at Lehigh he could carry on his investigation only during weekends and holidays. Often after a strenuous Sunday in the field with one or two of his student assistants he would get back to the university on Monday morning only just on time to give his first lecture to his class in physics. When it was all done everyone acknowledged the importance of his contribution to science, but few were aware of the heroic effort behind the contribution.

Necessarily Ewing's cross sections of the shelf area based on his seismic study ended at the coast. This left a nagging question unanswered; what did the rock layers do at the edge of the continental shelf which lay some miles beyond the coast line and below some hundreds of feet of water? This question was basic to an understanding of the global architecture of the earth; it involved the distinction between the ocean basins and the continents. Small wonder then that Ewing came to be a seagoing geophysicist and geologist.

In 1940 Ewing foresaw the importance of underwater sound in submarine warfare. Accordingly he took leave of absence from Lehigh and went to the Woods Hole Oceanographic Institution. In 1941 he and his former student, J. L. Worzel, got a grant from the Bureau of Ships of the Navy Department for the study of underwater sound transmission. Out of this study came Ewing's discovery of SOFAR, short for "Sound Fixing and Ranging." SOFAR depends upon the fact that at a certain depth in the oceans, roughly between 600 meters and 1,200 meters (2,000 and 4,000 feet), there is a layer in which sound waves travel at a minimum velocity. Sound waves generated within this layer cannot leave it because they are refracted back by the water layers above and below which transmit sound waves at higher velocities. A sound, the report from four pounds of dynamite for example, detonated within the channeling layer can be heard by listening devices, also in the layer, after having traveled across an entire ocean. By triangulation from several listening stations the source of the sound may be determined to within about one mile. One of the practical uses of SOFAR is to locate aviators forced down at sea. It is also being developed for use in navigation at the Lamont Geological Observatory. The discovery of SOFAR brought Maurice Ewing the Navy's highest civilian honor—the Distinguished Public Service Award.

After joining the faculty of Columbia University, Ewing, from 1945 to 1949, inspired and directed a series of remarkably successful deep-sea expeditions from the center of oceanographic research at Woods Hole. These led to important discoveries on the Mid-Atlantic Ridge, the enormous submarine mountain range which lies about midway between the continents.

In 1949 Columbia University decided to make an estate which had belonged to the late financier, Thomas W. Lamont, into an oceanographic research unit. The estate on the west bank of the Hudson at Palisades, New York, thirteen miles northwest of the George Washington Bridge, had been given to Columbia by Mrs. Lamont. The research unit was named Lamont Geological Observatory and Maurice Ewing was appointed its director. Under his direction it has developed into one of the most important oceanographic research centers in the world.

Perhaps the most fateful day in the history of Lamont Geological Observatory was January 13, 1954, when the Observatory very nearly lost its director and guiding spirit.

In January of that year the three-masted schooner *Vema* hoisted sail, stood out of New York Harbor, and set a course for Bermuda. At that time the 202-foot schooner was the largest vessel engaged in oceanographic research. During the thirty-one years since her launching as a yacht at Copenhagen, the *Vema* had seen many vicissitudes of fortune; only a short time before gaining a new lease on life as an oceanographic vessel she had narrowly missed being broken up for scrap. In these days of high taxes no one can keep up a yacht like the *Vema*. On the other hand, her design for fast sailing and lofty rig unfitted her for life as a commercial vessel. But fortunately for her, in 1953 the Lamont Geological Observatory needed a ship, and at that time her Nova Scotian owner was willing to sell her at a reasonable price. In addition to her sails she has an 800 horsepower Diesel engine. She has the capacity to carry thirty-five scientists and seamen around the world, if necessary.

Having passed Sandy Hook the great white eagle, *Vema*'s figurehead, began to wet his beak; the weather was rugged and there was no improvement to the south. The deck was continually flooded and water came in badly through the deckhouses. Still there wasn't any real danger; it was more a matter of degree of discomfort than anything else.

On the morning of January 13 the *Vema* was pitching and rolling violently in a gale off Cape Hatteras. As Ewing crossed the deck to the chartroom to check the position by means of the loran, four drums of lubricating oil, each weighing 500 pounds, broke loose from their lashings and careened across the deck. Here was one of those sudden emergencies that put seafarers to the test; in seconds a state of relative security had changed to one of peril. The rampaging drums, like battering rams, would soon wreck all deck gear and probably stave in the deckhouses. This could let in enough water to endanger the life of the ship.

Ewing was now joined by his brother, John Ewing, a scientist, and the first and second mates, Charles Wilkie and Michael Brown. Together they managed to subdue the drums and get them back into place.

After a long blow such as had been harassing the *Vema*, the sea becomes confused; its motion includes waves of various periods, heights, and even directions of travel. At such a time two or more wave motions may happen to join forces for a few seconds. The combined effect is a single short-lived wave of monstrous power. Apparently this kind of a coincidence occurred as the attention of the four men was fixed on the job of lashing the last drum. In an instant a mass of blue water covered them and tore the drums loose again. As Ewing said later, he found himself part of an emulsion of men, drums, and sea water. Then as the *Vema* recovered from the staggering blow, the "emulsion" cascaded into the sea. When Ewing got his head above water he saw the two mates holding onto one of the drums, and his brother swimming toward the log line which dragged astern of the ship. Ewing himself was in bad shape, with a great deal of water in his lungs. He tried to reach an oil drum. Although normally a powerful swimmer, he had to give up the attempt because of the water he had taken in and the weight of his clothes. He concentrated on the job of getting rid of his clothes. Always the scientist, he wondered how long it would take his shoes to make the three-mile trip to the bottom. Then he thought how silly a shoe would look resting on the bottom in some underwater photograph that he might take. As he was struggling to get off his trousers, he heard a cry for help from Wilkie, but in the mountainous seas Ewing could not see where the cry had come from. Then the cries stopped and Ewing realized that Wilkie must have gone under.

By this time the *Vema* was about one mile away. Captain Gould had brought the schooner about, but in the spray and wind he could see nothing of the men in the water. Then Captain McMurray, the sailing master, took the wheel, while Gould climbed the foremast shrouds. From the crosstrees he sighted the men and signaled to McMurray to steer to them. They reached John Ewing first and stopped to pull him aboard. Unable to hold onto the fast-moving log line, he had found a ladder washed from the deck of the *Vema;* on this he floated comfortably—at such a time comfort is relative.

When Ewing, between buffetings by the ferocious waves, saw the *Vema* stop, the disheartening thought came to him that the steering gear had broken down, as it had the day before.

However, *Vema* soon started again, but now she turned away from the men in the water. Ewing supposed rightly that she did so in order to pass on another tack, but he wondered if he could last out the delay. Each time he fought his way to the surface for a gasp of air and a chance to look around another wave came crashing down and rolled him over and over; each time he took in a little more water. He gave up trying to swim and concentrated on just keeping afloat. Then everything went black.

Later in a letter to his family he wrote: "I guess you'd think that a person would be pretty much alone out there at a time like that. I wasn't alone a bit. It seemed as though all the good people I love and who love me were there, and were encouraging me." He seemed to see his wife and four children. They called to him and he tried to answer. It seemed to him that they were all about to drown and that he had to save them. Then only his youngest daughter's voice was there, calling to him to come. As he was trying to get to her, a clear voice shouted into his ear, "I could hold onto this barrel easier if you'd take hold of the other end," and there was Mike Brown pushing a drum toward him. Ewing took hold of the drum; after that it was easier for both of them.

Again the ship was coming toward them. Soon someone heaved them a line. Mike caught it. Holding onto the drum with one hand, and to the line with the other, he pulled the drum and Ewing to the ship's side.

At each roll the *Vema*'s gunnel almost went under. On a deep roll Mike flung his arms over the gunnel and the ship lifted him out of the water so that he could climb aboard, but the same roll knocked Ewing far under. However, just as he went down he grabbed a rope.

At the same time the steering gear went out of commission, leaving the *Vema* helpless to maneuver. For Ewing, though he did not know it, this was a critical moment; if he let go of the rope he could easily be carried away from the ship by the wash of sea. But when he came up at last he still held the rope. On the next roll the men got him aboard.

John Ewing's leg was banged up, but no bones were broken. Mike Brown took a shower, as if he had not been wet enough, and then stood his watch as usual. But in striking the ship's side, Ewing had suffered a brain concussion and his left side was partly paralysed. When they reached Bermuda he was flown back to New York, but after a few weeks he returned to finish the expedition.

What happened that fateful January 13, 1954, illustrates the difficulties and hazards connected with deep-sea research. Accidents can easily occur when you work with greasy, tarry, heavy equipment, instruments, and explosives through days and nights in rain and gale, even when the ship is rolling thirty-five degrees in order to carry out as much scientific investigation and sampling as possible with the limited financial support available.

Twice when we ourselves have been out on expeditions taking sediment samples from the deep-sea floor, the wire on which the heavy coring tube was being raised has parted, and what was left of it, taut as a bow string, has lashed back over the deck nearly killing us.

To gain an understanding of the processes and forces which have shaped the earth and determined its structure, Maurice Ewing decided to emphasize undersea studies for several reasons. For one thing much of the present land surface, including most mountains and even some of the higher parts of Mount Everest, is covered by sediments laid down in ancient seas. The origin of some of these great thicknesses of sedimentary rock has been a baffling problem, even a hopeless one without firm knowledge of the sedimentation process which is going on in our present-day oceans. And yet, surprisingly, this promising underwater field of research, as recently as the end of World War II, had hardly been investigated at all. To a scientist like Maurice Ewing it offered the chance of the greatest return in new knowledge in proportion to the investment of time and effort.

The seismic method developed by Ewing has become a principal survey method of oceanographers. And the *Vema*, working in cooperation with other vessels, has now gathered more than 250,000 miles of seismic profiles in all the oceans. Today there is more seismic shooting at sea for scientific purposes than on land. For one thing, there are fewer other ways of investigating submarine geology. For another, it is easier to do seismic shooting at sea; no permits are required for setting off the explosives and no holes have to be drilled. Good reflection signals can be obtained from below the ocean floor simply by dropping charges over the side of the ship and allowing them to explode in the water. Experienced scientists can obtain satisfactory records even in quite heavy weather; shooting must be discontinued only when work on deck becomes hazardous or when the shooting ship can no longer maintain enough speed to get away from its own charges.

The sound waves generated by the detonation of a charge travel outward radially in all directions from the site of the explosion. However, the radial paths may be bent more or less by refraction in the sediments and underlying rock.

Refraction of sound passing from one medium to another can be compared to that of light. According to a principle proposed by the Dutch natural philosopher Christian Huygens in 1690, each point on an incident wave front becomes a point source of wavelets. Because sound travels faster in a denser medium, the first wavelet travels farther in a given time than the next one, and so on; thus the direction of the new wave front is bent away from the vertical (light, traveling more slowly in a denser medium, is bent toward the vertical). Figure 44 shows the effect of refraction on a wave front.

The skidding of a car is a kind of mechanical refraction; when one wheel slips on an icy pavement, the opposite wheel pushes forward more strongly with the result that the car turns toward the "slow" side or the side of the slipping wheel.

Seismic observations are of two kinds depending upon whether sound waves are reflected back to the observer or refracted to another observer some distance away from the source of the sound. In the *reflection method* the geophysicist measures the

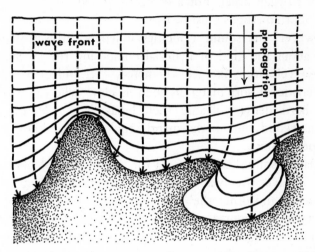

FIGURE 44 *Schematic representation of refraction of waves running on an irregular coast. Note concentration of energy on foreland and protection of beach in reentrant.*

time intervals between the arrivals of waves reflected from the boundaries between layers of sediment or rock of different densities. But, of course, geophysicists' interest is the thicknesses of the layers. To convert time intervals into thicknesses he must know the velocity of sound in each of the layers. This he can learn by means of the refraction method.

The paths of sound waves from an explosion are bent by refraction in such a way that parts of the sound energy travel horizontally through each of the layers of sediment or rock below the ocean bottom. At the same time some of the energy is refracted upward to the ocean surface, with the consequence that a listening ship miles from the sound source receives in its instruments a series of echoes each of which represents a distinct layer. From the time intervals between the explosion and the arrivals of each echo and the distance between the explosion and the listening ship, which is determined accurately by the sound wave transmitted directly through the water, the geophysicist can calculate the velocity of sound in each layer. These velocities can then be used to calculate the thicknesses of the layers from the reflection measurements. Thus the refraction and reflection methods are complementary to each other. For a complete picture of the sub-bottom geology both methods must be used.

However, the sound velocities independently provide information about the kind of material composing the layers. In general, low velocities like 1.8 kilometers (1.1 miles) a second are characteristic of soft materials such as clay, whereas the velocity in the hard dense volcanic rock basalt is 6.7 kilometers (4.2 miles) a second, and in the mantle rock it is 8.2 kilometers (5.1 miles) per second.

Today seismic shooting at sea for the purpose of observing the refracted waves involves two ships working together, one to do the shooting and other the "listening." One vessel proceeds along a predetermined course and drops explosives at selected intervals as it goes, starting as far as 60 miles away and continuing to fire as it comes up to the listening ship, passes it, and proceeds as much as 60 miles farther. The charges range in size from small boosters, for close-in firing, to standard 300-pound Navy depth charges, from which sound waves carry over longer distances. The listening vessel meanwhile remains still, with hydrophones in the water and engines and other noisemaking gear turned off to prevent interference. Figure 45 illustrates the method.

A radio signal notifies the listening ship of the instant at which a charge is exploded. The lines to the hydrophones are thereupon slackened in order to minimize local noise. Two hydrophones are used as a protection against failures. They are turned to pick up sound that comes through the sea bottom in the range from 3 to 30 cycles per second (at the very lower limit of the audible range). At any given distance, energy from a shot may reach the listening ship through one or two layers only; depending on the path of sound, as dictated by the critical angle of incidence, energy transmitted through other layers may be refracted right around the listening ship. To make sure that all layers are mapped, a series of shots must be fired at distances at least four or five times the depth of the deepest layers to be investigated.

The first sound waves to arrive from a shot fired at a great distance are those from the deepest and densest layer and hence the layer through which sound moves with the greatest velocity. Then comes the train of waves through the next layer above and then the train through the unconsolidated sediment on the ocean

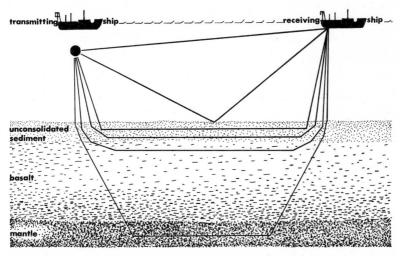

FIGURE 45 *Seismic refraction methods reveal much about the nature and thickness of rocks under the sea floor. One method uses two ships steaming away from each other to a maximum distance of about 180 kilometers (100 miles). One ship sets off underwater explosions every few minutes and the other receives the resulting sound waves after they are refracted in passing through the rock layers.*

floor. Finally, there come the direct water waves. Needless to say, the radial spreading of the sound energy and its splitting up to follow many paths results in its being spread very thin by the time it reaches the listening devices. On the average the energy received is less than one ten millionth of the original energy.

Each train of waves is recorded by an oscillographic camera as a train of oscillations of considerable duration. Interest centers on the first deflection written on the recording films by each train of waves. This records the "first arrival" of the refracted waves from a given layer and gives the travel time of sound through that layer.

The velocity of sound through the layer is found by plotting its travel time against the travel time of the direct water wave. Since the velocity of sound in water is known (approximately 1.5 kilometers or about one mile per second), the velocity of sound through the sediment and rock layers is thereby determined.

As has been pointed out earlier, the collection of deep-sea sediment cores at Lamont Geological Observatory exceeds the combined collections of all other laboratories in the world. The same is true of records of seismic-refraction surveys; more seismic shooting at sea has been done by Ewing and his co-workers at Lamont than the combined efforts of investigators from all other institutions. The results from Ewing's own work and from the method he developed have both given answers and raised questions of great importance about the structure and history of the earth.

Before World War II the Pacific Ocean was looked on by many earth scientists, because of its size and other features, as the only "real" ocean—real in the sense of being an early feature of the earth's surface and differing fundamentally in geology from the continents. Other oceans were regarded as secondary, formed later and by processes different from those that had formed the Pacific Basin. This was by no means a unanimous view, but the evidence to the contrary was inconclusive. The question was resolved in the first few years after the war by seismic-refraction surveys. The vessels *Atlantis* and *Caryn* (of the Woods Hole Oceanographic Institution) obtained refraction profiles in the Atlantic. Similar measurements were made in the Pacific by expeditions from the Scripps Institution of Oceanography. These surveys showed that the undersea crust in both the Atlantic and the Pacific is only 4 to 6 kilometers thick, compared with the 25- to 40-kilometer thickness of the crust beneath the continents. An analysis of the pathways followed by surface waves from earthquakes confirmed these results, showing that the crust below all the ocean basins is thin and that, in this fundamental aspect, one ocean basin is much like another and different from the land.

The division of the earth into distinct oceanic and continental provinces has since been sharpened in other ways, especially by investigations carried out by Ewing and his co-workers. As shown

in many refraction studies, the less dense granitic rocks characteristic of the continental crust are missing below the sea. The pre-
dominant oceanic basement rock is heavier basalt. Moreover, it
has been found that the continental margins act as a barrier to the
passage of some types of earthquake-generated surface waves;
such waves originating at sea often fail to reach the land and vice
versa.

Recent seismic shooting at sea by Ewing and his group of
associates has helped to illuminate the structure of the massive,
40,000-mile-long belt of underseas mountains called the Mid-
Oceanic Ridge. Refraction profiles show that the ridge is the site
of a great anomaly in the earth's crust. It is underlain by a belt of
rock with a velocity of 7.5 kilometers per second, about midway
between the 6.7-kilometer velocity of the basaltic rock of the
ridge and the 8.1-kilometer velocity of the earth's mantle. Rock
of this kind is not found anywhere else on earth in any quantity.

When in 1965 the Royal Astronomical Society of Great Britain awarded its first gold medal in geophysics to Maurice Ewing
and praised him for his leadership in developing Lamont Geological Observatory into the world's most comprehensive geological and geophysical research unit, the citation also said that
Ewing had planned Lamont's work "with great foresight and infectious enthusiasm . . . and the resultant scientific achievements
of the man himself and his devoted co-workers are enormous."

The marine geologist may be likened to a space traveler who
is trying to explore a planet into whose atmosphere he cannot
descend and whose surface is hidden by perpetual clouds. Yet by
making the most of every bit of information of many different
kinds, marine geologists have succeeded in sketching a general
picture of the ocean floor. Little by little they are piecing together the history of past epochs as it has been recorded in accumulated sediments. By timing the echoes of explosions they
trace the layers of rock and sediment, measuring their thicknesses, and estimate their densities. They thrust sensing probes
into the sediment carpet to measure the rate of flow of heat
energy from the deep interior. And they measure variations in the
pull of gravity in order to detect imbalances in the distribution of
mass below the sea floor. The story of Isaac Newton and the apple

is well known; a falling apple is a good example of the mutual gravitational attraction between two masses. Similarly a plumb bob is pulled toward the earth and the earth is pulled toward the plumb bob, and if there is a massive range of mountains nearby, it too will attract the bob and pull it a little to one side. In this sense a level surface, one perpendicular to the line of a plumb bob, is everywhere somewhat distorted by irregularities of topography and by local variations in the densities of rocks.

A simple way of measuring gravitational attraction is by timing the swings of a pendulum. The period, or time it takes a pendulum of given length to make a complete swing back and forth, is determined by the local pull of gravity. The pendulum swings faster where the pull is greater, just as a falling object falls faster where the pull, or acceleration, of gravity is greater.

In this way fortunes have been won by detecting small changes in the gravity field near great intrusions of salt known as *salt domes*. These are not valuable for the salt but rather for the petroleum which occurs particularly in the porous limestone that nearly always overlies such salt domes. It is the effect of the heavy limestone on the local pull of gravity that betrays the presence of the dome.

Thus the weight of a given mass varies from place to place on the earth's surface. In part the variation stems from the shape of the earth, which is not really spherical—because of the centrifugal effect of its rotation it is somewhat flattened at the poles and bulges at the equator. At the equator everything is a little lighter than at either pole, partly because of the centrifugal effect of the earth's rotation which works against gravity and partly because of the greater distance to the earth's center. Superimposed on the gradual increase in the gravitational field from the equator to the poles are local variations due to topographical irregularities and inhomogeneities of density of the upper layers of the earth. The local or regional variations are small; the unit used by students of gravity is the milligal, which is roughly one millionth part of the average pull of gravity. The object of gravity surveys is to detect anomalies in the field, that is departures above or below the normal value expected at the particular latitude.

The first significant advance in gravity work at sea was made by F. A. Vening Meinesz, a Netherlands geophysicist, in the

1920's. He developed a pendulum apparatus for making gravity measurements in submarines. Submerged beyond the play of wind and waves, a submarine is stable enough to work with a pendulum. Suitable conditions can normally be realized with a submarine able to dive to 75 meters (250 feet). Instead of recording the motions of a single pendulum, Vening Meinesz recorded the relative motions of two nearly identical pendulums used as a pair. Initially, one of these pendulums is at rest while the other is swung. The disturbing horizontal accelerations are the same for both pendulums and hence cancel out if the relative motion of the two pendulums is considered.

Vening Meinesz made his first gravity measurements at sea in 1923 and thereafter studied gravity in all the major oceans. His discovery of the belt of large negative-gravity anomalies associated with the oceanic trenches was one of the great contributions to contemporary geology and geophysics. Since their discovery, many geophysical investigations have been made by Vening Meinesz and others to try to delineate the structure related to these belts. In the East Indies, Vening Meinesz has evolved a detailed and complicated theory to account for the anomalies. He invokes a compression that causes a plastic downbuckle of the earth's crust, creating the earthquakes, negative-gravity anomalies, and fracture zones which serve as lanes for upwelling igneous rocks along the island arcs and facilitate the uplift of the islands.

The Vening Meinesz pendulum apparatus has proved to be an extremely reliable instrument. However, the length of time involved in making a single observation and reducing the data, as well as the necessity for making the observations in submarines, have proved to be serious drawbacks. Submarines are not readily available to oceanographers. Therefore, strenuous efforts were made to develop an instrument that could be used on surface ships.

In November 1957, J. Lamar Worzel of Lamont Geological Observatory made the first successful measurements of gravity from a surface ship in the open ocean. He used an instrument designed by Anton Graf of Munich, Germany, which was mounted on a gyro-stabilized platform on board the Navy ship, U.S.S. *Compass Island*. Unlike the pendulum whose bob responds to the slightest roll or pitch of the ship, the Graf instrument detects gravity variations by measuring slight shifts up or down in the end of a horizontal aluminum boom. The small boom is suspended and pivoted near one end by specially designed springs. These both support the boom and allow its other end to move up or down with changes in local gravity. This arrangement is much less susceptible to outside interference than a pendulum, yet it is sensitive and accurate. Combined with the gyro-stabilized platform, it has mastered the problems of measuring gravity at sea. The technique of gravity surveying at sea was thus revolutionized.

When we find gravity values that are out of the ordinary, we try to imagine some picture of the rock layers to fit the results. In this way we learn a little more about the slow changes that are going on all the time within the earth. The deep ocean trenches, for instance, are below average in their gravitational attraction. This is probably because they have been formed by a downward buckling of the lightweight crustal rocks. Because the light crust has pushed away some of the heavier mantle rock—in a way we do not yet understand—the gravitational attraction in the deeper trenches is below average. But just as a piece of wood tends to bob back to the surface when you press it underwater, so too the light crustal rock of the trenches is subject to an upward push. Gravity gives us a measure of the amount of the upward push. The fact that trenches do not respond to the upward force is significant evidence that they do not arise from tension—that is, a drawing apart of the crust-like mid-ocean ridges—but rather to compression or thrusting which is still active and holds them down against their natural buoyancy.

The combined information from the seismic method which reveals thicknesses of deep rock layers and from gravity measurements, which show where vertical forces are out of adjustment, can give interesting hints about what has happened to the earth's crust in the past. Scandinavia is an example. Under the weight of millions of tons of ice that covered Scandinavia during the last ice age the land was pushed down deeper into the dense mantle like a heavily laden ship. Now the ice has gone and the land is rising. Sea level observations show that it is still rising at a rate which reaches a maximum of a little more than a centimeter per year near the center where the former ice was thickest. Gravity measurements prove that the Scandinavian region is still deficient in mass; the land will continue to rise until enough dense mantle material will have flowed under it to make up for the deficiency. That it is a slow process need not be surprising. Intuitively we feel that the flowing material should have enormous viscosity. In the words of Galileo, who discovered laws governing the motion of pendulums and thereby paved the way for early gravity measurements, *"Eppure si muove!"*—nevertheless it does move! That is the important lesson to be learned from the slow rise of formerly ice-loaded lands. If mantle material can flow under Scandinavia, there is no reason why it cannot flow under the stress of density changes brought about by differential heating by radioactive substances.

The up-and-down movements of the continents expose their rocks to the grinding attrition of erosion; this creates *detritus*, the raw material of new sediment layers, some of which comes to rest in shallow seas, and some in the deep oceans. But more important to the question of the origin of continents and ocean basins is the possibility of lateral drift of continents. If the material below the continents moves laterally, why not the superposed continents? Under the circumstances it would be astonishing if they had not changed their relative positions.

If the crust under the oceans were as thick as it is under the continents, the ocean bottom should float as high as the land. But with a thin, somewhat heavier crust, the ocean basins would be expected to float lower. Both gravity and seismic measurements show that the thin crust of the oceans is indeed heavier than that under the land. The lower layer may be volcanic rock, basalt, while the upper layer might be some kind of sedimentary rock, such as limestone, or even a lava. In any event, the studies show that, on the whole, the ocean crust is nicely balanced against the continents just as a relatively thin and dense block of wood floats lower in the water than a thick, lighter one. Finding this *isostatic balance*, as it is called, is the important main conclusion drawn from the results of gravity surveying at sea.

One of the more recent developments in marine geophysics is the development of techniques of measuring the heat flowing out of the ocean bottom. The quantity measured is the amount of heat emerging from the earth's interior per unit area per unit time through the floor of the ocean. Many lines of evidence suggest that in most areas a state of thermal equilibrium exists at the ocean bottom in deep water, that is, neither the water nor the bottom sediment are being heated or cooled. Measurement of heat flow is actually more difficult on land—one has to use a deep borehole that has been abandoned for a considerable length of time. This accounts for the fact that many more measurements of heat flow have been made at sea than on land.

A large percentage of the heat flow measurements at sea have been made by the cylindrical probe method devised originally by Sir Edward Bullard at Cambridge University in England. The instrument is simple. It is essentially a probe about 3 meters (10 feet) long and 25 to 40 millimeters (1 to 1.6 inches) in diameter, which measures the temperature difference in the sediments at points near its top and bottom. A bottom sediment core is recovered by a separate lowering of a coring apparatus as close to the site of the thermal gradient measurement as practical. Back in the laboratory, the rate at which the material in the core conducts heat is measured. By using the observed temperature difference, the heat flow in the sediments can then be calculated. Thus, an important geophysical effect that cannot be measured directly can be determined indirectly by using the physical laws of heat conduction to interpret other characteristics that can be measured.

Recently, an apparatus in which the temperature gradient is measured by an attachment to a piston corer has been developed at the Lamont Observatory. This has the great advantage that the total time taken is greatly reduced and the core is obtained at the exact point where the temperature measurement is made.

To maintain a heat flow as large as that observed requires very large amounts of heat if it is to be continued through geological time. The only adequate source of heat that has been suggested is radioactivity within the earth. The observed heat flow is about that which would be expected from the uranium, thorium, and potassium contained in an earth built up from stony and iron meteorites. If the earth was, in fact, built up from meteorites, the radioactivity would initially have been distributed through the mantle. This would have lead to melting and probably to an upward migration of the radioactive elements, which tend to be concentrated in the materials crystallizing late in the process of solidification. However, the transmission of seismic shear waves through the earth's mantle argues against melting at present. The values of conductivity in the mantle are not known reliably, and it is quite possible that the values are much higher than those generally assumed. Another solution that has been suggested is the possibility of heat transfer in the mantle by convection currents, in which case melting would not occur. Still another solution requires the oceanic mantle to be made up of rocks which are much more radioactive than the ultrabasic rocks measured in the laboratory. In this case, the part of the oceanic mantle that contributes to heat flow would be confined to the top 200 kilometers and it can be shown that even with the normal values of thermal conductivity no melting would result.

The high heat flows over the ocean ridges can hardly be accounted for by local concentrations of radioactive material and it has been suggested that their immediate cause is the intrusion of igneous rocks beneath the ocean floor. It has also been suggested that big heat flow values along the ridges may be explained by assuming that mantle convection currents are effective in bringing hot material closer to the surface below the ridges.

In some areas where closely spaced observations of heat flow values are available, very high and very low values seem to occur within a few kilometers of each other. This may cast doubt on the deduction based upon the relatively few observations elsewhere, that large areas exist where the heat flow values are systematically higher or lower than average. However, if future detailed observations show that such areas do indeed exist, these results may be very important in deducing the horizontal distribution of radioactivity within the mantle and even, perhaps, in deciding whether convection currents exist in the mantle or not.

Some very careful earthquake measurements have shown that there is a layer about 80 to 160 kilometers (50 to 100 miles) inside the earth—well into the mantle—where the seismic waves travel more slowly than expected. This may mean that a band of rock in the mantle has been growing soft. As more and more radioactive heat is produced and stored inside the mantle, this soft band may move upward until it is near enough to the surface to break through in an enormous outburst of volcanic activity. This would release a great deal of heat very rapidly, so that the earth would settle down to another period of slow warming up. In the meantime, the more fluid mantle might allow the continents to drift about, while the sea-bed sediments were being baked to form a hard rock.

We do not know whether these things have happened in the past, or whether they are probable in the future. All we can do is continue to make observations, and measure such things as the heat flow through the sea bed and so to gather more figures to use in our calculations. Then at some stage we shall have enough information to know which theory is right, or whether we shall have to develop a new theory. Much of the history of the oceans and of the earth itself is bound up in the rock layers hidden beneath the sediment carpet of the sea floor.

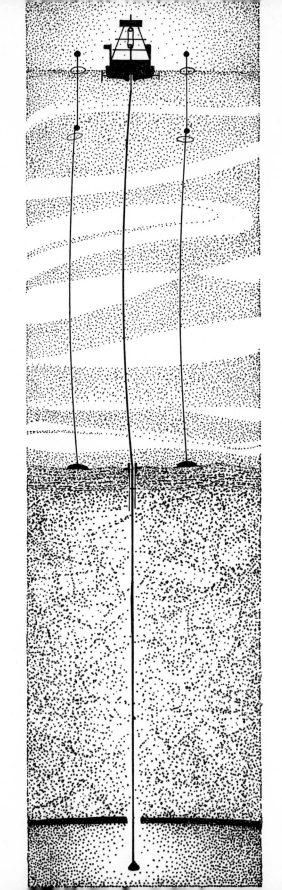

CHAPTER 9

THE MOHOLE

E VER SINCE MAN BEGAN TO THINK, HE HAS SPECULATED ABOUT HIS cosmic home, his own particular planet. Until recently, however, he had only hypotheses based on scanty facts and speculative assumptions. The relatively limited scale of scientific research and the modest scale of technical probings until recently were in no way commensurate to the importance of the problem of studying the deep interior of the earth. Automatic laboratories have reached Venus and the moon, but as yet man has penetrated only a little into the interior of the earth. So far, the deepest hole ever drilled, a well in west Texas, penetrated a little less than 8,000 meters (26,000 feet) of ancient marine sediments in search of deep-lying oil and gas deposits. Thus, the deepest drilling has penetrated only a fraction more than one thousandth of the radius of the earth; the layer of the earth's crust from which samples of rocks have been obtained amounts to a thin film on the surface of our planet. On a globe representing the earth on the scale of 1:10,000,000, with a diameter of a little more than a meter, the thickness of this film would be less than 1 millimeter.

The unexplored depths of the earth not only conceal the riddle of the origin and development of the thin layer of the earth's crust known to us, and the explanation of the laws that govern the concentration in this layer of deposits of useful minerals, but most probably also the unknown riches and natural forces that could increase the productivity of human society enormously. To penetrate into the depths of the earth is not merely the subject of a dream; it is an urgent and necessary next step in the progress of applied geology, for only from the depths of the earth can we meet the demands for ever greater quantities of the most varied kinds of minerals needed by a really vigorous industrial development.

The countries with sufficiently developed scientific resources have made a beginning in the study of the deep interior of the earth. The American project to drill into the depths of the earth is called the *Mohole Project*. (The name springs from the puzzling discontinuity between the mantle and the crust, called *Mohorovičić discontinuity*, or "Moho", in honor of its discoverer, a Yugoslav geophysicist, Andrija Mohorovičić—see pages 266–8. Thus, any deep hole projected to the mantle is known as a Mohole.)

The Mohole Project is a plan to explore inner space by drilling a hole 5,000 to 10,000 meters (15,000 to 30,000 feet) deep through the crust beneath the oceans. The primary goal is to reach the Mohorovičić discontinuity, but at the same time it will yield evidence on a number of basic questions regarding the origin, development, and constitution of our planet. It will probe into that unexplored region deep below our feet about which we know less in some respects than we know about outer space. For daring and magnitude of conception nothing approaching this adventure in earth science has ever before been undertaken. What will be won in knowledge and understanding of our home in the universe will be worth far more than the cost. The practical value of the new knowledge can hardly fail to be richly rewarding.

To appreciate why geologists, geophysicists, and paleontologists, or geonomists in general, anticipate a flood of fundamental information from the Mohole, and why they believe that the drilling site ought to be in an ocean basin rather than on a continent, one must consider the various competing hypotheses to explain the earth's features and the tenuous evidence upon which they have been constructed.

The earliest hint as to what might lie below the earth's solid crust came from volcanoes. The incandescent molten rock that flowed from them seemed to give the answer; at some depth below the surface of the earth the temperature was so high that all material was liquid. Miners knew that the deeper they delved, the higher the temperature. From the rate of increase of temperature with depth one could calculate that below a depth of about

100 kilometers or 60 miles the temperature must be high enough to melt any known rock.

This view of the state of the earth's interior was generally accepted until examined more critically by Sir William Thomason, Lord Kelvin (1824–1907), the British physicist and electrical engineer who was responsible for the research that made possible the laying of the first transatlantic cables. From the small distortion of the earth's shape by the tide-raising forces of the sun and moon he proved that the earth's interior could not be liquid; on the contrary, his calculations showed that the earth behaved as if more rigid than steel. Since then the study of earthquake waves passing through the body of the earth has settled the question beyond doubt as described later on in this chapter; no continuous layer of liquid material occurs anywhere between the earth's surface and its core at a depth of 2,900 kilometers (1,800 miles). However, Kelvin agreed that the earth must once have been much hotter, and therefore liquid; solidification had come later as it cooled. This surmise has also been born out by studies of earthquakes; it is reasonably certain that the materials of the deeper layers of the earth become denser with depth. So much so that the density of the core can be explained only by supposing that the core is composed of a mixture of nickel and iron. This segregation of different materials according to density can be explained only by the supposition that the whole earth was at one time liquid.

Kelvin then went on to calculate how long ago the earth had become solid. From what he knew about the temperatures at which rocks melt, and from reasonable estimates of the rate at which rocks conduct heat, he concluded that consolidation had probably occurred 98 million years ago, and under no circumstances longer ago than 400 million years. On the assumption that the earth is slowly cooling, he argued in his essay *On the Secular Cooling of the Earth* (1864) that volcanic activity should be diminishing:

> It is as certain that there is now less volcanic energy in the whole earth than there was one thousand years ago, as it is that there is less gunpowder in the *Monitor* after she has been seen to discharge

shot and shell, whether at a nearly equable rate or not, for five hours without receiving fresh supplies, than there was at the beginning of the action. Yet this truth has been ignored or denied by many of the leading geologists of the present day, because they believe that the facts within their province do not demonstrate greater violence in ancient changes of the earth's surface, or do demonstrate a nearly equable action in all periods.

As it happened, the geologists were right; in the record of the rocks there is no trace of evidence that the earth's fund of energy is wasting away. Kelvin made his picturesque comparison between the earth and the *Monitor* in 1862; at that time there was no conceivable way of explaining replenishment of the earth's stock of heat energy. As a physicist Kelvin was more impressed by the seemingly inexorable laws of thermodynamics than he was by the geological record.

The discovery of radioactivity has been to the earth sciences, or geonomy, what Mendel's laws of inheritance have been to biology and the theory of evolution; each has led to revolutionary advances which in turn have pointed the way to enlightening hypotheses. The radioactive clock tells geologists that sediments were accumulating on the floors of shallow seas longer ago by tenfold than Kelvin's extreme date for the solidification of the earth. At the same time, continuous generation of heat within the earth by the decay of radioactive substances explains away the mystery that confronted Kelvin and the geologists of his day, namely the youthful vitality of ancient mother earth.

The origin of the earth is an unsettled question, largely because knowledge of the materials of the interior and the distribution of radioactivity with depth is lacking. For information geologists have turned to the rocks ejected by volcanoes. The lava of the Hawaiian Islands is basalt, a heavy, black rock rich in iron, calcium, and magnesium, which is characteristic of oceanic islands. However, the lava of the Hawaiian Islands as it rises to the surface sometimes entrains lumps of a rock called *dunite* consisting almost entirely of the mineral olivine, a silicate of iron and magnesium. At the earth's surface dunite melts at about $1,200°$ Celsius, but at a depth of a few kilometers great pressure would prevent it from melting at even higher temperatures. This is interesting because earthquakes preceding a Hawaiian volcanic eruption start at depths as great as 32 kilometers (20 miles). Then during a period of several days subsequent shocks occur at decreasing depths. Presumably these shocks result from dislocations, or adjustments by fracture, which release the pressure keeping the heated material at depth solid and at the same time open up fissures by which the liquid lava can rise. But the evidence of the behavior of earthquake waves in the rocks beneath the Pacific shows that the crust in the region of the Hawaiian Islands is not thicker than about 16 kilometers (10 miles). Although the premonitory quakes originate at twice that depth, it is unlikely that the basaltic lava comes from such depth because basalt is not dense enough to account for observed velocities of earthquake waves in the mantle. On the other hand, dunite is dense enough, and therefore the lumps of it in the Hawaiian lavas may very well represent detached fragments of the mantle, but the fact that so little dunite reaches the surface is puzzling.

Meteorites from interplanetary space give another hint about the composition of the deep layers of the earth. They are probably samples of the material with which the earth and other inner planets were built. Meteorites are classified as either stony aerolites or nickel-iron siderites, but all gradations between these extremes also occur. The average composition from analyses of many meteorites is 13 per cent nickel-iron and 87 per cent peridotite, which is essentially an impure dunite. Thus the overall composition of these immigrants from space includes the same materials and in about the same proportions as the hypothetical composition of the earth inferred from independent evidence.

Much information about the earth's crust has been gained, as we have seen, by measuring variations, or anomalies, in the pull of gravity from place to place. Since gravitational attraction is proportional to the masses involved, one would expect to find slightly greater gravitational pull in high, mountainous regions. However, this is not the case; on the contrary, gravity in elevated regions is slightly less than in lowland areas of similar surface rocks. The only reasonable explanation for this deficiency of gravity is to suppose that the elevated crustal material is supported by a downward projection of rock of low density into the dense material of the mantle. Over the ocean basins gravity values are greater than they should be in view of the replacement of kilometers of rock by much less dense water. Evidently the oceanic crust is relatively thin and the dense mantle material must lie at a shallower depth than it does under the continents. Such variations in gravity and their relations to the broad features of the earth have led to recognition of the principle of *isostasy*, or "equal balance," according to which elevated mountainous regions float like icebergs; they are supported by large volumes of relatively light material extending downward and displacing denser material. Permanence of the continents follows from the principle of isostasy. The less dense continents float like vast rafts on the dense mantle material; like drifting rafts they may change position with respect to each other and to the earth's poles, but they cannot sink and become part of the ocean floor any more than an area of the ocean floor of continental proportions can emerge from the sea and become a continent. This does not exclude some vertical movement; we know from the evidence of guyots and coral atolls that a broad region of the floor of the southwestern Pacific subsided by between one and two kilometers during the last 100 million years, and ancient marine sediments on the continents show that they have stood lower with respect to sea level than they do now during much of geological time, but from the nature of these sediments we can be sure that they accumulated in shallow seas. Nowhere do we find evidence that parts of the continents have ever been depressed to oceanic depth.

Isostatic balance implies that the earth's mantle has no strength or rigidity. How can this be reconciled with Kelvin's conclusion that the earth as a whole has greater rigidity than steel? The answer lies in the time dimension. Kelvin's calculation delt with distortion due to the tide-raising forces having cycles of about twelve hours. The rate of flow within the mantle is probably in the order of a few centimeters a year as one may judge from the slow rise of the formerly glaciated regions of North America and Scandinavia.

Just as a physician can learn something about the condition of certain internal organs by tapping a patient and listening to the reflected sounds, so a geophysicist can take advantage of tremors set up in the interior of the earth by fracturing within the crust and mantle to learn about the interior of the earth.

Earthquakes and volcanic eruptions are the surface manifestations of forces at work deep below. For billions of years these forces have been raising vast mountain chains on the continents and vaster chains on the ocean floor, and, if present-day thinking is correct, these same forces have shifted the continents about with respect to each other and to the poles.

The process that converts heat energy into the flowing motion of the mantle is probably quite similar to that which keeps the atmosphere circulating. The difference is only one of degree; the rate of flow of the mantle can hardly exceed a few centimeters a year, whereas that of the atmosphere is measurement in kilometers per hour.

The sun's rays heat the earth's surface which in turn heats the lower part of the atmosphere. As the temperature of the air rises, it expands, becomes less dense or lighter. Wherever the heating is most intense, as in low latitudes, the warm, light air rises. At the same time cool air moves horizontally into the region to take the place of the rising air, the cool air being replaced by sinking cold, heavy air from the upper atmosphere.

Earth scientists conjecture that heat is generated in the lower part of the mantle by radioactive substances more rapidly than it can be carried off by conduction, with the result that, like the heated air, the material of the lower mantle expands and becomes less dense. On the other hand, the upper part of the mantle by reason of its proximity to the earth's surface loses heat by conduction faster than it gains heat by radioactive decay. Wherever the loss of heat is greatest, there the mantle material will be densest and therefore it will tend to sink. As it does so, it will push aside the hotter, lower part of the mantle which will rise and then spread horizontally into the regions of sinking, denser mantle material.

Figure 25 shows the pattern of flow that should result. Each closed circuit of flow is called a *convection cell*. It is the horizontal motion at the tops of convection cells that is believed to have created the irregularities of the earth's surface, as well as all those changes of its relief in the geological past for which evidence is found in the record of the rocks.

Apparently flow within the deeper part of the mantle, that is below 725 kilometers (450 miles), is smoothly continuous; the sudden dislocations that make themselves felt at the surface as earthquakes never occur at greater depths. Such deep disturbances, which originate within the upper part of the mantle, characterize the descending limbs of convection cells, along the west coast of South America for example, where mantle material moving from the Pacific Basin dips down and under the margin of the westward-moving continent.

Many quakes originate within the crust. As the upper part of the moving mantle drags against the under surface of the rigid crust it causes strain to accumulate in it. When the strain surpasses the strength of the rocks of the crust, crumpling, fracturing, and sudden movement along old fractures occur with disastrous consequences for men's anthills. On a miniature scale we see the same thing happen when the water of a frozen-over river flowing beneath the ice causes it to buckle and break, and thereby generates "icequakes" and the booming sounds that startle skaters.

When the energy of a large accumulation of strain is released by sudden movement, the whole globe quivers and inner space resounds with echoes to which seismologists listen with their highly sensitive instruments.

In 1906 an earth scientist, R. D. Oldham, from the study of records of the reverberations within the earth drew the conclusion that there must lie at a great depth below the surface a *discontinuity*, or level of abrupt change in the physical properties of the sound-transmitting material. The surface of a stone wall is a familiar example of a discontinuity. When sound waves traveling in the air encounter the surface of the wall with its very different density and elasticity, a small part of their energy sets up vibrations within the wall, but most of the energy is reflected back through the air as an echo. This is why one can "hear" a nearby wall when one passes it in a car.

Thirteen years after Oldham's observation, Beno Gutenberg, then in Germany and later professor of geophysics at the California Institute of Technology, was able to calculate that the depth to the discontinuity, or surface of the earth's core, was 2,900 kilometers (1,800 miles).

Since then geophysicists have observed that seismic waves that reach the earth's surface after passing through the core are exclusively of the kind called longitudinal, that is, waves in which the particles of the transmitting material vibrate back and forth in the same direction as the wave itself travels.

Apparently, the core is incapable of transmitting transverse waves or those in which the motion of the particles is at a right angle to the direction of travel of the wave. Since liquids at the earth's surface do not transmit transverse waves, it is evident that the core, or at least the outer part of it, must have some of the properties of a liquid, but we must keep in mind that the temperature of the core, according to geophysicists' calculations, is at least 2000° C. and it is certainly under an enormous pressure which cannot be reproduced in the laboratory. Since no one has seen matter under such extreme conditions, it is possible that the material of the outer core is in a state rather different from that of the fluids with which we are familiar.

As records of earthquakes accumulated and the sensitivity of recording instruments became keener, other fainter echoes apparently from within the core itself were observed. In 1936 Miss I. Lehmann, a Danish seismologist, pointed out that a small inner core could account for these otherwise inexplicable echoes. Except that earthquake waves seem to travel at a greater speed in the inner core, there is no good evidence regarding the nature of its composition. However, K. E. Bullen, British geophysicist, has concluded from a long line of reasoning that the inner core is solid.

For many years earth scientists have believed that the core is composed of iron and nickel, but recently they have turned to the theory that the outer core may consist of material chemically like that of the mantle, but transformed in its physical properties by the enormous pressure on it. However, the theory that the inner core consists of iron and nickel is still popular.

As we have said, according to present-day theory the earth consists of three main concentric layers: the crust, the mantle, and the core. If we compare the earth to a soft boiled egg, the yolk corresponds to the core, the white, to the mantle, and the shell, to the earth's crust. The radius of the earth is 6,340 kilometers or about 4,000 miles. The core extends from the center to about 3,500 kilometers (2,200 miles). The mantle accounts for most of the remaining 2,900 kilometers (1,800 miles) of the radius. The crust, or shell, is relatively thin; it varies from about 5 kilometers (3 miles) to more than 60 kilometers (40 miles) in thickness.

Although geophysicists disagree about the composition of the core, they agree that the enveloping mantle, which makes up more than 80 per cent of the volume of the earth, is dense rock. The crust is separated from the mantle by the Mohorovičić discontinuity, at which the velocity of earthquake waves changes abruptly from about 6.6 kilometers per second above to 8 kilometers below. Because the velocities of these waves increase with increasing density of the rock through which they travel, it is evident that the material of the mantle must be denser than that of the crust. Regardless of much speculation by experts, there is still little agreement about the nature and origin of the Mohorovičić discontinuity. As we said earlier, meager evidence and theory suggest that the mantle may be largely or entirely composed of dunite or olivine, a dense silicate of magnesium and iron, but the abrupt change at the discontinuity remains somewhat of a puzzle. According to the older, static conception of the earth's constitution, the change in density at the discontinuity came about through differential settling of various substances according to their densities, but such a process implies gradational change. As a way out of this dilemma some geonomists have conjectured that the abrupt discontinuity is not due to chemical change but rather to a change of phase or physical state resulting from the increase in temperature and pressure with depth. The primary objective of the Mohole Project is to drill through the Mohorovičić discontinuity and obtain samples of the mysterious material below it (see Figure 46).

The earth's crust itself is roughly layered with respect to the velocities of earthquake waves. The crust below the oceans includes a so-called "first layer" varying in thickness from a few hundred meters to more than 2,000 meters. This layer of low sound velocity consists of unconsolidated or nearly unconsolidated sediment. Below that a "second layer" of small and variable thickness can sometimes be recognized. Presumably it consists of hardened sediments, volcanic rocks, or both. Finally there is the

"third layer," some 5 kilometers thick, which may be regarded as
oceanic crust. The velocity of earthquake waves in this layer
averages about 6.6 kilometers per second, from which geophysicists infer that it is composed of basalt. However, another rock
that could equally account for the earthquake wave velocities is
serpentine. Chemically serpentine is really nothing but dunite,

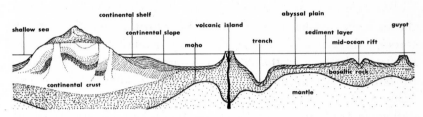

FIGURE 46 *Cross section of the earth's crust showing typical land and
sea forms. The sketch also demonstrates the theory of isostasy; if a land
mass stands high, the crust below it must be correspondingly thick. Beneath continents, the crust and mantle bulge down; elsewhere the crust
is thinner and the mantle is relatively closer to the surface. In effect, the
crust reflects a reverse image of the surface above. All continental crust
is light granitic rock; all sea basins are floored with heavier basaltic rock.
The crust is separated from the mantle by the Mohorovičić discontinuity
(the Moho).*

the hypothetical material of the mantle, combined with some
water, which reduces its density. A hint that the third layer may
be serpentine has been found by investigators of the Lamont Geological Observatory, who have dredged up masses of that material from three places where there are steep cliffs resulting from
fracturing along the Mid-Atlantic Ridge.

Proof that what is called *oceanic crust* is chemically the same
as mantle rock would be strong evidence in favor of the theory of
renewal of the floors of the oceans by convectional flow of the
mantle. Conversely, evidence that the "oceanic crust" and mantle
are quite different in chemical composition will deal the theory a
staggering blow. Samples of rock from the third layer and the
mantle, therefore, will be much more than mere mineralogical
curiosities. Upon their composition hang the answers to some
basic questions about the origin of ocean basins, continents,
folded mountain ranges, and volcanoes (see Figure 46).

The distinction between the crust and the deeper portions of the earth was first found by Andrija Mohorovičić in 1909 as an outcome of his study of records of earthquakes. The records, or *seismograms*, showed the arrivals of two series of waves separated by a time interval that increased as the distances from the centers of disturbance increased. To explain the dual arrivals Mohorovičić conjectured that there must be a layer beneath the crust which transmitted seismic waves at a greater velocity than the crust. Accordingly, the first wave to reach a seismometer has traveled through the deeper channel of high velocity, and the second, through the crust. Thanks to the sharp definition of the discontinuity at the base of the crust, seismograms provide information by which seismologists can calculate the thickness of the crust. Many such measurements show that the thickness varies a good deal from place to place. The crust is thickest under regions of high mountains where it may extend down 60 or 75 kilometers. Under the oceans its thickness varies from 7 to as little as 3 kilometers. This is one reason why American scientists have elected to try to reach the base of the crust by drilling in an ocean basin. The thickness of hard rock to be penetrated will be much less, but it is equally certain that by going to sea the drillers will take on other difficulties and unforeseeable hazards. Nothing like this has ever been attempted before. On the other hand, the information from a hole in an ocean basin will unquestionably be of greater interest and value to geonomists than one drilled through a continent; many deep oil wells have probed much of the deep structure of the continents, but nothing is known about the ocean basins below the few tens of meters reached by coring tubes. Moreover, recently acquired evidence has accentuated the fundamental difference between the ocean basins and the continents in their structure and history of development. A Mohole at sea should provide crucial evidence regarding this fascinating question.

The depth of water will surely not be less than 3,600 meters (12,000 feet) and it may be as much as 5,500 meters (18,000 feet) depending upon the choice of the drilling site. Beneath that thickness of water the drill will have to penetrate at least the same thickness of crustal rock. Unless the information from the first hole is far more complete than is at all likely, earth scientists are sure to want to have holes drilled at other sites. The drill stem, or heavy pipe to which the drill bit is attached and by which it is rotated, will have to be much longer than any ever used before. It will be lowered and the power applied to it from some kind of a floating platform that will be exposed to all the hazardous conditions of the open ocean in the form of waves, currents, and storms. Other difficulties not encountered by drillers of oil wells will be hard igneous rock instead of sediments, enormous pressure, and high temperature. Because much of the section to be penetrated will be in igneous rock such as basalt, the rate of progress will be held back by the necessity of changing the drilling bits at frequent intervals.

The project will severely test present-day techniques of drilling. The challenge will surely lead to various improvements and innovations in ways of doing a variety of things, quite apart from deep drilling, which will have wide and important applications in the future.

The name of the project, Mohole, tends to overemphasize the importance of the Mohorovičić discontinuity, as if reaching that were its only important objective. In reality the Mohole will probe a whole series of the most basic problems of the earth sciences. We have seen that the fundamental question of the differentiation between the continents and ocean basins also involves the hypothesis of continental drift, the permanence of continents and ocean basins, a still-disputed point, and the part played by flow of mantle material in the form of great convection cells powered by heat generated by atomic fission. The Mohole may not answer all these questions; instead it may yield evidence of wholly undreamed of past and present processes that will compel geonomists to rebuild their working hypotheses from the ground up. All we can be certain of is that it will yield a wealth of knowledge about this earth on which we must live. Every bit of information from the Mohole will not necessarily be of practical use; it may be that much of what we learn from it will not be convertible into material wealth, but the probability that the Mohole will yield useful knowledge we unhesitatingly assess at a thousandfold greater than that of exploring the moon, and at a good deal less than one tenth the cost.

The apparent thinness of the layer of sediments on the floors of the oceans is another tantalizing problem. According to measurements by seismic waves the thickness of unconsolidated sediment in the Atlantic is only about 700 meters (2,300 feet); in the Pacific it is only about half that amount. If we assume even very conservatively slow rates of sediment accumulation in the past, we find that these thicknesses cannot represent much more than the time since the latter part of the Mesozoic Era, when the giant lizards held sway, about 100 million years ago. Yet the first appearance of life is more than six times as remote in time. Some event of oceanwide effect seems either to have destroyed all older sediments or to have altered their physical properties to such an extent that they no longer react to sound waves like unconsolidated sediment. A further suggestion that something happened in late Mesozoic time is the fact that although coring and dredging in both oceans have brought up many samples of sediments containing the remains of extinct animals going back into the Cretaceous Period, the last of the three time divisions of the Mesozoic Era (see Figure 3), as yet no older sediment has been found. Possible explanations for the absence of older sediments come to mind; perhaps the ocean floors were flooded by vast outpourings of lava that either destroyed the older sediments or covered them up in such a way as to make their presence undetectable by the seismic method. Or the older sediments may have been swept toward the continents by movement of the sea floor in response to convective flow within the mantle. One way, probably the only way, to find out what happened is to drill to the bottom of the sediment layer.

We think that there is little probability that the Mohole will provide a continuous record of life going back to the very beginning; various lines of evidence strongly suggest that such a long record does not exist, at least not in the ocean basins, but we cannot really know until one or several Moholes have been drilled. On the other hand, there is every reason to expect a continuous record of life extending back into the Mesozoic Era, and the value of that to science would be worth the cost of a dozen Moholes.

To obtain a continuous sedimentary section, however, it will be necessary to choose the drilling site with care. We know from our study of many relatively short cores from all the oceans that discontinuity because of the loss of some part by slumping is almost the rule. To avoid elision by slumping the site ought to be either in the bottom of a basin or near the center of a broad, flat-topped rise. Moreover, if the depth of water much exceeds 4,500 meters (15,000 feet), there is a probability that the value of the record will be very much impaired by solution of calcareous organic remains.

The critical importance of the site suggests the desirability of drilling one Mohole at a site selected particularly for the purpose of reaching the Mohorovičić discontinuity, and then drilling one or more non-Moholes at sites more favorable for other objectives. Since non-Moholes would not need to be so deep, they could be drilled at considerably less expense of time and money.

Drilling at a site somewhere on the deep-sea fan of the Hudson Submarine Canyon should give results of the greatest interest even though carried down to a depth of only a few hundred meters. Another promising area for a shallow hole would be the Sigsbee Plain, the deep, nearly flat floor of the Gulf of Mexico. In both areas deposition by turbidity currents has dominated during much of the Pleistocene Epoch. According to the evidence in piston cores from these areas, turbidity currents were relatively infrequent during the times of mild climate between the ice ages. The sequence of Pleistocene sediments ought therefore to consist of an alternation of thick zones composed of graded layers almost devoid of the shells of planktonic organisms and much thinner zones of clay with abundant microfossils. Many piston cores have been taken in both areas, but none has been long enough to reach sediment deposited during the Sangamon Interglacial, that is, the interval of mild climate directly preceding the last ice age, presumably because accumulation of sediment during the last ice age was ten or more times faster than normal accumulation in the deep sea. In these areas the Mohole drilling equipment could do a good job and probably quite a rapid one, because the entire thickness of the Pleistocene section is no more than about 300 meters. The Pleistocene sedimentary records from these areas would be doubly valuable in that the climatic history would be defined not only by foraminifera, as in the record we have already established, but also by changes in the physical nature of the sediments themselves.

Deeper drilling into the "second" and "third layers" would

certainly bring rewards of the greatest scientific interest, and might return final answers to such questions as are there really any consistently distinguishable "second" and "third layers"? Is the "second layer" a combination of indurated sediments and volcanic rocks? Is there a thick series of older sediments masked by lava flows? Or have all pre-Mesozoic sediments been wholly destroyed or swept away by convective flow in the mantle?

The interest of paleontologists and students of evolution of course is centered entirely upon the fossil-bearing sediments. For them an ideal drilling site would be one of the lowest spots on the original primeval surface of the earth, where the first waters and sediments accumulated. There one might expect to find a continuous history layer by layer of the oceans and the creatures that have lived in them. Once, and not so long ago either, the existence of portions of the earth's original crust under the oceans was assumed by geologists as a matter of course; it was an assumption that naturally followed from the static theory of the development of the earth's features. Now the tide of thinking among geologists is turning. Various shreds of evidence hint that the floors of the oceans in the course of development of the earth's surface have been subject to either continuous or periodic renewal. If this is so, every trace of the earth's primeval surface must have been obliterated, at least within the areas now covered by the oceans. If any remnants of the primeval surface exist at all, they probably lie somewhere within the nuclei of the continents. However, only drilling can provide the final proof one way or the other.

Geophysicists, on the other hand, are more interested in the deeper-lying hard rocks under the carpet of sediment. They want samples to test for heat conductivity, electrical properties, density, elasticity, and magnetism.

As a mass of lava cools, certain iron-bearing minerals in it become magnetized in such a way as to conform to the earth's magnetic field at the time of cooling. Unless reheated, the lava retains its magnetism indefinitely regardless of subsequent changes in the positions of the earth's magnetic poles. Studies of the magnetic properties of ancient rocks show that the polarities of the magnetic minerals in such rocks point like little compass needles in various directions depending upon the ages of the rocks. In general, the polarities of rocks of any one age on any one continent agree in defining the former positions of a pair of magnetic poles, which, as a rule, are quite different from the present positions of the magnetic poles. But rocks of the same age on other continents have polarities which, though they agree among themselves, point to different positions of the North and South Poles. Since it is most improbable that there were ever several north and south magnetic poles at the same time, we are left with the only other alternative, that the continents have changed position with respect to each other since the time when the rocks were magnetized. These recent findings in paleomagnetism provide powerful evidence for continental drift. Students of this problem look forward with intense interest to the opportunity of testing the remanent magnetism of samples from the Mohole (see Figure 47).

Furthermore, students of paleomagnetism have found that the north and south magnetic poles have exchanged positions repeatedly and at fairly short intervals of time. By dating igneous rocks showing reversed polarity by means of the potassium-argon method, geophysicists and geochemists have worked out a schedule of polarity reversals extending back several million years. The time intervals between reversals have varied from a few tens of thousands of years to almost a million.

In 1962 H.M.S. *Owen*, a British oceanographic ship, found a strange pattern of abrupt changes in the intensity of the local magnetic field in the Indian Ocean. The region of magnetic anomalies included the Carlsberg Ridge, a range of submarine mountains extending roughly north and south. Since then similar patterns of anomalies have been found in other oceans, and similarly related to ridges. Apparently such magnetic patterns are as characteristic of ocean basins as the mid-ocean ridges themselves. They consist of zones or strips tens of kilometers wide and hundreds of kilometers long in the direction of the associated ridge. The boundaries between the zones or strips are defined by abrupt changes in the intensity of the local magnetic field. Recently two British geophysicists, F. J. Vine and D. H. Matthews of Cambridge University, have suggested that the anomalies may be due to reversals in the polarity of magnetization of strips of lava that have issued from fissures along the crests of the ridges and have flowed out on both sides of the ridges to distances of a few tens of kilometers. In cooling, the strips of lava would take on the polarity of the earth's field at the particular time. Now let us suppose that the sea floor spreads away from the median ridge carried on the moving mantle material as if on a conveyor belt, as R. S. Dietz has proposed. As time passes the pairs of strips of lava will be carried farther and farther from the ridge; at the same time reversals in the earth's magnetic polarity will cause each new pair of strips of lava to have reversed polarity. The result will be a pattern of magnetic anomalies similar to that observed by scientists on the *Owen*. As yet all this is purely hypothetical; no one knows whether the observed magnetic anomalies are really due to reversed polarity of strips of lava. Proof would go a long way toward establishing the validity of Dietz's hypothe-

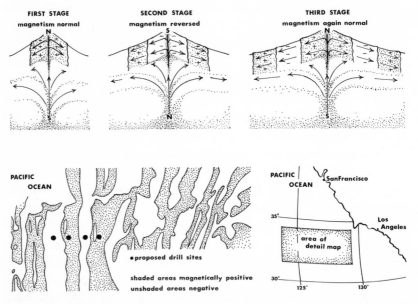

FIGURE 47   *The Mohole Project included the drilling of four holes in the floor of the Pacific west of San Diego (maps and lower sketches) to find out if the volcanic rocks there are magnetized in bands of opposite polarity. According to theory, lava extruded from submarine ridges should be magnetized in conformity with the earth's magnetic field at the time of extrusion. If the polarity of the earth's field reversed periodically, as indicated in the upper sketches, the reversals should be recorded as alternations of polarity of the bands of volcanic rock paralleling the ridges. The plus signs indicate normal polarization, the minus signs reverse polarization.*

sis of sea-floor spreading, and all that that theory carries with it, such as strong support for the hypothesis of convective flow in the mantle. Proof can be had by drilling, and not very deep drilling either. The lavas can probably be sampled by holes not deeper than about 300 meters. To get reliable evidence it will be desirable to drill several holes along a profile perpendicular to the long axes of the anomalies. Scientists associated with the Mohole Project have suggested that drilling four shallow holes in the region of anomalies off California would be a rewarding way of testing the gigantic floating drilling rig to be built for the Mohole Project.

Geologists whose chief interest is in the discovery of mineral deposits will have their own ideas about drilling sites. For example, geological and geophysical studies of the broad plain lying two miles below the surface of the Gulf of Mexico suggest the probable presence there of oil pools, beyond the reach of present drilling methods. The discovery and development of a new petroleum province there could easily repay the cost of the Mohole Project and yield a good profit as well.

No one drilling site or single hole will satisfy geologists, geophysicists, paleontologists, stratigraphers, and those in quest of mineral wealth. Since the design and building of the drilling equipment will represent a large part of the total cost, it will be good business to utilize the equipment fully rather than to dismantle it after drilling a single Mohole. Our own area of interest, the sequence of sediments, provides an example of the desirability of planning for drilling at several sites. Only by the most improbable good luck will the first Mohole pass through a continuous sequence of sediments representing all geological time. As we have said earlier, it is far more likely that the drill will encounter hard igneous rock or serpentine beneath sediment of age no greater than the Mesozoic Era. But such evidence at a single site will not be conclusive; only the finding of the same evidence at several other carefully chosen sites will justify the conclusion that the floors of the ocean basins are truly not older than the Mesozoic Era.

To explore the earth by drilling is not altogether a new idea. During the middle of the last century Charles Darwin regretted the unavailability of a millionaire willing to pay for the drilling of holes 500 to 600 feet deep into coral atolls. He realized that only by drilling could his theory of the origin of atolls by subsidence be tested conclusively.

In 1902 G. K. Gilbert of the Carnegie Institution in Washington suggested drilling a 10,000-foot (3,000-meter) hole to study the earth's heat. He appreciated the critical significance of evidence regarding the earth's heat budget to theories of the origin of the earth and that of its major features. In those days the record depth reached by drilling was only 2,800 feet (850 meters). Gilbert found a company that was willing to try to drill to 6,000 feet (1,830 meters), but at a cost of $110,000. As the money was unavailable, the project withered.

In 1939 Thomas A. Jagger of the United States Geological Survey and National Park Service proposed that petroleum engineers ought to design and build a special rig to mount on a ship for drilling at sea. Maurice Ewing has often said that the dream of his life was to drill a hole 2,000 feet (600 meters) into the ocean bed to obtain samples for study in the laboratory. In 1953 and 1954 he tried to get money for drilling, but an organization with enough money as well as a burning desire for scientific discovery and adventure did not come forward and so Ewing had to put off the realization of his dream. He estimated that the first hole would cost $1 million, but once the ship had been equipped and drillers trained he thought that additional holes could be drilled for only $200,000 each.

Frank B. Estabrook of the United States Army's Basic Research Branch should be credited with the first proposal to penetrate the crust and procure a sample of the mantle for laboratory study. He proposed that the drilling could be done on some island in the ocean where the mantle comes to within about 10 miles (16 kilometers) of the surface.

In the meantime insatiable demand for petroleum has stimulated ever deeper drilling. For a hundred years geology and geophysics have helped the petroleum industry select the best places to drill. The amount of money saved through the application of scientific knowledge to prospecting for petroleum, in place of the shotgun approach, has been enormous. The "useless" study of fossils, for example, has proved to be eminently useful in petroleum

finding. After all, is there any knowledge of any part or aspect of
our planet that is not likely to be useful?

But with the Mohole Project the tables will be turned; the
best brains of the oil, drilling, and engineering companies will
repay their debt to pure science by helping to provide the technical knowledge and experience necessary to reach the Mohole's
goal. Knowledge for its own sake will be the primary objective,
and not a mere byproduct, of this hole. In return, the oil industry
will receive a bonus in the form of new developments in methods
of drilling in deep water, the means of tapping eventually the
great wealth that probably lies beneath the seas.

The story of the Mohole began in 1957. At that time Walter
Munk, a geophysicist at the Scripps Institution of Oceanography,
and the geologist Harry Hess of Princeton University, proposed a
scheme for solving some basic problems of geology by drilling
through the earth's crust to the mantle. Other geophysicists and
geologists became interested, with the outcome that the project
attained "official" status early in 1957.

The first step of the Mohole enthusiasts was to determine
whether drilling to the mantle was really possible at all, and if so,
where the mantle might be most accessible. Geophysicists had
already shown through the study of earthquake waves that the
earth's crust under the oceans is thin, in many places being no
more than 8 and in some as little as 5 kilometers thick, whereas
under the continents it is much thicker. The region of Puerto Rico
is a good example; the crust under the island is about 32 kilometers thick, yet under the Atlantic north of the island it is only 3.2
to 6.5 kilometers thick but with 5.5 kilometers of water on top of
the crust.

By 1959 the protagonists of the Mohole had done much research, and had even carried out several geological and geophysical investigations to determine the feasibility of the project. To
find the necessary funds they had had to attain recognition as a
formal organization. This had been arranged by the National
Academy of Sciences-National Research Council which gave the
quite informal Mohole Committee a respectable home and formal
status. Numerous possible sites had been pin-pricked. Early in the
planning led by Gordon Lill and Willard Bascom, all sites on

continental shelves, volcanic ridges, oceanic deeps, areas of high heat flow, as well as those of prevalent cold and stormy weather, strong currents, and remote from bases of supply, were eliminated from consideration. The planners considered not only the geophysical and topographical conditions at the various possible locations but also the hazards due to wind, waves, swells, and surface currents. The final report pronounced the Mohole Project to be both "feasible and highly desirable."

For preliminary experimental drilling two sites were considered: the North Atlantic Basin near Puerto Rico; and the waters off Guadalupe Island, a couple of hundred miles southwest of San Diego. Not satisfied with the then available information, a reconnaissance survey sponsored by the National Science Foundation and the Office of Naval Research was carried out in the Atlantic north of Puerto Rico. For nearly a month four research vessels crossed and recrossed the area exploding depth charges and measuring the thicknesses of the rock layers by means of the refracted echos. The conduct of this survey was an innovation in itself. Instead of the usual single listening ship, there were three. This made possible more accurate measurements as well as more rapid coverage of the area.

The geophysicists soon found that a hole within a reasonable distance off Puerto Rico would have to penetrate 5,500 meters (18,000 feet) of sediment and rock before reaching the mantle. This thickness in itself is not a serious obstacle, but unpredictable weather and currents combine to make it probable that some other site of drilling will be chosen; one of the most trying problems of drilling will be to hold the 5,500 meters of unsupported drill pipe steady in the face of a strong current.

In the meantime, scientists on the west coast were also active. With the help of information accumulated earlier the geophysicists and oceanographers of the Scripps Institution of Oceanography were able to pick at least three locations near harbors and supply centers off southern California where the crust is also reasonably thin, and where weather, ocean currents, and heat flow in the sediment are favorable.

The next problem concerned the kind of ship to be used. As a beginning the obvious answer was to use equipment already developed by oil companies for offshore drilling. In 1957 a bargelike vessel called *Cuss I*—a name derived from the initials of the oil companies that owned it, Continental, Union, Shell, and Superior —had drilled holes in the sea floor, however only in the shallow water of the continental shelf.

After considering other possibilities, the Mohole group decided that a ship similar to the *Cuss I* would be suitable for practice drilling in water 300 meters (1,000 feet) to 3,000 meters (10,000 feet) deep.

At this point the Mohole Committee hired an engineering staff to get the experimental ship ready and to draw up plans for achieving the Mohole objective. Willard Bascom, who headed the staff of fifteen engineers, was made technical director of the project, with the responsibility of directing operations and carrying the job to completion.

In addition to the engineers and the fifteen or so scientists of the Mohole group, special panels of experts, numbering from five to fifteen, were selected to study various aspects of the project and advise the committee on them. These included a panel on naval architecture to deal with problems of design and construction of the drilling vessel; a panel on drilling techniques; a panel on site selection; and a panel on scientific objectives and measurements to decide what scientific measurements and observations should be made and by what means in order that the project may yield the greatest possible amount of new information about our planet.

By September 1959 these men had agreed upon a plan of action for the Mohole Project. Their approach included three phases. The drilling of practice holes with a *Cuss* type of ship was to be the first phase; this would give the engineers and drillers experience and prepare them for deep ocean drilling; at the same time equipment and methods could be tested in actual practice. The practice holes, though very shallow in comparison with the ultimate Mohole, would be deeper than any previously drilled at relatively great depths and distances from the continents, and therefore could be expected to yield enough scientific information to repay their cost.

The new technical and engineering information gained from Phase I would be used to design an improved drilling vessel and special drilling equipment. Phase II would include testing the equipment and drilling through the crust to the mantle. Phase III, which would go on at the same time as Phases I and II, would involve the collecting and analyzing of the scientific information and its publication. It would begin with the results of the first holes and would continue until the last sample had been fully studied.

As an experimental ship the Mohole group obtained the use of *Cuss I*. This 3,000-ton craft, a 260-foot converted Navy freight barge, had by the beginning of 1959 drilled more than 30 kilometers (100,000 feet) of hole, but always in depths of water not exceeding 110 meters (360 feet). In the hands of the Mohole group she was to be put to a more severe test.

Briefly, the *Cuss* method is as follows. Six anchors hold the ship in position. A prefabricated "landing base" bearing a short length of large diameter tubing (called casing by oil men) hangs under the ship. The drill pipe with drilling bit is lowered through the casing to the bottom; after drilling several hundred feet of hole, it is partly raised, and the landing base and initial casing are lowered down the drill pipe on guide cables to the bottom where they are cemented into place at the top of the hole.

A "conductor" that slides on the guide cables and is precisely centered on the landing base by conical sockets directs the riser-pipe (the casing above the sea bottom) to the mouth of the hole. As always in rotary drilling, the bit must be replaced at intervals depending upon the hardness of the rock encountered. The rock chips cut by the bit are removed from the hole by pumping a fairly heavy fluid mixture of clay and water, the drilling mud, down through the drilling pipe and then up between the drilling pipe and the wall of the hole or casing.

The fact that the *Cuss* had been quite successful in shallow, more or less sheltered water, where the bottom was hard, really proved very little about its effectiveness in the open ocean at depths greater than 3,000 meters and where a thick layer of yielding sediment carpeted the bottom. Obviously a number of entirely new procedures would have to be thought out, among which were a way of maintaining the ship's position, of bringing casing from the sea bottom to the surface, of circulating the drilling mud, and, most important, of recovering cores or samples of the rocks penetrated.

To begin with, the Mohole engineers did not know how much the ship could move without breaking the drilling pipe. From experience in shallow water they made the guess that the pipe would be endangered if the ship moved away from the hole by a distance greater than 3 per cent of the water depth. This meant that when drilling in 4,000 meters of water, she would have to remain within a circle of 120 meters or 395 feet radius centered over the hole. Conventional anchoring was out of the question. The problem called for an entirely new approach.

The solution as finally worked out involved two phases. One, some way of knowing the position of the hole several kilometers below the ship, and two, a means of maintaining the ship's position over the hole against wind, waves, and current. Determining the position of the hole was achieved by "fencing off" a circle of convenient radius with aluminum buoys held closely to position by taut wires attached to heavy anchors. Sonar and radar signals from the buoys constantly informed the pilot of the ship's position with respect to the hole, while he controlled this position by means of four immense outboard motors capable of driving the ship in any direction necessary.

Six anchors held the buoys in place. The lengths of the connecting wires were such as to hold the buoys about 45 meters or 150 feet below the surface, where they could not be tossed about by waves. The upward pull of the submerged buoys kept the connecting wires under a considerable tension. The steel piano wire holding the buoys was so thin that it offered little resistance to currents, and the buoys being streamlined were not seriously displaced by currents either, with the result that the buoys changed position by not more than about 12 meters or 40 feet.

Six surface floats were attached to the buoys by slack wires, so arranged that the radius of movement of each did not exceed 30 meters (100 feet) from the point directly over the anchor. The surface floats carried flags and lights for the benefit of the pilot, who could also use radar and sonar in case of fog.

The first phase of the Mohole Project ended in the early part of 1961. Five holes were drilled off La Jolla, California, from *Cuss I* in water 917 meters (3,109 feet) deep, and to a maximum depth of 316 meters (1,035 feet) below the bottom, after which five more holes were drilled between Guadalupe Island and the coast of Baja, California, in water 3,570 meters (11,700 feet) deep and to depths below the ocean floor of as much as 170 meters (560 feet). Drilling at the Guadalupe site went through only 170 meters of unconsolidated sediment overlying basalt. One of the holes was drilled 13 meters into the basalt.

Coring was done through the drill pipe by lowering four kinds of core barrels on a cable. The first kind, a conventional punch barrel, was locked into the bit with about 1.5 meters of the core barrel projecting below the bit; the weight of the string of drill pipes forced the barrel into the sediment. The second type of coring device, a hydraulic punch barrel, was locked into place above the bit and was forced into the sediment by hydraulic pressure from the mud pumps. The other two corers were a 6-meter rotary barrel and a turbo core barrel. The rotary barrel was the most successful in recovering cores; it drilled 9 meters into the sediment on each run without circulation of the drilling fluid.

The sediments were mostly greenish-gray clays with abundant siliceous and calcareous skeletons of microscopic plankters. On the evidence of the microfossils the entire thickness of sediment sampled was not older than Late Cenozoic, the uppermost section being of Pleistocene age, and that directly above the basalt, of Late or possibly Middle Miocene age.

Probably the most significant result of the drilling was a direct measurement of sound velocity through the unconsolidated sediment; the rate was 1.6 kilometers per second, well below previous estimates of 2.2 kilometers per second. If this is really representative of unconsolidated sediments in general, it means that the layer of sediment on the floor of the ocean is even thinner than previously supposed.

The scientific results of the preliminary phase of the Mohole Project are not of any great importance. As an achievement in drilling technique it was a greater success; it proved that a drilling ship can be held in position without anchors; that cores of unconsolidated sediment as well as hard igneous rock can be recovered; and that geophysical measurements can be made in holes drilled into the ocean floor. On the other hand, the rate of penetration of the basalt was discouragingly slow, particularly when one considers that almost certainly the Mohole will have to

go through kilometers of basalt. Futhermore, before the drilling
was done it became glaringly apparent that a *Cuss I* ship was not
even nearly adequate for Mohole drilling. For oceanic drilling a
much more stable, seaworthy craft will be needed.

More drilling at sea has not been attempted under the project
since the conclusion of the Guadalupe campaign in 1961. The
next step is to concentrate attention on the design of a larger
specialized drilling craft, probably more in the nature of a floating platform than anything like a conventional ship. Similarly, the
drilling equipment needs much improvement to cope with kilometers of hard rock. If all goes well with present plans the newly
designed gear will be ready for operation in 1968. Drilling will
then start in the Pacific.

The first phase has proved that drilling in deep water is feasible. With equal force it has proved that makeshift gear is not
good enough; the *Cuss I* was never intended for work in the open
ocean and the drilling equipment was designed to penetrate relatively soft sediments, not basalt. The successful completion of the
Phase I drilling without mishap was probably due more than
anything else to the courage, skill, and resourcefulness of the men
who ran the *Cuss*—that and a dash of good luck!

Both much time and many millions of dollars will have to be
allotted to this adventure in inner space before a sample of the
mantle is won. And success will require much hard thinking by
ingenious men.

Then there is the question of choosing a site that will yield the
greatest amount of scientific information. The region most favored by present opinion is that of the Hawaiian Islands. After
drilling has begun the time needed to reach the mantle will probably be from two to three years.

At this point the most encouraging progress is the organization of a group of experts to deal with the many problems connected with the Mohole. It includes scientists and engineers from
the government, universities, and private companies. The National Science Foundation is in over-all charge of the Project. The
National Academy of Sciences supervises the scientific work and
advises the Foundation. The building of the drilling platform and
the drilling operation itself will be the responsibility of a large
engineering firm in Texas, Brown and Root. The company will

have the cooperation of universities, and the help of drilling, oil, electronic and other firms in all parts of the country.

The United States is not alone in its plan to seek basic knowledge about our planet by deep drilling. The Russians also have a plan to drill, but they have elected to drill on land, probably somewhere on the Kola Peninsula, which they will survey in 1966 in order to select the actual site. They expect to begin drilling in 1967.

The Russian project will not duplicate the Mohole. Their goal is not to reach the Mohorovičić discontinuity, but to sample instead the basaltic layer of the lower part of the crust. Completion of both projects is most desirable because of the abundant indirect evidence of a basic difference between the crusts of the ocean basins and the continents.

We believe that the Mohole Project will be by far the more rewarding of the two, not only because it will reach the mantle but particularly because it will explore the oceanic crust. According to persuasive indirect evidence and recently elaborated hypotheses the key to an understanding of the origin of the ocean basins, the continents, the upheaval of mountain ranges and volcanoes, and the cyclical course of the history of our planet lies in the geology of the ocean floors rather than in that of the continents.

Shortly after writing the foregoing, we turned on the radio to learn what was going on in the world.

"The Appropriations Committee has trimmed from the National Science Foundation's budget for 1967 the entire $19,700,-000 to continue Project Mohole. The Committee said the project has greatly exceeded original cost estimates and the money could be better used for other scientific activities," announced the commentator.

By every reason exploration of this planet on which we must live should have priority, and yet the same Committee has approved nearly $5 billion dollars in 1967 for manned flight to the moon, the cost of which will eventually exceed $20 billion.

Truly this is lunacy!

LIFE

N GREAT DEPTHS

S O RECENT IS OUR KNOWLEDGE OF THE DEEP SEA THAT ONLY A little more than a hundred years ago a distinguished naturalist, Edward Forbes, could seriously announce to the scientific world that life did not exist in the oceans at depths greater than 550 meters (1,800 feet). Since then exploration of the world beneath the sea has advanced at a constantly increasing rate. Although zoologists and marine biologists have put most energy into studies of the inhabitants of the easily accessible shallow waters where valuable food-fishes abound, curiosity has driven others to lower trawls and nets to the greatest depths.

There is still much to be learned about creatures that dwell below reach of sunlight, and no doubt some surprises will turn up as improved gear and more effective methods are devised, but within recent years an outline of what the deep inhabitants look like, how they behave, and how they subsist has taken shape. We already know that it is a world of glaring contrasts where some of the largest animals that have ever existed fight to the death; where grotesque, goblinlike creatures compete with some of the most beautiful products of evolution.

The deep sea is a cold, unpleasant environment. What has driven a diversity of creatures, representing nearly all the major classes of animals, to resort to such a seemingly unfavorable habitat? Apart from chance strays, peopling of the depths has probably been enforced by the pressure of competition. Then as selection took effect, weeding out the least successful individuals, new and, to us, grotesque forms, well endowed to cope with the peculiarities of the environment, evolved.

Life in the ocean falls into distinct realms, each with its own peculiar creatures that are interdependent in various ways. Of these realms there is first the tidal zone, where land and sea meet. Then there are the shallow seas covering the shelves surrounding the continents, where depths do not much exceed 150 meters (500 feet). These two realms include by far the largest part of all marine life.

In the deep ocean there are two other realms. One is distinguished by receiving sunlight; the other is totally dark, or would be except for the phosphorescence of many of its inhabitants. Aquanauts in the *Trieste* as they descended 7 miles down into the clear waters of the western Pacific could see a faint glimmer at a depth of 600 meters (2,000 feet), and measurements by instruments show that in tropical regions the light threshold is as deep as 1,000 meters (3,000 feet). But practically speaking the lower boundary of the lighted zone lies at about 200 meters (600 feet). Deeper than that there is too little light to support the photosynthesis of diatoms and the other minute planktonic plants that with the aid of sunlight put together carbon dioxide and water to form sugars and starch.

These microscopic plants are the foundation of the vast food pyramid of the ocean. They are the fodder of the smaller number of vegetarians, among which are small crustacea, particularly copepods, themselves only a few millimeters long; and these in turn are fed upon by a still smaller number of larger carnivores. At the top of the pyramid are a relatively few large fish and other creatures that could not exist without some or all of the intervening levels of the pyramid. The scale of this life and death drama is staggering. A medium-sized humpback whale may have as many as 5,000 herring in its stomach. Each herring may have 7,000 small crustaceans in it, each of which may contain 130,000 diatoms. When we multiply through this chain we find that it takes about 400 billion diatoms to fuel a medium-sized whale for only a few hours. However, this calculation does not bring out the real numerical relationship between the links of the food chain because there is a continual loss of organic matter in passing from link to link.

Because a part of the substance eaten at each stage disappears in the form of energy expended, and part in repairing the wear and tear of tissues, only a small part goes into the building of new protoplasm. Experiments with rates of assimilation suggest that a loss of organic matter of at least nine tenths occurs at each stage. Consequently, the weight of the herbivore population will be less than one tenth of the weight of the plant production, and the weight of the first tier of carnivores less than one tenth of the production of herbivores, or one hundredth of the original weight of plant production, and so on. At the level of the second-rank carnivores, including some important food fish, productivity has tapered down to one thousandth of the original weight of organic substance produced by photosynthesis.

We have mentioned Edward Forbes's conclusion based on pure theory that life could not exist at depth greater than about 550 meters (1,800 feet). He assumed that this must be so because of the high pressure and absence of light at greater depths. His theory, published in the early 1840's, was widely accepted but not for very long. During the world-encircling expedition of the *Challenger*, the trawls and dredges brought up living organisms from depths almost ten times deeper than the upper limit of Forbes's azoic zone. Not only invertebrates but also fishes were caught down to depths of 4,400 meters (15,000 feet). At the beginning of this century Prince Albert I of Monaco at a point northwest of Madeira brought up a bottom-dwelling fish from a depth of about 6,000 meters (20,000 feet). Quite properly it was named *Grimaldichthys profundissimus*, "the deepest fish of Grimaldi," in honor of the Prince's family. Nearly half a century passed, and then in 1948 O. Nybelin of the Swedish Deep-Sea Expedition with the *Albatross* obtained bottom-living organisms from a depth of about 7,600 meters (25,000 feet). Only three years later this record was broken by the Danish *Galathea* expedition, which found organisms on the bottom of the deepest oceanic depression, the Philippine Trench, at 10,190 meters.

In this way during the past hundred years the lower limit of marine life, the 550 meters posited by Forbes, has been pushed downward to the greatest known depths. Evidently under normal conditions there is no lower boundary. As long as there is oxygen and a rain of organic matter from above, life can exist in spite of cold and pressure and absence of light. Where stagnation occurs, as in the Black Sea, bacteria generate hydrogen sulphide, and life, except for the bacteria that do not need oxygen, is utterly absent even at very moderate depths; but apparently under present conditions stagnant basins do not occur in the open oceans. Whether or not stagnation has occurred in the past is a question with interesting implications for the origin and evolution of deep bottom dwellers.

Pressure even at the greatest depths is not a limiting condition because it is equalized throughout an organism's tissues. A fish adjusted to live at depth is no more distressed by a pressure of 600 kilograms per square centimeter (about 4.5 tons per square inch) than we are by the 1 kilogram per square centimeter under which we live, although a moonling, hearing of the crushing atmospheric pressure on earth, might suppose it to be deadly in effect. A large change in pressure is quite a different matter. If a deep-sea fish rises above the depth to which it is accustomed, the gas in its swim bladder, or buoyancy organ, will expand and may thereby increase its buoyancy to such an extent that the fish helplessly "falls upward," with disastrous results. Deep-sea fish brought up in trawls are often in sorry shape because of too rapid expansion; in particular their swim bladders are apt to expand out through their mouths.

Darkness at depth precludes photosynthesis by plants. Many inhabitants of the deep are carnivores, but even so no community of animals can survive indefinitely by eating each other. There is of course, manna from heaven, the perpetual snow of dead and disintegrating plants and animals from the upper sunlit layer of water. Without doubt such material could support some bottom life; whether it is the sole source of provender is a question. C. E. ZoBell and R. Y. Morita found various species of bacteria in a series of sediment samples collected by the *Galathea* expedition from the Philippine Trench, Java Deep, Webber Deep, New Britain Trench and the Kermadec-Tonga Trench. Now many species of bacteria can derive nourishment entirely from inorganic substances, and they can do this without benefit of energy in the form of light. Then they have another advantage over most marine animals; some thrive on organic substances dissolved in sea water. Furthermore, it is known that protozoans, worms, sponges, filter-feeders, and mud-eaters ingest and digest bacteria. Just what proportion of the food of deep-sea animals consists of bacteria is not known, but ZoBell and Morita think that they may supply an appreciable part.

By now enough deep-sea trawling and dredging have been done to show that the population density at considerable depths is less than that at relatively shallow depths. Doubtless a restricted food supply is the limiting condition; after all, the environment is rather remote from the enormous blooms of planktonic plants in the surface waters and under any circumstances loss of organic matter occurs on the way down because of feeding by the inhabitants of intermediate depths and decomposition by bacteria.

However, whatever deep-sea populations may lack in numbers, they make up for by amazing variety and curious adaptations. The lenses of some fishes' eyes bulge out to such an extent that the field of vision of each eye exceeds 180°. Since the fields overlap forward these fish have binocular vision, a distinct advantage in gauging distances to their prey. The light organs of some fishes emit more than a mere glow; they can direct beams of light like searchlights sidewise, downwards or forwards, as they search for prey. Others lure their victims by means of lights. Some look like mere heads with a little tail and no body in between. And yet these all head and tail creatures have extraordinary capacities by virtue of their distensible stomachs; they swallow creatures twice their size as a matter of course. Others possess what amounts to fishing rods baited at the end with a light that dangles a short distance in front of their mouths.

In important ways the deep-sea environment is uniform over great distances. It lacks the drastic contrasts of the continents such as parched deserts and soggy swamps, steaming lowlands and chilly, wind-swept high plateaus; neither are there the strongly defined seasonal changes that have such a marked effect on terrestrial creatures. In consequence, assemblages of species in the deep sea range more widely than highly specialized populations on the continents. At one time, before much collecting had been done, some marine biologists assumed on theoretical grounds that almost all deep-sea species ranged throughout the ocean. More extensive collecting in recent years shows that this is not quite true; in fact, some populations of bottom dwellers, particularly invertebrates, now appear to have surprisingly restricted geographical ranges in spite of an apparent absence of clearly defined barriers. Perhaps this is because of their slow rate of spreading due to the elimination of an easily dispersed larval stage from their life histories. But in the course of millions of years they ought to have spread widely even at the slowest of dispersal rates. One is compelled to conclude that conditions on the bottom have changed, perhaps fairly recently. We know that conditions in the upper water layers changed repeatedly during the last one and a half million years, since the onset of the Pleistocene Epoch, and that the last rather drastic change occurred not more than about 11,000 years ago. Probably the influence of the Pleistocene changes on near-surface conditions extended downward to a greater extent than we are accustomed to suppose. Local oxygen depletion during warm intervals of the Pleistocene may have been responsible for the restricted geographical ranges of species bound to the sea floor.

A condition that varies regularly with depth is the hydrostatic pressure; it increases by one atmosphere (1.033 kilogram per square centimeter or 14.7 pounds per square inch) for each 10-meter increase in depth. At a depth of 10,000 meters the pressure is about 1,000 atmospheres or a little more than 1,000 kilograms per square centimeter (roughly 7 tons per square inch). Great as this pressure is, we may be sure that the 25 sea anemones, 75 sea cucumbers, 5 bivalves, amphipods, and bristle worms drawn up in the *Galathea*'s trawl from the bottom of the Philippine Trench lived quite comfortably; what must have caused acute distress was the change of pressure upon being brought to the surface. However, even that seems to be no serious problem to simple organisms such as bacteria; some of these dredged from the greatest depths lived and reproduced at atmospheric pressure. It is true that when subjected to a pressure comparable to that of their natural habitat they reproduced more rapidly and became luminescent, as if expressing their pleasure. Apparently their organic catalysts, or enzymes, worked most efficiently at a pressure of one metric ton per square centimeter, clear evidence that they belonged to a strain that had evolved on the deep-sea floor.

As light penetrates deeper below the surface of the sea, its intensity decreases because of absorption and scattering, and at a rate largely influenced by the amount of material in suspension. The ultra-violet and red rays are absorbed nearest the surface, whereas green and blue light penetrates most deeply. Observers in a bathyscaph could detect light at a depth of only 600 meters (2,000 feet), but the specially adapted eyes of deep-sea creatures can probably see at greater depths. The eyes of many deep-sea fishes have much in common with the eyes of owls that are known to work at intensities of light as low as one tenth to one hundredth of the amount necessary for human vision. In general, the eyes of deep-sea fishes differ from our own by having greater apertures and more transparent media. In addition, the light-sensitive pigments of the retina of the fish's eye absorb a greater fraction of the light than do those of the human eye.

Direct measurements of light intensity by light meters lowered at various places and under various conditions show that blue rays from the sun may penetrate to a depth of 1,000 meters (3,000 feet) in the clearest tropical waters. Therefore it is reasonable to suppose that at least some kinds of fishes, with their great owl-like eyes in bowl-shaped orbits that occupy from one quarter to almost one half the skull length, can see by faint glimmers of sunlight at depths of at least 1,000 meters. Oddly enough there is no evident relationship between the development of eyes and depth among fishes of the deep-sea floor. A single catch by a bottom trawl may include both fishes with well-developed eyes and others with degenerate eyes or even with no eyes at all. Unfortunately, association in a trawl is not proof that all were caught on the bottom; some may have entered the trawl as it was being hauled up. As a rule fishes that live at depths greater than about 2,000 meters (6,000 feet), that is, quite below the deepest penetration of sunlight, have small or degenerate eyes, whereas those living in shallower waters have large eyes with a wide pupil and broad lens.

To dwellers on the lightless sea floor vision would be useless in food gathering, the pursuit of which is confined to a single plane and thereby much simplified. Touch, taste, and smell must serve their purpose quite effectively. And yet in spite of insecure evidence of large-eyed fish in unclosed trawls, and in spite of a general tendency for the known deep dwellers to have small or degenerate eyes, there are a few species with moderately large eyes that unquestionably live at depths well below the slightest glimmer of sunlight. To these, keen sight must have some advantage. There seems to be no other explanation than that the extraordinary prevalence of luminous organisms even at great depths makes vision worthwhile for at least some of the deep dwellers.

Phosphorescence, or more properly bioluminescence, is a striking peculiarity of life in the oceans. It is not by any means confined to deep-dwelling organisms, as anyone who has watched the ocean's surface from a ship on a dark night will know. We remember one night at Ostend when each wave as it rolled in from the North Sea and crashed on the beach was marked by a flickering, greenish glow along its crest. In this case the display was due to myriads of glowing microscopic organisms.

Bioluminescence is brought about by the interaction of a substance, *luciferin*, with an enzyme, or activating substance, called *luciferase*. Apparently the biochemistry of luminescence is more complex than is suggested by the naming of the light-making substances. It has been found that luciferase from one animal will not always activate luciferin from another; evidently, the substances that go by names of luciferin and luciferase are not always the same. Difference in composition of the chemicals involved is also suggested by differences in the color of the light generated by various species that may be purplish-orange, yellow, yellowish-green, or blue-green.

Although not much is known as yet about bioluminescence in the depths of the oceans, what evidence there is indicates that the amount of light produced locally by living organisms may equal or exceed that of sunlight from the surface. Luminescence above the threshold of animal perception has been recorded at all depths down to 3,750 meters (11,500 feet). Like lighthouses, different species have characteristic rhythms of flashes or emit a continuous glow. From these patterns it is apparent that many different kinds of creatures are responsible for illumination at the various depths. The characteristics of light emission, almost as if coded, make it seem probable that bioluminscence occupies an important place in interrelationships between individuals of different species.

On the average among fishes caught in deep-ocean waters some four fifths or more of the individuals possess light-producing organs and about two thirds of the species are luminescent. This luminous contingent is dominated by the *Myctophidae* or lantern fishes (*Gonostomatidae, Sternoptychidae, Melanstomiatidae, Astronesthidae, Malacosteidae*) and *Ceratioidea* or deep-sea angler fishes. The design and arrangement of light organs combined with whatever is known about behavior of luminous fishes indicate that the lights serve a variety of purposes; some certainly serve as lures, some like flashlights are used to light the visual field, others to confuse an enemy, and still others as stimuli and recognition signals between the sexes.

There is a harmony between color or lack of color of marine animals and the changing spectral composition and distribution of light with changing depth. In the upper well-lit layer of water many invertebrates are transparent or tinted with blue to blend into their background, while fishes at the same level conform to the coloration pattern common among land animals, dark above and light or silvery below, a scheme that counteracts the effect of lighting from above and thereby reduces their visibility. Below the zone of abundant light many fishes are silvery and reddish, dark and black animals appearing in increasing numbers. At still more gloomy depths red and black are dominant colors. The occurence of many bright red animals at depth seems strange until one considers that the only light to reach great depths is blue which is entirely absorbed by red pigments; an animal like *Sergestes,* the deep-sea prawn that is bright red in daylight, appears quite black in the light of the deep sea.

Another condition of environment that restricts the geographical distributions of the various kinds of sea creatures is temperature. Except in polar seas where surface water is near or at the freezing temperature and certain restricted basins like the Red Sea, the temperature drops by an important amount from the surface to the bottom. The trend of temperature change with increasing depth varies with latitude and also, in temperate regions, with the time of the year.

A high temperature layer in the tropical and subtropical oceans is maintained by the inflow of radiant heat from the sun. The thickness of this warm layer of low density varies from 20 to 200 meters. Directly below lies a zone of discontinuity, the thermocline within which the temperature falls rapidly and a corresponding increase in density occurs. From here on down the temperature decreases more slowly, although a deeper discontinuity or zone of abrupt temperature change is sometimes found between 500 and 1,000 meters. In tropical regions between the surface and lower boundary of the thermocline at about 150 meters the temperature may fall from 29° C. to 15° C., whereas from 150 meters to 500 meters a gradual decrease to about 9.5° C. occurs. Below that level a very gradual drop to about 4° C. at 1,500 meters takes place. At 2,000 meters and deeper prevailing temperatures range from 3.5° C. to below zero values.

In a temperate region west of Scotland there is during the summer a discontinuity layer in the upper 100 meters within which the temperature falls from 13° C. to somewhat less than 10° C., then from 100 to 1,500 meters the water gradually cools from 9.5° C. to about 4° C. However, during the winter the cooling of surface water and the setting up of convection currents leads to vertical mixing that eliminates the zone of discontinuity.

In Antarctic waters there is actually a rise in temperature with depth. From the surface to 400 meters the temperature goes from −1.7° to +0.5° C. From 400 to 1,500 meters the water cools to 0° C.

Interesting parallels between the distributions of deep-sea animals and ocean temperatures can be found. Many species living between the surface and a depth of 500 meters have ocean-wide ranges between the north and south temperate zones. To understand why this may be so, let us take an animal living in the equatorial region of the Atlantic, that spends the day at a depth of about 400 meters and rises to the surface toward nightfall. This means that it passes the day in water of a temperature between 8° to 10° C. whereas after sunset it will enter the upper layer of water with a temperature above 20° C. But if the same animal remained in the surface water it would have to travel from the equatorial region to the area off Iceland to encounter such large differences in temperature. Since temperature is probably an important condition influencing the distribution in time and space of deep-water animals, it is not surprising that many species have vertical ranges of only about 1,000 meters and yet spread over thousands of miles in the north and south dimension.

An interesting consequence of the fairly large vertical temperature gradient in oceans is what is called *submergence*. It has been found that certain animals of the open ocean, as well as bottom dwellers that live in relatively shallow waters in the cool northern and southern seas, live at greater depths in low latitudes. Presumably their biochemistry is best suited to a cool environment; in tropical and subtropical regions they find agreeable temperature well below the warm surface layer. The jellyfish *Periphylla periphylla* is a good example; it is most abundant between depths of 500 to 1,500 meters below the warm surface water of the Atlantic, whereas it is common in the cool surface waters off Norway, Greenland, and Iceland. Another is the nemertean worm *Nectonemertes mirabilis*, which lives at a depth of about 500 meters in the seas around Greenland, but occurs only at depths of 1,300 to 1,800 meters in the vicinity of Bermuda.

A problem of scientific as well as practical interest is the fact of much variation in abundance of sea life from place to place. Some regions abound in life, while others are little better than oceanic deserts. On the continents, as we have mentioned, there is almost always some quite evident reason for local differences in population, but as one sails over the blue waters of the Sargasso Sea, to cite an example, the reason for the bareness of the clear water does not strike the eye.

A partial answer lies in an interplay between the chemistry of water, particularly the presence of two kinds of substances, nitrates and phosphates, and the life processes underway in the sunlit surface waters. Each has a critical influence on the other. But as so often happens when life is involved, the problem is not so simple. The raw chemicals are essential but not sufficient to ensure high productivity, as shown by the observation that adjacent areas where the chemistry of phosphates and nitrates is similar may differ greatly in their productivity; while one supports dense blooms of planktonic photosynthesizers, equally rich supplies of phosphate and nitrate in the other seem to be of no avail. A similar problem comes up in culturing marine organisms. Often it would be convenient to fill aquariums with artificial sea water, that is, a solution containing the right proportions of the various mineral salts known to occur in salt water; but the animals in such water never thrive unless another ingredient is added, called "soil extract," the very name of which is an admission of ignorance. Presumably "soil extract" contains small amounts of complex organic chemicals, metabolites, vitamins and the like, which are vitally important to marine life. The practical importance of the identity of these substances is obvious, if we hope to farm the sea. To attack the problem, special biochemical techniques will be needed. In many ways the oceanic world is still little known and less well understood.

Admittedly, we have been at a disadvantage in studying the oceanic world. When one thinks about it, to expect to learn much about the complex society of the oceans by lowering little nets and bags is almost ridiculous. To hope to gain an adequate picture of life on the North American continent by dragging a few little nets over its surface from an airship is almost analogous, but not quite. We have already mentioned the sharply defined variations in conditions on land. Fortunately, for the marine biologist life in the oceans is much more uniform in distribution; there are local variations but on an entirely different scale. Furthermore, new instruments and more effective methods of study are on the way.

As yet the most efficient gear for collecting animals from great depths is the trawl. Essentially, it is a widely open sack of netting that is dragged over the bottom on the end of a steel cable. Shapes and sizes vary widely. The width of the otter trawl used by the Norwegian *Michael Sars* expedition in the North Atlantic more than fifty years ago was about 15 meters (50 feet). This great width was kept open by means of otter boards. Each wing of the net was fastened by a bridle to a rectangular iron shod board. When towed, the otter boards like a pair of kites sheered away from each other and in that way kept the mouth of the net or bag fully open. This expedition, which gathered a wealth of material in the North Atlantic, was largely due to the generosity of Sir John Murray. Much impressed by the ability of the young Norwegian oceanographer Johan Hjort, Murray proposed that if the Norwegian government would provide a research ship with Hjort as leader, he would pay the scientific expenses of the expedition.

Another kind of trawl is kept open by an iron frame usually with runners so that it can slide over the bottom much like a sledge, from which it gets its name, sledge trawl. Naturally, the width of the opening is much less than that of the otter trawl. That used by the *Galathea* had a width of only 3 meters (10 feet). Trawls are intended to sample the bottom; if they catch anything above the bottom it is only by accident as they are being hauled up.

The deep-sea environment includes two distinct populations: first, the creatures that have reached abyssal depths, that is deeper than 1,000 meters, by creeping along the bottom; these bottom dwellers are known collectively as *the benthos*. Then there is the community of swimmers or drifters that occupy the midwater, the great space between the surface and the bottom; they are the pelagic animals.

Among the benthos are the echinoderms, animals without backbones that spend adulthood attached to the ocean floor or burrowing in the sediment. Only a few kinds ever make excursions above the sea floor. Very few of the phyla, the first broad subdivisions of the animal kingdom, belong exclusively to the sea. The phylum Echinodermata, which includes starfish, sea urchins, brittle stars, sea cucumbers, and sea lilies, is such a one. An outstanding characteristic of echinoderms is radial symmetry, and a strange, one might almost say perverse, preference for the number 5. However, there is some latitude of form; some starfish have many more rays than five, and many echinoids have well-developed bilateral symmetry. Since the larvae of all forms commonly have bilateral symmetry, it is probable that the typical radial symmetry of the adults is an evolutionary adaptation to a sedentary existence on the sea floor, where, all horizontal directions being much the same, there is little point in having a head end. A starfish will move in any direction where one of its arms happens to point. It moves by means of thousands of little sucking feet. That such a meagerly endowed creature should be able to coordinate its many feet so as to move at all is rather extraordinary. Echinoderms are remarkable for their great depth ranges. The scarlet sea star *Henricia sanguinolenta* ranges from shallows out to abyssal depths, and the brittle star *Ophiacantha bidentata* may be found between shallows of 4 or 5 meters and abyssal depths down to 4,500 meters (15,000 feet). The echinoderms are an ancient lineage in the fossil record; the early members antedate the first vertebrates by something like 100 million years. In fact, some paleontologists hold that the first vertebrates evolved from an echinoid; certain early fossil fish were encased in armor that has a suggestive resemblance to the calcareous plates of echinoids.

Regardless of the essentially sedentary nature of echinoderms, a few sea cucumbers have been found swimming in the mid-water. The first to be discovered was *Pelagothuria natatrix*, a rose-colored animal with a dark violet hindpart, about 10 centimeters (4 inches) long. The first find in 1891 was off the west coast of Central America. Since then it has been found several times by deep-fishing expeditions in tropical parts of the Pacific and Indian oceans. Two other species of deep-sea swimming sea cucumbers of the genus *Enypniastes* have been known for many years from such widely separated regions as the Bay of Bengal and the Great Australian Bight. The *Galathea* expedition found a third species of *Enypniastes* in the China Sea at a depth of more than 3,350 meters (11,000 feet). In the same area the *Galathea* caught a fourth species that was new to science. It was broadly oval in shape, 23 centimeters (9 inches) long, 15 centimeters (6 inches) wide, and dark violet in color. It has been named *Galatheathuria*, after the ship.

The commonest of all deep-sea bottom-living fishes are the rat-tails of the family *Macrouridae*. There are many kinds. Character-istically they have a big head from which the body tapers to a long tail, which is flattened in the vertical plane and often ends in a long filament. The head is heavily armored and is pitted with prominent canals that contain the long-distance sense organs of the "lateral-line." The lateral-line organs pick up vibrations in the water at a distance and enable the fish to find the source of the disturbance. All fish possess these organs but they are particularly well developed in deep-sea fish that must find their prey in darkness. The mouth, usually armored, is sometimes blunt, but more often extends forward—occasionally as a wide tube. The dorsal fin on top of the body is long and low and practically continuous with the long anal fin. The common lengths of rat-tails vary from 30 to 60 centimeters (1 to 2 feet). In nearly all species the eyes are a dominant and striking feature. Specimens from 25 to 75 centimeters long may have eyes with diameters ranging from 1.2 to 3.8 centimeters. Young rat-tails live in shallower water; then as they approach adulthood they seek greater depths, but apparently they keep the ability to swim upward at will, as is the case with many other deep-sea fishes. To help them in their upward trips they have well-developed swim bladders.

Why should these fish that spend so much of their lives in darkness have such remarkably sensitive eyes? Strangely enough the eyes become larger as the fish grow older and migrate to deeper water. Quite a number of rat-tails have an open gland along the belly that contains luminous bacteria. Is it possible that the light of luminous benthic invertebrates and bacteria enable rat-tails to find food?

When Jacques Piccard and Lieutenant Donald Walsh of the United States Navy dived to the bottom of the Marianas Trench in the bathyscaph *Trieste* in 1960 they saw a living fish on the floor of the trench at the great depth of more than 10,000 meters. "Slowly, very slowly, this fish, apparently of the sole family, about one foot long and half as wide, moved away from us, swimming half in the bottom ooze, and disappeared into the black night, the eternal night which is its domain."

This fish was a flatfish, one of the major groups that spend their adult lives lying directly on the sea bottom. The shallow-water species of flatfish are valuable catches in many countries. Halibut and flounder are familiar representatives in American waters; in Europe plaice and sole are best known. The flatfish exemplify a beautiful adaptation to life on the sea floor. Rays are flattened also, but in a different manner, as if they had been compressed from above in such a way as to retain their bilateral symmetry. The true flatfish start out in life as quite normal little fish that swim about on an even keel, but before long they take to lying on their sides on the bottom. If any ordinary fish did that it would lose the use of the eye that happened to be downward, but with the flatfish an extraordinary transformation takes place; the eye on the under side gradually migrates around to the upper side. As a result one eye is higher and farther forward than the other, but this does not impair their usefulness. At the same time the underside loses all color, while the upper side takes on an almost photographic reproduction of the appearance of the sandy bottom. While lying still they are really invisible. The fins, supported by numerous soft rays, extend around the whole body like a fringe. When disturbed they can dart away with lightning speed.

Although most flatfish live at shallow depths, a few species, like that seen by Piccard and Walsh, go down to great depths. The *Galathea* caught a strange kind of flounder, *Azygopus pinnifasciatus*, at a depth of 600 meters (2,000 feet) in the Tasman Sea. It is remarkable for having dark spots on its tail, two of which resemble eyes. According to theory the eyelike spots mislead its pursuers into mistaking the tail for the head. However, there is not much light at 600 meters in the Tasman Sea. Can its pursuers see the spots? From here one can theorize a bit further; perhaps the spots are vestigial from a time when its ancestors lived on the continental shelf. Thus the spots may be evidence that this deep-sea fish, and by inference others, originated on the continental shelf.

The *Galathea* caught a brotulid in the Sunda Trench in 1952 in water about 7130 meters (23,400 feet) deep, which set a depth record for a live fish that lasted until 1960 when it was broken by Piccard and Walsh. This little brotulid, only 17 centimeters (6.5 inches) long, broke a record that had stood for half a century— the one set by the Prince of Monaco's *Grimaldichthys profundissimus* from a depth of 6,000 meters. This fish was also a brotulid.

Next to the rat-tails, the brotulids are the most common of deep-sea fishes, and they are strangely similar to the rat-tails; they have the same large heads tapering to long, flattened, and pointed tails, and the dorsal and anal fins are continuous with the tail fin. Many species of the family Brotulidae have large and prominent eyes, again like many rat-tails. They are mostly rather small, that is from a few centimeters to about 30 centimeters (1 foot), with a maximum length of about 100 centimeters (3 feet).

The members of these two families of fishes are so much alike that it is difficult for anyone but an expert to tell them apart. However, they are probably not really closely related; the rat-tails are relatives of the cods, whereas the brotulids are closer to the live-bearing blennies of shallow waters. Clearly the rigorous selection of the deep-sea environment has, as it were, pressed different materials into the same mold, a phenomenon found elsewhere in the organic world and to which the name *convergence* has been given. What survival value the odd shape and other characters common to the two families have is anything but clear; but that they do somehow contribute to the success of their possessors is a certainty.

The ray fins of the family Sudidae long ago excited the interest of zoologists because of their amazingly elongated "feelers." The biologists of the *Challenger*, who caught many of these odd fishes, speculated about the possible uses for the fantastic appendages. That they were organs of touch seemed probable, but it was difficult to see why they should be so extravagantly long.

The ray fins differ from the rat-tails and brotulids in having a large tail instead of a long, pointed filament, and in having very small eyes. Like salmon and trout they have a small, fleshy fin on top of the tail. Their peculiarity is the long rays or feelers that project from the fins. These are really a part of the fins, being the much-elongated first fin rays of the pectoral fins, the paired fins on each side behind the head. Apparently, the feelers are used to probe the soft sediment for food. They also support the fish on the bottom like stilts according to observers in the bathyscaph *Trieste* who saw a ray fin at a depth of 7,000 meters (23,000 feet). Although a few species of ray fins have been caught on the continental slopes, most have been found at great depths.

The stomiatoids comprise a large group of deep-swimming fishes. Included among them are the so-called viper fishes. Some kinds give the impression of being all head with a little tail added as an afterthought. With their disproportionately large jaws and extensible stomachs they are voracious predators. In hunting their prey some kinds have the advantage of large light organs behind the eyes set in a pocket covered by transparent skin. During the day stomiatoids swim at a depth of about 1,500 meters (5,000 feet), but rise almost to the surface at night. Biologists have described them as beautiful, fearsome, and appalling; odd they surely are, but their appallingness is much tempered by their small size, mostly from 15 to 18 centimeters (6 to 7 inches) and at most only 30 centimeters.

A group of deep-swimming fishes that conform more nearly to what one expects in a fish is that known as lantern fish. They spend their days at depths of about 1,000 meters (3,500 feet) and,

like the stomiatoids, their nights at or near the surface. They earn
their name from their bright taillights and the rows of dimly glowing lights on their flanks. One species has lights on its tongue,
perhaps to lure prey into its mouth. Except for eyes that are a
good deal larger than those of most fish of their size, they are not
remarkable in form. Most are not more than a few centimeters
long and the largest reach a length of only 15 centimeters (6
inches).

The hatchet fish are well named; with a thin, straight-edged
belly as the blade and the tail as a handle, one of these strange
fishes looks a good deal like a hatchet, that is, a very little
hatchet; many are not more than 2.5 to 5 centimeters (1 to 2
inches) long, and the giants among them are only 10 centimeters
long. They live at depths between 270 and 500 meters (880 and
1,600 feet). They have curious tubular eyes that point upward,
and a series of colorful light organs.

Although some true eels, such as *Histiobranclaus infernalis*,
have been found at depths between 1,800 and 3,000 meters
(5,900 and 10,000 feet), the so-called spiny eels of abyssal depths
are not really eels at all. They belong to the family Notacanthidae.
Their only eel-like attribute is the unpaired fin along the top of
the body that consists of a series of free spines, unconnected by
skin or membranes as in most kinds of fishes. In other respects
they are like many other deep-sea fishes on the ocean floor in
having long tapering tails, many-rayed fins, and jaws slung beneath a projecting snout. A peculiarity of the mouth is a sharp
spine concealed at each corner. The food found in their stomachs
confirms what their underslung mouths suggest; that they feed on
the bottom sediment. The spiny eels are found at depths of about
2,000 meters (6,500 feet) or deeper.

The pelican eels, or gulpers (see Figure 48), are another group
of deep-sea fishes that are not really eels. They live in tropical
and subtropical oceans mostly below 2,000 meters (6,500 feet).
As machines for the purpose of seizing, holding, and swallowing
prey in order that there may be more gulpers in their dark, cold
world, they are not far from perfection. The huge mouth studded
with teeth, the distensible jaws, the belly that can expand to
several times its normal capacity, are some of the remarkable
adaptations of gulpers. Their eyes are quite small; a specimen of

the genus *Eurypharynx*, 25 centimeters long, has an eye not more than 0.15 centimeters in diameter. As deep-sea fishes go, gulpers are large; *Saccopharynx ampullaceus* measures about 180 centimeters (6 feet), though most are less than 60 centimeters (2 feet) long. The slender, whiplike tail accounts for a large part of a gulper's length; the rest of a gulper is really little more than mouth. A gulper with a body length of 15 centimeters (6 inches) can engulf a 23 centimeter (9 inch) fish.

However, in voraciousness, the gulpers take second place to

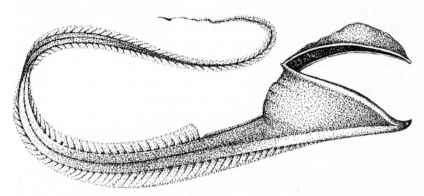

FIGURE 48   *Gulper, or pelican eel. This fish is all mouth and practically no brain.*

the swallowers. A black swallower, *Chiasmodus niger*, is only about 10 centimeters long and yet it is known to swallow fishes 25 centimeters long.

As an example of extraordinary adaptation the angler fishes are unsurpassed. Unlike most fish whose bodies are deeper than broad, the anglers are as wide as they are deep. The mouth is gigantic; much of the head consists of jaws that slant downward in such a way as to make the fish a caricature of grimness when the mouth is closed. With the mouth open the effect is compounded by long, curved, and sharp teeth. The roughly rectangular tail is insignificant in comparison with the head. As if to enhance the nightmarish appearance, the jet-black or dark-brown skin is covered with folds, warts, furrows, and various kinds of excrescences. The eyes are poorly developed.

But what sets the anglers apart is their fishing apparatus. This apparatus varies much among the species, being stubby in some, and several times the body length in others. Again, it may be straight or bent in a right angle. The fishing line, or illicium, is really a greatly overgrown and modified first ray of the dorsal fin. On the end of the illicium is what amounts to bait, a light organ to attract prey. The angler is a poor swimmer; after all, it has no need to dash after its prey. Instead it hovers motionless except for a flutter of its fins or tail and keeps its position somewhere between 1,000 and nearly 4,000 meters (3,000 and 12,000 feet) below the surface. There in the black depths it angles for its game by fluttering and twitching its rod and lighted bait and by displaying colored lights to attract the curious. When it gets a "nibble," it draws in the bait to induce the victim to move closer to its jaws. When it has played its quarry close enough, the gulf of the mouth suddenly opens and in pops the victim, helplessly sucked in by the current created by the opening jaws.

So far we have described only female anglers. For many years marine biologists were puzzled by the apparent nonexistence of males. Actually they had found them without knowing it; the males were so different that zoologists had mistakenly assigned them to a different family. Only recently has it been possible to pair off the various species. The difference between the sexes arises from their different ways of life; the male does not angle. At an early stage he attaches himself to the body of the female (see Figure 49) and thereafter spends his life as a parasite. Although he continues to grow he never attains much size, a fortunate circumstance for the female. The largest male of *Ceratias holboelli* ever found was only one third as long as his mate. Normally the males are much smaller, some being only one twenty-fifth as large. The disparity in weight is even greater, with the result that the puny male, parasitically gaining sustenance from the female's bloodstream, does not put too great a strain on his mate. Woe to him if he does, for her welfare is also his. Thus by a curious turn of evolutionary events the success of the species is enhanced by the reduction of the male to a miserable weakling.

The squids and octopuses are an uncanny tribe. Our innate repugnance for snakes is aroused eight- or tenfold by the snakelike arms of an octopus or squid. Small wonder that the octopus with its baleful eyes has inspired horror legends and horror pictures of ships being drawn down by huge sucker-studded arms reaching out of the deep. Of course, such horrors do not exist and neither does the ferocious creature described by Victor Hugo in *Toilers of the Sea.* In reality, octopuses are small, timid animals. The cephalopods, the group to which squids and octopuses belong, are members of the phylum Mollusca which includes clams and snails. Anyone who has eaten squid will probably have noticed the clamlike flavor.

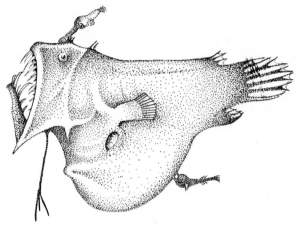

FIGURE 49 *Female angler fish and a parasitic male. The male, attached permanently to the belly of the female, gets his sustenance from her.*

The name *octopus* comes from the eight muscular arms. A mantle of thick skin and muscle surrounds a dome-shaped or egg-shaped body. An opening in the mantle at the neck leads into a cavity containing the gills. The animal breathes by dilating the mantle, thereby drawing water into the mantle cavity to bathe the gills; then the mantle opening closes and contraction of the mantle sends the water out through a siphon or funnel. At will the creature can jet itself about by means of the powerful stream of water from its siphon. Squids are swift swimmers and can go into reverse instantly by merely turning the siphon so as to direct their water jet in the opposite direction. Octopuses get about by crawling with their arms, and use jet motion only to dart away when startled.

In addition to the eight arms of the octopus, squids have two somewhat longer tentacles, often with club-shaped ends. The fairly long body is cigar-shaped and, in swiftly swimming species, beautifully streamlined.

Some species of squids and octopuses live at great depths. Squids have been caught at least as deep as 3,500 meters (11,500 feet), and in the Weddell Sea off Antarctica an octopus, *Grimoteuthis*, lives on the bottom some 2,750 meters (9,000 feet) down.

In fantastic modifications the deep-sea squids probably outdo all other groups of animals. In some the head sticks out on a long stalk. Others have their eyes on long stalks armed with searchlights. Some are so nearly transparent that their nerves can be easily seen. No other group of deep-sea creatures is quite so brilliantly lighted. In addition to having many different colored photophores, or light organs, squids seem to be able to control them with spectacular effect.

The extraordinary similarity between the human eye and the squid's eye is a brilliant example of evolutionary convergence; they are alike in almost every detail. Both have a transparent cornea, an iris diaphragm, a clear lens, a chamber filled with liquid, and muscles to control the focus of the lens and movement of the eyeball. The arrangement of the retinal cells of the squid's eye appears more efficient, however, than the human eye. The light-sensitive cells of the retina in the human eye are covered by the nerve cells that intervene between them and the lens, but this is not so for the squid's eye, which should therefore have a wider field of clear vision. The eyes of most squids are large in proportion to the head. The eye of the giant squid *Architeuthis* achieves the prodigious diameter of 40 centimeters (15 inches). This species reaches a length of at least 15 meters (50 feet), which is about the length of the largest of all fishes, the whale shark. A puzzling evolutionary development is the great disparity in size of the two eyes of some squids. In *Histioteuthis* and *Calliteuthis* the left eye has about four times the area of the right. A possible explanation for this strange assymetry is that the animal uses its large eye in the dim light of the deep sea and its small eye in the bright light of near-surface waters.

The arms of squids and octopuses bear suckers. Recent experiments with octopuses at the marine biological station in Naples show that in addition to being able to distinquish tastes by means of the suckers, they can also distinguish between objects of different textures and shapes, providing the scale does not much exceed the diameters of the individual suckers.

One of the strange tactics of cephalopods is the use of what amounts to smoke screens, that is, ink clouds, to confuse the enemy. The squid *Ommastrephes pteropus* goes so far as to squirt from the siphon a cigar-shaped cloud of ink roughly of its own dimensions that coagulates in the water enough to hold its shape for several minutes. The ink is a thick, dark-brown fluid. Artists, particularly in China and Japan, have used it in pen and brush drawings for centuries. It has also been used in Europe where it is known as sepia.

Squids are also remarkable for possessing nerve axons, or communication lines of the nervous system, of giant diameters. A squid's axon may be a millimeter in diameter, which is about two hundred times the diameter of a human axon. Through the laboratory study of squid axons much has been learned about what happens when an electrical impulse passes along a nerve fiber. The speed of transmission of the impulse is proportional to the diameter of the axon. Presumably the giant axon is useful to the squid in coordinating its escape responses. However that may be, the squid's axon is proving most useful in research for better understanding of the functioning of human nerves.

Monsters have always fascinated people. To fill this need imaginative men have invented cyclopses, unicorns, dragons, and a whole menagerie of mythical beasts. And the mystery of the ocean has encouraged some of the wildest and most persistent flights of fancy.

Exploration and world-wide communication have laid low the unicorns and chimeras of the Middle Ages, but the oceans are still a vast unknown; they remain a potential home for monsters. Moreover, conditions at sea sometimes make cold-blooded, objective observations rather difficult. The prototype of the mermaid may have been a dugong, manatee, or sea cow, mammals that bear and suckle their young in the sea or at the mouths of rivers. To be sure, these animals are not noted for beautiful tresses of hair, but no doubt wishful thinking and some Jamaica rum could make up for the deficiency. Similarly, the perennial sea serpents may have some basis in fact. Somehow sea serpents refuse to be downed, as witness the monster of Lock Ness in Scotland. Many explanations for the Loch Ness monster have been put forward but none is really satisfactory.

Many, if not most scientists reject the idea that sea monsters of large size will ever be discovered in the deep sea, and yet Anton Bruun held the theory that such creatures do really exist. One of the important missions of the *Galathea* expedition of 1950–2 was to test his theory. Naturally, oceanographic observations and the gathering of marine biological material were the basic purposes of the expedition. However, support for the expedition was stimulated when a Danish author, Hakon Mielche, took up Bruun's argument that the evidence against the existence of sea serpents is all negative; the fact that a sea serpent has never been caught does not prove that they do not exist.

In addition to Bruun, another distinguished marine scientist firmly believes that sea serpents exist in the deep sea. He is J. L. B. Smith of South Africa, famous as an ichthyologist and well known for his description of the coelacanth, a kind of fish originally known only as a fossil and supposedly extinct some 70 million years ago, until living specimens were caught off the coast of South Africa in 1938. Smith cites a number of instances in which reliable observers have reported seeing "monsters" and have been able to give impressive details. Smith regards the existence of the Loch Ness sea monster as being beyond reasonable doubt.

Some biologists believe that if sea serpents are ever found they will turn out to be giant squids. There is good evidence from sporadic finds that truly enormous and powerful squids exist in deep water. Individuals measuring 17.4 meters (57 feet) have been found and competently examined. An encounter with the giant squid *Architeuthes* took place in 1861 between Madeira and Tenerife, Canary Islands. A French corvette found the creature on the surface of the sea. Estimated to be about 5.5 meters (18 feet) long, it was described as "frightful, its color brick red . . . this colossal and shiny embryo presented a repulsive and terrible figure." There is another record of an encounter in 1873 in the waters off Newfoundland. When it attacked three cod fishermen in a dory one of its tentacles, 5.8 meters (19 feet) long, was cut off. In the same year, near the place where it had first appeared, four herring fishermen caught a squid in their net. According to a clergyman of St. Johns, who took an interest in natural history, the tentacles were 7.3 meters (24 feet) long and the over-all length was 9.8 meters (32 feet). During succeeding years other great squids were caught off Newfoundland, and from 50 to 60 were encountered by fishing boats. Then for some unknown reason they ceased to appear in that region.

The most ferocious and dangerous of giant squids are those of the Humbolt Current off Peru. Big-game anglers have sometimes lost their prize marlins to *Dosidicus gigas,* the squid of the Humbolt Current. It is well-named "gigantic," being 3 to 3.7 meters (10 to 12 feet) long and weighing up to 160 kilograms or 350 pounds. As we have said, *Architeuthis* is larger but probably not more ferocious. Actually a large part of the length of an *Architeuthis* is in the two longest tentacles. The tentacles of a giant squid found off New Zealand measured 15 meters (49 feet, 3 inches), whereas the total length of the animal was 17.4 meters (57 feet). But the proportions of this species are exceptional—as recorded in its name *Architeuthis longimanus.* Sir Alister Hardy lists specimens of *Architeuthis princeps* 16.8 meters (55 feet) and 15.9 meters (52 feet) long whose trunks were 6.1 meters (20 feet) and 4.6 meters (15 feet) long respectively, and a specimen of *Architeuthis harveyi* 15.9 meters (52 feet) long with a trunk of 3 meters (10 feet).

Very large eels have not been found but there is suggestive evidence that they may exist. During the cruise of the *Dana* around the world in 1928–30 an eel larva 184 centimeters long was caught. If a larva of that size grew up according to the larva-to-adult size ratio of common eels, it would attain a length of 21 meters (70 feet), which could be a good substitute for a sea serpent. As yet no one knows what such giant larvae become at maturity.

It may well be that in the vast expanses and depths of the oceans there are eels and squids that greatly exceed in size and power any so far caught or found dead. To catch such animals with even the most effective gear will be difficult; more probably their hiding places will be found through exploration of the deep sea by small submarines.

With the appearance in 1859 of Darwin's *On The Origin of Species* the theory of evolution became popular almost overnight.

The theory was old, but until that year there had been no plausible mechanism to explain evolution. The simplicity and compelling logic of Darwin's theory of natural selection was enough to raise evolution from the status of a vague hypothesis to that of a near certainty. Fossils took on a popular interest they had never had before.

The thought occurred to scientists that living descendants of some of the creatures whose shells were common in ancient sediments might occur in the deep oceans, where they had found refuge from competition against more efficient animals. Only five years after the publication of Darwin's book, G. O. Sars dredged from a depth of 550 meters (1,800 feet) a sea lily, or crinoid, unlike any previously known to be alive but the same as familiar forms abundant in sediments laid down during the Jurassic and Cretaceous periods more than 100 million years ago. This hangover from the past was named *Rhizocrinus lofotensis*, after the place where it was found, the Lofoten fjords. Sea lilies are not plants as the common name implies, but echinoderms related to starfish and sea urchins. They have a skeleton composed of many ossicles of calcium carbonate that occur in great numbers in many ancient sediments.

Sars set a fashion. After 1864 many other explorers of the sea found crinoids. Wyville Thomson on the *Porcupine* found some in 1870; the *Challenger* dredged them up in 1872–76, and so did the French *Talisman* in 1880–3. These fascinating finds seemed to confirm the guess that the more nearly unchanging conditions of the deep ocean had indeed permitted the survival of many "living fossils."

However, in the years that followed few other archaic forms were brought to the surface in spite of eager search. The majority of the creatures collected from great depths proved to be closely related to the well-known forms of shallow waters. The excitement among biologists subsided and they went on with the routine job of describing and cataloguing. For some reason the oceans had not been such a safe refuge after all; we can be sure now that whole assemblages of archaic forms will not be found in them. Nevertheless, as collecting has accelerated, some fascinating finds of the close relatives of otherwise long-extinct tribes of animals have been found in the seas. Among these are a fish belonging to a group previously thought to have become extinct many millions of years ago, and an ancestrial snail, or "presnail," whose youngest fossil relative is 350 million years old.

In 1938 a great event in the history of zoology occurred. A fisherman off the east coast of South Africa caught a fish of a kind that he had never seen before. When J. L. B. Smith (page 310) saw

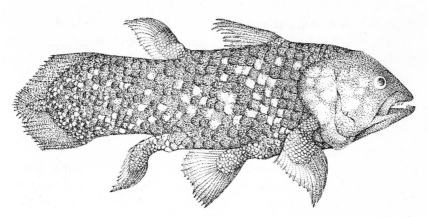

FIGURE 50 *The most famous of living fossils, the coelacanth fish* Latimeria chalumnae. *Its fellows were abundant 220 million years ago, but the last one was thought to have died 70 million years ago. Yet in 1938 a specimen, very much alive, was caught off the east coast of South Africa.*

the fish he recognized it as a coelacanth, a very ancient class of fishes that was supposed to have disappeared some 70 million years ago (see Figure 50). These fishes were distinguished by lobed fins, forerunners of the limbs of higher animals. Here was an opportunity to study at first hand a living link in evolution. Unfortunately, the specimen when it reached Smith had been mutilated and was partly decomposed.

Zoologists all over the world were eager to find more speciments, but in spite of a search by Smith and others, fourteen years passed before a fisherman found another, but again it was in deplorable condition by the time it reached Smith. At this point a system of catching, preserving, and transporting the fish by air was set up by the Madagascar Institute of Scientific Research. Since then nine more coelacanths, all in good condition, have been caught. These good-sized fishes, from 120 to 170 centimeters

long and weighing as much as 80 kilograms (180 pounds), have
been named *Latimeria chalumnae* by Smith. Their fins set them
apart from all other living fishes; they are borne on scaly stalks
and the bones articulate through a single structure, just as the
limbs of a quadruped hinge on a single bone. Furthermore, the
skull is constructed in the same general way as that of primitive
amphibians. These characters have led paleontologists to regard
the group to which the coelacanths belong as the common stock
from which sprang the amphibians and from them all land and air
vertebrates. Oddly enough all coelacanths have been caught in
fairly shallow water, that is, at depths between 150 and 365
meters (480 and 1,200 feet). Probably they descent to greater
depths; little fishes found in their stomachs belong to species that
live at depths between 550 and about 1,000 meters, but even so
they are not really deep-sea fishes. It seems strange that they have
not been caught long before.

If the *Galathea* did not catch a sea serpent, she caught something else, less spectacular but equally interesting. Near the end
of her cruise, off the coast of Costa Rica in the Pacific, from a
depth of 3,590 meters the *Galathea*'s dredge brought up ten live
specimens of a limpetlike little creature belonging to a group
previously known only to paleontologists as the Monoplacophora,
and supposedly extinct since the Devonian Period, 350 million
years ago. It was named *Neopilina galatheae* in honor of the ship.
Neopilina is an archaic mollusc, neither clam nor snail, being
more primitive than both. The oval, spoon-shaped shell, at most
38 millimeters long, is thin and fragile, semi-transparent, and
yellowish white. It rises to a little peak, with the point tilted over.
An almost circular "foot" of a bluish color, with a diffuse pink
central area, makes up a large part of the animal. Five pairs of
primitive gills surround the "foot."

In 1958 the research vessel *Vema* of the Lamont Geological
Observatory made another catch of neopilinas off the coast of
northern Peru at a depth of 5,840 meters (19,200 feet), southeast
of the *Galathea*'s locality. They proved to be of a different species
from those found by the *Galathea*, and have been named *Neopilina ewingi* in honor of Maurice Ewing.

To biologists, paleontologists, and students of organic evolution finds such as these are profoundly stimulating and illuminat-

ing; they are like a dream of vastly ancient things come true. Whereas before the student of evolution had only the bones of coelacanths to guide him in his reconstruction of the evolution of limbs, he now has the muscles, nerves, and coordinating brain as well.

The Pogonophora are other evolutionary curiosity yielded up by oceanic depths. They are not "living fossils"; instead they are remarkable as representatives of a completely new phylum, or primary division of organisms. One expects to find new species, new families, even new orders in the deep sea, but to find a creature representing a new phylum, after centuries of collecting from all environments, is an epoch-making occasion. The very improbability of finding a new phylum delayed recognition of the Pogonophora. The first specimens were dredged up off Indonesia by the Netherlands research ship *Siboga* during her expedition of 1899–1900. These strange, elongated, wormlike animals (see Figure 51) puzzled the *Siboga* scientists, without impressing them with their great biological importance. In 1955, however, A. V. Ivanov of the Soviet Union was able to show that they represent a distinct and previously unrecognized phylum.

The deep oceans have many facets, but none is quite so fascinating as the vast diversity of life that they contain. The catalogue of kinds of organisms in the depths is far from finished; in fact, it has hardly begun. Every new expedition finds an abundance of new species, and sometimes representatives of ancient lineages. Although whole communities of archaic forms, such as trilobites, eurypterids, and ammonites, have not been found, and probably will not be, it now seems clear that the proportion of ancient animals to those of recent origin is much greater in the deep sea than in shallow areas. Russian scientists have estimated recently that approximately 16 per cent of the species of animals found in depths greater than 4,000 meters (13,000 feet) are archaic, whereas no more than 0.00005 per cent of those of the shelf environment are archaic.

In some respects the scale of life in the oceans is quite different from that on land. The individual's chance of survival to reproductive maturity is, at least in many species, just a little bit better than zero, or something like 1 in 10 million. Violent death in the jaws of a predator is not merely a probability, it is a near certainty. In the course of development from egg through larva to adulthood each creature must elude ever larger enemies whose voraciousness knows no satiety. Here is natural selection in its rawest expression. To survive, a population must include individuals that are either very successful at the game of eluding, or who are so massively prolific that at least a few of their offspring

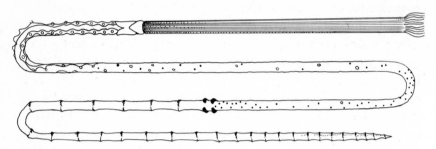

FIGURE 51   *This thin, wormlike animal is one of the Pogonophora, or beard worms. Pogonophora were not recognized until the twentieth century, largely because they live in the deep sea.*

out of millions survive to reproduce in turn. In the oceanic environment the latter expedient is particularly successful as a means of perpetuating the species. The codfish swimming about today are the descendants of fishes that produced 5 million eggs at a time for the good reason that in the long run it takes that many eggs to ensure the survival of two mature fish to perpetuate the species. Wasteful? Waste in this context has no meaning. After all, wasteful of what by whom? Codfish that are prodigal of progeny leave descendants; those that are parsimonious presumably do not, and thus their genes are eliminated from the gene pool of the population. But the results stagger the imagination of slow-breeding man. With 100 per cent survival the Atlantic would be filled solidly with cod in six years. And yet sea hares, which are large snails with a very small, almost internal shell, can lay eggs at a rate of 41,000 a minute, or a total of 5,000 million per season. At 100 per cent survival the descendants of a single sea hare after four generations would occupy a space of about six times the volume of the earth.

Some biologists hold that growth of aquatic animals, liberated from the impeding effect of gravity by the dense supporting medium in which they float, may continue throughout life. Accordingly a fish protected from predators may grow by simple enlargement year after year, and so long as it does so it escapes senility. If this is the case, what an irony of evolution that the environment that confers potential immortality should also ensure violent death in the jaws of a predator.

THE OCEAN

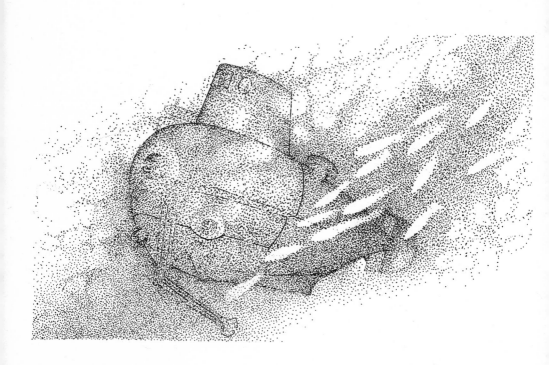

CHAPTER II

AND THE FUTURE

FROM AN EARLY TIME THE WORLD OCEAN HAS SERVED MAN AS A highway. In the last hundred years the efficiency of transportation by sea has rapidly increased, but it has resulted primarily from improvements in the vehicles themselves; more powerful and at the same time more economical engines and larger, stronger hulls have made the difference, because since Maury's important improvement of sailing routes the science of oceanography has been little used by mariners. Accumulated knowledge of the varying strengths of ocean currents, winds, and waves could probably improve upon ship-routing and the design of ships as much again as the revolution brought about by Maury over a century ago. According to estimates, improved routing of ships could save American shippers $250 million a year by shortening the time of crossings, while the cost of building new ships could be reduced by 10 per cent or $40 million a year by application of wave statistics.

Another innovation of the future will probably be increasing travel below the interface between the ocean and atmosphere, where interference of waves, winds, and ice may be avoided. Already submarines have proved their worth in research; with improved design they will undoubtedly find an important place in commerce. Admittedly there will be navigational problems under water, but these can be solved, as the successful cruises of the *Nautilus* and *Skate* under the ice of the Arctic Ocean prove. For navigation under water charts of bottom topography, local variations in the magnetic field, and the nature of the sea floor will be needed as well as instruments to detect variations of these properties. For routine crossings a system of sonic beacons should reduce navigation to nothing more complicated than passing from one beacon to the next.

Physical oceanography, the study of water masses and their dynamics, has been hampered by rather primitive instruments. A good deal of what is known about ocean waters has been measured with instruments that were designed thirty or more years ago. Use of most instruments requires that the ship stop and occupy a "station" often of several hours. Then the data normally require laborious processing. This has been particularly true of the determination of the chemical properties of ocean waters. The standard practice has been to take a series of water samples at various depths, but analysis of the samples had for the most part to await the return of the ship to her home laboratory. The ideal instrument would be one that recorded several properties continuously with the ship underway. Some progress has been made in this direction; unquestionably much more is needed.

The acoustic wave meter for measuring the heights of waves while underway is an example of the new trend in instrumentation. Another is the seismic reflection profiler for measuring the thicknesses of sediment layers on the ocean floor. The recently developed sound velocimeter system records sound velocity, temperature, and depth numerically by printing numbers on adding machine tape. The data may also be recorded as coded holes punched in paper tape, or may be recorded on magnetic tape. This system has two outstanding advantages; three different properties are measured simultaneously and are recorded in a form suitable for analysis by modern electronic computers.

As all seamen know, the oceans are ever changing. A single set of measurements at a given station may be more misleading than anything else; conditions may have been quite exceptional at the time. A unique set of measurements can give an indication of how much conditions vary at a particular place during a day, month, or year, but under normal circumstances a ship cannot remain for long at one place; she must move on to the next station. Unmanned buoys (see Figure 52) solve this important problem. Provided with suitable instruments they may be anchored on station for months at a time, either accumulating data on tape or transmitting them by radio to shore stations.

Another problem has been that of making numerous meas-

urements simultaneously and scattered over fairly wide areas—
that is, *synoptic surveys*. A surface ship is too slow even to approximate to a synoptic survey and fleets of ships are not ordi-
narily available. But now an airplane equipped with an infra-red
sensor pointed downward and flying at 60 meters (200 feet) or a
little higher can measure the surface temperature of sea over a

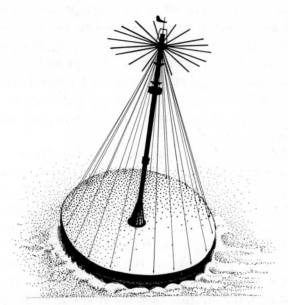

FIGURE 52 *Buoy which can be anchored in the deep sea to collect
oceanographic data over long periods of time.*

wide region in such a short time as to amount for all practical
purposes to a synoptic survey. Such rapid surveys of temperature
will probably revolutionize our understanding of the behavior of
the Gulf Stream.

Unmanned satellites will doubtless play their part in future
study of the oceans. Already they are useful as an aid to navigation, in determining with sharper precision the geographical positions of oceanographic stations. This is particularly important in
the detailed study of the ocean floor. The use of satellites as
collectors of oceanographic data (by mounting sensors in them)
is at least worth consideration, but because of their height it
seems unlikely they can be made to yield information of any

precision. Probably their role will remain that of navigational aids and communication links to relay information from ships and buoys to distant land stations; as recorders of cloud conditions they can be at least ancillary to oceanography by way of meteorology.

Oceanography is today at the threshold of a new era. Our charts of the oceans are covered with vast areas that are all blank; the data from such regions are so few as to provide no more than mere hints about prevailing conditions. Our present-day oceanographic information about these regions is roughly equivalent to geographical information at the time of Captain Cook's voyages. The rapid development of new devices, new methods and ways of applying them will change our picture of the oceans within a few decades, and with the changed picture will come solutions to many fundamental problems.

The whole approach to oceanography is evolving rapidly. It began with single expeditions; typically a naval vessel was "borrowed" for one or two years. At the end of the expedition the ship went back to her original duties and the staff of scientists scattered to their respective laboratories to study the material and data gathered during the expedition. Inevitably in such a purely exploratory stage of a science, far more questions were raised than answers found. The new and suggestive finds cried out for further research, but by that time the ship was no longer available and the scientific staff was disorganized. Then early in this century oceanographic institutions were founded here and there, of which the Woods Hole Oceanographic Institution is a brilliant example, with oceanographic ships continuously in commission, and in the case of the *Atlantis* built specifically for oceanographic research. The *Atlantis*'s powerful trawl winch was built into her as an integral part. The staff and scientists, technicians, the ship maintenance people went into the work as a career. Exploration of the seas was no longer a one-shot affair. If a piece of apparatus failed to work on its first try it was brought back, improved, and tried out again until it did work. Regions of particularly interesting conditions were revisited and conjectures tested, revised, and tested again. However, at this stage of development of oceanography, except for such special work as seismic refraction studies, the exploration was carried on by single ships.

Now oceanography is advancing beyond the expedition stage. One relatively new development is the multiple ship attack. Five or more ships working in coordination can accomplish in two weeks what a single ship could never achieve. The essential difference of course being the time dimension. The oceanographer is trying to paint the portrait of a model which is constantly in motion. The multiple ship approach is analagous to a snapshot of the model that takes in all parts at the same instant.

But still more effective for many kinds of measurements will be networks of moored buoys. Their relatively low production cost will allow the use of large numbers of them, which will greatly increase the resolution of the information obtained. Furthermore, securely moored, seaworthy buoys should be able to record throughout the year. The information from such arrays will be much better than a snapshot; it will be more like a cinema film of the moving model, and with enough buoys it can be a sharply focused one as well. Such arrays of buoys could at the same time record weather conditions to supplement those of the land-based network of weather stations. Summation of the two kinds of information would probably lead to the realization of firm theories of weather and shortly enable meterologists to make reliable long-range forecasts. As yet no more than a feeble beginning in the use of buoys has been made because of lack of funds, while billions of dollars go into the attempt to reach the moon.

The classical methods of winning data by lowering instruments on ropes and wires are no longer good enough for the needs of modern oceanography. In less than twenty years geophysical methods using sound waves, gravity, and magnetic measurements have revolutionized our thinking about the geology of the ocean basins, and in turn our ideas about the origin and structure of the continents. The next big advance is almost certain to come through the use of underwater vehicles capable of reaching the great depths. The proof that no depth is too great to be reached has been confirmed by the bathyscaph *Trieste* in descending to 10,915 meters (35,800 feet) in the *Challenger Deep* off Guam in the Pacific Ocean in 1960. Descents to lesser depths have become almost routine, but as yet collection of data by underwater vehicles has been confined almost entirely to what a man inside can see or photograph through the vehicle's portholes.

In the meantime hundreds of manned and unmanned vehicles designed for exploration are in various stages of planning and production. Among these the *Aluminaut* (see Figure 53) has been completed. The Reynolds International Company supplied money and metal (high-strength aluminum alloy) for its construction. The Electric Boat Division of General Dynamics Corporation was the builder. In 1965 it passed its tests and is now ready to carry out the exploratory work for which it was designed. It is 15.5 meters (50.9 feet) long, large enough for two scientists in addition to the pilot. It can cruise under water for 72 hours and has a working depth range of about 4,600 meters (15,-000 feet). The helplessness of the scientists inside will be relieved

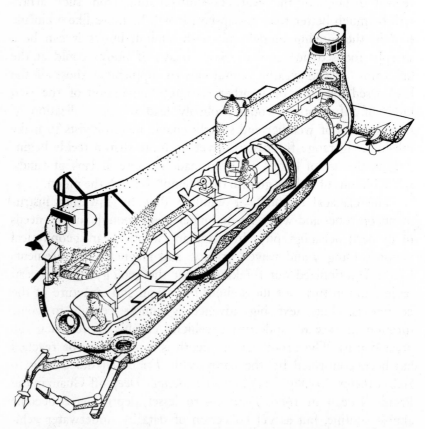

FIGURE 53 *The Aluminaut. Deep-submergence research and operations craft; the world's first aluminum submarine.*

to a certain extent by mechanical arms for collecting samples from the ocean floor. It also has sonar, television, and other up-to-date underwater equipment.

Recently the United States has decided to build a small atomic submarine for exploration of such relatively shallow water regions as the continental shelf. She will be about 18 meters (60 feet) long in contrast with the 76-meter (250-foot) length of a military submarine, and will have space for a crew of six. Her working depth will be only 300 meters (1,000 feet). Very practical uses for this craft are foreseen. With a fairly wide cruising range in the horizontal plane she will probably be a satisfactory vehicle for prospecting the shelf region for minerals, including petroleum, and for finding new fishing grounds.

1965 was marked by successful experiments in underwater living. Off the coast of southern California three groups of men lived for fifteen-day periods in the U.S. Navy's *Sealab II* at a depth of 62.5 meters (205 feet). The experiment, which lasted forty-five days, was under the direction of Commander George Bond. Two of the men spent two periods of fifteen days underwater. Off Cape Ferrat on the French Riviera Captain Jacques-Yves Cousteau, the French pioneer in underwater exploration, directed the three-week mission *Con Shelf III* (for Continental Shelf). In depths the French achievement outdid the American; the six men of the *Con Shelf III* lived at a depth of 100 meters (330 feet) and worked at even greater depths. Never before in history had men lived so long at such depths. It is most significant that the men were able to do their assigned jobs effectively and at the end of the experiments were in excellent health.

Just what the success of these experiments in underwater living portend for the future is hard to say. Certainly it opens the possibility of mining some kinds of underwater deposits of minerals, particularly those requiring shafts and tunnels. Perhaps underwater living may lend itself to experiments in physiology and marine biology. It will probably be an effective way of studying underwater archeological sites occupied during the last ice age when sea level was lower by something like 100 meters. In tropical regions the underwater "landscape" is very beautiful; that, and the novelty, should attract tourists for short stays in underwater hotels; and then for a writer with a book to finish the bottom of the sea might prove to be a suitable retreat. We do not think that living under water offers a solution to the problem of overcrowding above sea level as has been suggested; the only solution for that lies in limiting our numbers.

However, the sea does have a bearing on the population problem as a future source of food. Area for area, according to marine biologists, the sea is about as fertile as the land. With malnutrition already prevalent and with population growth out of balance with food supplies in two thirds of the world, it is rather amazing that at present only 2 or 3 per cent of the world's food comes from the sea.

According to the United States Department of Agriculture's annual survey world agriculture production in 1965 rose 1.5 per cent over that of 1964. But the world population increased by about 2 per cent in 1965. The real story is worse than these figures imply; food production, as distinct from total agricultural production, increased by only 1 per cent in 1965. Food production increased more rapidly than population growth only in North America and western Europe. In the meantime the American stockpiles of surplus food, carried over for many years, are nearing exhaustion.

According to a popular misunderstanding the present food crisis in India is said to be due to particularly unfavorable weather in 1965. Actually, the emergency promises to become chronic. According to United States officials, shipments to India in 1967 will match 1966's "emergency" rate of $1 billion worth of food. Heavy shipments of grain will be needed at least until 1970. What then? With ever-increasing population it is most probable that by the time 1970 arrives the situation will be even more difficult, unless new sources of food are tapped.

Studies by the United Nations Food and Agriculture Organization and World Health Organization point to protein deficiency as the most critical problem of the century. It is an appalling fact that more than 80 per cent of the world population receives insufficient protein and about 60 per cent is close to actual protein starvation.

According to a recent task force report to President Johnson about half the infants and pre-school-age children in developing countries suffer from protein malnutrition. A vicious aspect of this is the evidence that protein deficiency permanently impairs the mental and physical development of 10 to 25 per cent of these children.

In addition to water and minerals, the human system needs three elements: fats, carbohydrates, and proteins. Supply of fats and carbohydrates is not much of a problem; the body can synthesize both from proteins. But it cannot make proteins from fats and carbohydrates. Furthermore, the essential amino acids necessary for human growth are more plentiful in animal proteins than in plant proteins. The best sources of animal proteins are milk, eggs, and meat, but it is particularly these foods that are in limited supply in tropical regions where most of the developing nations lie.

Although the oceans are an obvious source of animal proteins, they are inadequately exploited. The annual catch of fish from the waters around the United States is about 5 million tons. Fisheries experts say that this could be easily raised to 12 million tons. The total world catch is about 50 million tons, according to a study by the National Academy of Sciences. The Japanese, who have an almost adequate diet, catch 6 million tons of fish annually. In contrast, India with five times as many people has an annual catch of less than 1 million tons. Presumably there is much room for expansion of fishing in Indian waters. A tenfold increase could at least temporarily relieve the protein shortage and thus provide a breathing spell during which population controls could be put into effect.

An effective way of increasing catches is by the use of underwater acoustics. Both echo sounders and SONAR devices similar in principle to those used by the U.S. Navy in detecting submarines are rapidly coming into use. By sweeping surrounding waters with SONAR a fisherman can not only detect shoals of fish, but also determine their distance and bearing. Acoustics studies of fish populations show that many fishes make characteristic noises which presumably serve some purpose in their activities. This suggests the possibility of using sound to lure fishes into traps or to herd them into nets.

Improvements in the ancient method of straining the fish out of water with nets are being developed. Russian fishermen in the Caspian Sea pump sardines on board through a large diameter pipe. Lights hanging below the boats attract the fish to the mouths of the pipes and an electric current paralyses them so that they cannot escape (see Figure 54). The use of lights by Japanese fisherman is an old custom. The recent innovation made possible by electricity is remarkably ingenious; lights mounted on rows of stakes extending at right angles to the shore are switched off and

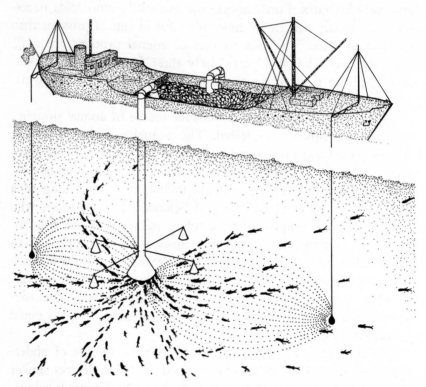

FIGURE 54 *In this fishing system fish are attracted by underwater lights, paralyzed in an electric field, and then sucked into a tube and pumped into the ship's hold.*

on like the stop lights of a one-way street, so that the fish are led from the most distant light toward the shore and into waiting nets.

Fishing is still in the hunting–food-gathering stage. In exploiting the food productivity of the land our ancestors turned to farming thousands of years ago. By analogy we ought to farm the seas.

One way to augment the ocean's harvest artificially is to transplant food fishes to more favorable environments. Walter Garstand, a British biologist, more than fifty years ago collected young plaice (the European flounder) in the crowded shoals off the Netherlands coast and took them to an area of similar bottom, but free of plaice, in the middle of the North Sea. Each time he tried this experiment he found that the transplanted plaice grew to three times the size of those left behind in the crowded waters off the Netherlands. Other examples include the transplantation of striped bass, shad, and soft-shelled clams from the east to the west coast of North America. The North American Chinook salmon is also being transplanted successfully to New Zealand.

Shallow waters and embayments offer the best chances for successful cultivation of sea foods. Research on the breeding of oysters and clams has made good progress in the United States and Japan in the last few years, and the Japanese are now working on the artificial propagation of shrimp.

But formidable obstacles stand in the way of farming the more open coastal waters. The very substance of the blue pastures of the ocean is constantly in motion; the soil of the wheat farm remains in one place so long as it is intelligently cultivated to avoid wind and water erosion. Probably for a long time to come the most efficient way to exploit open waters will be to let the fish propagate and feed naturally and then gather them with the most effective modern equipment.

Just as on land, the primary sources of food are the green plants. Only they can combine the inorganic substances—nitrates, nitrites, phosphates, and so forth—with dissolved carbon dioxide to form carbohydrates, proteins, oils, and fats. But these photosynthesizers, the first links in the food chain, thrive only so long as the nutrient substances within the sunlit upper layer of water are replenished. Because of the sinking of vast quantities of waste products, including dead animal and plant tissues that are broken down into simple chemicals by bacteria, the deep waters are rich in nutrients. According to estimates, 90 per cent of the nutrient in the sea is trapped in the greater depths where it cannot be used by plants because of absence of sunlight. Wherever upwelling of deep water brings nutrients within reach of sunlight, diatoms and other tiny planktonic plants bloom prolifically. Since the time interval between generations of diatoms under favorable conditions is a matter of minutes, the growth of a diatom crop is rapid.

Whereas the addition of fertilizers to ocean waters will probably not be economical for a long time to come, if ever, it may be feasible to induce upwelling of nutrient-rich deep waters. Columbus Iselin of the Woods Hole Oceanographic Institution has suggested some interesting possibilities. One way could be to pump compressed air through long tubes to considerable depths; the rising air bubbles would set upwelling in motion. Or large planes, like the otter boards of fishing trawlers, might be suspended from submerged buoys in the Florida Strait. Tilted at right angles these planes would deflect deep water upward. The result would be to turn the Gulf Stream off the southeastern United States into a rich stream of life. What of the side effects? That the Gulf Stream influences the weather of our east coast is a certainty. If Iselin's otter boards really lowered the average surface temperature of the Gulf Stream, it is likely that a change in climate along the east coast would follow, and the gain in fish might be offset by a loss of productivity on land.

Although the upper layer of the sea is most prolific of food and most accessible, the deeper layers are worth consideration as a source of food. Populations of edible animals large enough to yield considerable catches exist at fairly great depths. Russian fishermen have had success at depths as great as 650 meters (2,100 feet.) Their catches include cod, rat-tails, flatfish, and shrimp. But really profitable fishing at depth must wait for more powerful and efficient gear than that available to American fishermen.

Because the mass of plankton in the sea is many orders of magnitude greater than that of fish, the direct consumption of plankters by humans seems a simple solution of the food problem. Experts estimate that the annual production of plants in the seas of the world amounts to roughly 150,000 million tons. However, at each link in the food chain 90 per cent is lost; 100,-000 tons of plants yield 10,000 tons of herbivorous planktonic animals; these support 1,000 tons of carnivores, leaving only 10 or even 1 ton of fish which feed at one or two stages farther along in the chain. In the intensively fished waters of the North Sea and the Icelandic Shelf about 0.2 or 0.3 per cent of the original crop of photosynthesizers is converted into fish. Low as it is, this is better than the world average, partly because the catch includes a large proportion of herring which feed mostly on herbivores, being thus a little closer to the primary production.

Undoubtedly to utilize the primary production directly would be one way of tapping a tremendous source of protein. But the primary plankters are very small, generally measuring only a few thousandths of a millimeter. Filtering them out of the water would be a problem. Nets with meshes fine enough to catch them become clogged almost at once. In fact, the small size of the photosynthesizers is probably the reason why fish do not feed on them directly but instead through intermediaries, mostly very small crustacea, which are themselves small enouth to harvest the primary grass of the sea. The problem of concentrating plankton is an engineering one; by present methods the cost would make plankton as expensive as the best caviar. Furthermore, tests of nutritional value of plankton show that it is not a particularly wholesome diet for people; it contains over-rich fats and excessive amounts of vitamins which, in the long run, can be fatal. Probably we had better leave plankton to those marine creatures which through millions of years of selection have become able to thrive on it, and concentrate our efforts in the gathering of fish, the end members of the food chain.

We still have far to go in the efficient utilization of fish. For example, scientists in the United States have in the last few years developed a method of making a concentrate of fish protein that could end "protein starvation." The history of the product is strange. A similar but less refined product was banned from interstate commerce in 1962 by the Food and Drug Administration because it was "polluted and filthy." But the process of concentration was such as thoroughly to sterilize the final product, and, therefore, it was "polluted and filthy" only in an aesthetic sense. In the same sense raw clams, oysters, and uncleaned sardines are "polluted and filthy." In December 1965, the Bureau of Commercial Fisheries of the Interior Department announced the development of a new process for making a "clinically pure" fish concentrate.

By the new process the whole fish is ground to a kind of fish hamburger, which then goes through a moving bath of cold isopropyl alcohol to eliminate most of the water and fat. Next it gets a double treatment with hot isopropyl alcohol to remove the last traces of fatty substances and most of the remaining water. What remains after spray drying is an off-white, flourlike material that is 80 per cent protein. The last 20 per cent includes such beneficial minerals as calcium, phosphate, and a trifle less moisture than is chemically present in wheat flour. The concentrate is almost odorless and tasteless. Intended as a food supplement or additive, it is said to mix readily with baked goods, noodles, or beef gravy mix without any trace of fish taste. The National Academy of Sciences and the National Research Foundation have pronounced it "pure and wholesome." From feasibility studies it seems that if the unharvested fish in the coastal waters of the United States were converted into the concentrate, the amount would supply the normal protein needs of 1 billion persons for 300 days at a production cost of half a cent per person daily.

Better understanding of the climate and weather of the oceans will also help to increase the production of food from the sea. This involves learning more about the influence of chemical and physical conditions in the ocean on the behavior and abundance of fish populations. Knowing how to anticipate the changes should increase catches of fish by an order of magnitude. The data will probably be gathered by devices that are suspended from moored buoys and in continuous radio communication with shore stations. The same arrays of buoys used for oceanographic observations would be available for this purpose. The volume of data received would be enormous, but not overwhelming if handled by the new data-processing machines. From the integrated information it should be possible to supply fishermen of the future with predictions and the location of important concentrations of fish.

But regardless of how efficiently we may exploit the oceans in the future to meet the vast needs of an exploding world population, the annual yield of food from them has an upper limit. The oceans are finite in area. Efforts to increase productivity from the oceans must be thought of purely as stopgap measures that may serve to stave off the political collapse which is sure to follow wholesale starvation. Really effective means must be taken to reduce the rate of population increase. The alternative to intelligent control of population growth will be brutal and final control by starvation. As the British biologist James Fraser has put it: "Without population control, more effort to find more food merely means that instead of starving millions eventually there will be starving multimillions."

In reality the food supply is only one of several limitations upon population growth. Most of the people now alive could get along without any food from the sea, but populations cannot get along without fresh water. In the long run all fresh water comes from the oceans, naturally distilled by energy from the sun, and condensed to rain or snow over the lands. For the United States a shortage of uncontaminated water is rapidly becoming a critical problem, especially in the cities. The problem of converting brackish and sea water into fresh water is a subject of much research. With advances in technology the cost of conversion will go down; at the same time increases in population will raise the value of fresh water. It is only a matter of time before conversion becomes economical.

Water, as we pointed out earlier, is extraordinary in its chemical properties. In changing state from liquid to vapor it absorbs a remarkable amount of heat, and for this reason making pure water by distillation will remain expensive unless some way of applying heat from the sun or cheap nuclear energy can be found. Simple freezing leaves much of the salt in pockets in the ice, but some modification of the method, similar to the zone refining of metals, may be feasible. At least it would require only about one sixth as much energy as distillation. Other possible methods are the use of semi-permeable membranes that permit the water to pass through but not the salt, ion exchange, or even some kind of salt-modifying bacteria.

An interesting suggestion comes from the Scripps Institution of Oceanography. Antarctic icebergs, being part of the continental ice cap, are free of salt. To relieve the water shortage of Los Angeles, why not tow north a big iceberg? The Scripps scientists calculated that three ocean-going tugs could maneuver a 10-mile-long, half-mile-wide berg into the Humboldt Current flowing north along the west coast of South America. In order to take advantage of other currents beyond the range of the Humboldt the berg would have to be guided in a rather roundabout course that would detour almost to Hawaii before reaching Los Angeles. The trip would require about a year, in the course of which the berg would dwindle, probably to half its original size, but it would still include a great deal of fresh water. For example, even a small berg, as Antarctic icebergs go, after melting to half size could still contain 1 billion cubic meters or 220 billion gallons of fresh water. There would remain the problem of getting the ice water into the city's mains. The Scripps scientists propose that the berg, having been grounded on an offshore shoal, should be surrounded by a floating dam extending some 7 meters or 20 feet below the surface. The less dense melt water would float on the salt sea water and could be drawn off as needed through pipes leading to the city. The advantage of this Jules Verne method of getting water would be the surprisingly low cost, something like one third of a cent per 1,000 gallons. That is a very small part of what Los Angeles now pays for its drinking water.

For many millions of years the oceans have received dissolved chemicals from the lands. Because water is a close approximation to the alchemist's universal solvent, sea water and the sediments on the ocean floor contain quantities of every known mineral. As yet little has been done toward exploring this great wealth.

The most obvious and abundant of these substances is common salt, the extraction of which by flooding shallow areas and letting the sun's heat evaporate the water is an ancient industry. It is still carried on in parts of Europe and in the West Indies, but in this country it is cheaper to work deposits of salt laid down in shallow seas that flooded the continent hundreds of millions of years ago.

Stimulated by the brisk demand for magnesium needed for aircraft construction during World War II, metallurgists of the Dow Chemical Company perfected a process of extracting magnesium from sea water. Sea water contains not more than 0.13 per cent magnesium, but pumping sea water through an extraction plant is cheaper than mining ore.

Bromine is another useful mineral successfully extracted from sea water. Again the percentage, 0.038, is small, but the total amount in the oceans is gigantic, and therefore the reserve is truly inexhaustible. When, through an improved method of extraction or a rise in price, it becomes economical to extract a mineral from sea water, the problem of future supply vanishes. Deposits on land are usually richer, but with rare exceptions they are exhaustible; America's rich iron ore deposits were large, but they were used up within a lifetime.

At present potassium is obtained from salt deposits, the residues of ancient seas on the continents, and from the highly saline water of the Dead Sea. Potassium in combination with other substances is an essential part of fertilizers; the demand is sure to rise steeply in coming years. Although the percentage of potassium in sea water is low, a new process promises to make its extraction from sea water profitable. Of course, for maximum efficiency and reduction of the cost of pumping the large volume of water needed, the extraction of magnesium, bromine, and potassium should be combined in a single plant operation.

Another substance essential to modern agriculture is phosphorite, an impure phosphate of calcium. Great quantities of phosphorite are mined in central Florida and Idaho but with a rapidly rising need throughout the world, comparably rich deposits on the continental shelves off Australia, Japan, South Africa, Spain, and both coasts of America will become critically important to world agriculture. Unlike substances dissolved in sea water, these bottom deposits are not inexhaustible, but they are certainly very large.

Even diamonds occur in exploitable deposits off southwest Africa, where one company has already won a rich reward by dredging them. They occur in gravels brought by streams and rivers from the original source rocks. A hopeful forecast sets the future rate of production at 75,000 carats a month in sizes up to 10 carats.

Ever since the days of the *Challenger*, peculiar black nodules have been appearing in deep-sea dredge hauls and biologists' bottom trawls. Photographs of the sea floor show these potatolike concretions forming an almost continuous pavement covering vast areas, particularly in the Pacific. They are composed primarily of manganese and iron oxides, with manganese making up from one fifth to one half by weight. Minor amounts of copper, nickle, and cobalt are also present. Metallic manganese is most valuable in making special steels, and the oxide has important uses in chemical industry. According to recent estimates the values of some of these deep-sea deposits run to as much as $10 million per square mile. But the cost of recovery will be a problem; the average depth at which they lie is about 4,300 meters or 14,000 feet. One suggestion is to suck them up with hydraulic devices somewhat like large vacuum cleaners, as illustrated in Figure 55. Once picked up by suction heads moving over the bottom, the nodules would be raised to the ship in a stream of water pumped through a pipe. Although oceanographers fail to agree about the origin of the nodules, measurements of their rate of growth (based on the decay of contained radio-

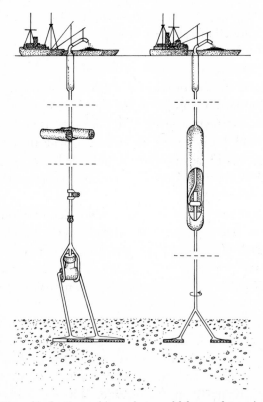

FIGURE 55　*Two kinds of machines that could be used to mine manganese nodules. The left works like a vacuum cleaner, with motor and pump above the suction heads. Two floats, equipped with propellers, move the machine along the bottom. The right-hand dredge has motor and pump inside a single float. Its suction heads sweep in circles.*

active substances) strongly suggest that they are forming fast enough to take care of the world's present consumption of the metals which they contain. In the future these nodules will probably prove to be a less expensive source of manganese, with nickel, cobalt, and copper as byproducts, than our dwindling mines on land.

Much of the world's oil and gas comes from the shallow sea floor off the coasts of the United States and Europe, and in the Persian Gulf. Exploratory drilling for hydrocarbons is under way in the North Sea and some gas has already been found.

It is a reasonable guess that oil deposits under the sea may exceed in quantity those on land. Even sketchy present knowledge of the geology of the sea floor indicates that 40 per cent of all known oil reserves lie beneath the continental shelves. K. O. Emery of the Woods Hole Oceanographic Institution from preliminary evidence gathered during a current geological investigation of the continental shelf has concluded that three large areas of the continental shelf and upper part of the continental slope off the Atlantic coast of the United States are favorable sites for prospecting for petroleum. One of these is a seaward extension of Cape Fear Arch northeast of Charleston; another is southeast of New York City; and a third is the outer part of the continental shelf from south of Boston northeastward to the Grand Banks of Newfoundland.

The origin of petroleum is still a good deal of a mystery, but the consensus among the experts is that most, if not all, deposits formed in the sea. All deposits either occur in or are closely associated with sediments that accumulated on the floors of ancient seas. The most plausible explanation is that petroleum is the residue of more or less chemically altered remains of marine plants and animals. The presence of at least some once-living matter in petroleum is conclusively proved by the occurrence of substances having asymmetrical left- or right-handed molecules in petroleum. Chemical reactions within organisms, when they produce such asymmetrical or chiral molecules, always put together exclusively right-handed or left-handed molecules, and never both together. For example, all plants always build right-handed molecules of common sugar or sucrose. Since the chiral molecules in petroleum are never mixed right- and left-handed forms, they must have been molded by the organic template process. A really successful explanation of the origin of petroleum would be most useful in the search for new pools. Future oceanographic research appears to be the most promising route to such a theory.

A homely but nonetheless valuable resource found in great quantities on the continental shelves is sand and gravel for aggregate in concrete. K. O. Emery's current study of the continental shelf off the east coast shows that large, almost inexhaustible, deposits of sand and gravel occur there. The annual value of sand and gravel quarried on land in the United States is about $900 million, or about 20 per cent of the total value of all nonmetallic minerals other than fuels. Sampling shows that sand suitable for construction is present throughout most of the length of the continental shelf off the Atlantic coast of the United States, lying at depths ranging from 20 meters (60 feet) to 140 meters (450 feet) near the edge of the shelf. The thickness of the sand reaches 60 meters (200 feet) locally. Gravel is much less abundant, but from preliminary sampling it should be plentiful in two areas. One of these is a large fan of gravel off New York City, and the other is in the northern margin of Georges Bank, a projection of the shelf southeast of Boston. Exploitation of these deposits of sand and gravel will depend upon future developments in marine engineering; factors that would distinctly favor their economical utilization are the wide distribution of the sand, and cheap transportation by barge.

With increasing knowledge of the oceans comes a growing realization that oceanic circulation has a powerful effect on man, upon all of his activities and his general well-being. The pattern of flow of ocean waters together with the movements of air masses are responsible for determining the climates of the various parts of the world.

The critical level of action is the interface between sea and atmosphere. Here moisture passes from the sea to the air, later to become clouds, and finally to fall as rain on the continents. This involves exchange of great quantities of energy constantly replenished from the sun. The steady inflow of solar heat raises the temperature of the ocean's surface; the air at the atmosphere-ocean interface is then heated by contact. This gives rise to atmospheric circulation in turn imparting motion to the ocean's waters. The vast reserve of heat energy in the moving oceans regulates climate much as the momentum of a flywheel regulates the motion of an engine. In fact, the intermeshed oceanic and atmospheric circulations constitute a great heat engine, which is kept in motion by constant flow of heat energy from low latitudes, to high latitudes where it is dissipated by radiation into space.

Air is very transparent to radiant energy. To the same extent that we receive a flood of light through the atmosphere from the sun on a cloudless day, so does the ocean's surface receive a flood of radiant energy of longer wave length that we cannot see but can easily feel through the heating effect on the skin.

On reaching the ocean's surface the radiant energy from the sun goes over to kinetic energy of the molecules of water; the velocity of their random motion increases; the temperature, a measure of the average kinetic energy of the molecules, rises. Exchange of much energy from the heated water to the atmosphere takes place by direct contact at the air-water interface. At the same time an important part, about one third, enters the atmosphere through the condensation of water vapor. A single gram of water at 20° Celsius absorbs 580 calories of heat in changing from liquid to vapor, and the same amount is given out when the vapor condenses to liquid again. Thus the condensation of water vapor is an important factor in heating the atmosphere, particularly in high latitudes.

Because of the large heat capacity of water and the massiveness of the oceans, their temperature can change only very slowly. The persistence of weather patterns over weeks to years is due to the thermal inertia of the oceans. Studies of thermal interactions between the oceans and atmosphere and frequent information on the distribution of temperature in the oceans should go a long way toward solving the problem of long-range weather predictions. At present the accuracy of even short-range forecasting is low, as most of us know from inconvenient experience. Improvement would benefit us all. Long-range forecasts would be of inestimable value to farmers, permitting savings in the planning of seasonal fuel transportation and storage, facilitating the timing of building and road construction, and acting as a protection against floods and droughts.

The close intermeshing of oceanography and meteorology

arouses the hope that eventually we may be able to some extent to control the weather of our planet. For example, tropical storms, known as hurricanes in the Atlantic and typhoons in the western Pacific, originate over oceans. They have their beginnings in exceptionally massive transfers of heat and water vapor from the sea to the atmosphere. This suggests that some means of dissipating anomalously large concentrations of heat energy at the ocean's surface would block their development. The elimination of these storms would save the United States at least $140 million, the average annual cost of damage by hurricanes in the eastern and southern parts of our country during the period between 1940 and 1957.

Before the explosion of the first hydrogen bomb, the atmosphere and the world ocean contained only a few pounds of tritium, the heavy, unstable isotope of hydrogen with atomic weight 3. After the United States and Soviet Union had finished their atmospheric testing of hydrogen bombs at the end of 1962, tritium content of atmosphere and ocean had risen to about 600 pounds (275 kilograms). Since tritium is relatively harmless the increase was not a matter of concern; on the contrary it proved useful to the science of meteorology by leading Gote Ostlund of the University of Miami's Institute of Marine Science to the conclusion that hurricanes instead of gaining most of their power from the condensation of water vapor in the atmosphere, as meteorologists then believed, derive their energy by sucking vapor up from the sea.

As a form of hydrogen, tritium combines with oxygen to form water. According to Ostlund's report, published in 1965, the proportion of this so-called *tritiated water* in sea water was under normal conditions ten times less than that in the air, but under the exceptional condition of a hurricane the concentration of tritiated water vapor in the winds over the sea dropped by as much as one quarter of its usual value. This means that the swirling air of a hurricane receives water vapor from the sea about twice as fast as it receives it from the surrounding atmosphere.

Ostlund's discovery has an interesting implication for at least partial control of hurricanes. By preventing or reducing evaporation from the sea's surface (using a film of some kind of chemical), it should be possible to deprive an embryonic hurricane of a large part of its source of energy. Such films are in use to prevent evaporation from reservoirs, but they break up under winds exceeding velocities of 15 meters per second or about 35 miles per hour, in contrast to velocities of as much as 45 meters per second or 100 miles per hour in hurricanes.

The importance of weather, even to primitive people, is shown by the elaborate ceremonies performed to ensure rain at certain seasons. Modern men have tried thousands of devices and methods for rain making. Although some methods supported by sound theory do modify clouds and yield some precipitation, modification and control of weather in general has not made much progress yet. It will come eventually, but probably not before we have learned a good deal more about the complex reactions underlying the perpetual turmoil of atmosphere and ocean that we call weather.

In 1966 a presidential science panel, appointed by the National Academy of Sciences, having spent two years studying the scientific aspects of weather control, recommended that research in the subject be increased sevenfold. The panel emphasized its importance as "a new and enormous power to influence the conditions of human life." But the panel concluded that most of the money and manpower at present "is being dissipated by support of subcritical or substandard efforts." The fastest computer presently available for weather research "is 50 times too slow," the panel found. It recommended that the computer industry endeavor to fill the need "as a matter of national urgency." More coordination, more money, more research, and more field tests of techniques are "mandatory to ensure orderly and rapid progress in the future." To this end the panel urged that the money spent for research on modification of weather should be increased from $4.09 million in 1965 to $30 million by 1970. The objectives of weather control "are as ambitious as any ever confronted by physical science" and "the scope of intellectual efforts needed in this field is correspondingly large," the panel concluded. This declaration is a good deal more positive than any previously expressed by scientific groups; unquestionably the subject of weather control is gaining peoples' interest.

The oceans are a mighty reservoir of energy. The very size of the problem of harnessing this energy has balked its utilization. Because an oceanic source once brought under control would be practically inexhaustible, ocean-derived energy may eventually be competitive with nuclear energy which requires the replacement of expensive fuel elements and the disposal of dangerous waste products.

A potential source of energy in the oceans is the temperature difference between surface water and deep water, which may be as much as 28° Celsius or 50° Fahrenheit. During the depression years of the 1930's Georges Claude, who had made a fortune with his invention of the neon light, spent a large part of it in an attempt to turn the oceanic temperature gradient into mechanical power. To do so he had a conduit laid on the south slope of the Puerto Rico Trench and extending down to a sufficient depth to tap cold water. His conversion mechanism, in essence, consisted of two chambers connected through a turbine; flow of vapor from one chamber, which received warm surface water, into the other chamber where cold water from the conduit caused condensation, turned the turbine. As a test of the principle, the experiment was a success; the turbine actually generated some electric current. However, the feasibility of generating current at a profit was not properly tested because almost immediately after a preliminary test the conduit, the most expensive part of the installation, was destroyed by a hurricane, and the project was abandoned. There is still talk in the French government of reviving Claude's idea.

In the meantime, the French government is going ahead with a plan to generate electric power from the rise and fall of the tide off the coast of Brittany. A dam 710 meters (2,329 feet) long has been built in the Rance Estuary, 3.2 kilometers (2 miles) upstream from Saint-Malo. The dam has two-way turbines that work on both the incoming and outgoing tides. The maximum tide range is 11.3 meters (37 feet); the basin into which the water flows in the rising tide has an area of 20 square kilometers (7.75 square miles). Some electricity has been generated there since 1960. When in full operation the Rance complex will contribute about 565 million kilowatt hours annually to France's total production of electricity, enough to save half a million tons of coal per year, providing the scheme lives up to hopes. This large-scale undertaking, which will ultimately cost not less than $100 million, is still in an experimental stage. At least the natural conditions in the Rance Estuary are highly favorable, something that can be said of only a few other places in the world. To serve as a source of power tides must rise at least 3 meters (10 feet) and the water must flow into a large basin through a narrow opening to the sea. Another favorable location is Passamaquoddy Bay in the Bay of Fundy on the Maine-New Brunswick border. During the depression a project to develop power by damming Passamaquoddy Bay was eventually abandoned as too expensive after the United States government had poured millions of dollars into it. However, if the Rance Estuary experiment succeeds, revival of the Passamaquoddy scheme may be considered. Other suitable settings are the Severn Estuary on the east coast of England, Cook Inlet in Alaska, the San José and Deseado rivers in Argentina, the Penzhinskaya Bay in Siberia, and on the shores of the White Sea where development of tidal power is said to be under way. Eventually the French plan to build a dam across the bay of Mont-Saint-Michel, as mentioned earlier. It is hoped that this grandiose construction will fill nearly half France's present electrical needs.

Remedies from the sea have been known for a long time. Sometimes, as so often with old traditions, the believed beneficial properties of certain algae and marine animals have some foundation in fact. If the medicinal value of agar, a gelatinous substance derived from an alga, is not of much importance, it has played an important part in the study of disease-causing bacteria; it is an ideal substance upon which most bacteria can be cultured in the laboratory. The so-called Irish moss *Chondrus crispus*, a beautifully iridescent alga, provides another gelatinous substance. Once it was used by New Englanders to make blancmange and now it enters into a surprising variety of foods such as custard pies, ice cream, and jellies. Manufacturers of drugs and cosmetics put this same versatile material into toothpastes, mascara, calamine lotion, permanent wave lotions, and syrups. It is particularly effective in preventing medicines in suspension from settling; thanks to this extract of *Chondrus crispus* the once-familiar direction "shake well before using" is now almost forgotten.

Among remedies derived from marine animals is cod-liver oil, whose early use depended upon the empirical principle that "it worked." Today we know that it is a valuable source of vitamins A and D together with iodine.

For a long time the magnesium, bromine, and iodine used in pharmacy have been obtained from the sea. A quaint remedy for thyroid disorder, still in use only thirty years ago, consisted of a powder made of oven-dried sponges. Whatever efficacy this treatment may have had was probably due to the iodine in the sponges.

Actually, however, relatively few substances of marine origin are used in medicine. The reason for this neglect is easy to understand; we are still profoundly ignorant of the properties of myriads of agents produced by living things in the sea. But a beginning has been made, and encouraging discoveries are adding momentum to the search for more.

Some kinds of staphylococci, infectious yeasts, and fungi are immune to pharmaceuticals derived from land sources. Furthermore, various deadly microorganisms are evolving into resistant strains in response to the selective effect of penicillin and other formerly effective antibiotics. Among the billions of individuals in a population of pathogenic microorganisms it sometimes happens that a few differ from the herd enough in their physiological chemistry to be able to survive a dose of penicillin. These survivers then propagate and transmit to their descendants the genetically determined chemical peculiarities that confer immunity to penicillin. This is why there is a crying need for new antibiotics.

On theoretical grounds substances synthesized by marine organisms may be expected to be particularly effective against pathogens that have evolved on land. All else being equal, land pathogens should be most susceptible to organic substance derived from an environment alien to their own and to which they cannot have been exposed for many millions of years.

It is reasonably certain that such substances do occur in the oceans, but only recently has a concerted effort been made to find them. The results so far are promising. For instance, Paul R. Burkholder and his co-workers at the Lamont Geological Observatory have found a new antibiotic in the form of a marine bacteriophage, a strain of microorganisms that feed on pathogenic bacteria. Furthermore, Burkholder and his group of investigators (including his wife) have separated three different antibiotics from the single-celled, ultra-small planktonic plants of the genus *Gonyaulax*. When conditions in the surface waters are just right, *Gonyaulax* and a few similar forms sometimes suddenly bloom in enormous numbers and give rise to "red tides." *Gonyaulax* secretes a powerful toxin. These red tides frequently contain enough poison to kill off large numbers of fish, and the poison carried ashore in spray can cause irritation to human beings. A common sequel to a red tide is a flood of poisonous hydrogen sulfide, generated by the action of sulfur bacteria on the dead fish.

The Lamont group led by Burkholder are now screening about sixty other potential pharmaceuticals from seaweeds, corals, sponges, and venomous fishes.

Among other miscellaneous research projects, an anti-viral drug, one of the most sought-after pharmaceutical substances today, is being perfected by C. P. Li at the National Institute of Health at Bethesda, Maryland. Li found the substance, called Paolin II, in the body fluids of abalones, clams, and oysters. Discovery of a chemical that slows the heartbeat of animals to a few throbs per minute has prompted intensive research at the Los Angeles County Hospital. The drug, a potential aid in surgery, occurs in venom of the weever fish. Another chemical that lowers blood pressure in animals, and which may prove to be useful in treating hypertension, has been discovered by doctors at the University of Southern California. It was isolated from the poison secreted by the venomous stonefish. Scientists at the World Life Research Institute in California have purified a chemical that greatly reduces coagulating time of blood; again the source was venom secreted by a marine organism.

The paradoxical fact that powerful poisons may be turned into valuable drugs holds much hope for the successful treatment of some of mankind's most troublesome diseases, and it would seem that the best place to look for them is among marine organisms; it is there that the most virulent toxins occur. For example, the puffer fish secretes a poison that is 3,000 times more effective than our most deadly war gas.

Thus marine pharmacology is one of the most promising fields in the medicine of today. But it involves the collection of marine organisms that manufacture biologically active substances, the separation and purification of these substances, and study of their possible applications in the treatment of diseases. As yet only a beginning has been made; probably no more than 1 per cent of all sea organisms known to produce biologically active chemicals has so far been investigated.

At present the attention of workers in marine biochemistry is almost entirely devoted to the study of the chemical nature of the secretions and substances of marine organisms. And yet other aspects of life in the sea are probably equally worthy of attention. One of the strange capabilities of marine animals that seems to set them apart from those on land is their way of growing new parts. The starfish is an example. Deprived of an arm, the starfish simply grows another, but what seems really grotesque is the ability of the amputated arm to grow into another starfish. Research into the enzymes, hormones, genetical set-up, or whatever it is that makes this possible could hardly fail to increase our understanding of that all-important life process—growth. Perhaps it is expecting too much to look forward to the time when a person can grow a new limb, but insight into the controlling biochemistry of the process may some day enable physicians to induce the partial renewal of a damaged heart or kidney. Moreover, an understanding of the chemistry of growth may show the way to control the wild proliferation of cells that occurs in some forms of cancer.

The behavior of *Bonellia*, a marine worm, is suggestively pertinent. The young larvae swim close to their mother before taking to independent life. Any larvae that touch the mother become males and cease to grow; those that do not touch her settle to the bottom and become females. This sea magic is due to a water-soluble hormone that determines the transformation of the larvae that touch their mother. Biochemists have already isolated this growth-arresting hormone. The next step will be to find out how it works, knowledge that may well bring the control of cancer a step nearer.

Just how life started no one knows, but it is very probable that it started in the sea. If life began in the sea, marine biology is the essence of all biology; and the marine environment offers the best opportunity to study some of the basic problems of life. One of these is the extraordinary biological rhythms of marine organisms, rhythms that are synchronized with the tides and therefore with motions of the moon and sun. Of these rhythms, hardly any is more fantastically well regulated than the spawning schedule of a little fish called grunion. This animal lays its eggs on the beaches of California at the time of highest monthly tide; consequently, the eggs remain undisturbed by waves until just one month later, by which time the newborn grunions are ready to take advantage of the peak tide and swim into the sea.

Another fascinating subject is bioluminescence, so prevalent among sea life from bacteria to some of the largest fish. The process appears to be highly efficient; little, if any, chemical energy is wasted in the form of heat, something not at all true of man's light-making apparatus all of which not only waste energy as heat but also raise the problem of disposing of heat. It seems we have much to learn from the illumination engineers of the deep sea.

In the sea, life goes to extremes unknown on land. In size the great blue whale exceeds the largest dinosaurs. Some sea snakes are more venomous than cobras. There are killers more ferocious than tigers. The brilliant phosphorescence of many kinds of sea life outshines our fireflies. In beauty of color and form a coral reef with jewel-like fish darting in and out outdoes the best that a tropical garden with its birds can offer; at the other extreme are the hideous forms that prowl the unlit depths. And yet it is doubtful if we know more than a hundredth part of the strange life that swarms in the sea.

The most plausible hypotheses of the origin of life hold that life began by a spontaneous synthesis of certain complex molecules in the oceans of the primitive earth, which contained quantities of substances composed of carbon, hydrogen, oxygen, nitrogen, and other elements that seem to be essential to life. S. L. Miller, while working at the University of Chicago with H. C. Urey, synthesized a variety of organic molecules by passing an electric discharge through a mixture of methane, hydrogen, ammonia, and water vapor—a mixture similar in Urey's opinion to the earth's primitive atmosphere. However, Miller's experiment did not produce living organisms.

At what point can one draw the boundary between a living organism and nonliving matter? Perhaps there is no clear-cut division. Certainly the first appearance of replicating molecules of ribonucleic acid and deoxyribonucleic acid was a fateful moment in the earth's history. However, experiments with viruses containing ribonucleic acid prove that replication can occur only within the cell of some other organism. Apparently, the existence of molecules of ribonucleic and deoxyribonucleic acids is not enough to set the life process going; substances in protoplasm of living cells are also essential. Protoplasm, the living cell substance, is a mixture of many complicated organic molecules. The principle ingredients are carbon, oxygen, nitrogen, and hydrogen. A substance present in the protoplasm of most plants has an additional atom of the metal magnesium; this is chlorophyl, which gives green leaves their color, a material of essential importance to all higher life because of its catalytic role in converting carbon dioxide and water into the sugars and starches needed as food by higher animals.

So we see that life possessing a level of sensitivity above that of bacteria depends upon the existence of several complex molecules. Apparently in the very early days of our planet, when conditions were different, not just one but several improbable chemical reactions occurred. This implies a long period of time.

Within the past few years paleontologists have succeeded in pushing back the fossil record of life to a remote period previously thought of as devoid of life. In November 1965, E. S. Barghoorn of Harvard University reported that he had found the remains of bacterialike cells in sediments known to be 3 billion years old by radiometric dating. If the earth is not older than 4.5 billion years, as is generally supposed, self-replicating life had already come into existence one and a half billion years after the solidification of the earth's crust. This may be encouraging to those biochemists who endeavor to recreate life in the laboratory. Possibly, under suitable conditions, the coming together of the right atoms into the right configurations is not so improbable as we used to think.

Naturally, we land dwellers know about and take a greater

interest in the part of the earth that lies above sea level. Our planet is the only sample of the universe with which we can become familiar; but the oceans cover three quarters of that sample. To attain the fullest possible awareness and understanding of our little speck of the universe we shall have to turn more and more to the study of the oceans.

BIBLIOGRAPHY

Arrhenius, G.: *Sediment Cores from the East Pacific*. Reports of the Swedish Deep-Sea Expedition 1947–1948, Vol. V, Fasc. I. Göteborg: Elanders Boktryckeri Aktiebolag; 1952.

Arx, W. S. von: *Introduction to Physical Oceanography*. Reading, Mass.: Addison-Wesley Publishing Company, Inc.; 1962.

Barnes, H.: *Oceanography and Marine Biology*. New York: The Macmillan Company; 1959.

Bascom, W.: *A Hole in the Bottom of the Sea*. Garden City, N.Y.: Doubleday & Company, Inc.; 1961.

Bramlette, M. N.: "Significance of Coccolithophorids in Calcium Carbonate Deposition." *Geological Society of America Bulletin*, Vol. LXIX (1958), pp. 121–6.

Bramlette, M. N., and Bradley, W. H.: *Geology and biology of North Atlantic deep-sea cores between Newfoundland and Ireland. Pt. I Lithology and geologic interpretations*. United States Geological Survey, Professional Paper 196 (1940), pp. 1–34.

Bramlette, M. N., and Riedel, W. R.: "Stratigraphic Value of Discoasters and Some Other Microfossils Related to Recent Coccolithophores." *Journal of Paleontology*, Vol. XXVIII (1954), pp. 385–403.

Brunn, A. F., Greve Sv., Mielche, H., and Sparck, R., eds.: *The Galathea Deep Sea Expedition 1950–1952*. London: George Allen & Unwin, Ltd; 1956.

Burke, W. T.: *Ocean Sciences, Technology, and the Future International Law of the Sea*. Columbus, Ohio: Ohio State University Press; 1966.

Carson, R. L.: *The Sea Around Us*. New York: Oxford University Press; 1951.

Chapin, H., and Smith, F. G. W.: *The Ocean River*. New York: Charles Scribner's Sons; 1952.

Charlesworth, J. K.: *The Quaternary Era*, 2 vols. London: Edward Arnold (Publishers) Ltd.; 1957.

Colman, J. S.: *The Sea and Its Mysteries*. New York: W. W. Norton & Company, Inc.; 1950.

Coon, C. S.: *The Origin of Races.* New York: Alfred A. Knopf; 1962.

Cowen, R. C.: *Frontiers of the Sea.* Garden City, N.Y.: Doubleday & Company, Inc.; 1960.

Curtis, G. H.: "A Clock for the Ages: Potassium-Argon." *National Geographic,* Vol. 120, No. 4 (October 1961), pp. 590–2.

Daly, R. A.: "Origin of Submarine Canyons." *American Journal of Science,* Vol. XXVII (1936), pp. 401–20.

Darwin, C.: *On The Origin of Species.* New York: Collier Books; 1962.

Deacon, G. E. R., ed.: *Seas, Maps, and Men.* Garden City, N.Y.: Doubleday & Company, Inc.; 1962.

Defant, A.: *Physical Oceanography,* 2 vols. New York: Pergamon Press; 1961.

Dietrich, G.: *General Oceanography.* New York: John Wiley & Sons, Inc.; 1963.

Dietz, R., and Piccard, J.: *Seven Miles Down.* New York: G. P. Putnam's Sons; 1961.

Emiliani, C.: "Pleistocene Temperatures." *Journal of Geology,* Vol. LXIII, No. 6 (November 1955), pp. 538–78.

Engel, L., and the editors of *Life: The Sea.* New York: Time, Inc.; 1961.

Ericson, D. B.: "Pleistocene Climatic Record in Some Deep-Sea Sediment Cores." *Annals of the New York Academy of Sciences,* Vol. XCV (October 1961), pp. 537–41.

Ericson, D. B., Ewing, M., and Heezen, B. C.: "Turbidity Currents and Sediments in the North Atlantic." *American Association of Petroleum Geologists Bulletin,* Vol. XXXVI (1952), pp. 489–511.

Ericson, D. B., Ewing, M., Heezen, B. C., and Wollin, G.: *Sediment Deposition in the Deep Atlantic.* Geological Society of America, Special Paper 62 (1955), pp. 205–20.

——: "Atlantic Deep-Sea Sediment Cores." *Geological Society of America Bulletin,* Vol. LXXII (February 1961), pp. 193–286.

Ericson, D. B., Ewing, M., and Wollin, G.: "Pliocene-Pleistocene Boundary in Deep-Sea Sediment Cores." *Science,* Vol. CXXXIX, No. 3556 (1963), pp. 727–37.

——: "Sediment Cores from the Arctic and Subarctic Seas." *Science,* Vol. CXLIV, No. 3623 (1964), pp. 1183–92.

——: "The Pleistocene Epoch in Deep-Sea Sediments." *Science,* Vol. CXLVI, No. 3645 (1964), pp. 723–32.

Ericson, D. B., and Wollin, G.: "Correlation of Six Cores from the Equatorial Atlantic and Caribbean." *Deep-Sea Research,* Vol. III (January 1956), pp. 104–25.

——: "Micropaleontological and Isotopic Determinations of Pleistocene Climates." *Micropaleontology,* Vol. II, No. 3 (July 1956), pp. 257–70.

———: *The Deep and the Past.* New York: Alfred A. Knopf; 1964.

Ericson, D. B., Wollin, G., and Wollin, J.: "Coiling Direction of *Globorotalia truncatulinoides* in Deep-Sea Cores." *Deep-Sea Research,* Vol. II (1954), pp. 152–8.

Ewing, M.: "Marine Geology." *Ocean Sciences.* Annapolis, Md.: United States Naval Institute; 1964, pp. 156–71.

Ewing, M., and Engel, L.: "Seismic Shooting at Sea." *Scientific American,* Vol. CCVI, No. 5 (May 1962), pp. 116–26.

Flint, R. F.: *Glacial and Pleistocene Geology.* New York: John Wiley & Sons, Inc.; 1957.

Gaskell, T. F.: *World Beneath the Oceans.* Garden City, N.Y.: The Natural History Press; 1964.

Guenther, K., and Deckert, K.: *Creatures of the Deep Sea.* New York: Charles Scribner's Sons; 1956.

Hamilton, J. L.: *Sunken Islands of the Mid-Pacific Mountains.* Geological Society of America, Memoir 64 (1956).

Heezen, B. C., Tharp, M., and Ewing, M.: *The Floors of the Oceans. I. The North Atlantic.* Geological Society of America, Special Paper 65 (1959).

Hill, M. N., ed.: *The Sea: Ideas and Observations.* 3 vols. New York: John Wiley & Sons, Inc.; 1962.

Idyll, C. P.: *Abyss.* New York: Thomas Y. Crowell Company; 1964.

Kuenen, Ph. H.: *Marine Geology.* New York: John Wiley & Sons, Inc.; 1950.

Kullenberg, B.: *Bottom Investigations. No. 2. Deep-Sea Coring.* Reports of the Swedish Deep-Sea Expedition 1947–1948, Vol. IV, Fasc. I. Göteborg: Elanders Boktryckeri Aktiebolag; 1955.

Long, E. J., ed.: *Ocean Sciences.* Annapolis, Md.: United States Naval Institute; 1964.

Marshall, N. B.: *Aspects of Deep Sea Biology.* London: Hutchinson & Co., Ltd.; 1954.

Martini, E., and Bramlette, M. N.: "Calcareous Nannoplankton from the Experimental Mohole Drilling." *Journal of Paleontology,* Vol. XXXVII (1963), pp. 845–56.

Menard, H. W.: *Marine Geology of the Pacific.* New York: McGraw-Hill Book Company; 1964.

Moore, H. B.: *Marine Ecology.* New York: John Wiley & Sons, Inc.; 1958.

Murray, J., and Hjort, J.: *The Depth of the Ocean.* London: Macmillan and Co., Ltd.; 1912.

Nicol, J. A.: *The Biology of Marine Animals.* New York: John Wiley & Sons, Inc.; 1960.

Pettersson, H.: *Westward Ho with the Albatross.* New York: E. P. Dutton & Co., Inc.; 1952.

Phleger, F. B: *Ecology and Distribution of Recent Foraminifera.* Baltimore: The Johns Hopkins Press; 1960.

Phleger, F. B, Parker, F. L., and Peirson, J. F.: *Sediment Cores from the North Atlantic Ocean. No. 1. North Atlantic Foraminifera.* Reports of the Swedish Deep-Sea Expedition 1947–1948, Vol. VII, Fasc. I. Göteborg: Elanders Boktryckeri Aktiebolag; 1953.

Raitt, H.: *Exploring the Deep Pacific.* New York: W. W. Norton & Company, Inc.; 1956.

Raymont, J. E.: *Plankton and Productivity in the Oceans.* New York: The Macmillan Company; 1963.

Sears, M., ed.: *Oceanography.* American Association for the Advancement of Science, Publication No. 67; 1961.

Shapley, H., ed.: *Climatic Change.* Cambridge, Mass.: Harvard University Press; 1953.

Shepard, F. P.: *The Earth Beneath the Sea.* Baltimore: The Johns Hopkins Press; 1959.

——: *Submarine Geology,* 2nd edn. New York: Harper and Row; 1963.

Simpson, G. C.: "Ice Ages." *Nature,* Vol. CXLI, No. 3570 (1938), pp. 591–8.

Smith, J. L. B.: *The Search Beneath the Sea.* New York: Holt, Rinehart and Winston, Inc.; 1956.

Stewart, H. B., Jr.: *The Global Sea.* Princeton, N.J.: D. Van Nostrand Company, Inc.; 1964.

Stommel, H.: *The Gulf Stream.* 2nd edn. Berkeley and Los Angeles: University of California Press; 1965.

Sverdrup, H. U., Fleming, R., and Johnson, M. W.: *The Oceans.* Englewood Cliffs, N.J.: Prentice-Hall, Inc.; 1942.

Vening Meinesz, F. A.: *The Earth's Crust and Mantle.* New York: Elsevier Publishing Co.; 1964.

Wilson, J. T.: "Continental Drift." *Scientific American,* Vol. CCVIII, No. 4 (April 1963), pp. 86–100.

Yasso, W. E.: *Oceanography.* New York: Holt, Rinehart and Winston, Inc.; 1965.

Zeuner, F. E.: *The Pleistocene. Its climate, chronology and faunal successions.* London: Bernard Quaritch; 1945.

——: *Dating the Past.* 2nd edn. London: Methuen & Co., Ltd.; 1950.

INDEX

abyss: defined, 9; topography of, 10–11; ocean currents of, 82–8
abyssal hills province, 159
abyssal plains, 159, 167–8
Adriatic Sea, 138
Aegean Sea, 143
Africa, 59, 67, 134, 162
Aftonian Interglacial, 220, 225–6
Agassiz, Alexander, 8, 125
age determinations: *see* dating methods
Agulhas Current, 59
Alaska, 69, 108, 136–7; 1958 earthquake, 113
Albatross (research vessel), 8, 177, 195–6, 199–200, 289
Albatross Plateau, 8
Aldrich, Pelham, 156
Aleutian Current, 69
Aleutian Islands, 6, 111, 146
Aleutian Trench, 110
algae: of Sargasso Sea, 65–6; importance of upwelling to, 67, 71; of Humboldt Current sediment, 71
Altair (research vessel), 82
Aluminaut (deep-submergence research craft), 324–5
Amazon River, 108
amphidromic points, 106
Andes, 134
Antarctic Circumpolar Current, 74–6
Antarctic Ocean (Southern Ocean): convergence, 73–4; thermal influence, 75–7
Antarctic West Wind Drift, 71
Antarctica, 26, 33, 73–7, 141, 147, 160
Antilles, 6, 63
Antilles Current, 63
Appalachians, 22, 206
Arabian Sea, 76
Arago, François, 150
Architeuthis, 308, 311
Arctic Ocean, 6, 26, 62, 63, 194
Arrhenius, Gustaf, 200–1
Arrhenius, Svante, 81
Atlantic Ocean: rift valley, 5, 170–1; areal surface, 6; deepest trench of, 6; thickness of unconsolidated sediment in, 14, 181, 185; and continental drift theory, 25, 169–70; currents, 62–8, 78–9; tides, 105–6; during ice ages, 137; average depth, 149; continental shelves, 155, 167; floor, 159–60; mantle flow beneath, 169–70; crust, 246
Atlantis (research vessel), 55–6, 64–5, 187, 246, 322; 1951 expedition, 211–14
Atlantis legend, 163–4, 171
atmosphere of earth, 19, 41; reaction of, to solar energy, 46, 62; circulation of, 46, 48–51, 62–3
atolls, 123–5, 160
Australia, 23, 60, 70, 146, 155
Azores, 170

Bache, Alexandre, 149
bacteria of deep oceans, 290, 292
Baffin Bay, 53
Bahama Islands, 221
Baltic Sea, 116
Barghoorn, E. S., 348
Bascom, Willard, 277, 279
basins of oceans, 6; topography of, 10–1, 121–2, 125–7; evidence of age of, 14–15; theories of formation of, 19–27; oxygen depletion in, 67–8; floor subsidence in, 123–5, 127–8, 140; 148; crust thickness of, 242–6, 266, 268; crust layers of, 266–7; *see also* floors of oceans
bathyscaph, 288, 301, 323
bathythermograph (BT), 56
Bay of Bengal, 76
Bay of Biscay, 148
Bay of Fundy, 106–7
Benguela Current, 59, 67–8, 71
benthic foraminifera, 192
benthos, 299
Bering Sea, 68
Bering Straits, 136–7
Bermuda Islands, 160
Bermuda rise, 159–60
Bigelow, Henry B., 53–4
bioluminescence, 294–5, 347
Bjerknes, Wilhelm, 47, 53
Black Sea, 289
Blake (research vessel), 36
Blake Plateau, 221–2
Bond, Cmdr. George, 325
Bonellia, 346
Bonneville, 135
bore, 108–9
Borneo, 9
Brazil, 161
Brazil Current, 63, 68, 82
British Isles, 133
Brittany, 109, 342
Broecker, W. S., 228
Brooke, J. M., 147
Brown, Michael, 239, 240–1
Brussels, 1853 oceanographic conference in, 31

Bruun, Anton, 310
Buchanan, J. Y., 79
Bullard, Sir Edward, 252
Burkholder, Paul R., 344–5

California, 36–7; Ekman theory exemplified in coastal waters of, 50
California Current, 69–70
Calliteuthis, 308
Cambrian Period, 16
Cambridge University, 252, 273
Campeche Peninsula, 191
Canada, 23, 218
Canaries Current, 61, 79
canyons, submarine, 11, 156, 165–71, 187
Cape Cod, 55, 155
Cape of Good Hope, 59
Cape Hatteras, 60, 64, 221
Cape Horn, 26, 31
Cape Johnson Deep, 6
Caribbean Sea, 6, 63, 185
Carlsberg Ridge, 8–9, 273
Carnegie (research vessel), 8
Carnegie Institute, 276
Caryn (research vessel), 246
Caspian Sea, 134
Cenozoic Era, 16, 206–7, 223
Central America, 164
Ceratias holboelli, 306
Cerigo, 143
Chain (research vessel), 79
Challenger (research vessel), 8, 32–6, 79–80, 148–9, 174, 182, 194, 289
Challenger Deep, 6, 323
"Challenger Reports," 174
Chamberlin, Thomas C., 17
Chance (research vessel), 54–5
Charleston, 63–4, 337
chemicals, sea as source for, 334–6
Chiasmodus niger, 305
Chien Tang River, 108
Chile, 112–13
China, 108
Claude, Georges, 342

coelacanth (*Latimeria chaluminae*), 310, 313–15

Compass Island, U.S.S., 249

Con Shelf III, 325

Congo River, 156

continental drift theory, 19–23, 169–70

continental margins, 154; slope, 9, 155–6, 165; shelf, 154–5; rise, 156, 167; trenches, 156–7, 169; deltas, 184

continents: theories of origin of, 12–13, 19–27; "floating" character of, 13, 19–27, 128–33, 169–70; effect of glacier weight on, 23–4, 141–3, 250–1; symmetrical distribution of, 26; changes in relative heights of, 119–43, 251; inundation of, 133–4; boundaries of, 154–6, 165; crust of, 246–7; and isostasy principle, 262

convection cells, 131, 134, 263

convection flow, *see* heat convection theory

corals, 103, 123–5, 155

core collections, 187, 191, 200; Lamont, 210–11, 227

core of earth: defined, 18; theoretical composition of, 120, 259, 265; size of, 120; surface of, 264; inability to transmit transverse waves, 265; temperature, 265; radius of, 265–6

cores: from clay sediments, 208; from calcareous sediments, 209; retrieval of, 210, 213–14; analysis of, 214–20, 226–7; coarse fraction of, 215–16; record of climatic changes in, 216, 218–21; faunal change record in, 221–2; discoasters in, 222–4; zonal correlation of foraminifera in, 226–8; complete record of Pleistocene in, 228; *see also* sediment

cores of currents, 77

coring expedition, described, 211–14

coring methods, 82, 173–4, 182, 197, 208; Piggot gun, 194–5; Hvorslev-Stetson free fall, 195, 209; Pettersson-Kullenberg vacuum, 197; Kullenberg piston, 197, 201, 209; Ewing piston, 209–10; of Mohole Project, 282

Coriolis effect, 48–9, 58, 68

cotidal lines, 105–6

Cousteau, Jacques-Yves, 325

creta, 133

Cretaceous Period, 127–8, 140, 160, 181; flood, 132–4; sediments, 193

Cromwell Current, 77–8

Cromwell, Townsend, 77–8

crust of earth: interaction of parts of, 5–6, 12–13; floating character of, 13, 19–27, 128–30, 169–70; defined, 18; verticle movements of, 23–4, 128–9, 250; thickness of, 120, 266, 268; subocean thickness of, 242–6, 266, 268; subocean gravity measurement of, 247–51; isostatic balance of, 251, 167; subocean layers of, 266–7; discontinuity at base of, 264, 268

Cuba, 56

currents of oceans: early studies of, 27–31; energy sources of, 45–6, 62; influence of, 46–7; seasonal character of, 47, 58; subsurface motions of, 47, 77–88; wind-driven, 48–51, 58, 62; related to earth's rotation, 48–9, 58, 62; major hemispheric, 58–62; equatorial, 63; effect on sea levels, 63; influence of salinity, temperature on, 84–5; measurement of oxygen content of, 85; tidal, 107; *see also* turbidity currents

Cusanus, Nicolaus, 147

Cushman, J. A., 216

Cuss I (drilling vessel), 279–80, 283

Cyclades, 143

Daly, R. A., 138, 166, 201

Dana (research ship), 8, 311

Darwin, Charles, 123–5, 232, 275–6, 311–12

dating methods, 4, 103–4, 229–30; radiocarbon, 4, 15, 104, 137–8, 141, 208, 228; protactium-ionium, 228; protactium-*231*, 228; thorium-*230*, 228–9; uranium-*234*, 229; potassium-argon, 273; *see also* dendrochronology

Davidson Current, 70

Davis, William Morris, 155

"dead water," 115

deep drilling, *see* Mohole Project; petroleum

deep-sea animals: depth zones of, 287–8; food pyramid of, 288–9; phosphorescent, 288, 294–5; requisites for life of, 289; of lightless depths, 290–5; reaction to pressure changes, 290, 292; bacteria, 290, 292; adaptations of, 291–3; range of, 291–2, 295–6; eyes of, 291, 293–4; colors of, 295; reactions to temperature, 295–7; reactions to ocean chemistry, 297–8; collections of, 298–9; varieties of, 299–315; monster, 306–11; living fossil, 312–15; new phylum, 315

Delos, 143

deltas, 184, 190–1

deluge legends, 119–20, 143

dendrochronology, 226

Denmark, 133, 229

Devon Island, 224

Devonian Period, 103, 314

diatom ooze, 176

diatoms, 65, 71, 80, 329–30

Dietz, Robert S., 133, 169, 274–5

discoasters, 222–34

Dogger Bank, 136, 138

Donau Ice Age, 230

Donn, B. D., 12

Donn, W. L., 12

Dosidicus gigas, 311

Dover cliffs, 133

dunite, 260–1

Dutton, Clarence E., 128

earth: present epoch, 4–5, 205–6; energy sources, 5, 13, 24–7, 62, 73, 252; areal water surface, 6; theories of origin of, 16–18, 120; layers of, 18–19; atmosphere, 41–6, 62, 121; origin of features of, 18–27, 120; polarity of, 22–3, 272–3; patterns of water and land masses on, 26, 120–44; hydrosphere, 41–6; rotation of, 48–9, 62, 67, 103; heat flow, 252–4; consolidation of, 259–60; primeval surface of, 272; age of, 348

earthquakes, submarine, 110–15, 158–9, 261, 263–4; *see also* seismic sea waves

eddies (gyres), 58

Edinburgh, 34–5

Eemian Interglacial, 229

Eemian Sea, 229

Egeria, H.M.S., 156

Ekman spiral, 48–51, 69

Ekman, Vagn Walfrid, 48, 115

El Niño current, 51, 72–3

Elbe River, 136

electric power generation, *see* ocean energy conversion

Emery, K. O., 337–8

Eniwetok Atoll, 125

Enypniastes, 300

Eocene Epoch, 134

Equatorial Counter Current: of the Atlantic, 63; of the Pacific, 68

equatorial currents, *see* North Equatorial Current; South Equatorial Current

Estabrook, Frank B., 276

Euboea, 143

eustatic change, 127–41

Ewing, John, 179, 239–41

Ewing, Maurice, 9, 83, 162, 167, 178, 187, 209, 228, 236–42, 246–7, 276, 314

fauna of deep oceans, *see* deep-sea animals; sea foods

faunal change, 221–2
faunal zones, 287–8
fetches, 96
fish, *see* deep-sea animals; sea foods
fisheries, 35
fishing, 77; Baltic, 116, 327–9
Fleming, R. H., 37
Flint, Richard F., 139, 160
flood, global, 133–4; *see also* deluge legends
floors of oceans: major features of, 7–11, 152, 159–62, 235; sediment patterns of, 83–4; current scour on, 84; subsidence of, 123–5, 127–8, 160; and convection flow theory, 131–3, 169–70, 274–5; abyssal plains of, 159, 167–8, 185; abyssal hills province, 159; rises of, 159–60; asymmetrical ridges in, 160–1; crust thickness of, 242–6, 266, 268; basement rock of, 247–51; *see also* sediment; turbidity currents
Florida Current, 68
Florida Straits, 63–4
foraminifera: of Antarctic convergence vicinity, 74; planktonic, 79–80, 176, 193–4, 216; of Canary Island vicinity, 79; shells of, 80, 83, 192–3; calcium carbonate secretion by, 80, 192; of Hudson Canyon region, 167; benthic, 192; life cycles of, 192–3; depth, temperature ranges of, 193–4, 216, 218; right- and left-coiling species of, 218, 221; reversal in coiling direction of, 221–2
Forbes, Edward, 148, 287

Galápagos Islands, 78
Galathea (research vessel), 289–90, 299, 302, 310, 314
Galatheathuria, 300
Galveston, 114
Gauss (research vessel), 7
Gazelle (research vessel), 35, 148

Geophysical Institute of Bergen, 53
German South Atlantic Expedition, 36, 81
Gibraltar Strait, 84
Gilbert, G. K., 276
glaciers: vertical earth movements effected by, 23–4, 128–9, 141–2, 250–1; thermal properties of water related to, 42–4; retreat of, related to climate change, 73, 137–8, 141; formation of, 135–7, 140–1; detritus, 155, 207; *see also* ice ages; Pleistocene Epoch
globigerina ooze, 191
Globigerinoides sacculifera, 217
Globorotalia menardii, 79, 217–18, 221–2
Globorotalia truncatulinoides, 217–18, 222, 224
Gondwanaland, 13
Graf, Anton, 249–50
Grand Banks of Newfoundland, 9, 60, 64
gravity survey methods, 247–8; Vening Meinesz pendulum, 248–9; Graf horizontal boom, 249–50
Great Barrier Reef, 146, 155
Great Salt Lake, 135
Greenland, 53, 62, 160
Grimaldichthys profundissimus, 289
Grimoteuthis, 308
ground swell, 98
Guadalupe Island, 278
Guam, 6
Guantánamo, 56
Gulf of Alaska, 69, 106, 126
Gulf of California, 106
Gulf of Mexico, 63, 114–15, 133, 185, 190, 271
Gulf of Naples, 142–3
Gulf of St. Malo, 109
Gulf Stream, 36, 58, 330; main extension of, 60; North Atlantic extension of, 60–1; paths of branches of, 61–4, 69; southern counterpart of, 63; and Sargasso Sea, 65–6; in Pleistocene, 66;

Gulf Stream (*continued*)
  nature, influence of, 66–7; currents below, 82
Gullmar Fjord, 115, 195, 197, 199
Günz Ice Age, 230
Gutenberg, Beno, 264
Guyot, Arnold, 126
guyots, 125–7, 133

Haber, Fritz, 81
Halimeda, 187
Hardy, Sir Alister, 311
Harvard University, 4, 53, 195, 348
Hawaiian Islands, 70, 260–1; 1946 seismic wave, 110–12
heat convection theory, 24–7, 131–3, 169–70, 252–4, 263, 267, 274–5
heat flow measurement, 251, 253; cyclindrical probe method, 252
Heezen, Bruce C., 9, 84, 162, 168, 170
Helland-Hansen, Björn, 48
Henbest, L. G., 216
Henricia sanguinolenta, 299
Hess, Harry H., 125–6, 152, 277
Heyerdahl, Thor, 71
Himalayas, 134
Histioteuthis, 308
Hollister, Charles, 84
Holocene epoch, 206
Hooke, Robert, 147
Hopkins Marine Station, 36
Horizon (research vessel), 157
Hudson Submarine Canyon, 155, 156, 167, 191, 271
Humboldt, Alexander von, 81
Humboldt Current, 71, 73, 311, 333
hurricanes, 340–1
Huygens, Christian, 242
Hvorslev, M. J., 195
Hydrographer (research vessel), 162
hydrostatic pressure, 292

ice ages, 65, 71–3, 163; theories of causation of, 135–7, 140–1; areas glaciated during last, 136–7; inter-

glacial flooding, 137–9; interstadial, 139; *see also* Pleistocene Epoch; glaciers
icebergs, 52–3; as possible water source, 333–4
Iceland, 61, 146; recent volcanic activity of, 170
Illinoian Ice Age, 220, 229
India, 326
Indian Ocean, 126, 148; areal surface of, 6; trench, 6; ridge, 8–9; theory of origin of, 13–14; gyre, 58; effect of seasonal winds on, 59–60; 1959 expedition, 60, 79; equatorial undercurrent, 79; depth, 149; floor, 159
interglacial, 137–40
International Council for the Exploration of the Sea, 35, 115, 196
International Geophysical Year, 1957–8, 74–6
International Ice Patrol, 53
International Indian Ocean Expedition, 60, 79
interstadial, 139
Irish Sea, 148
Irminger Current, 62
Irving, E., 23
Iselin, Columbus, 54–6, 330
isostasy principle, 128–30, 251, 262, 267
Ivanov, A. V., 315

Jagger, Thomas A., 276
Japan, 112–13
Japan Current, *see* Kuroshio
Java, 6, 9
Java Deep, 290
"John Murray" Expedition, 162
Johnson, M. W., 37
Joly, John, 4–5
Jüngere Hauptterrasse, 230

Kansan Ice Age, 220
Kelvin, Lord, 149, 259–60

Kermadec Islands, 157
Key Largo Limestone, 229
Kola Peninsula, 284
Kon-Tiki Expedition, 71
Krakatoa, 114
Kuenen, P. H., 181
Kullenberg, Börje, 197–8
Kuroshio, 68, 70, 78

Labrador, 54–5, 142
Labrador Current, 55, 64, 69
Labrador Sea, 53
La Jolla, 37, 57
Lamont Geological Observatory, 9, 74, 83, 84, 152, 162, 167–8, 177–9, 187, 191, 210–11, 215, 229, 236, 238, 246–7, 267, 344–5
Lamont, Thomas W., 238
Lane, Capt. Adrian, 213–14
La Romanche (surveying ship), 7
Leclerc, Georges-Louis, 16
Lehmann, I., 265
Li, C. P., 345
Lill, Gordon, 278
Linné, Carl von, 142
Loch Ness monster, 310
lomas, 72
Long Island, 155
Los Alomas Scientific Laboratory, 125
Lower California, 70
Luskin, Bernard, 168
Lyell, Sir Charles, 139, 142

Macrouridae, 300
Madagascar Institute of Scientific Research, 313
magnetic anomalies, 273
magnetic polarity, 22–3, 272–4
Maine, 141
Malacca, 9
mantle of earth: defined, 18; and convection flow hypothesis, 24–7, 131–3, 169–70, 252–4, 263, 267, 274–5; thickness of, 120, 266; and isostasy principle, 128–30, 251, 262,

267; composition of, 260–1, 266; rate of flow within, 262–3; heat conversion process in, 263; discontinuities in, 264, 266; *see also* Mohole Project
Marianas Trench, 301
marine biochemistry, 346–8
Marine Biological Association Laboratory of the United Kingdom, 36
Marine Biological Association of San Diego, 37
marine pharmacology, 343–6
Martha's Vineyard, 57, 107, 155
Mascaret, the, 108
Matthews, D. H., 273
Maury, Matthew F., 28–32, 46–7, 147–8
medicines, 343–6
Mediterranean Sea, 6, 139, 148, 163–4; current patterns of, 84
Melville Bay, 53
Mercury, 17
Merz, Alfred, 81
Mesozoic Era, 15, 122–3, 133, 205
Metcalf, W. G., 79
Meteor (research ship), 8, 36, 81, 152, 161, 194
meteorological observation, beginnings, 30–1
Miami Oolite, 229
Mid-Atlantic Ridge, 7–9, 161–3, 169–70
Middle Devonian Period, 104
Mid-Indian Ridge, 162
Mid-Ocean Ridge, 7–8, 9, 161–2, 247
Mielche, Hakon, 310
Miller, S. L., 347
Mindanao Trench, 6
Mindel Ice Age, 230
mining, underwater, 202, 325, 334–6
Mississippi River, 156, 190–1
Mohole Project: objectives of, 266–7, 269; reasons for drilling in ocean, 268; contributions to be derived from, 268–70, 272–5; site for, 270–2, 275, 283; precedents for,

Mohole Project (*continued*)
275–7; preparations for, 277–80; three-phase plan for, 279–80; Phase I of, 280–3; plans for Phase II of, 283; 1967 withdrawal of funds for, 284
Mohorovičić, Andrija, 258, 268
Mohorovičić discontinuity, 258, 266, 284
Monaco, oceanographic museum of, 36
Monsoon Current, 59
moon: theories of origin of, 12; tidal effects of, 99–102, 116–17
Moore, Usborne, 108
Morita, R. Y., 290
mountain building, 5, 11–12, 123, 125–6, 206, 263
mountain range, submarine, *see* Mid-Ocean Ridge
Munk, Walter, 277
Murray, John, 35, 174, 195–6

Nansen, Fridtjof, 47, 62, 145
Nansen bottles, 47, 56
Nantucket, 155
Naples, 36
National Academy of Sciences, 55
National Academy of Sciences Research Council, 277
National Science Foundation, 277, 283–4
Nautilus (submarine), 319
navigational research, first formal, 28–32
Nebraskan ice age, 220, 225
Nectonemertes mirabilis, 316
Neopilina ewingi, 314
Neopilina galatheae, 314
Netherlands, 229
New England, 55
New Orleans, 115
New York, 139
New Zealand, 70
New Zealand Plateau, 76
Newell, Norman D., 229

Newfoundland, 9, 60, 64, 184
North America: Cretaceous age flood of, 133; during ice ages, 136–7; 170, 218
North Atlantic Drift, 61–2
North Atlantic Ocean, 36, 56; great gyre of, 58, 60, 63–5, 79; currents of, 62–7, 82; during last ice age, 137; abyssal plains, 167
North Equatorial Current, 59; of the Atlantic, 63–4; of the Pacific, 68, 70
North Pacific Ocean, 126, 148; great gyre of, 58, 70; current system, 68–70
North Pole, 22–3, 272–4
North Sea, 6, 35, 136
Norway, 36, 50, 146
Norwegian Sea, 36, 63
Novia Scotia, 155
nuées ardentes, 185
nummulites, 192
Nybelin, O., 289

ocean energy conversion, 109, 341–3
oceanic crust, 267–8
oceanic rises, 159–60
Oceanographic Institute of Göteborg, 197, 200
oceanography: founding of modern, 28–32; first circumglobal expedition, 32–5; first study of single ocean, 36; first research institution for, 36–7; World War II defense research in, 37–8, 56–7; innovations in data gathering, processing, 320–5
Oceans, The (Sverdrup, Johnson, and Fleming), 37
Oldham, R. D., 264
Ommastrephes pteropus, 309
Ophiacantha bidentata, 299
Ostlund, Gote, 340
Ovey, C. D., 216
Owen, H.M.S., 273–4
Oyashio, 68–9, 70

Pacific Antarctic Ridge, 76

Pacific Grove, 36

Pacific Ocean: surface area, 6; basin origin theories, 12, 24; thickness of unconsolidated sediment in, 14, 181; currents, 58, 68, 70–8; tides, 106; volcanic islands in, 133; during Pleistocene, 137; depth, 149; trenches, 156, 169–70; floor, 159–60; turbidity currents, 169; crust, 246

paleomagnetism, 22–3, 272–3

Paleozoic Era, 205

Paris, oceanographic institute in, 36

Parker, F. L., 216

Parr, Albert E., 65

Passamaquoddy Bay, 343

PDR (Precision Depth Recorder), 152, 168

Pelagothuria natatrix, 300

Pennsylvanian age, 103–4

Periphylla periphylla, 297

Permian Period, 205

Peru, Ekman theory exemplified in coastal currents of, 50–1, 71–2

Pet, Capt. Arthur, 146

petroleum, 178, 202; probable first stage of deposit of, 67–8; indicated by salt domes, 248; deep drilling for, 257, 275–7; sea drilling for, 268, 276, 278, 337; origin of, 337, 341

Pettersson, Hans, 168, 195–7, 199–200

Pettersson, Otto, 35, 115, 195

Philippine Islands, 6, 68

Philippine Trench, 289–90

Phipps, Capt. C. J., 146

Phleger, F. B, 216

photosynthesis, 288, 290, 329–31

Piccard, Jacques, 301

Piggot, Charles, 194

plankton, 176, 213, 330–1

Plato, 163–4, 171

Pleistocene Epoch, 65–6, 134, 160, 163, 166; record of, in sediment cores, 82–4, 137, 139, 208, 215, 219–20; periods of glaciation, 135–7, 139–41, 206, 220, 225–6, 229–30; interglacials, 137–41, 206–7, 220, 225–6, 229–30, 271; as time of geological revolution, 205–6; emergence of man during, 207, 228, 230–2; depositional process during, 207–8, 271; discovery of boundary between Pliocene and, 220–8; duration of Pliocene transition, 224; thickness of composite core of, 228; duration of, 228–9

Pliocene Epoch, 220–4

Plymouth, 36

Pogonophora, 315

poles, *see* magnetic polarity; North Pole; South Pole

Polynesia, 71

Pozzuoli, 142–3

Pre-Cambrian geological revolution, 205

Puerto Rico, 277–8

Puerto Rico Trench, 6, 187

Radiolaria, 71

Rance Estuary project, 342–3

Red Sea, 162

reefs, 123–5, 155, 160

Renard, A., 174

Revelle, Roger, 127

Rhine River, 136, 230

Rhizocrinus lofotensis, 312

Rhodesia, 4

Richards, Horace, 167

Rift Valley, 162

Rio Grande Ridge, 161

Robertson, W. A., 23

Rockefeller Foundation, 55

Rocky Mountains, 206

Romanche Deep, 6–7

Ross, Sir James C., 147

Ross Sea, 76

Royal Astronomical Society, 247

Sable Island, 155

Saccopharynx ampullaceus, 305

Sahara desert, 134
salinity, 84–5; and thermal reaction of ocean water, 43–4; related to latitude, 51
salt domes, 248
Sandström, Johan, 48
Sangamon Interglacial, 220, 229, 271
Sargasso Sea, 64–7, 145, 163
Sars, G, O., 312
satellite data collection, 321
Scandinavia, 22–4, 142, 250–1
Schott, W., 194, 216
Scoll, P. M., 23
Scotland, 22, 148
scour, 14 and *n.*
Scripps Institute for Biological Research, 37
Scripps Institute of Oceanography, 36–7, 57, 77, 126, 133, 157, 166, 177, 277–8, 333
sea foods: cultivation of, 326–31; protein concentrate, 331
Sea of Okhotsk, 68
sea water conversion, 333
Sealab II, 325
seamounts, 83, 117, 168; defined, 11; minimum rise of, 153
sediment, 11; fossil-bearing, 14, 22, 74, 181, 192–3, 215–16, 272; unconsolidated, 14–15, 133, 166, 181, 201, 208; accumulation rate, 15, 228, 271; in oxygen-depleted waters, 67–8, 292; of seamounts, 83; effect of internal waves on, 117; accumulation processes, 122, 174–6, 201–2; missing pre-Mesozoic, 122–3, 133, 193, 202, 270, 272; of submarine canyons, 167; composition, 175–6; colors, 176; calcareous, 176, 193; seismic reflection measurement of, 177–81, 199; quartz sand, 182–3; clay, 185, 208; graded, 185, 187, 190; slumping, 185–6, 221, 270–1; relative distribution of, 188–9; *see also* cores; turbidity currents
Seine River, 108, 109

seismic sea waves (tidal), 109–14, 253–4; *see also* storm surges
seismic survey methods, 149, 236–7; reflection, 177–81, 243–4, 320; refraction, 242–6
seismic warning systems, 111–12
seismic wave velocities, 244, 246, 253–4, 265–8, 320
seismograms, 268
Serapis "temple," 142–3
Sewell, R. B. S., 162
shear wave, 129
Shearwater, H.M.S., 148
Shepard, Francis P., 166
Shimbara Bay, 113
Siboga (research vessel), 315
Sigsbee Plain, 271
Simpson, Sir George, 137
Skagerak (research vessel), 177
Skate, 319
slumping, 14 and *n.,* 185–6, 221, 270–1
Smith, Edward Hanson, 53
Smith, J. L. B., 310, 313
SOFAR (sound fixing and ranging), 237
solar energy: reaction of oceans to, 45–6; reaction of atmosphere to, 46; related to glacier retreat, 73
Solomon Island, 78
Somali Current, 60
SONAR (sound navigation ranging), 56, 327
sonoprobe, 178
Soule, F. M., 53
sounding methods: weighted line, 8, 10, 33–4, 145–9; echo, 8, 9–10, 36–7, 56, 82, 149–54, 168; automatic profile transcription, 10, 152–3; *see also* seismic survey methods
South America, 9, 71–3, 134
South Atlantic Ocean, 22, 148; profile of, 10–11; theory of origin of, 13; *Meteor* expedition study of, 36, 81–2; great gyre of, 58, 67; currents of, 63, 67–8; asymmetrical ridges of, 161
South Equatorial Current, 62; of the

South Equatorial Current (*cont.*)
Atlantic, 63, 68; of the Pacific, 70, 77–8

South Pacific Ocean, 126, 148; great gyre of, 58, 70–1; current system, 70–8

South Pole, 22–3, 272–4

South Sea Islands, 70

Southern Ocean, *see* Antarctic Ocean

Soviet Union, 134, 284

Spain, 9

Spence, Lewis, 164

Stanford University, 36

Stetson, Henry H., 166, 195

Stommel, Henry, 66, 86–7

storm surges, 114–15

submergence of sea animals, 297

Sudidae, 303

Sumatra, 9

Sverdrup, H. U., 37

Sweden, 35, 115, 134, 142

Swedish Deep-Sea Expedition, 168, 195, 199–200, 289

synoptic surveys, 321

Tahiti, 71

Talisman (research vessel), 35

Tasman Sea, 76

Teh-Lung Ku, 228

Tekniska Högskola, 35

Thames River, 136

Tharp, M., 162

thermal properties: of water, 42–4; of oceans, 43–6

thermocline, 45

Thomson, Wyville, 32–5, 312

tidal energy, *see* ocean energy conversion

tidal waves, *see* seismic sea waves

tides, 98, 116; equilibrium theory of, 99–100; dynamic theory of, 100–2; spring, 101; neap, 101–2; causes of inequalities of, 102, 104; effect of friction of, on earth's rotation, 102–4; prediction of, 104; in-fluence on shape of ocean basins, 105–6; ranges of, 106–7; reversing currents of, 107; bore, 108–9; exploitation of energy of, 109, 341–3; period of interval of maximum, 116

Tirey, G. B., 179

Titanic, 52–3

Tofua, 156

Tonga Islands, 156–7

Tonga Trench, 157–8, 290

trade winds, 46, 58, 62–3

Travailleur (research vessel), 35

trawling, 298–9

trenches, 6, 156–7, 169–70; deepest, 289

Tricker, R. A. R., 109 and *n.*

Trieste (bathyscaph), 288, 323

Tristan da Cunha, 161

tsunami, 109–15

Tuamotu Islands, 146

turbidity currents, 166–7, 169, 184; erosion by, 166–9; destruction of sediment record by, 184, 191; "snow-balling" effect of, 184–5; creation of deltas by, 184–5, 190–1; created by slumping, 185–7; sediment deposited by, 187–90; characteristic flow of, 190–1; during interglacials, 271

turbidites, 187, 190

Tuscarora (research ship), 35, 148

Uddevalla, 142

Ungava Bay, 106

Unimak, 110

United Nations Food and Agriculture Organization, 326

United States Coast and Geodetic Survey, 36, 149, 152; warning system, 111

United States Geological Survey, 125, 276

upwelling, 67, 71–2

Urey, H. C., 347

Valentine, W. G., 12
Vema (research ship), 9, 178, 238–42, 314
Vening-Meinesz, F. A., 26, 169, 248–9
Vesuvius, 143
Vine, F. J., 273
volcanoes, 133, 143, 158–9; *see also* seamounts; guyots

Walfisch Bay, 67
Walsh, Donald, 301
Walvis Ridge, 161
water: molecular structure of, 41–2; thermal properties of, 42–6
wave recorders, 94–5, 97–8
waves, 91; measurement of, 92, 320; formal motions of, 92–3; wind-driven, 93; formal variations of, 93–4; heights of, 95–6; periods of, 96; velocities of, 96–8; breaking effect of, 96–7, 106, 110; distances traveled by, 111; compression, 110; internal, 115–17; *see also* tides; seismic sea waves; storm surges
weather control, 338–41

Webber Deep, 290
Wegener, Alfred, 19–22
Weibull, Waloddi, 177, 199
Wells, John, 103–4
Weser River, 136
Wilkie, Charles, 239
Wilson, J. T., 169
Wisconsin Ice Age, 136–41, 220
Wiseman, J. D. H., 162, 216
Woods Hole Biological Laboratory, 55
Woods Hole Oceanographic Institution, 54, 56–57, 61, 79, 86, 152, 166, 177, 179, 195, 211, 237, 322, 330, 337
Woolfson, M., 17
World Health Organization, 326
World War II, 37–8, 56, 84
Worzel, J. L., 237, 249
Wüst, Georg, 51, 76, 81

Yarmouth Interglacial, 220, 225–6
Yucatán Channel, 63

ZoBell, C. E., 290
Zoological Station of Naples, 36

A NOTE ABOUT THE AUTHORS

DAVID B. ERICSON, Senior Research Scientist at the Lamont Geological Observatory of Columbia University, was born in New York City and received his B.S. at the Massachusetts Institute of Technology and his M.S. in geology and paleontology at the California Institute of Technology. Until 1938 Mr. Ericson worked as geologist for various oil companies and served for two years as petroleum geologist for the Turkish government. Subsequently he was Assistant State Geologist for the Florida Geology Survey and Marine Geologist at the Woods Hole Oceanographic Institution before taking up his present post in 1947. He was Vice President for Oceanography of the Seventh Congress of the International Association for Quarternary Research in 1965. Mr. Ericson is co-author with Mr. Wollin of *The Deep and the Past*, published in 1964.

GOESTA WOLLIN, born in Sweden and educated at the University of Lund and at Columbia University, has been associated with Lamont Geological Observatory since 1949. He has continued to collaborate in the Observatory's projects as Research Consultant, while carrying on his own career in social welfare and mental health. Mr. Wollin was an Intelligence officer and paratrooper in the 82nd Airborne Division of the U. S. Army from 1943 to 1945 and entered the journalism field after the war. He had two novels published before he joined the Lamont group, and currently he is devoting full time to his oceanographic research at Lamont. Mr. Wollin is married and has one daughter.

A NOTE ON THE TYPE

The text of this book was set on the Linotype in Janson, a recutting made direct from type cast from matrices long thought to have been made by the Dutchman Anton Janson, who was a practicing type founder in Leipzig during the years 1668-87. However, it has been conclusively demonstrated that these types are actually the work of Nicholas Kis (1650-1702), a Hungarian, who most probably learned his trade from the master Dutch type founder Kirk Voskens. The type is an excellent example of the influential and sturdy Dutch types that prevailed in England up to the time William Caslon developed his own incomparable designs from these Dutch faces.

Composed and bound by The Haddon
Craftsmen Inc., Scranton, Pennsylvania. Printed
by Halliday Lithograph Corporation, West Hanover, Massachusetts.
Typography and binding design by GUY FLEMING